Psycho-Criminological Perspective of Criminal Justice in Asia

This book offers both theoretical and practical examinations of the psycho-criminology of criminal justice in Asia, with particular emphasis on the Hong Kong and Singapore contexts. It is designed to present the current state of the field, which addresses key topics in three major sub-areas: policing and legal system, offender rehabilitation and treatment, and research and future directions. Written by academics with extensive research experience in their respective topics and senior ranking practitioners in their fields, topics include psychologists' involvement in different aspects of forensic investigation, police emotional reactions to major incidents, the application of psychological approaches in developing offender rehabilitation and treatment modules to address different offender's criminogenic needs, and legal issues related to the insanity defence, fitness to plead, the jury system, and procedural justice and legitimacy. An important reference for post-graduate courses, this book will be of special interest to criminologists and psychologists working in forensic settings, mental health professionals, policy-makers, police personnel, prison officials, and legal executives.

Chapters include:

1 Youth gang offenders in Singapore
2 Offender rehabilitation: The Hong Kong Correctional Services Department
3 Juries as decision-makers in East Asian judicial systems: Hong Kong, Mainland China, South Korea, and Japan
4 The psychology of violent extremism: What we know and what else we need to do

Heng Choon (Oliver) Chan, PhD, is an assistant professor of criminology at City University of Hong Kong, Hong Kong, SAR. He was the recipient of the 2012 Outstanding Criminology Ambassador Award presented by the University of South Florida, and the honorary title – Early Career Award – by the Hong Kong Research Grants Council (RGC) in 2014. His research focuses on criminological issues related to the Asian population, and violent and sexual offence topics (e.g., sexual homicide and offender profiling). Chan published widely on these topics and presented at numerous academic conferences. His most recent single-authored research monograph, "Understanding sexual homicide offenders: An integrated approach", is published by Palgrave Macmillan (2015). Chan is an associate editor of *International Journal of Offender Therapy and Comparative Criminology* and editorial review board member of *Advancing Corrections Journal* (the official journal of the International Corrections and Prisons Association).

Samuel M.Y. Ho, PhD, is a professor of psychology at the City University of Hong Kong, Hong Kong, SAR. He is an honorary professor of the University of Hong Kong and the honorary advisor of the Hong Kong Correctional Services Department Women Offender Working Group. His primary research interest is in traumatology and resilience, in developing an in-depth knowledge about the factors that facilitate adjustments to life-threatening illnesses (e.g., cancer) and traumatic events (e.g., infectious disease epidemic). As a registered clinical psychologist and a researcher, Ho benefits from conducting basic research to help understanding of applied problems as well as taking applied issues for explorations in empirical research. Ho has been conducting invited training workshops and presentations regularly in Hong Kong, China, Taiwan, Europe, and North America to share his research findings and clinical expertise.

Routledge Studies in Asian Behavioural Sciences
Series Editor: T. Wing Lo, City University of Hong Kong

Archaeology of Psychotherapy in Korea
A study of Korean therapeutic work and professional growth
Haeyoung Jeong

Hidden Youth and the Virtual World
The process of social censure and empowerment
Gloria Hongyee Chan

Psychoanalysis in Hong Kong
The absent, the present, and the reinvented
Diego Busiol

Psycho-Criminological Perspective of Criminal Justice in Asia
Research and Practices in Hong Kong, Singapore, and Beyond
Edited by Heng Choon (Oliver) Chan and Samuel M. Y. Ho

Routledge Studies in Asian Behavioural Sciences

Psycho-Criminological Perspective of Criminal Justice in Asia

Research and Practices in Hong Kong, Singapore, and Beyond

Edited by Heng Choon (Oliver) Chan and Samuel M. Y. Ho

Routledge
Taylor & Francis Group
LONDON AND NEW YORK

First published 2017 by Routledge

2 Park Square, Milton Park, Abingdon, Oxfordshire OX14 4RN
711 Third Avenue, New York, NY 10017

Routledge is an imprint of the Taylor & Francis Group, an informa business

First issued in paperback 2018

British Library Cataloguing-in-Publication Data
A catalogue record for this book is available from the British Library

Library of Congress Cataloging-in-Publication Data
A catalog record for this book has been requested

ISBN: 978-1-138-68065-4 (hbk)
ISBN: 978-1-138-36587-2 (pbk)

Typeset in Galliard
by Apex CoVantage, LLC

To the Chan Family:
With deep appreciation of your unconditional love, endless support, and encouragement
In loving memory of my mother
Heng Choon (Oliver) Chan, PhD

I dedicate this book to my wife Georgiana and my children Joyce, and Kevin, without whom this book would not come true.
Samuel M.Y. Ho, PhD

Contents

Figures

Tables

About the editors

Heng Choon (Oliver) CHAN, PhD, is an assistant professor of criminology at City University of Hong Kong, Hong Kong, SAR. He received his PhD in criminology from the University of South Florida, and was the recipient of the "2012 Outstanding Criminology Ambassador Award." Chan has also been awarded the honorary title – "Early Career Award" – by the Hong Kong Research Grants Council (RGC) of University Grant Committee (UGC) in 2014, and "The President's Award 2016" by City University of Hong Kong in early 2017. His research focuses on criminological issues related to the Asian population (i.e., Asian criminology); and violent and sexual offending topics such as sexual homicide, offender profiling, sexual offending, homicide, and stalking behaviour. Chan has published widely on these topics, with over 65 peer-reviewed journal articles and books chapters; and presented in numerous international, regional, and local academic conferences. His most recent single-authored research monograph, "Understanding sexual homicide offenders: An integrated approach" is published by Palgrave Macmillan (2015). Chan is an associate editor of *International Journal of Offender Therapy and Comparative Criminology* and editorial review board member of *Advancing Corrections Journal* (the official journal of the International Corrections and Prisons Association). He has also been regularly interviewed by electronic media and quoted in print media on criminological issues; and consulted on the offending behaviour of violent offenders by television programme scriptwriters and movie producers.

Samuel M.Y. HO, PhD, is the Associate Provost (Institutional Initiatives) and a professor of psychology at the City University of Hong Kong, Hong Kong, SAR. He is an honorary professor of the University of Hong Kong and the honorary advisor of the Hong Kong Correctional Services Department Women Offender Working Group. His primary research interest is in traumatology and resilience, in developing an in-depth knowledge about the factors that facilitate adjustments to life-threatening illnesses (e.g., cancer) and traumatic events (e.g., infectious disease epidemic). As a registered clinical psychologist and a researcher, Ho benefits of conducting basic research to help understanding of applied problems as well as taking applied issues for explorations in empirical research. Ho has been conducting invited training workshops and presentations regularly in Hong Kong, China, Taiwan, Europe, United Kingdom, and North America to share his research findings and clinical expertise.

Contributors

Samuel Adjorlolo, Doctoral Candidate, Department of Applied Social Sciences, City University of Hong Kong, Hong Kong, SAR.

Jansen Ang, Senior Principal Psychologist and Deputy Director, Immigration Checkpoint Authority Psychological Services Branch, Immigration Checkpoint Authority; Assistant Director, Police Psychological Services Division, Singapore Police Force; and (Adjunct) Assistant Professor, Division of Psychology, Nanyang Technological University, Singapore.

Ka Po Jessica Chan, Clinical Psychologist, Hong Kong Correctional Services Department, Hong Kong, SAR.

Samson Chan, PhD, Honorary Lecturer, Department of Sociology, The University of Hong Kong, Hong Kong, SAR.

Sook Yee Chang Lam, Social Worker, Hong Kong, SAR.

Kevin Kwok Yin Cheng, PhD, Assistant Professor, Faculty of Law, The Chinese University of Hong Kong, Hong Kong, SAR.

Hung Kei Cheung, Clinical Psychologist, Hong Kong Correctional Services Department, Hong Kong, SAR.

Jeffery Chin, Senior Psychologist and Assistant Director, Crime, Investigation, and Forensic Psychology Branch, Home Team Behavioural Sciences Centre, Home Team Academy, Singapore.

Chi Meng Chu, PhD, Deputy Director and Senior Principal Clinical and Forensic Psychologist, Centre for Research on Rehabilitation and Protection, and Centre for Evaluation, Ministry of Social and Family Development, Singapore.

Leevia Dillon, Behavioural Sciences Research Analyst, Home Team Behavioural Sciences Centre, Home Team Academy, Singapore.

Siew Maan Diong, Principal Psychologist and Deputy Director, Home Team Behavioural Sciences Centre, Home Team Academy; and Commander, Emergency Behavioural Sciences and CARE Unit, Singapore Civil Defence Force, Singapore.

Ciping Goh, Psychologist, Resilience and Counselling Psychology Branch, Police Psychological Services Division, Singapore Police Force, Singapore.

Hui Fen Ho, Senior Psychologist and Head, Resilience and Counselling Psychology Branch, Police Psychological Services Division, Singapore Police Force, Singapore.

Cora Y.T. Hui, Doctoral Candidate, Department of Applied Social Sciences, City University of Hong Kong, Hong Kong, SAR.

Shuk Han Hui, PhD, Senior Clinical Psychologist, Hong Kong Correctional Services Department, Hong Kong, SAR.

Majeed Khader, PhD, Senior Consultant Psychologist and Director, Home Team Behavioural Sciences Centre, Home Team Academy; Deputy Director, Police Psychological Services Division, Singapore Police Force; and (Adjunct) Assistant Professor, Division of Psychology, Nanyang Technological University, Singapore.

Wing Yan Kung, Clinical Psychologist, Hong Kong Correctional Services Department, Hong Kong, SAR.

Regina Wing Yin Kwong, Clinical Psychologist, Hong Kong Correctional Services Department, Hong Kong, SAR.

Yuk Ip Kindy Lam, PhD, Clinical Psychologist, Hong Kong, SAR.

Kit Shan Yvonne Lee, PhD, Clinical Psychologist, Hong Kong Correctional Services Department, Hong Kong, SAR.

Rong Cheng Lee, Psychologist, Operations and Forensic Psychology Branch, Police Psychological Services Division, Singapore Police Force, Singapore.

Timothy Hee Sun Leo, Chief Psychologist and Director, Singapore Prison Service, Singapore.

Wing Ling Li, Clinical Psychologist, Hong Kong Correctional Services Department, Hong Kong, SAR.

Ching Chuen Lu Chan, Honorary Consultant (Psychological Services), Youth Outreach, Hong Kong, SAR.

Vivian Wai Ming Mak, Clinical Psychologist, Hong Kong Correctional Services Department, Hong Kong, SAR.

Carolyn Misir, Principal Psychologist and Head, Operations and Forensic Psychology Branch, Police Psychological Services Division, Singapore Police Force, Singapore.

Loo Seng Neo, Senior Behavioural Sciences Research Analyst, Home Team Behavioural Sciences Centre, Home Team Academy, Singapore.

Samantha Hui Fang Neo, Psychologist, Resilience and Counselling Psychology Branch, Police Psychological Services Division, Singapore Police Force, Singapore.

Gabriel Ong, PhD, Principal Psychologist and Assistant Director, Resilience, Safety, and Security Psychology Branch, Home Team Behavioural Sciences Centre, Home Team Academy; and Senior Assistant Director, Singapore Prison Service, Singapore.

Barbara Ka Yan Pau, Clinical Psychologist, Hong Kong Correctional Services Department, Hong Kong, SAR.

Li Li Poh, Principal Psychologist, CNB Psychological Unit, Central Narcotics Bureau, Singapore.

Yining Tham, Psychologist, Resilience and Counselling Psychology Branch, Police Psychological Services Division, Singapore Police Force, Singapore.

Ming Hwa Ting, PhD, Manager and Senior Research Specialist, Centre for Research on Rehabilitation and Protection, Ministry of Social and Family Development, Singapore.

Ephraem P. W. Tsui, PhD, Lecturer (Clinical Psychology), Department of Psychology, The University of Hong Kong; and (retired) Police Clinical Psychologist, Hong Kong Police Force, Hong Kong, SAR.

Wing Ki Winnie Wong, Clinical Psychologist, Hong Kong Correctional Services Department, Hong Kong, SAR.

Chin Pang Woo, Clinical Psychologist, Hong Kong Correctional Services Department, Hong Kong, SAR.

Vincent Yeh, Psychologist, Operations and Forensic Psychology Branch, Police Psychological Services Division, Singapore Police Force, Singapore.

Gerald Zeng, PhD, Manager and Senior Research Specialist, Centre for Research on Rehabilitation and Protection, Ministry of Social and Family Development, Singapore.

Acknowledgments

The editors wish to thank all chapter contributors for sharing their expertise and valuable experience. They have worked tirelessly on their chapter regardless of their hectic schedules. Without their significant contribution, this edited volume could not have been made possible. We would also like to thank our undergraduate students – Christy Hoi Yu Tsang, Annie On Ling Wong, and Eason Yik Shun Chui – for their assistance in this book project.

In addition, we are very grateful to the editors at Routledge, particularly Christina Low, for believing in this book project and for their guidance and support throughout the process. We are also indebted to the external reviewers for their thoughtful and astute comments to make this volume much stronger. Finally, we would like to express our appreciation to the Department of Applied Social Sciences at City University of Hong Kong for the strong support of our work.

Introduction

Exploring criminal justice in Asia from a psycho-criminological perspective

Heng Choon (Oliver) Chan and Samuel M. Y. Ho

Introduction

Psychological criminology is referred to as the convergence of psychology and criminology in that psychological criminology is concerned with the use of psychological knowledge to explain or describe (with the attempt to change) criminal behaviour (Hollin, 2012). With personality and social influences, this field of study stresses the individual criminal behaviour, on how the behaviour is acquired, evoked, maintained, and modified (Bartol, 2002). This is particularly relevant to the focus of this edited volume. In this book, we aim to explore the different aspects of the criminal justice system (e.g., police, correctional, and legal) in Asia from a psycho-criminological standpoint, with particular emphases on the Hong Kong and Singapore contexts.

The book structure

With a combined theoretical- and practical-oriented approach, this volume attempts to introduce readers to the core areas of research and practice in this field. This text is arguably the first to explore the Asian criminal justice from a psycho-criminological standpoint in three main sections (i.e., policing and legal system, offender rehabilitation and treatment, and research and future directions). Written by experienced field practitioners and researchers, each section aims to address different topics relevant and unique to Asian criminal justice.

Five chapters are structured under the first section on the policing and legal system. In Chapter 1, Ming Hwa Ting and Chi Meng Chu introduce the historical background on Chinese youth gangs and how the group dynamic changes over time in contemporary Singapore. The authors argue that the contemporary youth gangs in Singapore are less likely to be politically driven and no longer organised strictly along ethnic or dialect lines. However, they assert that continual needs for rehabilitation and enforcement efforts are required as research has shown that youth offenders involved in gang activities are more likely to reoffend than their non-gang affiliated counterparts. In Chapter 2, Ephraem Tsui et al. first review the literature on the current understanding of children's testimony from a psychological perspective. They further offer the readers with suggestions on how investigators and legal professionals in Hong Kong could adopt a child-friendly approach in assisting child witnesses to provide their best evidence to the court. The chapter concludes with a case study to illustrate a child-friendly interview process.

Chapter 3 and Chapter 4 by Samuel Adjorlolo and Heng Choon (Oliver) Chan are devoted to topics relevant to criminal responsibility and fitness to plead in Hong Kong. These chapters provide the readers a thorough insight into the insanity defence and fitness to plead legislations. Specific emphasis is given to Hong Kong legislation, including the adjudication of defendants pleading insanity, the insanity verdict, disposition associated with the verdict, and the fitness to plead provisions and applications. In Chapter 5, Cora Hui et al. provide a review of the court and jury systems in four East Asian jurisdictions (i.e., Hong Kong, Mainland China, South Korea, and Japan). Specific attention is paid to discussing the factors that affect jury decision-making and the impact of a defendant's confessions on East Asian lay decision-makers.

The next seven chapters are organised under the section on offender rehabilitation and treatment. These chapters are written by experienced correctional practitioners from Hong Kong and Singapore to share their best practices in rehabilitating different types of offenders. In Chapter 6, Samson Chan presents a historical background of the correctional services in Hong Kong. The development of offender rehabilitation at different eras with the establishment of different programmes over the years is discussed in detail. Chapter 7, written by Ching Chuen Lu Chan et al., builds on the previous chapter by introducing the development of psychological services in the Hong Kong correctional services. They first offer a background on the development of different psychological services provided to persons-in-custody (PIC) and the criminal justice system as a whole, including forensic assessments, psychological treatment programmes, and consultation services to management of PIC, staff, and the organization. The chapter concludes with the discussion on essential elements for the development of effective offender psychological treatments.

In Chapter 8, Vivian Mak et al. introduce the development of a unique treatment programme for female offenders in Hong Kong. The "Psychological Gymnasium" (PSY GYM) is established to adopt gender-responsive approaches that include the formation of a therapeutic community and the incorporation of an everyday life perspective into psychotherapy in addressing the gender-specific needs of female offenders. Core features of PSY GYM are discussed and a case study is presented to illustrate gender-specific treatment approach. Chapter 9 by Yvonne Lee et al. is devoted to the psychological assessment and treatment of serious violent offenders (e.g., homicide offenders) in Hong Kong. Specific emphasis is given to the development and delivery of the Violence Prevention Programme (VPP), which aims to reduce the recidivism risk of the offenders as preparation for their release back to the community. A case study is offered to illustrate the delivery of VPP and treatment outcome. In Chapter 10, the focus of Jessica Chan and Chin-pang Woo is on how the Sex Offenders' Evaluation and Treatment Unit (ETU) adopts different psychological approaches in developing its treatment programmes for convicted sex offenders in Hong Kong. Over the years, the unit's treatment approach has progressed from the relapse prevention model to the current strength-based and goal-oriented intervention strategies (e.g., the Good Lives Model and other positive psychological approaches). Special attention is paid to the establishment of ETU and the tasks performed by its team of clinical psychologists. The chapter concludes with a case illustration to provide the reader with a run-through of its programme.

In Chapter 11, Timothy Leo provides a review of the development of offender rehabilitation and treatment in the Singapore Prison Service. The incorporation of psychological knowledge into the correctional services in Singapore (e.g., risk assessment, risk reduction intervention, organisational and system change, and community engagement) has evidenced to be effective in rehabilitating and managing offenders. Chapter 12 by Chi Meng Chu and Gerald Zeng is written to introduce the readers to the assessment and management of youth offenders in Singapore. With the adoption of the risk-need-responsivity framework, the authors discuss local research findings on the associated risk assessment measures (i.e., Youth Level of Service measures) that facilitate the systematic evaluation and effective management and rehabilitation of youth offenders.

The final section of the book, with four chapters, focuses on the research and future directions of the psycho-criminology of criminal justice in Asia. In Chapter 13, Rong Cheng Lee et al. empirically examine the psychological well-being of 84 Singaporean police officers who responded to the Little India riot – first major riot in over 40 years – that occurred on 8 December 2013, which involved about 400 Indian migrant workers. Findings indicate that only a minority of officers were found to display symptoms of post-traumatic stress disorder and the overall officers' coping strategies were consistent with previous international studies (i.e., adaptive coping strategies). Similarly in Chapter 14, Vincent Yeh et al. analyse the crowd behavioural characteristics during the Little India riot using interview transcripts of the involved parties, incident video footage, and scene photographs. Overall findings suggest that the crowd was rational and organised in three distinct groups, and the group identity was present within the crowd. The authors further offer implications for public order policing with emphasis on the dynamic interactions between and within groups.

In Chapter 15, Leevia Dillon et al. first synthesise the literature on the psychology of violent extremism from 2011 to 2015. Seven themes have emerged (i.e., violent extremist tactics, online discourse, public perception of violent extremism, counter violent extremism efforts, use of Internet by violent extremists for recruitment, group dynamics, and risk assessment). The authors further discuss the research conducted in Singapore and provide future research directions on the topic. Finally in Chapter 16, Kevin Cheng highlights important work that has been conducted in the area of procedural justice and legitimacy, with emphasis on the perceptions of young people towards legal authorities in Hong Kong. The author subsequently suggests future research directions on the topic in Hong Kong and Asia in general, including the effectiveness and moral alignment and perceptions of other legal authorities (e.g., the police).

Exploring criminal justice in Asia from a psycho-criminological perspective

The style of writing combines with valid and up-to-date case illustrations, and supported by empirical and theoretically-driven research findings, we hope that this edited volume, contributed by experienced field practitioners and academics, could contribute greatly to the limited literature in the psycho-criminological study of Asian criminal justice. Such knowledge is prerequisite for the effective operation of an impartial criminal justice system (i.e., police, correctional, and legal), particularly in crime prevention and offender rehabilitation (Chan, Lo, & Zhong, 2016; Chan, Lo, Zhong, & Chui, 2015). In the words of Westen and Weinberger (2004):

> Collaboration between clinicians and researchers could substantially improve the quality of scientific research . . . The scientific mind and the clinician mind can coexist, in a single field – indeed, in a single person – and that the dialectic between the two may be essential for a scientific [psycho-criminology].
> (p. 610)

References

Bartol, C. R. (2002). *Criminal behaviour: A psychosocial approach* (6th ed.). Upper Saddle River, NJ: Prentice Hall.

Chan, H. C. O., Lo, T. W., & Zhong, L. Y. (2016). Identifying the self-anticipated reoffending risk factors of incarcerated male repeat offenders in Hong Kong. *The Prison Journal, 96*(5), 731–751. doi: 10.1177/0032885516662640

Chan, H. C. O., Lo, T. W., Zhong, L. Y., & Chui, W. H. (2015). Criminal recidivism of incarcerated male nonviolent offenders in Hong Kong. *International Journal of Offender Therapy and Comparative Criminology, 59*(2), 121–142. doi: 10.1177/0306624X13502965

Hollin, C. R. (2012). Criminological psychology. In M. Maguire, R. Morgan, & R. Reiner (Eds.), *The Oxford handbook of criminology* (5th ed., pp. 81–113). New York, NY: Oxford University Press.

Westen, D., & Weinberger, J. (2004). When clinical description becomes statistical prediction. *American Psychologist, 59*(7), 595–613. doi: 10.1037/0003-066X.59.7.595

Part 1

Policing and legal system

1 Youth gang offenders in Singapore

Ming Hwa Ting and Chi Meng Chu

Introduction

Youth gangs are an important focus of contemporary research into youth crime and delinquency due to the fact that gang-affiliated youths are responsible for a disproportionate amount of serious and violent criminal offences (Thornberry, Krohn, Lizotte, & Chard-Wierschem, 1993) with their concomitant social, legal, and criminal justice costs (Covey, 2010). Although the expansion of youth gangs across the United States and Europe is well documented with gang activities (Klein & Maxson, 2006), it is clear that the transmission of youth gangs and gang culture is a worldwide phenomenon that is not limited to Western contexts. Studies have reported the existence of youth gangs in North and South America (Decker & Pyrooz, 2010; Shelden, Tracy, & Brown, 1997), Europe (Gatti, Haymoz, & Schadee, 2011), Africa (Covey, 2010) Australia (White & Mason, 2006), and Asia (Pyrooz & Decker, 2012).

Research suggests that prevalence rates for youth gang membership in the United States vary between 2% and 37% depending on the nature of the sampling population and the definition adopted (Klein & Maxson, 2006; Thornberry et al., 1993). In addition, prevalence estimates for youth gang membership vary greatly across countries in Europe, from 0.4% of youths in Armenia to 16.8% of youths in Ireland (Gatti & Haymoz, 2011). Similarly, the prevalence of gang membership in Asia varies widely. For example, Chu, Daffern, Thomas, and Lim (2012) found that 35% of a sample of 165 incarcerated youths could be classified as gang-affiliated offenders in Singapore. In another sample of institutionalised youth offenders in Singapore, 63.7% of a sample of 168 youth offenders was classified as gang-affiliated (Chu et al., 2015). In contrast, a study of 654 incarcerated youth offenders in China found that 47% had been convicted for gang-related crimes (Zhang, Messner, Lu, & Deng, 1997). Lower prevalence rates were found among a sample of 2,163 school students in China; only 11.4% were classified as having either former or current gang involvement (Pyrooz & Decker, 2012). Importantly, the variation in prevalence estimates across these studies demonstrates how changing the definition of gangs or the sample population can dramatically influence prevalence rates.

Definition of youth gangs

There is little consensus among scholars on what constitutes a gang and what the defining features of youth gangs are (Esbensen, Winfree, He, & Taylor, 2001; Howell, 1998). Dissimilar definitions of gang involvement can lead to challenges in assessing the scope and nature of gang problems and identifying the predictors of gang membership and the direction of anti-gang strategies (Esbensen et al., 2001). Importantly, overestimating or underestimating gang problems can affect the allocation of resources and lead to inaccurate depictions of gangs that influence perceptions about the extent of local gang problems (Matsuda, Esbensen, & Carson, 2012).

A recent conceptualisation developed through cross-national collaboration between gang researchers (the Eurogang network) specifies five defining characteristics of youth gangs. This definition asserts that "a street gang is any durable, street-oriented youth group whose involvement in illegal activity is part of its group identity" (Klein & Maxson, 2006, p. 4). Other characteristics (e.g., ethnicity, tattoos, and gang names) are *descriptors* that delineate particular gangs or elements that describe specific groups rather than necessary *definers* of youth gangs (Klein & Maxson, 2006; Wood & Alleyne, 2010). Consistent with the Eurogang definition, many definitions of youth gangs have included illegal activity as a defining feature (Klein & Maxson, 2006; Miller, 1975; Thrasher, 1963). However, other researchers have debated the importance of including criminality as a necessary criterion for defining youth gangs (Ball & Curry, 1995; Howell, 1998; Short, 1996). They emphasise the importance of a shared identity, solidarity, and identified territory as more critical determinants of youth gangs (Esbensen et al., 2001) and note that most criminality among young people occurs in concert (Chu, Daffern, Thomas, & Lim, 2012).

Research suggests that as the definition or scope of gang involvement changes, prevalence estimates of gang membership and the qualities and activities of youth gangs shift (Esbensen et al., 2001; Matsuda et al., 2012; Winfree, Fuller, Vigil, & Mays, 1992). Despite the differences associated with the conceptualisation of youth gangs and the lack of agreement about the necessary criteria for gang membership, most definitions include the following characteristics: "(1) a self-formed group united by mutual interests (2) that controls a particular territory, facility or enterprise, (3) [that] uses symbols in communication, and (4) [that] is collectively involved in crime" (Howell, 1998, p. 4). Importantly, Wood and Alleyne (2010) argue that the inclusion of criminality as a criterion for defining gangs is compelling because the parties involved in studying gangs are mostly interested in the adverse criminal behaviour associated with gang involvement.

Youth gangs and criminal activities

Gang-affiliated youth offenders engage in a wide variety of criminal activities, including but not limited to violent and drug offences (e.g., Curry, 2000; Curry, Decker, & Egley, 2002; see O'Brien, Daffern, Chu, & Thomas, 2013 for a review). Gang-affiliated youths are more likely to use weapons (Curry, 2000;

Curry et al., 2002; Esbensen & Huizinga, 1993; Huff, 1998; Thornberry et al., 1993; White & Mason, 2006) and to reoffend at higher rates than their non-gang-affiliated peers (Bendixen, Endresen, & Olweus, 2006; Curry et al., 2002; Esbensen & Huizinga, 1993; Huff, 1998; Thornberry et al., 1993; White & Mason, 2006). Notwithstanding that youth gang members contribute disproportionately to violent and general crime rates and that the differences between gang and non-gang youth offending rates are most noticeable for serious and violent crimes (Esbensen & Huizinga, 1993), gangs do not specialise in violent offending to the exclusion of other types of offending. In fact, it is rather apparent that gang-related offending behaviour is generalist in nature, and this includes significant engagement in both minor and serious criminal activities such as drug use, public disorder and nuisance behaviours, and property, drug-related, and violent crimes (Esbensen & Weerman, 2005; Sharp, Aldridge, & Medina, 2006; Thornberry et al., 1993).

Research suggests that youth gangs have been found in almost all highly populated continents and that the association with crime and gang membership is strong across the globe (Pyrooz & Decker, 2012). However, patterns of involvement in crime vary between countries. The level of gang violence between countries appears to be influenced by access to firearms; higher gun violence is found in countries with greater access to firearms (Decker & Pyrooz, 2010). Asian gang youths are typically found to engage in less aggravated violence (e.g., assault, robbery, and extortion offences are most common) than gang youths in America, where shootings, gun violence, homicide, and aggravated assaults appear to be more common (Chin, 2000; Chu, Daffern, Thomas, & Lim, 2011; Tsunokai & Kposowa, 2002).

In any case, their rehabilitation is multifaceted and demanding (Benda & Tollett, 1999; Klein, 1995). The extent of association with youth gangs appears to have a linear relationship with criminal behaviour; youths associated with gang members but who are not fully-fledged gang members report more delinquency than youths who are not associated with gang members at all but considerably less delinquency than fully fledged gang members (Curry et al., 2002). There is unfortunately little consensus as to the best approach to the rehabilitation of gang-affiliated youth offenders and whether the focus of intervention with this particularly challenging population should be on encouraging desistence and/or targeting their so-called criminogenic needs (i.e., dynamic risk factors that affect the likelihood of reoffending when changed; Andrews & Bonta, 2010).

In the following sections of this chapter, we will delve deeper into the origins of triad societies and the "evolution" of youth gangs in Singapore. In addition, this chapter will review the research on youth gangs in Singapore and discuss the rehabilitation strategies within the local context.

Brief history of triad societies

In brief, both triads and secret societies are unlawful organisations. The main point of departure between the two organisations is that triads can trace their roots back to the Hung League and adopt elaborate initiation rituals. Secret societies, on the other hand, do not have links with the Hung League, and they also do not adopt such elaborate rituals. However, over time, the distinctions between the two types of organisations are not as clear as they have evolved to escape law enforcement efforts. For ease of reference in this chapter, the term *triad society* is used as shorthand to refer to both types of organisations.

Chinese triad societies could be thought of as a "political organisation". They were first formed as a reaction to the foreign political rule in China when the Manchus came into political power at the expense of the Ming rulers. With their professed objective of overthrowing the foreign rulers and reinstalling the House of Ming, it was unsurprising that the Manchu ruling elites regarded members of this group to be politically subversive, and attempts were made to suppress it, thereby driving it underground. Given the clandestine nature of their activities, it was unsurprising that triad societies had to be sure that prospective members were committed to the organisation. This was done through the use of elaborate rituals that served as a signalling action that was costly to fake. Given the illegal nature of such organisations, it was imperative that prospective members were screened to ensure that they were committed and loyal to the organisation. Almost invariably, individuals opting to join triad societies were young and marginalised males. They were not only searching for adventure but also, more importantly, for an identity, solidarity, and protection.

Initiation rituals constituted a major part of premodern societies. Rituals are important, especially if they are difficult to fake, as they can be very effective in promoting intra-group solidarity as well as minimising free-ridership (Sosis, 2004). In order to enjoy the benefits associated with membership, individuals must pay the price of admission. In the context of Chinese triad societies, participating in the initiation ritual meant that the individual identified with the outlawed beliefs, goals, and values of the organisation, thereby setting himself against the Manchu governing elites. In short, rituals can be regarded as "symbolic behaviour that is socially standardised and repetitive" and that "follows [a] highly structured, standardized sequence and is often enacted at certain places and times that are themselves endowed with special symbolic meaning" (Kertzer, 1988, p. 9).

Over time, as the Manchu rulers consolidated their rule in China, the goal of overthrowing them became less realistic. Hence, the overt political overtures receded into the background and triad societies performed additional roles as China underwent a series of major socio-economic and political changes such as the highly destructive Taiping Rebellion in the latter half of the Qing dynasty. From being organisations animated by a strong political ideology, triad societies slowly turned into *kongsi* and *hui*, organisations that could be thought of as "outgrowths of traditional village mutual-assistance societies" (Kuhn, 2008, p. 168). For instance, during the 1800s, difficult economic conditions served as a major push factor in causing economically impoverished Chinese males to seek out better employment prospects overseas.[1] As more and more Chinese sought out better conditions in other countries, these sojourners brought their culture and social values with them. Unsurprisingly, they also set up *kongsi*, and this was how triad societies were introduced into Singapore, Malaya, and other parts of Southeast Asia.

Triad societies in colonial Singapore

Organised along dialect lines, newly arrived immigrants would often seek out the support of their *tongxiang* – individuals who had resided in the same village back in China – upon disembarkation. With limited prior knowledge of Singapore and the ways of the British colonial authorities, these newly arrived sojourners looked to these *kongsi* to help them navigate their way in a foreign environment (Warren, 2003). As noted by Freedman (1960), these groupings provided a buffer for the Chinese against the colonial authorities, and they allowed them to exercise a certain degree of autonomy in an unfamiliar social and political culture.

With the passage of time, triad societies' political ideology weakened due to the evolving social and political contexts. Even though many Chinese immigrants still regarded China as their homeland, dynastic politics were becoming less relevant to them. This was because from the mid-1800s, there was a growing nationalist movement in China, one that sought to replace monarchy rule with civilian rule.[2] Although these organisations did have some prosocial elements to them, it has to be pointed out that they were also involved in criminal activities such as running protection rackets, guarding lucrative economic sites such as mines and prostitution dens (Warren, 2003), and competing among themselves to control the expanding market in coolies and opium. By the early 1800s, such groups became more prominent, bolstered in part by the large influx of Chinese emigrants into Southeast Asia (Trocki, 1990). A list of known triad societies in 1860 is shown in Table 1.1. Even though the colonial British administrators regarded these groups as a threat to public order, their existence was tolerated. This was because in the early years, the colonial administrators needed to manage the peace between the Chinese labourers from different dialect groups who came to Singapore in large numbers to seek out better prospects (Yen, 1985).

However, as the colonial authorities in Singapore became more competent in dealing with the Chinese community in Singapore over time, the British soon changed their attitude from one of grudging acceptance to that of more active suppression to prevent the situation from worsening.[3] With triad societies implementing their own notions of justice to individuals who were deemed to have broken the blood oaths of brotherhood, they were directly challenging the state on the latter's "monopoly of the legitimate use of physical force in the enforcement of its order" (Weber, 1978, p. 54).

Many of the activities triad societies were involved in became criminalised, which then drove them underground. For instance, Sir Cecil Clementi, who was appointed Governor in 1887, passed the *Societies Ordinance* in Singapore in January 1890. In large part, the introduction of the *Societies Ordinance* was due to the attack on W.A. Pickering, the inaugural Protector of the Chinese, by triad society members in 1887. To send an even stronger message to triad society members, the colonial government also introduced the *Banishment Ordinance*,

Table 1.1 List of triad societies in Singapore in 1860

Name	*Estimated Membership*	*Dialect Group*
Ghee Hin	15,000	Hokkien
Hai San	6,000	Hokkien and Teochew
Ghee Hin	4,000	Macao
Cho Koon (Ghee Hin)	3,500	Teochew
Ghee Hin	2,500	Hainanese
Ghee Khee	1,500	Hakka and Teochew
Ghee Sin	1,500	Teochew
Ghee Soon	1,500	Hokkien and Hainanese
Chen Chen Kow (Tsung Peh Society)	1,000	Hokkien and Hakka
Ghee Hok	800	Teochew
Hok Bing (Hok Hin)	600	Hokkien and Hainanese
Hen Bing	500	Hokkien
Choo Leong	500	Hokkien
Ang Bang	400	Hokkien

Source: Adapted from Lim (1999)

which gave them the authority to banish any non-British subjects who posed a serious threat to public order. Given that triad societies were invariably ethnic Chinese, they were deported to China. As China was also cracking down on triad societies, anyone deported there on such grounds was likely to be punished by the Chinese government. However, as more and more members of triad societies were born in Singapore over time and could not be banished, the *Banishment Ordinance* became ineffective. This was not to say that there were no legal innovations being implemented to put continual pressure on triad societies and their members.

Gangs in modern Singapore

As Singapore moved towards self-governance and independence, the hard-line stance towards triad societies was maintained. For instance, the *Criminal Law (Temporary Provisions) Ordinance* of 1958 was passed; this allowed for the detention without trial of individuals suspected of being members of triad societies. As Comber noted, this was adopted "to overcome the difficulties experienced in coaxing witnesses to come forward and risk their lives giving evidence against secret society gangsters in open court" (Comber, 2009, p. 63). With the passage of this ordinance, the expanded powers of the police made them more effective. For instance, the number of incidents associated with triad societies decreased from 416 in 1959 to just 12 in 1983. In 1996, there were only five such incidents (Lim, 1999).

As seen above, with law enforcement agencies in Singapore becoming more effective in combating triad societies, these underground organisations in Singapore have evolved. To avoid unnecessary attention and detection, they have largely moved away from traditions such as having elaborate initiation rituals for new members and this has blurred the lines between triads and secret societies. To a large extent, such moves away from traditions are necessary as these overt displays would inevitably result in action being taken against them. Hence, many of the traditions and rituals have either been simplified or done away with. Writing about triad society members in the 1950s, Comber noted that they were different from their predecessors in the 1800s; he noted that these individuals were "to a large extent 'Westernized'. The gaudy shirts and jeans they wear, their unruly mops of hair, all point to the influence of the cinema, comic strips and cheap detective novels" (Comber, 2009, p. 79). More importantly, it is highly plausible that they have little knowledge of the historical and political ideologies of the triad societies of the past (Morgan, 1989).[4] Hence, it does appear that triad societies have "undergone a steady deterioration of purpose" (Morgan, 1989, p. xiii) as their contemporary counterparts have devolved into antisocial youth street gangs that lack the historical gravitas of their predecessors ("More Malay youth in gangs", 2012). In a further departure from the historical membership of triad societies organised along dialect lines seen in Table 1, contemporary groups tend to be ethnically agnostic in their recruitment and admission.[5] That said, the influence and threat of triad societies remains, albeit greatly diminished by tough laws and strong police suppression strategies ("20 secret society arrests", 1957; "Man pleads guilty", 2011; "MHA to study more police powers", 2010a; Tai, 2013; "Tattoo Crazy", 1958; "Teenager jailed for triad website", 1999).

To a large extent, this deterioration of purpose has also arguably picked up pace due to the effectiveness of enforcement action and the growth of the Internet. For instance, younger members of triad societies and street gangs have now shied away from having a strong street presence and now increasingly express their virtual bravado through online means (Kamaludeen, 2004). However, this change in *modus operandi* does not mean that these contemporary groups no longer pose a threat to public order. Nevertheless, it is clear that youth gangs, like any organisation, are not static entities. Compared to traditional triad societies, the activities and outlooks of youth gangs tend to be more general than their historical counterparts, which, as discussed above, tended to perform more specific roles. Ironically, the fact that youth gangs lack any political ideology or do not target their recruitment at specific dialect groups may make them more resistant to suppression efforts. From an organisational perspective, generalist entities are more likely to survive than specialist entities. For instance, by not restricting themselves to only accepting members from specific dialect groups, as was the case previously, youth gangs today are able to make themselves relevant to a societal context in which one's identity is not tied to one's dialect group. However, without strong underlying ties or a strong ideology, such groups are more prone to splintering (Weisel, 2002), which may render efforts to suppress these youth gangs even more difficult due to the diffused nature of the leadership.

The changing nature of youth gangs has direct implications for rehabilitation and policing efforts in Singapore. This is because the motivations to join these antisocial organisations have changed over time. Nevertheless, it is clear that youth gangs remain operational and continue to pursue criminal activities and engage in violence (Ministry of Home Affairs, 2006).

Youth gangs in Singapore

Even though, as discussed above, youth gangs in Singapore are different from their historical counterparts, they still tend to adopt the names of triads and secret societies as well as loosely modelling themselves after these organisations. However, they are different in several aspects (Covey, 2003). Triads and secret societies are considered organised crime groups that (a) are constituted mainly for economic gains through criminal activities and (b) operate as a whole group rather than subsets. In contrast, youth gangs in Singapore have largely abandoned the traditional initiation and rituals and tend to be loosely organised in terms of structure and hierarchy. Within the Singapore context, a study on youth gang offenders found that most (60.7%) youths reported that their gangs had between three and 10 members; 20.6% reported their gangs had between 11 and 20 members; and 15.9% reported their gangs had between 21 and 50 members (Chu et al., 2015). With regard to the structure of youth gangs, it appears that Singaporean youth gangs are generally small in size and comprised predominantly of teenagers who are possibly led by a young adult in their early twenties.

In Chu et al.'s (2015) study, about half of the youths stated that their gangs had regular meetings, but only 22.4% shared that their gangs had specific rules or codes. In fact, very few (4.7%) reported that their gangs required specific activities prior to joining, and more than three-quarters (78.5%) stated that their gangs did not have peculiar symbols to symbolise gang affiliation. Very few said their gangs wore special clothing (5.7%) or dedicated tattoos (15.9%). Overall, the self-reports from the youth gang members suggested that these organisations are loose in terms of structure and that compared with the triads and secret societies, they are much easier to join and leave (Chu et al., 2015). This observation is similar to Decker, Katz, and Webb's (2008) finding that youth gangs in an American context are not very well organised. These youth gangs appear to be different in terms of characteristics and structure from the traditional triads or secret societies that have been documented in the Singaporean context (Lim, 1999). Notwithstanding that these youth gangs are generally not described as being well organised, their propensity for crime and violence should not be underestimated (Chu et al., 2012; Decker et al., 2008). In general, youth gang membership serves a number of different functions; despite the presence of co-occurring delinquency, youth gang membership may primarily satisfy social (Decker & van Winkle, 1997) rather than economic needs. Consistent with research showing that many youths are "pulled" into youth gangs to satisfy a universal human need for affiliation (Decker & Van Winkle, 1996; Klein, 1995; Klein & Maxson, 2006) or relatedness/community (Ward & Brown, 2004), Chu et al. (2015) demonstrated that youth gang offenders overwhelmingly reported that they had joined gangs because of social-related reasons: for example, they had joined gangs because of their friends, to find a sense of belonging, to feel important, to participate in group activities, and to share experiences with others. In the next section, we will examine the individual characteristics of youth gang offenders.

Characteristics of youth gang offenders

The average age at entry to youth gangs in Singapore was 13 to 14 years old, with 56.8% of the sample being 13 years or younger (Chu et al., 2012, 2015). It was also noted that gang membership was rather transient (average length: < 2 years), and the average age at first charged offence was 15+ years old. Chu et al. (2012, 2015) also found that youth gang offenders were more likely than non-gang-affiliated youth offenders to have a history of substance abuse, prior offences, and weapon use.

Similar to local and overseas findings, gang-affiliated youth offenders in Singapore were more likely than their non-gang-affiliated counterparts to have friends in gangs, and the former were also more likely to hang out with friends even if they would get them into trouble at home with their guardians (Chu et al., 2015). In addition, gang-affiliated youth offenders were comparatively less likely than non-gang-affiliated youths to like school and to see education as important. In fact, they would rather enjoy themselves with friends than study to achieve academic excellence. Pertaining to the violence-related domain, gang-affiliated youth offenders were more likely than the non-gang-affiliated to (a) carry hidden weapons for protection purposes, (b) assault others, (c) assault others with weapons, (d) fight with others for pride reasons, and (e) engage in gang fights (Chu, 2010).

Notwithstanding that the youth gang offenders were being rated significantly higher on violence and general risk assessment measures, the differences in the severity of the ratings for the various subscales (within the risk assessment measures) were nonsignificant between gang-affiliated and non-gang-affiliated youth offenders (Chu et al., 2011). In addition, a study of "street corner" gangs in Singapore found that youths involved with street corner gangs were more likely to have lower self-esteem, higher levels of aggression, and poorer interaction with their mothers and to be over-controlled by their mothers (Kee, Sim, Teoh, Tian, & Ng, 2003). The gang-affiliated youth offenders were also more likely than the non-gang-affiliated youth offenders to have siblings in the gangs and family members who are/were previously in gangs (Chu, 2010).

Furthermore, Chu, Daffern, Thomas, Ang, and Long (2014) found that favourable attitudes toward gangs, violence, and criminal associates remained significantly associated with gang membership. Specifically, youth gang offenders were more entitled, had more pro-violence attitudes, and were more partial toward antisocial associates than their non-gang-affiliated counterparts. It is possible that youth gang offenders have been socialised into developing attitudes that may perpetuate their offending behaviour, and as the next section of this chapter will show, youth gang offenders have poor recidivistic outcomes. Importantly, Chu et al. (2014) showed that youth gang offenders also endorsed more favourable attitudes towards weapon use than non-gang-affiliated youth offenders – this is unsurprising given their penchant for using weapons in fights.

With this background information on youth gang offenders' pro-criminal and violent proclivities, the next section will examine their recidivistic outcomes.

Youth gang offenders and recidivistic outcomes

As with most countries around the world, youth violence is a major concern in Singapore. More recently, youth gang violence in Singapore was further spotlighted due to the widely publicised Downtown East ("Suspects in fatal Downtown East slashing arrested", 2010), Bukit Panjang ("Youths attacked by '369' gang members", 2010), and Orchard Cineleisure (Zaccheus, 2013) gang-related attacks. According to crime statistics, rioting[6] is one of the three most common youth crimes in Singapore, with almost 13% of all youth offenders being arrested for rioting offences in 2007 (Singapore Police Force, 2008). In a study of 300 youth rioters (aged 21 years and below), 87.6% were reportedly involved with gangs (Subordinate Courts of Singapore, 1998). A study examining gang affiliation and general criminal recidivism among youth offenders found that gang membership did not significantly predict general recidivism among youth offenders in Singapore (Ang & Huan, 2008). Further examination of an older subsample within this cohort revealed that youth offenders who were gang members were more likely to recidivate violently than those without gang affiliation. In addition, those who were not gang members but were associated with gang-affiliated peers were also more likely than those without gang affiliation, but less likely than full-fledged gang members, to recidivate violently (Ang, Huan, Chua, & Lim, 2012). In addition, those who were not gang members but were associated with gang-affiliated peers were also more likely than those without gang affiliation, but less likely than full-fledged gang members, to recidivate violently (Ang et al., 2012).

In another study on youth gang offenders, Chu et al. (2012) found that compared with non-gang-affiliated youth offenders, gang-affiliated youth offenders were more likely to have violent offending behaviours, substance use, and weapons use. Moreover, gang-affiliated youth offenders were also 1.71 and 2.46 times more likely to engage in general and violent recidivism, respectively, than their non-gang-affiliated counterparts, even after accounting for the potentially confounding effects of age at first charged offence, substance use, and time at risk. Further to the above-mentioned published local studies, an unpublished retrospective study on youth offenders who were ordered to reside in a youth offender institution showed that 69% of the sample was gang-affiliated and that gang affiliation was significantly associated with violent offending (Neo, 2010). Gang status was also shown to be predictive of assaultive institutional misconduct, but strong social support and resilient personality factors were protective factors against assaultive institutional misconduct (Long, 2015).

Desistance from youth gangs

Notwithstanding that friendship was the most common reason for joining a gang, the reasons given for leaving a gang mostly related to outgrowing the gang or becoming frustrated by the consequences of criminal activity, including incarceration and estrangement from family (Chu et al., 2015). Moreover, lower-level gang members described disappointment that gang affiliation brought few benefits and that they were exploited or disrespected by senior gang members. Those young people who left their gang typically did so (a) to avoid trouble, (b) because they did not see any value in remaining within their gang, (c) because they fell out with other gang members, (d) because they were bored by the gangs' activities, (e) because they wanted a bright future, and (f) they recognised that family bonds were more important to them than the friendships that initially drew them into the gang (Chu et al., 2015). However, there were also reasons that prevented these youth gang offenders from leaving gangs; these included not feeling able to leave the gangs due to fear of reprisals or other difficulties, concerns about losing relationships with other gang members, a sense of loyalty to the gang, and fear of losing status (Chu et al., 2015). Having an understanding headman or good relationships with the headman, having parents/police/friends to talk to the headman, and not keeping in touch with the gang were most important in making their exits from the gangs easier (Chu et al., 2015).

Prevention, suppression, and rehabilitation

There is a range of personal and social reasons for youths to join gangs, with the need for affiliation the primary reason for joining and remaining in gangs. Moreover, youths exit gangs due to emerging interests in satisfying alternative basic human needs (e.g., work and family) and an emerging awareness of the costs associated with gang affiliation, including harassment by the police, incarceration, and a realization that lower-level gang members are often exploited by senior gang members. Prevention programmes should target at-risk youths (those with (a) early exposure to gangs by way of family, friends, or neighbours who are gang affiliated, (b) family disruption, and (c) educational difficulties that may result in exclusion by prosocial groups) to ensure that adequate opportunities for prosocial affiliation are available. The pre-eminence of affiliation in this group might also be discussed with the youths, and interventions to enhance their enjoyment and mastery of other basic human needs, including education, are recommended. As many gang-affiliated youth offenders have difficult family circumstances and cite a desire later in life to repair family bonds, prevention programmes might also include family therapy to improve family relationships prior to youths joining gangs. Intervention programmes might have a similar focus, engaging community services to provide suitable prosocial activities that provide opportunities for friendship and to renew and strength family relationships.

Gaining cognisance of the reasons why youths join gangs is useful for intervention efforts since it can help social agencies target at-risk youths and assist the facilitators in terms of weakening the youths' bonds with their gangs by emphasizing the common disadvantages of affiliation and sources of disaffection (Chu et al., 2015). It is also important to target youths who are struggling with education and those who are desensitised to gangs through their neighbourhood presence within the Singaporean context. In particular, Pyrooz, Sweeten and Piquero

(2013) suggested that expediting the process of youths leaving gangs has positive effects in terms of reducing crime and victimisation and that school disruption features prominently in terms of gang affiliation and victimisation (Brunson & Miller, 2009). Youth gang members may have lost interest in education and may require intervention to motivate them to seek educational or employment-related opportunities that are more suitable. It is also possible that the lack of motivation to engage in education and existing ties to the gangs may pull or push youths toward gang involvement, but there is also a possibility that gang affiliation had led youths to lose interest in education and become even further entrenched in delinquency.

In addition to education and employment, it is also important to engage youths in other positive, developmentally appropriate activities that will provide the affirmation and personal life goals that youths are seeking. The reasons why youths choose to remain in gangs can also be used to develop strategies or interventions so that the factors inhibiting desistance (e.g., fear of retribution and safety concerns) are addressed at both the systemic and individual level. As Pyrooz, Sweeten, and Piquero (2013) note, even when members indicate a desire to leave the gangs, they may continually remain in a network of former gang members. Therefore, programmes need to help youths create distance from their gangs so that the urge to return to antisocial gang-related activities is reduced.

In the Singapore context, law enforcement authorities have also implemented various initiatives targeting at-risk youths to prevent them from joining gangs (Singapore Police Force, 2015). For instance, the Singapore Police Force (SPF) organises Project Camp ACE, which provides a platform for former gang members to share their experiences with at-risk youths on the dangers of joining such illegal and antisocial organisations, as well as the Prison Education Visits for Schools (PVEPS) scheme that seek to educate students about life behind bars.

Specifically, in the wake of the gang-related attacks in Bukit Panjang, Downtown East, and Orchard Cineleisure, the Working Group on Youth Gangs (WGYG) was formed so as to achieve enhanced coordination and collaboration between relevant agencies such as the Ministry of Home Affairs (MHA), the Ministry of Social and Family Development (MSF), the Ministry of Education (MOE), the SPF, and the Attorney General Chambers (AGC) in order to "deter youths from joining gangs and to disrupt existing youth gangs" (Singapore Parliamentary Report, 2013a). Furthermore, the SPF also set up the Youth Offenders Unit, which oversees initiatives "to prevent youth crime, monitors trends and coordinates public education and outreach efforts to youths" (Singapore Parliamentary Report, 2013a). At the same time, the SPF also conducts "visible patrols and enforcement checks" at various public, social, and recreational areas that youths frequent in order to serve as a deterrent against the activities of youth gang members (Singapore Parliamentary Report, 2013b). Hence, even though it may not be possible to completely eradicate such activities, the continual preventive and enforcement efforts resulted in a general downward trend in the number of juvenile delinquents arrested in Singapore between 2008 and 2014 (Ministry of Social and Family Development, 2015), which provides encouraging evidence for the efficacy of such efforts in recent years.

Chapter summary points

- Contemporary youth gangs in Singapore can trace their roots to Chinese triad societies.
- Youth offenders involved in gangs are more likely to recidivate than their non-gang counterparts.
- Rehabilitation and enforcement efforts need to evolve in tandem with societal changes to remain effective.

Notes

1 When Lee Hsien Loong (2008) was asked why his ancestors came to Singapore, he replied: "To find a livelihood and to get rich. My great-grandfather came from China to seek a living, just like the others".

2 From this vantage point, the formation of the Chinese Republic of China under Sun Yat-sen's leadership could be regarded as the realization of the goal set by the Triad Society, which was to replace foreign rule with indigenous rule.

3 "[S]ecret societies were dreaded organisations. They were the more dangerous because they used fire arms. Fights were frequent and there was much blood shed. The faction troubles arrived at such a state that Singapore came very near to being termed the 'Chicago of the East'" ("The Chicago of the East," 1929).

4 For instance, when writing about the situation in Hong Kong in 1960, Morgan (1989, p. xiii) argued: "Nowadays, the Triad Society as a co-ordinated body does not exist. It has disintegrated into hundreds of seperate (sic) societies all claiming membership of the Triad family but normally acting quite independently of each other. These modern societies might be defined as Chinese secret societies whose members bound by oaths of blood brotherhood, are pledged to assist one another and further the particular aims of their societies irrespective of the moral and civil laws of the country wherein they operate. Alternatively, and for all practical purposes, they might best be described as mainly criminal gangs who use the name and fragmentary rituals of the ancient Triad Society for their own nefarious purposes".

5 For instance, Hanif (2008) notes that Omega, a Malay Muslim-only gang, was set up due to the perceived notion that Malays recruited into Chinese-dominant triad societies face discrimination and are less likely to rise up in the ranks. http://scholarbank.nus.edu.sg/bitstream/handle/10635/16099/MA%20thesis2_nafis%20%28revised%29.pdf?sequence=1

6 Rioting is defined as a violent public disturbance whereby physical force or violence is used by an unlawful assembly (of five or more people), or any of its members, on another person or group (Singapore Penal Code, 1985).

References

Andrews, D. A., & Bonta, J. (2010). *The psychology of criminal conduct* (5th ed.). Cincinnati, OH: Anderson Publishing.

Ang, R. P., & Huan, V. S. (2008). Predictors of recidivism for adolescent offenders in a Singapore sample. *Criminal Justice and Behavior*, *35*(7), 895–905. doi: 10.1177/0093854808317270

Ang, R. P., Huan, V. S., Chua, S. H., & Lim, S. H. (2012). Gang affiliation, aggression, and violent offending in a sample of youth offenders. *Psychology, Crime and Law*, *18*(8), 703–711. doi: 10.1080/1068316X.2010.534480

Ball, R. A., & Curry, G. D. (1995). The logic of definition in criminology: Purposes and methods for defining 'gangs'. *Criminology, 33*(2), 225–245. doi: 10.1111/j.1745-9125.1995.tb01177.x

Benda, B. B., & Tollett, C. L. (1999). A study of recidivism of serious and persistent offenders among adolescents. *Journal of Criminal Justice, 27*(2), 111–126. doi: 10.1016/S0047-2352(98)00051-8

Bendixen, M., Endresen, I. M., & Olweus, D. (2006). Joining and leaving gangs: Selection and facilitation effects on self-reported antisocial behaviour in early adolescence. *European Journal of Criminology, 3*(1), 85–114. doi: 10.1177/1477370806059082

Brunson, R. K., & Miller, J. (2009). Schools, neighborhoods, and adolescent conflicts: A situational examination of reciprocal dynamics. *Justice Quarterly, 26*(2), 183–210. doi: 10.1080/07418820802245060

The Chicago of the East. (1929, 14 June). *Straits Times.* Retrieved from http://eresources.nlb.gov.sg/newspapers/Digitised/Article/straitstimes19290614-1.2.21.aspx

Chin, K. L. (2000). *Chinatown gangs: Extortion, enterprise and ethnicity.* New York, NY: Oxford University Press.

Chu, C. M. (2010). Towards an understanding of youth gangs in Singapore. *Social Research Digest, 2*, 1–2.

Chu, C. M., Daffern, M., Thomas, S. D. M., Ang, Y., & Long, M. (2014). Criminal attitudes and psychopathic personality attributes of youth gang offenders in Singapore. *Psychology, Crime and Law, 20*(3), 284–301. doi: 10.1080/1068316X.2013.772182

Chu, C. M., Daffern, M., Thomas, S. D. M., Ang, Y., Long, M., & O'Brien, K. (2015). Determinants of gang affiliation in Singaporean youth offenders: Social and familial factors. *Journal of Aggression, Conflict and Peace Research, 7*(1), 19–32. doi: 10.1108/JACPR-11-2013-0031

Chu, C. M., Daffern, M., Thomas, S. D. M., & Lim, J. Y. (2011). Elucidating the treatment needs of gang-affiliated youth offenders. *Journal of Aggression, Conflict and Peace Research, 3*(3), 129–140. doi: 10.1108/17596591111154167

Chu, C. M., Daffern, M., Thomas, S. D. M., & Lim, J. Y. (2012). Violence risk and gang affiliation in youth offenders: A recidivism study. *Psychology, Crime and Law, 18*(3), 299–315. doi: 10.1080/1068316X.2010.481626

Comber, L. (2009). *The triads: Chinese secret societies in 1950s Malaya and Singapore.* Singapore: Talisman Publishing.

Covey, H. C. (2003). *Street gangs throughout the world.* Springfield, IL: Charles C. Thomas.

Curry, G. D. (2000). Self-reported gang involvement and officially recorded delinquency. *Criminology, 38*(4), 100–118. doi: 10.1111/j.1745-9125.2000.tb01422.x

Curry, G. D., Decker, S. H., & Egley, A. (2002). Gang involvement and delinquency in a middle school population. *Justice Quarterly, 19*(2), 275–292. doi: 10.1080/07418820200095241

Decker, S. H., Katz, C. M., & Webb, V. J. (2008). Understanding the black box of gang organization: Implications for involvement in violent crime, drug sales, and violent victimization. *Crime and Delinquency, 54*, 153–172. doi: 10.1177/0011128706296664

Decker, S. H., & Pyrooz, D. C. (2010). Gang violence around the world: Context, culture and country. In G. McDonald (Ed.), *Small arms survey 2010* (pp. 101–128). London: Oxford University Press.

Decker, S. H., & van Winkle, B. (1996). *Life in the gang: Family friends, and violence.* New York, NY: Cambridge University Press.

Esbensen, F. A., & Huizinga, D. (1993). Gangs, drugs, and delinquency in a survey of urban youth. *Criminology, 31*(4), 565–587.

Esbensen, F. A., & Weerman, F. M. (2005). Youth gangs and troublesome youth groups in the United States and the Netherlands: A cross-national comparison. *European Journal of Criminology, 2*(1), 5–37. doi: 10.1177/1477370805048626

Esbensen, F. A., Winfree, L. T. J., He, N., & Taylor, T. J. (2001). Youth gangs and definitional issues: When is a gang a gang, and why does it matter? *Crime and Delinquency, 47*(1), 105–130. doi: 10.1177/0011128701047001005

Freedman, M. (1960). Immigrants and associations: Chinese in nineteenth-century Singapore. *Comparative Studies in Society and History, 3*(1), 25–48. doi: 10.1017/S0010417500000980

Gatti, U., Haymoz, S., & Schadee, H. M. A. (2011). Deviant youth groups in 30 countries: Results from the second international self-report delinquency study. *International Criminal Justice Review, 21*, 208–224. doi: 10.1177/1057567711418500

Hanif, N. M. (2008). *Prison in society, society in prison: Analysing Omega's racially structured realities within and beyond* (Unpublished master's thesis). National University of Singapore.

Howell, J. C. (1998). *Youth gangs: An overview* (Juvenile Justice Bulletin: Youth Gang Series). Washington, DC: US Department of Justice, Office of Juvenile Justice and Delinquency Prevention.

Huff, R. (1998). *Comparing the criminal behavior of youth gangs and at-risk youths: Research in brief.* Washington, DC: U.S. Department of Justice, Office of Justice Programs, National Institute of Justice.

Kamaludeen, M. N. (2004). Protected sites: Reconceptualizing secret societies in colonial and postcolonial Singapore. *Journal of Historical Sociology.* doi: 10.1111/johs.12072

Kee, C., Sim, K., Teoh, J., Tian, C. S., & Ng, K. H. (2003). Individual and family characteristics of youth involved in street corner gangs in Singapore. *Journal of Adolescence, 26*(4), 401–412. doi: 10.1016/S0140-1971(03)00027-7

Kertzer, D. I. (1988). *Ritual, politics, and power.* New Haven, CT: Yale University Press.

Klein, M. W. (1995). *The American street gang: Its nature, prevalence and control.* New York, NY: Oxford University Press.

Klein, M. W., & Maxson, C. L. (2006). *Street gang patterns and policies.* New York, NY: Oxford University Press.

Kuhn, P. A. (2008). *Chinese among others: Emigration in modern times.* Singapore: NUS Press.

Lee, H. L. (2008). *Speech by Prime Minister Lee Hsien Loong at the Internal Security Department 60th anniversary dinner.* Singapore: Prime Minister's Office.

Lim, I. (1999). *Secret societies in Singapore: Featuring the William Stirling collection.* Singapore: Singapore History Museum, National Heritage Board.

Long, M. (2015). *Determinants of assaultive institutional misconduct by juvenile offenders: The role of gang affiliation and protective factors* (Unpublished master's thesis). James Cook University.

Man pleads guilty to displaying secret-society related banner. (2011). *AsiaOne.* Retrieved from http://news.asiaone.com/News/AsiaOne+News/Crime/Story/A1Story20110921-300741.html

Matsuda, K. N., Esbensen, F-A., & Carson, C. C. (2012). Putting the 'gang' in 'Eurogang': Characteristics of delinquent youth groups by definitional approaches. In F. Esbensen & C. L. Maxson (Eds.), *Youth gangs in international perspective: Tales from the Eurogang program of research* (pp. 17–33). New York, NY: Springer.

MHA to study more police powers to curb youth gangs. (2010). *AsiaOne*. Retrieved from http://news.asiaone.com/News/AsiaOne+News/Singapore/Story/A1Story 20101124-248822.html

Miller, W. B. (1975). *Violence by youth gangs and youth groups as a crime problem in major American cities*. Washington, DC: National Institute for Juvenile Justice and Delinquency Prevention.

Ministry of Home Affairs. (2006). *The Criminal Law (Temporary Provisions) Act*. Singapore: Ministry of Home Affairs.

Ministry of Social and Family Development. (2015). *Juvenile delinquents: Juveniles arrested*. Singapore: Ministry of Social and Family Development.

More Malay youth in gangs. (2012). *AsiaOne*. Retrieved from http://news.asiaone.com/News/Latest+News/Singapore/Story/A1Story20121022-378957.htm

Morgan, W. P. (1989). *Triad societies in Hong Kong*. Hong Kong: Government Press.

Neo, L. H. (2010). *Risk, needs, and responsivity framework for Singapore Boys' Home* (Unpublished manuscript).

O'Brien, K., Daffern, M., Chu, C. M., & Thomas, S. D. M. (2013). Youth gang affiliation, violence, and criminal activities: A review of motivational, risk, and protective factors. *Aggression and Violent Behavior, 18*(4), 417–425. doi: 10.1016/j.avb.2013.05.001

Pyrooz, D. C., & Decker, S. H. (2012). Delinquent behavior, violence, and gang involvement in China. *Journal of Quantitative Criminology, 29*(2), 251–272. doi: 10.1007/s10940-012-9178-6

Pyrooz, D. C., Sweeten, G., & Piquero, A. R. (2013). Continuity and change in gang membership and gang embeddedness. *Journal of Research in Crime and Delinquency, 50*, 239–271. doi: 10.1177/0022427811434830

Sharp, C., Aldridge, J., & Medina, J. (2006). *Delinquent youth groups and offending behaviour: Findings from the 2004 Offending, Crime and Justice Survey*. London: Home Office Research Development and Statistics Directorate.

Shelden, R. G., Tracy, S. K., & Brown, W. B. (1997). *Youth gangs in American society*. Belmont, CA: Wadsworth.

Short, J. F. (1996). *Gangs and adolescent violence*. Boulder, CO: Center for the Study and Prevention of Violence, University of Colorado.

Singapore Parliamentary Report. (2013a, 8 July). Vol. 90, cols. 94–97.

Singapore Parliamentary Report. (2013b, 12 July). Vol. 90, col. 77.

Singapore Police Force. (2008). *Crime situation 2007 – Youths as perpetrators of crime*. Retrieved from http://www.spf.gov.sg/stats/stats2007_youtharrests.htm#

Singapore Police Force. (2015). *Youths against gangs*. Retrieved from http://www.police.gov.sg/yag/yag_initiatives.html

Sosis, R. (2004). The adaptive value of religious ritual. *American Scientist, 92*, 166–172.

Subordinate Courts of Singapore. (1998). Typology of youth rioters. *Research Bulletin, 10*. Retrieved from http://app2.subcourts.gov.sg/Data/Files/File/Research/RB 10Pg1-8.pdf and http://app2.subcourts.gov.sg/Data/Files/File/Research/RB10 Pg9-16.pdf

Suspects in fatal Downtown East slashing arrested. (2010, 8 September). *AsiaOne*. Retrieved from http://news.asiaone.com/News/AsiaOne+News/Crime/Story/A1Story20101102-245278

Tai, J. (2013, 21 June). Tougher anti-gang laws in the works. *Straits Times*. Retrieved from http://www.straitstimes.com/singapore/tougher-anti-gang-laws-in-the-works

Tattoo crazy? Secret society signs may put you in trouble. (1958, 7 December). *Straits Times*. Retrieved from http://eresources.nlb.gov.sg/newspapers/Digitised/Article/straitstimes19581207.2.70.aspx

Teenager jailed for triad website. (1999, 3 April). *New Straits Times*. Retrieved from https://news.google.com/newspapers?nid=1309&dat=19990403&id=RS1PAAAAIBAJ&sjid=ciEEAAAAIBAJ&pg=1240,2242708&hl=zh-TW

Thornberry, T. P., Krohn, M. D., Lizotte, A. J., & Chard-Wierschem, D. (1993). The role of juvenile gangs in facilitating delinquent behavior. *Journal of Research in Crime and Delinquency*, *30*(1), 55–71. doi: 10.1177/0022427893030001005

Thrasher, F. M. (1963). *The gang: A study of one thousand three hundred thirteen gangs in Chicago*. Chicago, IL: University of Chicago Press.

Trocki, C. (1990). *Opium and empire: Chinese society in colonial Singapore, 1800–1910*. Ithaca, NY: Cornell University Press.

Tsunokai, G. T., & Kposowa, A. J. (2002). Asian gangs in the United States: The current state of the research literature. *Crime, Law and Social Change*, *37*(1), 37–50.

Ward, T., & Brown, M. (2004). The good lives model and conceptual issues in offender rehabilitation. *Psychology, Crime, and Law*, *10*(3), 243–257. doi: 10.1080/10683160410001662744

Warren, J. F. (2003). *Ah ku and karayuki-san: Prostitution in Singapore 1870–1940*. Singapore: NUS Press.

Weber, M. (1978). *Economy and society: An outline of interpretative sociology, Volume I*. Berkeley, CA: University of California Press.

Weisel, D. L. (2002). The evolution of street gangs: An examination of form and variation. In W. L. Reed & S. H. Decker (Eds.), *Responding to gangs: Evaluation and research* (pp. 26–65). Washington, DC: National Institute of Justice.

White, R., & Mason, R. (2006). Youth gangs and youth violence: Charting the key dimensions. *Australian and New Zealand Journal of Criminology*, *39*(1), 54–70. doi: 10.1375/acri.39.1.54

Winfree, L. T., Fuller, K., Vigil, T., & Mays, G. L. (1992). The definition and measurement of 'gang status': Policy implications for juvenile justice. *Juvenile & Family Court*, *43*(1), 29–37. doi: 10.1111/j.1755-6988.1992.tb00717.x

Wood, J., & Alleyne, E. (2010). Street gang theory and research: Where are we now and where do we go from here? *Aggression and Violent Behavior*, *15*(2), 100–111. doi: 10.1016/j.avb.2009.08.005

Yen, C. H. (1985). *Coolies and mandarins: China's protection of overseas Chinese during the late Ch'ing period (1815–1911)*. Singapore: Singapore University Press.

Youths attacked by '369' gang members. (2010, 9 November). *AsiaOne*. Retrieved from http://news.asiaone.com/News/AsiaOne+News/Crime/Story/A1Story20101109-246475.html

Zaccheus, M. (2013, 17 June). Nine suspects in Orchard Road slashing case. *Straits Times*. Retrieved from http://www.straitstimes.com/singapore/nine-suspects-in-orchard-road-slashing-case-arrested

Zhang, L., Messner, S. F., Lu, Z., & Deng, X. (1997). Gang crime and its punishment in China. *Journal of Criminal Justice*, *25*(4), 289–302. doi: 10.1016/S0047-2352(97)00014-7

20 secret society arrests. (1957, 22 July). *Straits Times.* Retrieved from http://eresources.nlb.gov.sg/newspapers/Digitised/Article/freepress19570722.2.82.aspx

2 Hearing evidence from child witnesses

Hong Kong experience

Ephraem P. W. Tsui, Yuk Ip Kindy Lam, and Sook Yee Chang Lam

Introduction

Children are sometimes witnesses to crimes committed against themselves or against others. Occasionally, the sole evidence of a crime is a child's testimony. Some jurisdictions impose severe restrictions on the admission of children's testimony, which are justified by the position that children are not reliable or competent witnesses. Other jurisdictions, however, value the evidence of any child highly, to the degree that the verbal evidence of a child is sufficient to convict a defendant of a serious crime. In 1995, the *Evidence Ordinance* of Hong Kong, which was modelled on British criminal law of that time, was amended to remove nearly all restrictions against children's testimony, while the *Criminal Procedures Ordinance* was amended to facilitate children to testify in court concerning a broad range of violent and sexual crimes. Hong Kong law has since allowed:

- Children under the age of seven years to give evidence;
- Children under 14 to give unsworn evidence;
- The unsworn evidence of a child to be admitted without corroboration;
- Children to give their evidence-in-chief via a video recording, though they are still required to undergo cross-examination in court via live TV link;
- A police officer or government-employed social worker or clinical psychologist can conduct the video-recorded interview with the child witness; and
- Children giving evidence in court to be accompanied by a person acceptable to the court.

These legal changes reflected Hong Kong society's full trust in children's testimony. They were likely the first of their kind in Asia. Yet, the existence of these legal provisions does not mean that children's testimony is automatically admitted in court. The quality of the testimony and the way it is given may become major concerns in a court case. The evidence is best when collected fresh and uncontaminated. It must be clear and precise enough to be helpful to the court. However, it is optimistic to expect a child to give such good evidence. It requires motivation and cooperation on the child's part and understanding, patience, and skill on that of the investigators. It also requires that investigators avoid distressing the child during or after the investigation as this would breach the United Nations' *Convention on the Rights of the Child*, by which Hong Kong must abide.

Since 1995, thousands of child witnesses, mostly ethnic Chinese and Cantonese speakers, have given their testimony this way in Hong Kong and hundreds have testified in court. This chapter highlights the current understanding of children's testimony from a psychological perspective and illustrates how investigators and legal professionals in Hong Kong adopt a child-friendly approach and apply their knowledge to help child witnesses give the best evidence they can.

Characteristics of children's testimony

When dealing with child witnesses, investigators must remind themselves that children differ from adults in their understanding of the world and in the way they express themselves. Investigators cannot expect children to understand adult language, share adults' knowledge, or to follow adult rules or logic. Nor can investigators expect children to be as calm as adults when recounting their victimization or horrific experiences. While psychological research has demonstrated that children can be reliable witnesses, the qualities of their testimony cannot be compared to those of adults' testimony (Sas, 2002; Westcott, Davis, & Bull, 2002). This is because children may not have developed the range of essential cognitive, language, and emotional skills to meet the high standards of testimony. Certain allowances must be made to child witnesses. It is best for adults to follow children's perception, understanding, reasoning, and emotions when inviting children to tell them what they have experienced in a crime context.

Language development

The first essential difference between children and adults is in their language. What children are able to say increases with age and mental capacity. Normally, toddlers have a few hundred words at their disposal. They can name common things quite accurately. Yet they cannot join words together to make a sentence. A larger vocabulary helps them remember things. Words can enhance their visual or emotional memory of an event. Toddlers remember much more than they can tell. They can understand simple questions but can at most articulate only bits and pieces of their experiences. Since they cannot link words to form a full answer, they are often treated as incompetent witnesses. That is their disadvantage. Without their testimony, investigators must collect other evidence (Sas, 2002; Saywitz, Jaenicke, & Camparo, 1990; Steward, Bussey, Goodman, & Saywitz, 1993).

Preschool children have a much larger vocabulary and are able to use idiomatic expressions. Although preschoolers can speak in short full sentences, they still have great difficulty putting complex ideas into words and can only use words they know. They may link up words to form phrases that only they can understand. For example, they could describe semen as "white-coloured blood" and a penis the shape of a chicken's egg. Investigators may think child witnesses are talking nonsense or imagining things. Yet those may be the best words they have to describe what they have seen or experienced. Using idiosyncratic expressions does not necessarily mean that their perception or memory is faulty or their account fabricated. Because of their expressive language limitations, preschoolers are also at a disadvantage when testifying in court (Saywitz et al., 1990).

Early primary school children should have developed sufficient language skills to participate in everyday conversation using full sentences. Nevertheless, confusion often arises when abstract concepts such as time and dates, and spatial relations – "before and after", "above or under", "in and out", "first and last", "in front of or behind" – are used. Using these words requires skills of abstract manipulation in children's underdeveloped mind. Imprecision and errors are common, making their testimonies sound unreliable (Saywitz et al., 1990).

Late primary school children can make much better sense of the questions put to them. Yet they may interpret words literally or narrowly according to what they have learned. For example, they may understand the word "touch" to mean only contact with the hand and not with other parts of the body (Schumann, Bala, & Lee, 1999). If the child's body was contacted by the abuser's mouth or genitals, he or she may respond "no" to the question, "Did he touch you?" So, when investigators are familiar with the language characteristics of children, they can try alternative ways of asking questions in order to receive the nearest answers (Saywitz, 2002). It is also crucial to check what child witnesses are able to express before asking them important questions and to always check the meaning of their answers rather than accepting them literally (Cheung, 2001).

Children's memory

How much a child can recall often becomes the main basis of the evaluation of his or her competency as a witness. Investigators should try to understand how children's memory works before asking them to recall events. Generally speaking, children do have long-term memories of personal events and can provide an accurate account of these events under the right conditions. Young children recall fewer details of events than older children because they have not yet developed a good memory system to store or organise the details, nor do they have the language to express them fully. That is, although much of the memory of the event may be stored inside their mind, retrieving and articulating it is rather difficult (Ceci & Bruck, 1993; Sas, 2002; Westcott et al., 2002).

Unlike a film made with a video camera, events are not registered and stored completely in the human brain. In human memory, many details of an event will decay if left unused, yet its central elements are largely imprinted. These central elements, such as an act of sexual abuse, are the details most likely to emerge in free recall situations. Peripheral details, such as the clothes the perpetrator was wearing, the date and time of the crime, may not come out as freely, if at all. Such details may need to be sought with further probing. Older children have a more organised mind, and a greater number of such details are properly stored and remain accessible.

High anxiety during an incident can disrupt the storage of details (Peters, 1991). It causes fragmented memory traces, which are difficult to retrieve. On the other hand, high anxiety may also facilitate the storage of core details of an event, which will not go away even if the child tries to forget them. Therefore a child may recall vividly what happened to him or her personally during a horrific crime, but details of the surroundings may be very blurred. Expecting the child to remember all the details equally is unrealistic. Investigators should ask what the child can remember rather than frustrating him or her with questions about peripheral details.

Investigators cannot expect young children to provide a full account of a crime in free recall. Some researchers have pointed out that certain types of information are not encoded in the memory of young children because the relevant concepts have not yet been developed (Sas, 2002). These may include concepts of time, distance, height, age, body parts, sex, relative position, family relationships, and frequency. Asking young children such questions may not be fair to them.

Young children are not always aware of where or when they come to know something. They may confuse their personal experience with an observed experience or hearsay. Research findings suggest that children older than five are quite able to identify the source of their memories correctly (Sas, 2002). Nevertheless, it is important to always ask children if what they are reporting does indeed come from their own memory or was learned from somewhere else.

Suggestibility in children

Various studies have shown that children are more suggestible than adults and that the younger the child, the more suggestible he or she is. According to Ceci and Bruck (1995), young children's memories are easily rewritten under the influence of strong suggestions. Another research team (Thompson, Clarke-Stewart, & Lepore, 1997) found that children lack confidence and tend to look to adults for cues on how to interpret social behaviours. They found that young children tend to assume that adults have all the answers and submit to pressure from adults, modifying their answers. Investigators have to be aware that strong verbal and non-verbal expressions can influence children's confidence in their own perception.

Fortunately, research has demonstrated that children are not equally suggestible in every context. In forensic interviews, regardless of the child's age, it is much more difficult to mislead children to report sad or abuse-related events than to suggest funny, positive events (Eisen, Goodman, Qin, & Davis, 1998). This means that children are fairly resistant to suggestions that they have been victimised when they have not. Our field experience in Hong Kong has shown us that children rarely recount a convincing victimization experience when they have not experienced it personally. Thus, suggestibility lies mainly with the questioner rather than with the child. If investigators ask children the right types of question, and in the right manner, children will likely give truthful answers.

Telling the truth and telling lies

In forensic situations, it is important that children understand their duty to tell the whole truth. Child witnesses are often required to pass a test of truth and lies as if this can ensure they will tell only the truth. Research findings suggest, however, that although children are capable of telling lies from the age of four, there is no evidence that children have a greater tendency to lie than adults (Haugaard, Repucci, Laird, & Nauful, 1991). Research has also shown that children do not necessarily act according to what they know; that is, that they can tell the difference between telling the truth and telling a lie does not guarantee they will not lie (Talwar, Lee, Bala, & Lindsay, 2002). On the other hand, not knowing the difference between telling the truth and telling a lie does not necessarily mean that they will tell lies. Studies have shown that the simple act of promising to tell the truth motivates children to do so (Astington, 1988; Maas & Abbedutto, 1998).

Fantasy

Fantasy is another serious concern in children's testimony as it is commonly believed that children cannot differentiate fact from fantasy. It is true that fantasy sometimes intrudes into children's account of events, but it happens more often with younger children. There are two main types of fantasy. The first consists of highly implausible or impossible events, like "Superman flew down to rescue me". The second type consists of gross exaggeration of a plausible event, such as, "It was so painful, like I was shot by a laser gun".

In research involving a group of high-certainty sexual abuse cases, Dahlenberg (1996) found more fantasy statements in children who had suffered more severe abuse. This prompted further research and discussion of the possible causes of fantasy. First, children under four have more difficulty differentiating fact from fantasy or the source of information in their thought. They do not analyse their own thinking and thus do not tell others that ideas were invented by them. Second, traumatised children tend to use fantasy to cope with the stress because fantasy can both comfort and empower them to regain some psychological control. Third, children may introduce fantasy to help them express an unfamiliar experience (Dahlenberg, 1996; Gopnik & Graf, 1988). Since their vocabulary is still limited, they may have to borrow words or ideas from cartoons or fairy tales to help them articulate. Lastly, investigators can unintentionally encourage a child to construct a fantasy within the context of a forensic interview. For example, when a young child says, "Then Superman flew down to rescue me", instead of encouraging the child to continue her free narration of the crime, the interviewer starts to ask questions about this Superman: where he came from, what he looked like, how he fought the villains, and so on. These questions steer the child away from the account and she is glad that she does not have to talk further about her traumatic experience. The interview thus ends up with both parties co-constructing a new Superman story and the child says nothing further about the crime. So, when fantasy starts to intrude into a child's account of abuse, it does not mean that the account is not to be believed. The investigator has to understand the reason for the fantasy, and then encourage the child to continue with the account. To stop the child using the fantasy, the investigator must give him or her an easier way to recount the experience.

Overall, findings in child psychology research support the participation of child witnesses in the criminal justice system (Sas, 2002). Children as young as three have much to tell about their actual experiences but need help and support in testifying (Ceci & Bruck, 1995). Investigators and legal practitioners must have extra patience and make special allowances to children, modify and simplify their questions in order to encourage children to speak out. The main obstacles are investigators' failure to be patient while listening to children, and their expectation that children perform the witness role as competently as adults.

Difficulties of child witnesses in court

Before testifying in court

In order to understand children's difficulties when testifying in court, adults need to look beyond their appearance in court itself and try to appreciate the various difficulties they have faced before coming to testify in court. In cases of sexual abuse within the family, after a disclosure is made, children and their families are often swept up in a complex process that they may not understand. Children are not prepared for the stressful and demanding events that follow. For example, they are not prepared for the intrusive questioning by people in authority, the medical examination, or the strong reactions of people hearing their disturbing story. Research findings suggest that what most children want from disclosure is simply for someone to stop the abuse for them (Sas, Hurley, Hatch, Malla, & Dick, 1993). They do not expect to have to testify in court months later about what has happened to them. Some young children may not even know what a court or trial is. They are not prepared for the critical questioning they are submitted to in court. They do not foresee that their parents cannot be with them when they testify. All these experiences are unimaginable and emotionally taxing for children.

Testifying in court

Walker (1993) observed and outlined six basic expectations of child witnesses in court: (a) that they have actually observed or experienced the event in question; (b) that they can remember the event in question; (c) that they can recount the event from memory; (d) that they understand the questions put to them in the witness box; (e) that they can give intelligent answers to the questions put to them; and (f) that they are aware of their duty to speak the truth. Melton (1981) also suggested that a child witness must: (a) have the cognitive skills to adequately comprehend what they have experienced; (b) be able to organise that experience cognitively; (c) be able to differentiate the memory in question from other memories or fantasies; and (d) be able to maintain and demonstrate these skills under stressful conditions. Greenhoot and colleagues (1995) found that child witnesses' verbal reports of an event cannot fully reflect what they actually remember, mostly owing to the fact that they cannot meet the behavioural and cognitive demands of the forensic examination, which are greatly compromised by child witnesses' ability to withstand the emotional demands placed on them.

It is known that high anxiety has a negative impact on children's memory. However, child witnesses experience extremely high anticipatory anxiety as they do not know how the criminal justice system works. In court, child witnesses are often questioned about a stressful event by a lawyer who may employ a confrontational tone, particularly during cross-examination. The proceedings may also be carried out in what has been referred to as "legalese", which sounds like a foreign language to children (Quas, Goodman, Ghetti, & Redlich, 2000). Many legal terms are unfamiliar to children, the phrases are confusing if not incomprehensible, and the questions too abstract or critical, potentially making the task of testifying insurmountable for children. This defeats the original purpose of inviting children to tell the court what happened. There are other special challenges for child witnesses in court, as shown in Table 2.1.

1. Making inferences about others' intentions and taking another's perspective

Young children struggle to describe what others are feeling and are not very perceptive of others' intentions, particularly those of perpetrators. They tend to respond to questions on these areas by simply projecting their own feelings and perceptions onto others. Typically, children under the age of seven struggle unsuccessfully with the demand to make an inference about others' intentions, or take another person's perspective, while children under 10 can do so but need assistance (Sas, 2002).

Similarly, children find it difficult to deal with ambiguous verbal messages. They cannot distinguish between the superficial message in the question and the speaker's intention in asking it. This is particularly notable during cross-examination, when questions with assumptions and underlining meanings are

Table 2.1 Special challenges for child witnesses in court

1. Making inferences about others' intentions, and taking another's perspective
2. Dealing with hypothetical questions
3. Using scaled models to explain a situation
4. A tendency to attribute knowledge to adults
5. Not knowing what they do not know
6. Estimating duration and frequency of events, and dates
7. The concepts of court and justice
8. Fear and anxiety

often asked: “Did you weep when your uncle touched you?” or “Did you accept his gift?” As children tend to respond only to the superficial side of ambiguous questions, without the chance to elaborate, their answers can be used to create doubts later to the defendant’s benefit.

2. Dealing with hypothetical questions

Children under 10 have difficulty responding to hypothetical situations. They have not yet developed the abstract reasoning abilities to handle them. They are generally unable to follow *what if* questions. Some children will simply deny that the suggested scenario is an accurate description, while others may submit to giving answers to questions they cannot understand. Thus, not asking hypothetical questions would be a good step towards ensuring that the responses provided by children are accurate and within their cognitive development.

3. Using scaled models to explain a situation

Young children are often asked to explain something by referring to a drawing, a map, or a model. However, researchers have found that children have difficulty with the concept that a model is an object in its own right and simultaneously a symbol of something else (Sas, 2002). Moreover, children’s mental ability to reduce both distances and heights to scale in models takes time to develop. So, it may be difficult for a child witness to point out accurately, for example, “Where were you on this floor plan of the house (or in this map of the park)?” In forensic cases, children are sometimes permitted to use dolls or drawings to represent themselves or others. Caution should be exercised with children under three because they have not yet developed the sense of self as separate from others, and are unable to imagine that a doll can represent the self.

4. Tendency to attribute knowledge to adults

Owing to social desirability factors, children tend to view adults as omniscient (Saywitz & Camparo, 1998). Children tend to assume that if they know something, other people, particularly adults, must know it too. Because of this perception, children are reserved in offering spontaneous information. Moreover, they tend to fail to note the gaps when they explain what has happened. Their account of an event is typically very brief, jumpy, and incomplete as they expect adult listeners to know the rest of the story. However, in court, they are required to fill in every gap of their account. This can be a very frustrating process for the child witness. The gaps also tempt adults to make guesses and to ask leading questions. One way of overcoming this problem is to tell a child early and clearly that the adult listeners do not actually know what he or she knows and then invite him or her to recount everything that he or she can recall. This strategy has been shown to be useful in reducing leading questions and thus suggestibility (Mulder & Vrij, 1996).

5. Not knowing what they do not know

Another potential problem is that children do not know what they do not know. Markman (1979) found that children can have difficulty with "comprehension monitoring"; that is, they often fail to realise that they have not understood the material or questions put to them. They tend to think they should know the answer, which prompts them to give an answer. One way to minimise made-up answers is to ask children only simple, clear, and age-appropriate questions. Adults need to remind children that they can say, "I don't know" or "I can't remember" if that is the case. Another way is to check their comprehension by asking them to paraphrase or restate what they have been asked, or asking them to explain what they believe the words mean.

6. Estimating duration and frequency of events and dates

Children are frequently asked when an incident occurred and how long it lasted. Under optimal research and stress-free conditions, children at certain ages may be able to recall time or duration quite precisely. However, testifying in court certainly cannot be regarded as an optimal condition. Children have great difficulty recalling and estimating how many times an event has occurred. To them, every time is the same. They may be able to tell more about the first and last time it occurred, but they will struggle to discriminate between events that happened repeatedly.

Young children in particular struggle to tell how long an event lasted as they have not yet mastered the concepts of time and duration. Asking them about the duration of an event will likely yield an incorrect answer. With respect to dates, weeks, months, or seasons of the year, young children can rattle off the names of the days of the week, or the current calendar year, or the year they were born, yet still have difficulty placing an event along a time line. This is why they cannot tell if an event occurred a long time or a short while ago. For many preschoolers, there is no distant past, just a "yesterday". Primary school-age children are aware of the past, but it is very compressed.

Preschool children cannot tell the time accurately. If adults ask them, they will probably give a wrong answer. So it is more meaningful to ask young children to explain when an event occurred relative to major time markers of that specific day, such as breakfast time, after school, TV time, or just before bed. Thus, the rule of thumb should be that abstract questions – such as asking for the date and time an event occurred, the frequency and duration of an incident, the height and distance of different objects – should be avoided whenever possible when dealing with very young children.

7. Concepts of court and justice

Most children know very little about the criminal justice system and why they are going to court. Children tend to understand that the judge is a very serious person with the power to punish people. Some may anticipate punishment by the judge if they say something wrong. By the age of 10, most children understand the roles of the judge, witness, and police, and the meaning of breaking the law. Yet they still do not understand the roles of lawyers and the jury. They may have seen a trial in session on TV but they would not understand the spirit of the law or its process.

Children typically assume that all the adults in the courtroom will believe them when they explain what has happened, and that all adults want the same court outcomes as they do. They will also expect the defendant to tell the truth about the crime because no one is allowed to lie in court. Such feelings of goodwill and high expectations of the adults in court are extended to the judge. Children thus cannot understand why a judge would doubt them when they are telling the truth. Similarly, children do not appreciate the underlying rules of the trial. When a defence lawyer suggests misinformation to them, they tend to view it as an honest mistake rather than a tactic to discredit them. These phenomena are proven in child psychology research, which suggests that children under nine years old still adhere to the "sincerity postulate", that is, they expect a high degree of sincerity that is not present in the adversarial process (Sas, 2002). This explains why a child may easily acquiesce to misleading questions even though the facts are inconsistent with what they know.

8. Fear and anxiety

Finally, some researchers (Moston & Engelberg, 1992; Peters, 1991) have strongly suggested that when children are very anxious, when they feel intimidated and are made anxious by an unsupportive environment, or when they lack the necessary knowledge to interact appropriately in court, they perform less well in testifying.

In sum, children can have many forensically relevant details to offer the court. But they face various difficulties and challenges in doing so. To obtain the best evidence from children, adults have to take these limitations into consideration and adopt a child-centred and child-friendly approach to accommodate them. Applying adult rules to child witnesses is pointless and even unfair to them.

Questioning child witnesses in Hong Kong

One way to eliminate the undesirable factors affecting the credibility of child witnesses is to collect their verbal evidence through a skilled interviewer and to record the whole process on video soon after the crime is reported. The child's verbal evidence and demeanour are preserved on video which can be reviewed multiple times without requiring the child to repeat his or her testimony to different persons. A legal provision of 1995 provides that such video-recorded interviews are admissible in Hong Kong courts as the child's evidence-in-chief. The interview can be conducted by a police officer, a social worker, or clinical psychologist employed by the government. The recording is reviewed in court as if the child were giving the evidence inside the courtroom. The pre-recorded interview must satisfy all the rules of evidence and the interview environment must be friendly and sufficiently stress-free to facilitate the child to give the best evidence possible. This demands a high degree of sensitivity, knowledge, and skill from the interviewer.

Hong Kong's video-recorded interview approach and protocol were borrowed from the UK's *Memorandum of good practice on video recorded interviews with child witnesses for criminal proceedings* (Home Office, 1992) and subsequently *Achieving best evidence in criminal proceedings* (Home Office, 2001; Ministry of Justice, 2011; National Police Improvement Agency, 2007). Based on these blueprints and accumulated case experience over 20 years, Hong Kong has developed and fine-tuned questioning skills to form the interviewing protocol that is used today with nearly all child witnesses as prescribed by the law.

All video-recorded interviews in Hong Kong are conducted in designated child-friendly and undisturbed interviewing suites managed by the Hong Kong Police. All the equipment is standardised and satisfies the rules for evidence. A non-offending parent or guardian and the case social worker attend to hear the evidence through a live TV link outside the interviewing room.

Interviewing a child witness when he or she is not yet ready is unfavourable because the video recording cannot be paused or restarted in Hong Kong. In the spirit of good practice, there is usually only one chance to conduct a successful video-recorded interview. This requires interviewers to earn the trust of children to tell the whole truth and to possess the forensic interviewing skills to cover all the necessary evidence. To increase the chances of success and to ensure adequate coverage of evidence, the interviewer is backed up by an equally well-trained monitoring officer from the Hong Kong Police or the Social Welfare Department in the adjacent room, who can offer advice and assistance through a "bug in the ear" communications earpiece.

There are four stages in a typical video-recorded interview, which may last between half an hour to several hours, depending on the complexity of the account:

I. Rapport building
II. Free narration
III. Questioning
IV. Closing

Stage I: Rapport building

Rapport building is very important although it is not part of the child's evidence. This step must be short but effective in relaxing and engaging the child and preparing him or her to disclose the incident fully. After a brief introduction, the interviewer helps the child show how well he or she can talk about an ordinary event. The child's ability to describe the date, time, place, processes, and details of a neutral personal experience can normally be demonstrated by asking just a few open questions for the child to fill in. The subject may be a school event or a favourite activity that the child is happy to talk about. This stage also helps familiarise the child with the interviewer's questioning style. If the child shows particular weaknesses in narration, the interviewer can adjust the questioning approach.

As soon as the child has got used to the interview and is ready to talk about the crime, the interview will lightly interrupt to set the ground rules for the child. The interviewer will check the child's ability to differentiate between telling the truth and telling a lie. The interviewer has to ensure that the child understands the importance of telling the truth and promising to tell only the truth. The child is reminded that it is better to say, "I don't know", "I don't understand", "I don't remember", or "I don't know how to say it" when he or she finds it difficult to answer any question. The child is reassured that the interviewer can always rephrase a question to make it easier to understand. The interviewer must also attend to the emotional and other needs of the child, and also try to respond to the child's questions with care and sensitivity in order to alleviate his or her worries.

Stage II: Free narration

Child witnesses usually already know from their parents or guardians why they have come to the interview and what they are expected to talk about. Simple prompts such as "Tell me what happened", "Tell me more about that", "And then what happened?" can usually help older children to complete the free narration. Some witnesses may find it difficult to articulate, so moments of silence or reassuring words are given. The interviewer needs to find out the total number of incidents experienced by each witness in order to get an overview of the crime, and to make sure the child is narrating the crimes one by one. The interviewer must refrain from interrupting the child's free narration as any distraction can easily hinder his or her free recall. This free narration contains the core memory of the crime and children seldom include peripheral details. The interviewer needs to listen to this free narrative account with special care because gaps or conflicting facts have to be clarified later.

Stage III: Questioning

After the child has exhausted his or her free narrative account, a number of questioning skills are used to find out more about the incidents. The questions used usually move from the general to the specific. The usual skills involved are strategic use of:

i. Open-ended questions,
ii. Multiple-choice questions, and
iii. Closed-ended questions.

i. Open-ended questions

To prompt children to say more about a particular aspect of an incident, open-ended questions are the first choice. Typical open-ended questions start with "when", "where", "who", "what", or "how". For example, "When did that happen?", "Where was your mother at that time?", "Who is Uncle?", "What did Uncle say to you?", or "How did Uncle touch you?" Any answer may be followed by a free-narrative question, such as "Tell me more about that", so that the child feels free to elaborate. When children find it difficult to respond because a question induces embarrassment or anxiety, or simply because they do not know how to articulate an idea, alternative questioning skills are used.

ii. Multiple-choice questions

Multiple-choice questions are very useful when children struggle to express an idea. Children often find multiple-choice questions easier to answer and they lessen embarrassment when the topic becomes sensitive. However, multiple-choice questions may impose limits on the possible answers. Instead of just asking, "Did it happen in the morning, in the afternoon, or in the evening?" a free choice (". . . or at another time?") is always given so that all possible answers are covered. After answering an easy multiple-choice question, children are usually more able to continue their free narration. Multiple-choice questions must not be used for critical issues such as the identity of the perpetrator as they can be considered misleading.

iii. Closed-ended questions

A closed-ended question limits the child's choice to one or two answers. They can become highly suggestive or misleading if the child feels pressure to answer. Yet closed-ended questions can be useful when the interviewer foresees that there are only one or two possible answers. For instance, "Was there anyone else at home when your uncle touched you?", or "Did he talk to you when he grabbed your hand?", but this last would only be asked after the child has said that the uncle grabbed his or her hand. Closed-ended questions are also useful sometimes to help shy or quiet children speak up in the interview. They may find such questions easy to answer, and once they start to respond, more open questioning skills can be used.

Skilful interviewers will ask easier questions first, such as "who", "where", and "what". Children may find it difficult to answer when and how questions, so these may be asked later in order to avoid frustrating them. Since many clarifying questions may be asked in this questioning stage, child witnesses, particularly young ones, may get tired or stressed. The interviewer must also attend to the physical and emotional needs of every child. Short breaks, moments of silence, a cushion to hug, some water to sip, or adjustment of the room temperature may be offered to make children feel cared for and respected.

iv. Closing

After clarifying all the elements of the crime with the child, the interviewer thanks the child for his or her cooperation and explains what will happen next. A summary of the crime is unnecessary but the interviewer should address any questions or concerns raised by the child. The interview should end with the child feeling relieved and reassured. The video recording is stopped after the child has left the room to re-join the parent or guardian waiting outside.

QUESTIONS TO AVOID

With child witnesses, certain forms of question must be avoided (Cheung, 2001):

1) Two-part questions, such as "Can you tell me who kicked you?", which actually contains two questions, (i) "Can you tell me?" and (ii) "Who kicked you?", since children tend to answer the easier part (i.e. "No, I can't tell you"), providing a response that fails to answer the main question;
2) Multifaceted questions also contain two or more questions, but each of these embedded questions deserves separate attention, such as "What did you tell your mother and what did your mother do upon hearing it?", as children may not be able to handle the complication;
3) Questions that change the child's wording, for example, responding to the statement "Daddy kissed me" with the question "How did Papa kiss you?", because "Daddy" and "Papa" may mean two different people in a child's life;
4) Age-inappropriate questions, such as asking a toddler who has not learned to tell the time, "What time was it when it happened?", or asking "How big was the room?" when the child has no sense of dimensions;
5) Repeated questions, because children may think the earlier answer to the same question was unacceptable and thus try to adjust their response to please the interviewer;
6) Double-negative questions, such as "You didn't want to go but you didn't tell him, did you?", as these are difficult for any child to comprehend;
7) Leading questions informed by the interviewer's preconceived ideas about the crime asked before the child has said something related;
8) Interrupting questions, when the interviewer is too eager to clarify something before the child has finished his or her narration; and
9) Why questions, such as "Why didn't you shout for help?", because children may not be able to explain a particular behaviour and such questions may imply fault on the child's part.

All questions should be formulated considering the ability and characteristics of the child, and all should be short, simple, open, distinct, and to the point. If the interviewer needs to ask the same question again, he or she must make it clear that it is the interviewer's responsibility or absentmindedness rather than allowing the child to believe that he or she has given a wrong answer. Instead of starting a question with "why", the interviewer can start it with "what" or "how", for example, "What made you follow your uncle's instruction since you said you didn't like it?" It is important that the interviewer is patient and follows the pace, logic, and perspective of the child.

CAREFUL USE OF ANATOMICALLY DETAILED DOLLS, DRAWINGS, AND OTHER PROPS

Sometimes, when the child is too young to narrate details of an incident of sexual abuse, the interviewer may use anatomically detailed dolls and drawings to facilitate the narration (Cheung, 2012). However, it is very natural for non-abused children to play with anatomically detailed dolls in seemingly sexual ways when presented to them. For example, non-abused children will quickly discover that the clothes of these dolls can be taken off easily and that there are holes in the body that can admit their little fingers. Before long, these non-abused children will be seemingly "molesting" the dolls as if re-enacting an abusive act. Similarly, though well intentioned, the use of other props in the forensic interview, such as a ruler for measurement, colour samples to identify a colour, a doll's house or models, may be construed as a misleading gesture as they can limit the answers of the witness.

If children have not mentioned any abusive act, dolls and drawings should not be introduced as they can be highly suggestive of some sexual behaviours. Anatomically detailed dolls are used only when children find it too difficult to describe the posture and movements of a sexual act that they have already mentioned but not clearly enough. Drawings of human figures are used for children to mark body parts they had difficulty pinpointing. In Hong Kong, the use of anatomically detailed dolls and drawings in forensic interviewing follows a particular procedure that should help the child understand that it is not a toy or game, the purpose is clear, the interviewer will not make any suggestion, the child's free choice and narration are valued, the process is captured closely by the camera, and the child should feel respected if doll's clothes are removed.

VIDEO-RECORDED EVIDENCE

In Hong Kong, for every video-recorded interview, two digital video discs are made on site, one as the evidence copy, which will be sealed until opened in court, and the other as the working copy for use in the investigation. As their narration of the crime is recorded on video, child witnesses do not need to repeat the experience to different persons and can set it aside until called to court to testify. Those observing the interview via the live TV link should also have very clear ideas of what the child witness has experienced and said so that they can work to help and protect the child.

Occasionally, when new evidence is found, such as a tool or a video recording of the victimization process, it may be necessary to ask a child witness to clarify certain points or to identify the evidence. Re-interviewing child witnesses always requires special permission from the Department of Justice. All second interviews must be carefully planned by the investigators in order to avoid distressing the child witness, particularly when the materials are pornographic or shocking to watch.

Supporting child witnesses

Protective measures were built into the Hong Kong system for child witnesses in 1995, covering the process from investigation to court trial outcome. There are public policies and referral directives for handling cases involving victims of child abuse. A social worker is designated as the Case Manager on the day the crime is reported. A multidisciplinary case conference is held to devise a coordinated protection and welfare plan for every abused child with the involvement of parents/guardians. Regular multidisciplinary training on handling child witnesses and victims has been put in place, including specialised joint training for police officers and government-employed social workers and clinical psychologists, to investigate such cases and conduct forensic interviews.

The Hong Kong Police and the Social Welfare Department also work together closely to prepare and support child witnesses to testify in court. A Witness Support Programme has been established to help reduce child witnesses' fear and anxiety. A trained independent individual is assigned as a Support Person for every child witness. The main responsibilities of a Support Person are fourfold. First, before the court hearing, the Support Person will help the child witness to understand the court proceedings with the aid of the *Child witness pack* (Social Welfare Department, 2015). The pack contains information booklets for children and their parents/guardians. In children's language and with colourful drawings, the booklets illustrate what the court is like and the role of different parties in the trial. It also explains the duty of witnessing via live TV link. It reminds the child witness to tell the truth and how to express themselves if they have needs or requests. Second, upon the arrangement of the police, the Support Person accompanies the child to make a pre trial court visit to help familiarise him or her with the environment. Third, on the day the child gives testimony, the Support Person stays with the child inside the witness room. The Support Person is forbidden to communicate with the child during the testimony, even to offer comfort, without the judge's permission. The Support Person sits behind the child such that the child cannot even see any non-verbal gestures made by the Support Person. The Support Person is trained to approach the court usher if he or she observes that the witness is in need of assistance. Fourth, after the court hearing, if the child needs it, the Support Person arranges a final meeting to inform him or her of the trial's outcome in a supportive manner.

Other protective measures during court proceedings include: (a) a fast track in the Department of Justice to handle cases involving child witnesses; (b) designated passages and facilities for child witnesses in the court building; (c) removal of ceremonial wigs and gowns in court when the child is testifying; (d) allowing the child witness to use instant photographs to identify the perpetrator in court;

and (e) prohibition of the mass media to disclose the identity and address of the child. All these measures may help reduce the child witness' anxiety without sacrificing the fairness of the trial of the defendant.

Conclusion

To conclude, Hong Kong has 20 years of experience facilitating children to testify in criminal cases and maintaining a multidisciplinary child protection system. Conducting video-recorded interviews with child witnesses and helping them to testify in court have become daily practice for police officers, social workers, and other professionals working with children. Child psychology and social work principles are faithfully applied throughout the system and procedures. With the dedication of all those involved, the dual mission of satisfying the principles of criminal justice and child protection can be achieved. Although the laws of Hong Kong and the basic child protection system have changed little since 1995, the accumulated experience of 20 years' practice have helped refine the quality of each of the measures, thus facilitating child witnesses to give their best evidence and reassuring every child witness that he or she will be protected despite their unfortunate experience.

Case study

Kit is 10 years old and lives with her parents. This morning at school, she disclosed to her classmate that her father molested her at home. The classmate encouraged her to tell the school social worker. Upon hearing this, the school social worker called the Family and Child Protective Services Unit (FCPSU), the specialised unit of the Social Welfare Department, for a consultation. An FCPSU social worker advised the school social worker to ask Kit a few key questions to establish that it was indeed a suspected incident of child sexual abuse and then offered help to report the case to the police. Before long, the FCPSU social worker and the officers of Child Abuse Investigation Unit (CAIU), the specialised unit of the Hong Kong Police, visited the school together to meet the school social worker. They also called Kit's mother to come, but did not tell her the reason. After informing Kit's mother of the sexual abuse report, the joint investigation team, comprising FCPSU and CAIU, arranged a video-recorded interview with Kit the same afternoon without questioning Kit further.

The team arrived at the child-friendly interviewing suite and settled Kit and her mother. It was decided that the FCPSU social officer would interview Kit while a CAIU officer would monitor proceedings in the adjacent room. The interviewer built a rapport with Kit while the monitor prepared the recording equipment. When Kit was ready, the interviewer invited her to enter the interviewing room. Her mother witnessed the entire process from outside via live TV link with the company of another CAIU officer. At the beginning of the interview, the interviewer spent some time introducing the room and chatted with Kit about her daily life to help her get used to the interview and to demonstrate her ability in answering questions. Then the interviewer softly changed topic to ascertain Kit's ability to differentiate between telling the truth and telling a lie. The interviewer encouraged Kit to tell only the truth, but told her that she could always say so if she was unable to answer. Then the interviewer invited Kit to recount the incident in her own way and at her own pace without interrupting her. Next, the interviewer asked Kit how many times such a thing had happened and then requested details of the process, time, place, people involved, etc. for each incident that she could recall. The monitoring officer next door listened carefully and jotted down missing information which would be essential to establish a crime. Once the interviewer had exhausted her questions, the monitoring officer suggested supplementary questions to ask. As Kit could narrate quite clearly with words, no doll or drawing was used.

While Kit described the multiple incestuous incidents, her mother became very emotional outside. Hearing how her husband had been sexually abusing their daughter was devastating. The CAIU officer present comforted her and prevented her from interrupting the interview. Meanwhile, the CAIU officer contacted the Forensic Pathologist to prepare to collect medical evidence from Kit as soon as possible. The interview lasted over two hours. Kit rejoined her mother waiting outside. Following the interview, the FCPSU and CAIU officers immediately discussed how best to protect and help Kit. The CAIU officers then arranged Kit's forensic examination and proceeded to arrest and charge Kit's father and to collect crime scene evidence. Kit was safe from her father as he was detained by the court. As Kit had made a video-recorded statement, she did not have to recount her abuse again. The FCPSU social worker conducted a comprehensive social investigation of Kit's family and then arranged a multidisciplinary case conference to formulate a welfare plan for her and her family.

While waiting to testify in court, Kit received professional counselling from social worker and a psychologist who did not discuss the abuse incident with her. She was helped to resume a normal family and school life as far as possible. When the court trial was fixed, she was assigned a Support Person to help her prepare for witness duty. A week before the trial, Kit visited the court and reviewed her video-recorded statement. The Support Person accompanied her throughout the testifying period in the special room reserved for child witnesses. The judge and counsels greeted her in a friendly manner and she was required to review her statement while it was played in court. When being cross-examined, she was protected from unfair questioning by the judge. There ended her duty as witness. She was informed of the trial verdict and a counselling service was provided as long as she needed it.

Chapter summary points

- Children are reliable witnesses but their testimony is limited by their language, concepts, memory, vulnerability to suggestion and fantasy, anxiety, and respect for adults and authority.

- Children can give good evidence if adults understand their developmental limitations and adjust their forensic interviewing approach or questioning style as appropriate.
- Hong Kong has 20 years' experience of video-recording interviews with child witnesses and has developed its own child-friendly protocol that satisfies the rules of evidence as well as the psychological needs of children.
- Special measures in criminal procedures can facilitate children to give evidence in court without excessive fear and uncertainty, which would undermine the quality of their evidence.

References

Astington, J. W. (1988). Children's understanding of the speech act of promising. *Journal of Child Language*, *15*, 157–173. doi: 10.1017/S0305000900012101

Ceci, S. J., & Bruck, M. (1993). Suggestibility of the child witness: A historical perspective. *Psychological Bulletin*, *113*, 403–439. doi: 10.1037/0033-2909.113.3.403

Ceci, S. J., & Bruck, M. (1995). *Jeopardy in the courtroom: A scientific analysis of children's testimony*. Washington, DC: American Psychological Association.

Cheung, M. (2001). Critical issues in multidisciplinary child sexual abuse allegation investigation. *Hong Kong Journal of Social Work*, *35*(1), 13–33. doi: 10.1142/S0219246201000031

Cheung, M. (2012). *Child sexual abuse: Best practices for interviewing and treatment*. Chicago, IL: Lyceum.

Dahlenberg, C. (1996). Fantastic elements in child disclosure of abuse. *APSAC Advisor*, *9*(2), 1, 5–10.

Eisen, M. L., Goodman, G. S., Qin, J., & Davis, S. L. (1998). Memory and suggestibility in maltreated children: New research relevant to evaluating allegations of abuse. In S. Lynn & K. McConkey (Eds.), *Truth in memory* (pp. 163–189). New York, NY: Guildford.

Gopnik, A., & Graf, P. (1988). Knowing how you know. *Child Development*, *59*, 1366–1371.

Greenhoot, A. F., Ornstein, P. A., Gordon, B. N., & Baker-Ward, L. (1995). Acting out the details of a pediatric check-up: The impact of interview condition and behavioral style on children's memory reports. *Child Development*, *70*(2), 363–380. doi: 10.1111/1467-8624.00027

Haugaard, J. J., Repucci, N. D., Laird, J., & Nauful, T. (1991). Children's definitions of the truth and their competency to testify in legal proceedings. *Law and Human Behavior*, *15*, 253–271. doi: 10.1007/BF01061712

Home Office. (1992). *Memorandum of good practice on video recorded interviews with child witnesses for criminal proceedings*. London: HMSO.

Home Office. (2001). *Achieving best evidence in criminal proceedings: Guidance for vulnerable or intimidated witnesses, including children*. London: Home Office Communication Directorate.

Maas, F., & Abbedutto, L. (1998). Young children's understanding of promising: Methodological considerations. *Journal of Child Language*, *25*, 203–214.

Markman, E. (1979). Realizing that you don't understand: Elementary school children's awareness of inconsistencies. *Child Development*, *50*, 643–655. doi: 10.2307/1128929

Melton, G. B. (1981). Children's competency to testify. *Law and Human Behavior, 5*, 73–85. doi: 10.1007/BF01048573
Ministry of Justice. (2011). *Achieving best evidence in criminal proceedings: Guidance on interviewing victims and witnesses, and guidance on using special measures.* London: Ministry of Justice.
Moston, S., & Engelberg, T. (1992). The effects of social support on children's eyewitness testimony. *Applied Cognitive Psychology, 6*, 61–75. doi: 10.1002/acp.2350060104
Mulder, M. R., & Vrij, A. (1996). Explaining conversational rules to children: An intervention study to facilitate children's accurate responses. *Child Abuse and Neglect, 20*(7), 623–631. doi: 10.1016/0145-2134(96)00050-6
National Police Improvement Agency. (2007). *Achieving best evidence in criminal proceedings: Guidance on interviewing victims and witnesses, and using special measures.* London: Office for Criminal Justice Reform.
Peters, D. P. (1991). The influence of stress and arousal on the child witness. In J. Doris (Ed.), *The suggestibility of children's recollections: Implications for eyewitness testimony* (pp. 60–76). Washington, DC: American Psychological Association.
Quas, J. A., Goodman, G. S., Ghetti, S., & Redlich, A. (2000). Questioning the child witness: What can we conclude from the research this far? *Trauma, Violence and Abuse, 1*(3), 223–249. doi: 10.1177/1524838000001003002
Sas, L. (2002). *The interaction between children's developmental capabilities and the courtroom environment: The impact on testimonial competency.* Ottawa: Department of Justice Canada.
Sas, L., Hurley, P., Hatch, A., Malla, S., & Dick, T. (1993). *Three years after the verdict: A longitudinal study of the social and psychological adjustment of child witnesses referred to the child witness project.* London, Ontario: London Family Court.
Saywitz, K. (2002). Developmental underpinnings of children's testimony. In H. L. Westcott, G. M. Davis, & R. H. C. Bull (Eds.), *Children's testimony: A handbook of psychological research and forensic practice* (pp. 3–19). Chichester, UK: John Wiley & Sons.
Saywitz, K., & Camparo, L. (1998). Interviewing child witnesses: A developmental perspective. *Child Abuse and Neglect, 22*(8), 825–843. doi: 10.1016/S0145-2134(98)00054-4
Saywitz, K., Jaenicke, C., & Camparo, L. (1990). Children's knowledge of legal terminology. *Law and Human Behavior, 14*(6), 523–535. doi: 10.1007/BF01044879
Schumann, J. P., Bala, N., & Lee, K. (1999). Developmentally appropriate questions for child witnesses. *Queen's Law Journal, 1*, 251–304.
Social Welfare Department. (2015, revised). *Child witness pack* (in Chinese). Hong Kong: Hong Kong SAR Government.
Steward, M., Bussey, K., Goodman, G., & Saywitz, K. (1993). Implications of developmental research for interviewing children. *Child Abuse and Neglect, 17*(1), 25–37. doi: 10.1016/0145-2134(93)90005-P
Talwar, V., Lee, K., Bala, N., & Lindsay, R. C. L. (2002). Children's conceptual knowledge of lying and its relation to their actual behaviours: Implications for court competence examinations. *Law and Human Behaviour, 26*(4), 395–415. doi: 10.1023/A:1016379104959
Thompson, W. C., Clarke-Stewart, K. A., & Lepore, S. J. (1997). What did the janitor do? Suggestive interviewing and the accuracy of children's accounts. *Law and Human Behavior, 21*(4), 405–426. doi: 10.1023/A:1024859219764

Walker, A. G. (1993). Questioning young children in court – A linguistic case study. *Law and Human Behavior*, *17*(1), 59–81. doi: 10.1007/BF01044537

Westcott, H. L., Davis, G. M., & Bull, R. H. C. (Eds.). (2002). *Children's testimony: A handbook of psychological research and forensic practice*. Chichester, UK: John Wiley & Sons.

3 Criminal responsibility (insanity defence) in Hong Kong

Samuel Adjorlolo and Heng Choon (Oliver) Chan

Introduction

There are generally two categories of defendants involved in the criminal justice system or criminal proceedings depending on their mental health status: those without mental health issues and those with some degree of mental health problems (Adjorlolo, Chan, & Agboli, 2016). Whereas defendants without mental abnormalities are somewhat easy to deal with in terms of the complexity of the criminal proceedings, the converse is true for those with mental disorders. Notably, the presence of mental abnormality in the courtroom can affect criminal proceedings in several ways. One of the seemingly most important and well-discussed ways is blameworthiness or liability (insanity at the time of offence, diminished responsibility, and automatism). Given the scarcity of the insanity defence literature from Asian countries relative to Western countries, this chapter fills this gap by discussing the insanity defence and its application in Hong Kong.

This chapter is organised as follows. First, a brief overview of the concept of mental illness and criminal responsibility and the origin of the insanity defence law is provided. This is followed by a comprehensive discussion of the provision in Hong Kong with respect to the elements of the insanity defence legislation, adjudicating insanity defendants, the special verdict, and the disposition of insanity acquittees. The chapter concludes by offering some recommendations for research into the insanity defence.

Mental illness and the concept of criminal responsibility

In criminal law, finding a person guilty of an offence requires that he/she is criminally responsible for the offence in question. To be held criminally responsible, it must be proved that the person actually or attempted to commit a crime (i.e., the physical element; *actus reus*) and, in doing so, the person had and/or had acted on the requisite rational intent, knowledge, and free will (i.e., the mental element; *mens rea*) (Adjorlolo, Agboli, & Chan, 2016). In essence, the nexus between actus reus and mens rea must be established. Whereas both elements are the principal focus in criminal trials, there is a general and a common presumption that any person charged with an offence had the necessary mens rea (Allnutt,

Samuels, & O'Driscoll, 2007). However, the issue can also be raised, mostly by the defence counsel, that the defendant lacks the necessary mens rea. When there are reasons to believe that the offence was committed as a result of irrational or defective mens rea, consideration is given to whether a mental disorder contributed to the distorted or impaired mens rea. Where a mental disorder is reasonably suspected to have influenced the commission of the crime, a further consideration is whether the insanity defence is appropriate. Raising the insanity defence, therefore, implies that there is no contention regarding whether the defendant committed the offence but only on his mental state at the time the crime was committed. Thus, in insanity defence trials, the focus is on the mental element of the crime rather than the physical element.

Brief history of the origin of the insanity defence

The insanity defence may be raised by a defendant who supposedly suffered from a mental abnormality at the time of committing the alleged offence. This defence is one of the most controversial and well-debated defences in criminal law in many industrialised nations, particularly in the United States. The debate about holding mentally ill persons criminally blameworthy has a long history, appearing first in Roman law in the third century and later in the sixth century (Allnutt et al., 2007). Prior to the 1800s, the insanity defence laws were generally stringent, requiring a person's mind to be totally deprived, akin to that of "a wild beast" (Zhao & Ferguson, 2013). However, in 1843, a more generous test of the insanity defence was enacted following the case involving Daniel M'Naghten, who attempted to murder the then Prime Minister of England, Robert Peel, but mistakenly shot and killed the prime minister's private secretary. At the trial, it was concluded, on the basis of psychiatric and other circumstantial evidence, that M'Naghten was mentally incapacitated at the time of the alleged offence. Consequently, albeit he was acquitted of all the criminal charges on the basis of *not guilty by reason of insanity* (NGRI), he was committed for mandatory treatment. Even before the decision in M'Naghten, there had been an acquittal based on insanity in a high-profile case involving the attempted assassination of Queen Victoria (Gledhill, 2012). Given the tensions and the controversies that accompanied the outcomes of these trials, particularly the M'Naghten trial, the House of Lords sought clarifications from the judges of the common law concerning the law governing insanity and criminal acts. The Judges of the Queen's Bench responded to series of questions that eventually culminated in what universally became known as the M'Naghten rule (see Allnutt et al., 2007; Gledhill, 2012; Yeo, 2008 for historical details). Of interest, one of the questions asked was "in what terms ought the question [of insanity] to be left to the jury as to the prisoner's state of mind at the time when the act was committed" (*Queen v. M'Naghten*, 1843). Lord Justice Tyndal responded by asserting the following:

> the jurors ought to be told in all cases that every man is to be presumed to be sane, and to possess a sufficient degree of reason to be responsible for his

> crimes, until the contrary be proved to their satisfaction; and that to establish a defence on the ground of insanity, it must be clearly proved that, at the time of the committing of the act, the party accused was labouring under such a defect of reason, from a disease of the mind, as not to know the nature and quality of the act he was doing; or if he did know it, that he did not know he was doing what was wrong.
>
> (*Queen v. M'Naghten*, 1843)

This rule is the starting point for understanding the substantive test of the insanity defence in Hong Kong. Specifically, Hong Kong's insanity defence legislation is mirrored on the M'Naghten formulation. This is not surprising in view of the historical ties between Hong Kong and Britain; Hong Kong was a colony of Britain until 1997, when the territory was handed over to China under the "one country, two systems" arrangement and agreement.

Insanity defence legislation in Hong Kong

According to Hong Kong's *Criminal Procedure Ordinance* (CPO), an acquittal on the basis of insanity is possible

> [w]here in an indictment any act or omission is charged against any person as an offence, and it is given in evidence on trial of such person for that offence that he was insane, so as not to be responsible according to law for his actions at the time when the act was done or the omission made, then, if it appears to the jury before whom such person is tried that he did the act or made the omission charged, but was insane as aforesaid at the time when he did or made the same, the jury shall return a special verdict that the accused person is not guilty by reason of insanity.
>
> (section 74(1) of the CPO)

By closely examining Hong Kong's insanity legislation, one may quickly recognise that it provides scant information as to the elements of the insanity defence compared with the M'Naghten rule. Yet, it is interesting to note that all the essential elements in M'Naghten are expressly applicable in Hong Kong. One central feature of both English and Hong Kong legislation is the presumption that every man is sane and should be held accordingly for performing any act that contravenes the law. However, the criminal law in Hong Kong, just like in Britain, provides a rebuttal of the presumption of sanity. To claim insanity, the following essential circumstances must be satisfied (see Jackson, 2003; Roebuck, 1995): (1) the defendant was labouring under a defect of reason when the crime was committed; (2) the defect of reason was as a result of a "disease of the mind"; and (3) due to the defect of reason, the defendant either (a) did not know the nature and quality of the act or (b) did not know the act was wrong or contrary to law. These essential features of the insanity defence are briefly examined below.

Defect of reason

Defect of reason can be proven on the ground that the defendant's power of reasoning, as well as his or her ability to make rational choices and decisions, is severely compromised. Minor defects in reasoning such as absent-mindedness and mere confusion at the time of the crime would not suffice for the test of defect of reason. In *R v. Clarke* (1972), the court ruled that absent-mindedness resulting from diabetes and depression does not amount to a defect of reason. Defect of reason also includes absence of reason in circumstances such as when the defendant was unconscious (Jackson, 2003). The onus is on the defendant to demonstrate that he/she had severe reasoning impairment.

Disease of the mind

The defect of reason must arise from a disease of the mind. Essentially, whether a particular mental condition, as the defendant alleges, amounts to a disease of the mind is a fact for the court to determine (*R v. Li Lam*, 1966). Stated alternatively, disease of the mind, notwithstanding its superficial meaning, is a legal, not a medical, concept. What really qualifies as, or as what can cause, a disease of mind has troubled the courts. Consequently, the courts have tended to apply various criteria, with some focusing on the nature and aetiology of the defendant's mental abnormality and others adopting the common and criminal law proposition that offenders who act under the influence of a defective mental state should not be held criminally liable but rather should be committed for treatment (Jackson, 2003). Regardless of the criteria, the impact of disease of the mind (i.e., defective reasoning) on the commission of a crime in question is of paramount importance. This was echoed by Lord Denning in *R v. Bratty* (1963): "It seems to me that any mental disorder which has manifested itself in violence and is prone to recur is a disease of the mind" (p. 412). In *R v. Sullivan* (1984), the court also stated that "it matters not whether the etiology of the impairment is organic, as in epilepsy, or functional, or whether the impairment itself is permanent or transient and intermittent, provided that it subsisted at the time of commission of the act" (p. 172). This implies that both physical and mental illnesses can be interpreted widely as capable of causing diseases of the mind.

Indeed, the courts, over the years, have interpreted the terminology broadly to cover a wide range of conditions that affect individuals' mental capacity. In *R v. Kemp* (1957), the defendant was charged with causing grievous bodily harm after hitting his wife over the head with a hammer. At trial, the defendant alleged that he suffered from a physical condition known as arteriosclerosis (hardening and thickening of the walls of the arteries) which caused blackouts or temporary unconsciousness. The court was of the opinion that arteriosclerosis is capable of affecting the mental faculties of reasoning, memory, and understanding and hence is a disease of the mind. The jury involved with the case returned a verdict of insanity.

In another case, *R v. Quick & Paddison* (1973), the appellant was a nurse who attacked one of his patients while on duty. The appellant was subsequently charged with assault occasioning actual bodily harm. At trial, he provided evidence that he had suffered from a low blood glucose level (often termed hypoglycaemia) caused by the administration of insulin. The trial judge reasoned that hypoglycaemia can cause disease of the mind, and an insanity verdict was duly returned. On appeal, quashing the verdict, the court argued that hypoglycaemia was not caused by diabetes but by an external factor, namely insulin. This ruling brought yet another criterion for deciding what constitutes a disease of the mind. Accordingly, defective mental states resulting from the application of external factors such as violence (resulting in brain injury, e.g., concussion), drugs, alcohol, and hypnosis (resulting in altered mental states) do not appropriately qualify as being due to a disease of the mind (*R v. Quick & Paddison*, 1973). In general, it is absolutely necessary to prove that a disease of the mind resulted from internal, as opposed to external, factors. This criterion was applied in *R v. Hennessy* (1989). The defendant was a diabetic patient who had failed to inject insulin to normalise his glucose or sugar level. He consequently had a high glucose level in his blood, a condition referred to as hyperglycaemia. He was charged with stealing a car, a crime which he had no knowledge of (i.e., blackout). The court effectively ruled that hyperglycaemia amounts to a disease of the mind.

From the aforementioned cases, it seems that the courts are not necessarily interested in whether the disease of the mind could have been prevented from occurring if the individuals had taken the right course of action at the right time. For instance, it is possible that if Hennessy (*R v. Hennessy*, 1989) had adhered to the treatment regimen, there would have been a high probability of the disease of the mind being averted. Yet, this was overlook by the court when the judgment was delivered. In another case (*R v. Burgess*, 1991) of appeal against NGRI, the appellant, who was allegedly asleep, smashed a bottle over the victim's head before hitting her with a video recorder. Medical evidence showed that the appellant had a disorder called sleepwalking. According to the trial judge, the only defence available was insanity rather than the defendant's preferred defence of automatism. The jury returned a NGRI verdict. On appeal, it was said that sleepwalking is a malfunctioning of the mind caused by internal factors and therefore amounts to a disease of the mind. The NGRI verdict was upheld and the appeal was dismissed.

The notion that external agents or factors would not amount to a disease of the mind capable of producing defective reasoning was decided in a recent case in Hong Kong (*HKSAR v. Tang Kwok-wai*, 2000). In this case, the appellant was convicted of attempted murder and sentenced to six years' imprisonment. He appealed against the conviction as well as the sentence. The circumstances that led to the charge and subsequent conviction and incarceration were that the appellant assaulted the victim (his girlfriend) and threw her from the 18th floor of a building, but the victim managed to grip her hands on the railings, which prevented her falling. Prior to this, the victim reported that the appellant had experienced hallucinations and also heard voices. The appellant, who admitted to taking "ice", believed the victim was hiding something from him and demanded to know what it was. The appellant maintained that in the course of his actions, he had heard the voice of an old woman suggesting that the victim had betrayed him. The voice from the supposed old woman similarly commanded him to throw the victim and he knew the voice was telling him to kill her. Upon critically evaluating the evidence adduced, the trial judge did not direct the jury to acquit on the basis of NGRI. The judge instead instructed the jury to consider whether the defendant committed the offence intentionally. The Court of Appeal held that the judge was right not to direct the jury to quit on NGRI. The court reasoned on the basis of the House of Lords' decision in *R v. Quick & Paddison* (1973) that the appellant's defect of reasoning was the result of the ice (i.e., ice-induced psychosis). It further stated that the changes in reasoning were transient in nature and were caused by an external factor (i.e., ice) and would subside upon withdrawal from taking the drug. The court held that temporary changes in reasoning induced by ice do not sufficiently amount to a disease of the mind. The court further stated that a catastrophic and disastrous situation would have happened but for the victim's ability to firmly hold on to the rails and her steadfastness in doing so. Thus, the argument that the six years' imprisonment was manifestly excessive was explicitly rejected.

In a related case, the defendant in *Queen v. Fung Mui-lee* (1996) allegedly committed burglary and issued threats of violence to a fashion shop's attendants and a taxi driver. It was stated at the trial that she had taken too many Imovane tablets (used to relieve sleep disturbances), which raised doubts and questions about her intentions and mental state. The judge was of the opinion that the defendant took the tablets to further her criminal intentions. The judge also concluded that the defendant was in the right state of mind when she made all the necessary arrangements to rob the shop and issued the threats. The insanity defence was not successful in this case.

It is important to draw a distinction between defective reasoning resulting from life events (e.g., life stressors or self-induced; taking drugs) and defective reasoning that could possibly result from internal mental conditions and be exacerbated by life events. For example, in *HKSAR v. Tang Kwok-wai* (2000), the court took into account evidence of an existing defective mental condition prior to the substance abuse or exposure to stressful life events (e.g., loss of relationship, death of loved one). Evidence that the mental condition would persist in the event that the defendant stopped taking the drugs makes a strong case that an act was a by-product of defective reasoning. This was affirmed in *Queen v. Lam Ka Yiu* (1997). In this particular case, the defendant walked into a bank in Lai Chi Kok and suddenly started to shout "robbery"; he also claimed that he had a bomb. The police officers who arrived at the scene quickly immobilised him. Upon interrogation, the defendant alleged that he had been chased by someone who intended to kill him. He was subsequently charged with attempted robbery and arraigned before a district court. At trial, the judge accepted the medical evidence that he was insane at the time of the offence and a verdict of NGRI was returned.

A more recent case, *HKSAR v. Wong Hung Fai Joseph* (2008), similarly affirmed the above position. The defendant, a van driver, jabbed a traffic warden with his finger. He also allegedly tried to commit suicide with the gun of a police officer at the scene, with the reasoning that he had AIDS and this had brought great suffering to him. Medical evidence revealed that the defendant was suffering from a relapse of paranoid schizophrenia but not AIDS, as he alleged. Accordingly, the defendant's conduct was largely under the influence of his psychotic symptoms and poor mental state, which were precipitated by stressful life events. On this basis, the court found the defendant did not have the required mens rea and that his conduct resulted from a disease of the mind and consequently returned a NGRI verdict. In summary, not all mental conditions, such as a low or below average intelligent quotient (*HKSAR v. Cheung Yiu Kong*, 2007), will necessarily result in a successful insanity defence plea.

It follows from the above discussion that the definition of disease of the mind is not restricted to formal psychiatric diagnoses of mental illness but is also subject to legal guidelines and judgment: that is, the mere presence or diagnosis of a mental disorder does not translate into a disease of the mind.

Did not know the nature and quality of the act or that it is wrong

The last important element of the insanity defence legislation is lack of knowledge of the nature and quality of the act or that it is wrong. It follows that a disease of the mind must cause a defect in reasoning, which in turn must lead to this last element. It is a kind of hierarchically organised rule-based system. The mere existence of a defect of reasoning resulting from a diseased mental state may not be sufficient for an insanity verdict if the defendant is proved to possess knowledge about the nature and quality of the act or to know that what he/she was doing was wrong. The nature and quality of the act as used in the proviso primarily concerns the physical, not the moral, nature of the act (*R v. Codere*, 1916). The wrongness of the act has also been restricted to legal wrongness and excludes moral wrongness (*R v. Windle*, 1952).

The provision above can be likened to the performance of, for instance, a three-year-old child. Although the child performs or engages in some behaviours, the presumption is that he/she lacks knowledge of the nature and quality of the act. By the same token, the child cannot tell whether an act is wrong or not. Acts committed when the defendant is unconscious will necessarily be sufficient for an insanity defence as an unconscious person obviously would have no knowledge of the nature and quality of the act or even know that it is wrong (Jackson, 2003). In some instances, a defendant may appear knowledgeable of the nature and quality as well as the wrongness of the act and yet be committed for treatment rather than imprisonment. This was illustrated in *HKSAR v. Wong Hung Fai Joseph* (2008). In dismissing the appeal against a hospital order without limitation, Stuart-Moore VP, giving the judgment of the Court of Appeal, stated that medical evidence indisputably showed that the appellant suffered from a disease of the mind. He further stated that although the defendant equally knew the nature and quality of his act and was aware that the act was wrong, the trial judge was entitled to and made the appropriate decision in this particular instance. This case represents several of the unique circumstances when the need for detention for treatment is prioritised over criminal blameworthiness.

Knowledge of the nature and quality of an act and/or its wrongness explicitly precludes the act being done under irresistible impulse: that is, acts in which the individual is conscious of the offence but could not desist from committing same because of an inability to control himself/herself. In *R v. Pang Bing-yee* (1984), the defendant, on appeal against a murder conviction, attempted to prove with medical evidence that she was unable to control her behaviour. She primarily sought to argue that her inability to control her behaviour or impulse emanated from the maltreatment and abuse she had suffered as a child. Dismissing the appeal against conviction, the Court of Appeal stated:

> The applicant was fully aware of the nature of her acts, there was no suggestion of any recklessness, mistake or lack of a consciousness mind . . . The acts were clearly voluntary ones . . . Murder being a crime of specific intent, uncontrollable impulse, if it exists, does not go far as a defect of reason sufficient to negative intent by rebutting the presumption of insanity.
>
> (p. 304)

The recent case of *HKSAR v. Wong Hung Fai Joseph* (2008) also illustrated that irresistible impulse is not sufficient for a successful insanity defence. In this case, the appellant contended that the trial judge erred in law and in fact by failing to consider a defence of irresistible impulse or automatism. The Court of Appeal found no basis for this argument and reiterated the fact that irresistible impulse is not acceptable as a defence. The Court of Appeal stated that directing a jury to consider evidence of uncontrollable impulse as illustrating a defect of reason owing to a disease of the mind which precludes him or her from knowledge of the nature and quality of the act or its wrongness is wrong. The appeal against conviction was dismissed. On the other hand, where it is proved that the irresistible impulse was due to some underlying debilitating and major mental disorder and that the person did not know the nature and quality of the act or its wrongness, the insanity defence may suffice (Jackson, 2003). In circumstances such as this, the court may focus more on the disorder and its influence on the irresistible impulse and knowledge of the act rather than the mere existence of irresistible impulse.

In summary, in insanity defence trials, it is not enough that the defendant suffered from a defect of reasoning resulting from a disease of the mind. The defendant, in addition to demonstrating lack of knowledge of the nature and quality of the act, should demonstrate lack of knowledge of the wrongness of the act. Wrongness in the spirit of the law is confined to legal wrongness and excludes moral wrongness. Table 3.1 presents a summary of some selected cases on insanity defence.

Table 3.1 Summary of some selected cases on insanity defence

Case	*Decision by the Courts*
R v. Clarke (1972)	Absent mindedness resulting from diabetes and depression does not amount to a defect of reason.
R v. Kemp (1957)	Arteriosclerosis is capable of affecting the mental faculties of reasoning, memory, and understanding, and hence causing a disease of the mind.
R v. Bratty (1963)	A mental disorder which can cause violence and which can recur is a disease of the mind.
R v. Quick & Paddison (1973)	Hypoglycaemia (low blood glucose level) can cause a disease of the mind.
R v. Hennessy (1989).	Hyperglycaemia (high blood glucose level) amounts to a disease of the mind.
R v. Burgess (1991)	Sleepwalking is a malfunctioning of the mind and hence a disease of the mind.
Queen v. Fung Mui-lee (1996)	Changes in mental states resulting from Imovane tablets (used to relieve sleep disturbances) do not amount to a disease of the mind.
HKSAR v. Tang Kwok-wai (2000)	Temporary changes in reasoning induced by ice do not sufficiently amount to a disease of the mind.
Queen v. Lam Ka Yiu (1997).	Mental illness that persists after a defendant withdraws from taking drugs constitutes defective reasoning.
HKSAR v. Wong Hung Fai Joseph (2008)	The defendant had a disease of the mind and was knowledgeable of the nature and quality as well as the wrongness of the act. An insanity defence verdict was returned.
	Mental illness precipitated by stressful life events provides sufficient basis for an insanity verdict.
R v. Pang Bing-yee (1984)	Uncontrollable impulse does not amount to defective reasoning given that the defendant was aware of the nature, quality, and wrongness of the act although could not resist committing it.
HKSAR v. Cheung Yiu Kong (2007)	A low or below average intelligent quotient will not necessarily result in a successful insanity defence plea.

Adjudicating defendants with a mental illness

A notable characteristic of Hong Kong's judicial system is its adversarial nature mirrored on the British judicial system. In this system, both the defence and prosecution counsels present their facts on the case before the court and call witnesses and experts to testify when necessary. The witnesses and experts are mostly subjected to cross-examination. The ultimate goal is to assist the trier of law and/or fact to make appropriate legal decision as to the culpability, or otherwise, of the defendant in question. Although the key players in the criminal adjudication process may vary across cases and courts, insanity defence trials are prima facie constituted by the following: a judge, a jury, prosecutor, defence counsel, and medical experts (section 74(1) of the CPO).

Simplistically, the prosecutor brings a case that a crime has been committed to the attention of the court for trial. The defendant in this case is represented by the defence counsel, whose responsibilities include "exonerating" the defendant by legally rebutting any evidence that might implicate him or her. During preliminary proceedings, the trial or sitting judge, who functions as the gate-keeper of the judicial system, initially screens evidence presented by the prosecutor and defence counsel for its merits. The judge, with recourse to all the facts and the medical evidence laid before the court, decides whether a case merits consideration as insanity at the time of the offence (see *HKSAR v. Tang Kwok-wai*, 2000; *HKSAR v. Wong Hung Fai Joseph*, 2008). If the judge is satisfied that the evidence suggests a disease of the mind, the next phase involves determining whether the defendant suffered from the condition at the time of committing the crime. Consequently, the judge will instruct and direct jurors (see Chapter 5 for information about jurors in Hong Kong) that the defendant is entitled to acquittal on the basis of NGRI if they are satisfied that the elements of the insanity defence legislation have been proved. If the defendant alleges insanity, he/she bears the burden of disproving sanity on the balance of probabilities (*HKSAR v. Wong Hung Fai Joseph*, 2008; *R v. Queen v. Fung Mui-lee*, 1996; *Woolmington*, 1935).

Both the prosecution and defence counsels must present their arguments and counter-arguments to the jurors, who are the triers of fact and the ultimate decision-makers. In this adversarial system, the defendant's mental state is fiercely contested. In most cases, there is bound to be disagreement among experts: (a) between the defence and prosecution counsels and (b) between medical experts. Frankly speaking, trials in which defendants place their mental state at issue have sometimes being described as a battleground for experts (Adjorlolo & Chan, 2015a). It is not unusual for the medical expert called by prosecution counsel to testify in support of the prosecution counsel. Likewise, it is common for the defence counsel's medical expert to give testimony concurring with the counsel's claims. As a result, the trial process is mostly characterised by differing views, opinions, and submissions. To illustrate, in the case of *HKSAR v. Tang Kwok-wai* (2000), two psychiatrists gave contradictory testimonies regarding whether the defendant was capable of forming the intent to commit the crime. The medical expert brought by the defence counsel testified that the appellant was directed by an abnormal thinking process and perception. He could not form the necessary intent. In contrast, the medical expert called by the prosecution opined that the appellant was capable of forming the intent and that he knew what he did was wrong. The burden and challenge to the court is reconciling all the divergent opinions and subsequently ascertaining the facts in the case before a judgment is returned.

The issue of insanity may also be raised by the prosecutor or the trial judge (Jackson, 2003). The trial judge, for instance, may raise the issue of insanity even against the defendant's wish: that is, where the defendant may have chosen not to put his or her mental state at issue at trial (see *HKSAR v. Wong Hung Fai Joseph*, 2008; *R v. Chan Ming-luk*, 1962). If necessary, witnesses may be called to testify at the trial and the case left to a jury to make a decision. However, this is only possible in the event of medical evidence indicating that the defendant had a disease of the mind which has affected his/her reasoning so severely that he/she does not know the nature and quality of the act or that it is wrong. This is an example of instances where the need for treatment takes precedence over punishment for the crime committed. Nevertheless, this may occur rarely, especially when the efficiency of the criminal justice system is determined by the number of cases tried and prosecuted (Burke, 2012).

The complexities of the judicial process and the opposing views that characterise insanity defence trials sometimes create a situation where the law is wrongly applied: that is, the trial judge may wrongly direct a jury on how to apply the law (see *Queen v. Fung Mui-lee*, 1996). Thankfully, the system has made it possible for defendants to appeal against the decisions of the lower courts (e.g., district and magistrate courts) at the higher courts (e.g., Court of Appeal).

Special verdict and disposal of insanity acquittees

In principle, punishment meted out to criminal offenders must be proportional to the seriousness, severity, and degree of the offence. Traditionally, punishments are prescribed to offenders with the objective of achieving the following goals: deterrence, retribution, rehabilitation, and incapacitation (Burke, 2012). However, the goals of deterrence and retribution are not easily applicable to offenders whose crimes resulted from a mental disorder (Allnutt et al., 2007). Moreover, society has presumably accepted that punishing offenders whose crimes resulted from a mental disorder is inappropriate since they did not commit their crimes out of free will. Pursuant to section 74 of Hong Kong CPO, the special verdict of NGRI should be returned where the jury is satisfied on evidence given at trial that a defendant was insane at the time of the offence. All the requisite elements of insanity, as stipulated under section 74 of the CPO or in the M'Naghten formulation, must be proved and satisfied before the verdict is returned. It is possible to appeal against the special verdict, and the Court of Appeal may substitute a conviction or acquittal, subject to section 83k (4) of the CPO.

Obviously, the psychiatric needs of insanity acquittees take precedence over prescribing punishments for their criminal conduct. In consequence, the judge or magistrate hearing the case has several orders to make for treatment purposes when the verdict is returned. The type of order depends on several factors, including the type and severity of the mental disorder and the type of offence. Where the offence carries a fixed and mandatory sentence (e.g., murder), a hospital order for admission to a mental hospital for treatment is made. However, pursuant to section 76 of the CPO, two or more registered medical practitioners must testify that admittance to the Correctional Services Department Psychiatric Centre or a mental hospital is necessary for the welfare of the accused or for protection of others. Admission for treatment must be within 28 days of hospitalisation being made. The admission is treated as an admission under section 45 of the *Mental Health Ordinance* (MHO), and the provision of care and treatment is subject to the provisions of the MHO. The defendant could be detained for treatment indefinitely and could be discharged at such time as he/she no longer constitutes a danger to himself/herself and the public (*HKSAR v. Wan Pak-sing*, 2004; *HKSAR v. Wong Hung Fai Joseph*, 2008).

On the other hand, given the nature and circumstances surrounding the case, the judge or magistrate can make one of the following orders under section 76 (2)(b): (a) a guardianship order; (b) a supervision order and treatment order; and (c) an order to absolutely discharge the defendant. This last order is granted when the jury is satisfied on the basis of the evidence that the defendant did not commit the crime in question, although the same jury is satisfied that the defendant is insane (Jackson, 2003; *R v. O'Donnell*, 1996). There is a general right of appeal against a particular order imposed by courts. For instance, in the case of *Queen v. Lam Ka Yiu* (1996), the appellant requested that the court replace a hospital order with supervision and treatment order under the MHO: the appeal was allowed.

Conclusion and future directions

This chapter has provided a general overview of the concept of criminal responsibility and specifically highlighted the insanity defence, including its essential elements, the special verdict, and the disposition of insanity acquittees. The concept of insanity in the criminal justice system differs markedly from the ordinary medical meaning. The ultimate decision regarding whether or not a defendant committed a crime under the influence of a mental disorder is the purview of the key players of the judicial system (e.g., judges, magistrates, and jurors). Such decisions are made by taking into account the presence of a disease of the mind and its ability to produce a defect of reasoning. This must in turn cause the defendant to lack knowledge of the nature and quality of the act or that it is wrong. Thus, using the legal definition, it is important to note that not all persons, including those who clearly suffer from a mental disorder, may be acquitted on the basis of NGRI. The path to determining whether a defendant was mentally incapacitated at the time of the alleged offence is tortuous.

Unfortunately, relatively little is known about the insanity defence in Hong Kong and other Asian countries. Studies investigating this topical issue are obviously needed. Indeed, the potential for research is endless. For instance, jurors play key roles in insanity defence trials, and hence studies of their decision-making processes in Hong Kong are warranted. Because jurors have been shown to have their own biases and values before the legal proceedings commence (Peters &

Lecci, 2012; Skeem, Eno Louden, & Evans, 2004), identifying factors likely to bias their decision can be instrumental in empanelling an impartial jury: that is, to exclude from the adjudication process jurors whose decision-making is likely to be predictable. Potential research areas include the effects of judicial instruction, defendant characteristics (e.g., age, gender, and socioeconomic status), and extra-legal factors (e.g., demographic backgrounds, attitudes towards and perception and knowledge of mental illness) on jury decision-making. Another research area involves the explication of recidivism rates of insanity acquittees and the factors that are associated with the revocation of conditional release or recidivism (both violent and non-violent recidivism). Insights into these factors can inform empirical strategies to mitigate them, thereby contributing to preventing or reducing the likelihood of future reoffending by insanity acquittees. The characteristics of insanity acquittees in terms of gender, developmental trajectories, offence history, psychiatric history, socioeconomic history, and other salient demographics equally deserve research attention. Where possible, insanity acquittees should be compared and contrasted with non-insanity offenders. This can help in formulating preventive policies and programmes to reduce crimes resulting from mental disorder, particularly given the interdependence between researchers and policymakers (Adjorlolo & Chan, 2014, 2015b).

Chapter summary points

- Hong Kong has instituted insanity defence legislation to absolve from criminal liability defendants whose criminal behaviours resulted from mental illness.
- In insanity defence trials, the focus is on the mental element of the crime (mens rea) rather than the physical element (actus reus).
- The requirement for a successful insanity plea include: (1) the defendant was labouring under a defect of reason; (2) the defect of reason was as a result of a "disease of the mind"; and (3) due to the defect of reason, the defendant either (a) did not know the nature and quality of the act or (b) did not know the act was wrong or contrary to the law.
- An insanity defence can be raised by the prosecution counsel, the defence counsel, or the judge/magistrate on behalf of a defendant. The verdict associated with the insanity defence is not guilty by reason of insanity (NGRI). The disposition associated with the verdict is mostly commitment for treatment at a mental health institution.

References

Adjorlolo, S., Agboli, J. M., & Chan, H. C. O. (2016). Criminal responsibility and the insanity defence in Ghana: The examination of legal standards and assessment issues. *Psychiatry, Psychology and Law, 23*(5), 684–695. 1–12. doi: 10.1080/13218719.2015.1113606

Adjorlolo, S., & Chan, H. C. O. (2014). The controversy of defining serial murder: Revisited. *Aggression and Violent Behavior, 19*(5), 486–491. doi: 10.1016/j.avb.2014.07.003

Adjorlolo, S., & Chan, H. C. O. (2015a). Forensic assessment via videoconferencing: Issues and practice considerations. *Journal of Forensic Psychology Practice, 15*(3), 185–204. doi: 10.1080/15228932.2015.1015363

Adjorlolo, S., & Chan, H. C. O. (2015b). The nature of instrumentality and expressiveness of homicide crime scene behaviors: A review. *Trauma, Violence, & Abuse*. Advance online publication. 1–15. doi:10.1177/1524838015596528

Adjorlolo, S., & Chan, H. C. O. (2016). Determination of competency to stand trial (fitness to plead): An exploratory study in Hong Kong. *Psychiatry, Psychology and Law*. Advance online publication. 1–18. doi: 10.1080/13218719.2016.1247417

Adjorlolo, S., Chan, H. C. O., & Agboli, J. M. (2016). Adjudicating mentally disordered offenders in Ghana: Criminal and mental health legislations. *International Journal of Psychiatry and Law, 45*, 1–8. doi: 10.1016/j.ijlp.2016.02.001

Allnutt, S., Samuels, A., & O'Driscoll, C. (2007). The insanity defence: From wild beasts to M'Naghten. *Australasian Psychiatry, 15*(4), 292–298. doi: 10.1080/10398560701352181

Burke, R. H. (2012). *Criminal justice theory: An introduction*. Oxford: Routledge.

Gledhill, K. (2012). *Defending mentally disordered persons*. Hampshire, UK: Hobbs the Printers.

HKSAR v. Cheung Yiu Kong, HKLRD 362 (2007).

HKSAR v. Tang Kowk-wai, 2 HKLRD 744 (2000).

HKSAR v. Wan Pak-sing, 3 HKC 283 (2004).

HKSAR v. Wong Hung Fai Joseph, HKLRD 153 (2008).

Jackson, M. (2003). *Criminal law in Hong Kong*. Hong Kong: Hong Kong University Press.

M'Naghten, 10 CI & Fin 200; [1843–60] All ER Rep 229 (1843).

Peters, M., & Lecci, L. (2012). Predicting verdicts, adherence to judge's instructions, and assumptions about the disposition of the defendant in a case involving the insanity defense. *Psychology, Crime & Law, 18*(9), 817–831. doi: 10.1080/1068316X.2011.566872

Queen v. Fung Mui-Lee, 1 HKC 72 (1996).

Queen v. Lam Ka Yiu, HKLRD 445 (1997).

R v. Bratty, AC 386 (1963).

R v. Burgess, 2 QB 92 (1991).

R v. Chan Ming-luk, HKLR 651 (1962).

R v. Clarke, 1 All ER 219 (1972).

R v. Codere, 12 Cr App 21 (1916).

R v. Hennessy, 1 WLR 287 (1989).

R v. Kemp, 1 QB 399 (1957).

R v. Li Lam, HKLR 809 (1966).

R v. O'Donnell, Crim LR 121 (1996).

R v. Pang Bing Yee, HKLR 298 (1984).

R v. Quick & Paddison, QB 910 (1973).

R v. Sullivan, AC 156 (1984).

R v. Windle, 2 QB 826 (1952).

R v. Woolmington, AC 462 (1935).

Roebuck, D. (1995). *The criminal law of Hong Kong*. Beijing: Peking University Press.

Skeem, J. L., Eno Louden, J., & Evans, J. (2004). Venirepersons's attitudes toward the insanity defense: Developing, refining, and validating a scale. *Law and Human Behavior*, *28*(6), 623–648. doi: 10.1007/s10979-004-0487-7

Zhao, L., & Ferguson, G. (2013). Understanding China's mental illness defense. *The Journal of Forensic Psychiatry & Psychology*, *24*(5), 634–657. doi: 10.1080/14789949.2013.830318

4 Fitness to plead in Hong Kong

Samuel Adjorlolo and Heng Choon (Oliver) Chan

Introduction

Fitness to plead (FTP; also known as competency to stand trial, adjudicative competency, or fitness to stand trial) is a fundamental legal concept derived from old English common law (White, Meares, & Batchelor, 2014). FTP ensures the postponement of criminal proceedings for defendants who are not able to participate in and contribute to their own defence, particularly due to mental disease (Zapf, Roesch, & Pirelli, 2014). It is a concept of jurisprudence and a criminal procedural requirement that is instituted to uphold and maintain due process right, procedural fairness, and judicial integrity (Heilbronner & Frumkin, 2003). The essence of FTP was summarised by Lord Edmund-Davies in *R v. Podola* (1960) in Britain as "no man may be brought to trial upon any criminal charge unless and until he is mentally capable of fairly standing trial". Normally, at the beginning of or in the course of a trial, the question about a defendant's FTP may be raised. To uphold due process correctly, the court is required to make a determination of the defendant's fitness, regardless of the factors (e.g., mental disorder) that may have catalysed the commission of the crime (Jackson, 2003).

Although there is paucity of data on the frequency of fitness evaluation requests in Hong Kong, such requests are frequently and substantially made more often than insanity evaluations. In the United States, for instance, some analysts estimated that about 60,000 fitness evaluations are requested annually (Bonnie & Grisso, 2000), with an estimated annual expenditure of $300 million (Zapf et al., 2014). Notwithstanding the steady increase in referrals for fitness evaluations (Sakdalan & Egan, 2014), it was estimated over a decade ago that approximately 20% of defendants were found unfit to plead (Roesch, Zapf, Golding, & Skeem, 1999). A more recent meta-analytic study reported an unfitness base rate of about 27.5% (Pirelli, Gottdiener, & Zapf, 2011).

This chapter focuses specifically on FTP in Hong Kong. Firstly, it provides a brief overview of FTP as well as its applications in England and the United States. This is followed by an extensive discussion of FTP in Hong Kong, highlighting the legal admissibility standards and law students' views regarding the composition of FTP legislation, the approaches to determining FTP used by the courts, and finally the outcomes of fitness decision-making and the disposition of unfit defendants. Discussions and recommendations for future research are provided.

Fitness to plead legislation

Generally, every jurisdiction (e.g., the United States, Australia, and Canada) has its own legislation for determining whether a defendant is fit or unfit to plead. In the United States, this involves the Supreme Court decision in *Dusky v. US* (1960). According to the *Dusky* standard, a defendant's orientation to time and place and ability to recollect some events are not enough: whether he has (a) the sufficient present ability to consult with the defence counsel with a reasonable degree of rational understanding and (b) a rational as well as a factual understanding of the proceedings against him are also important. The *Dusky* standard has raised a number of questions relating to, for instance, the meaning of "sufficient present ability" and how to determine that a defendant "has a rational and as well as factual understanding" (see Zapf et al., 2014).

In England and Wales (henceforth, the United Kingdom), FTP is determined on the basis of the *Pritchard* (1836) criteria: (a) ability to plead; (b) ability to understand evidence; (c) ability to understand the court proceedings; (d) ability to instruct a lawyer; and (e) knowing that a juror can be challenged (Rogers, Blackwood, Farnham, Pickup, & Watts, 2008). The *Pritchard* criteria have also raised some concerns, particularly regarding the utility of ***knowing that a juror can be challenged*** and whether the criteria amount to a comprehensive construct to allow for fair trials. It has been recommended that the former be substituted with a defendant's ability to give evidence on his/her own behalf since that would ensure a fair trial (Gray, O'Connor, Williams, Short, & MacCulloch, 2001). With regard to the latter, an empirical study of criminal barristers revealed that the *Pritchard* criteria are not comprehensive enough and do not protect the interests of offenders with mental illness who are tried unfairly, a situation necessitating a reformulation of the criteria (Rogers, Blackwood, Farnham, Pickup, & Watts, 2009).

Hong Kong's legal provision concerning FTP is contained in section 75(1) of the *Criminal Procedure Ordinance* (CPO). Accordingly, a defendant is unfit to plead if he labours "under any disability such that apart from this Ordinance it would constitute a bar to his being tried". A more elaborate description was given in *R v. Leung Tak-Choi* (1995). The court, following English case law, specifically referred to "under disability" as a defendant's lack of ability to understand the charges, instruct the defence counsel, challenge jurors, understand the evidence against him, and to give evidence in defence. A very interesting question is whether there are presumably other indicators of FTP in addition to what was espoused by the court in *R v. Leung Tak-Choi* (1995): that is, whether "under any disability such that apart from this Ordinance it would constitute a bar to his being tried" encompasses several abilities aside those stated above. In this regard, a study by Adjorlolo and Chan (unpublished manuscript) revealed that participants in a juris doctor programme at the City University of Hong Kong endorsed the majority of the fitness indicators canvassed from the literature, particularly those from the United States (Melton, Petrila, Poythress, & Slobogin, 1997). By implication, Hong Kong's FTP legislation may encompass a wide range of fitness abilities. This study also suggested that FTP indicators may be universal, regardless of the jurisdiction of application.

Fitness issues are mainly raised when there are indications that a defendant is suffering from a mental disorder. This is also the case in several jurisdictions, including the United States (see Zapf et al., 2014), the United Kingdom (see Roger et al., 2008), Australia (White, Batchelor, Pulman, & Howard, 2012), and Ghana, a former British colony (Adjorlolo, Chan, & Agboli, 2016). Yet, across these jurisdictions, there are also indications that not all mental conditions are suggestive of unfitness. For example, in Hong Kong, the fact that the defendant is suffering from senile dementia may not be enough of a basis to warrant a declaration of unfit to plead (see *R v. Chiu Te-ken,* 1993; see Zapf et al., 2014 for a similar case in the United States).

Issues concerning FTP can be raised by the prosecution, the defence, or the trial judge. However, a judge intervenes only if there is a substantial question as to a defendant's trial fitness (*R v. Keung Sai-chung*, 1986). A judge is not obliged to raise the issue in instances of a mere possibility of unfitness (*R v. Keung-Sai-chung*, 1986). This places a huge burden and responsibility on attorneys, especially the defence attorney, to make known the suspicious behaviours of defendants that might suggest unfitness. Unfortunately, many attorneys may not have the requisite training and knowledge in mental illness and its (subtle) influences on behaviours, including courtroom behaviours. Indeed, the detection of potentially unfit defendants is a major challenge in the quest to ensure fair trials, largely due to the absence of routine and mandatory screening of defendants appearing in court (Rogers et al., 2008). Thus, many unfit defendants may have been found FTP on a number of occasions and consequently processed via the judicial system without addressing their fitness issues (Grubin, 1991).

Approaches to determining fitness to plead in Hong Kong

Of particular importance is the procedure used to determine fitness issues in the courtroom. In Hong Kong, the CPO stipulates two discrete and independent pathways depending upon the court exercising jurisdiction over the case. At the magistrate and district courts, the trial or the sitting judges or magistrates hear and make a finding on FTP on the basis of the medical evidence adduced for that purpose. Conversely, at the high courts, juries are empanelled to ascertain fitness issues. This can be done in two different ways. If the issue is one that needs to be determined before or at the time of arraignment, then a jury must be empanelled specifically to make a decision. On the other hand, where the issue arises after the arraignment, the court may empanel a new jury to decide the issue or use the jury by whom the defendant is being tried (see Jackson, 2003 for details). This practice is the same as or similar to that in the United Kingdom (Rogers et al., 2008). In the lower courts (e.g., magistrate courts), judges or magistrates hear and make a decision on fitness issues. However, there is a two-stage procedure available to the crown courts. Under this requirement, the crown courts empanel two different juries: one is tasked to make a decision on the fitness of the defendant, whereas the other is charged with determining whether the defendant committed the crime in question.

In summary, both in Hong Kong and the United Kingdom, the two main "agents" involved in the legal decision-making pertaining to FTP are the judges and the jurors. The judges are concentrated in the lower courts, while the jurors are fact finders in the high courts. This lack of uniformity raises the concern of whether the judges and the jurors would differ significantly in their decision-making. This may not be inevitable and may arise from different sources, including differences in the interpretation and understanding of the legislation, the workload in the lower courts, and personal influences and biases. For example, the judges or magistrates in the lower courts may be preoccupied with the overwhelming number of cases, including those involving offenders with a mental illness (Exworthy, 2006), and hence may have little time to ascertain fitness issues. Secondly, although judges, given their professional education and training, may be regarded as capable of interpreting and making appropriate decisions on the fitness issue, their decisions may also be prone to bias. Some researchers (Yourstone, Lindholm, Grann, & Svenson, 2008), for instance, have reported situations where judges' decision-making was influenced by their own gender and the gender of the defendant: that is, male judges were more likely to find a male defendant insane compared to a female defendant, and female judges were similarly more likely to find a female defendant insane compared to a male defendant.

Regarding jurors, even though they are supposedly provided with clear, concise, and explicit guidelines to assist them to make impartial legal decisions, there is enough evidence that their decision-making can also be biased. In fact, studies conducted so far have revealed that legal decision-makers are not blank slates; rather, they have their own biases and values that influence the decisions they make (Skeem, Eno Louden, & Evans, 2004). It was documented over a decade ago that mock jurors who have been provided with instructions relating to a trial and those who have not received any instructions have similar verdict patterns (Finkel & Handel, 1988; Peters & Lecci, 2012). Studies have subsequently revealed the influence of extra-legal factors on legal decision-making; for example, compared with males, females have been found to be lenient in their decisions and willing to acquit on the basis of not guilty by reason of insanity (NGRI) (Breheney, Groscup, & Galietta, 2007; Finkel & Handel, 1988). In a meta-analytic study, Narby, Cutler, and Moran (1993) found that legal authoritarianism, which is the tendency to convict rather than acquit a defendant, both positively and strongly correlated with and moderated legal verdict decision-making. Another study (Daftary-Kapur, Groscup, O'Connor, Coffaro, & Galietta, 2011) reported that legal authoritarianism significantly accounted for 4.3% of the variance in not guilty by reason of insanity verdict decision-making. The first-ever study of factors influencing legal decisions on fitness determination in Hong Kong by Adjorlolo and Chan (unpublished manuscript) similarly reported that relative to the male participants, the female participants were more likely to find the defendant unfit to plead. In this study, high scores in legal authoritarianism and punitiveness significantly and negatively predicted whether or not the participants found the defendant fit to plead. These findings were generally consistent with the findings of studies on insanity defence noted above. In summary, in view of the possible biases in legal decision-making, there is the likelihood that some "genuine" unfit defendants would be found FTP.

Outcomes of fitness decision-making and the disposition of an unfit defendant

The issue of FTP brought before a court of competent jurisdiction can proceed in two ways. First, section 75(2) of the CPO grants a court exercising jurisdiction of a criminal case discretionary power to acquit a defendant of all the charges being tried "if having regard to the nature of the supposed disability" such an acquittal is in the best interests of the defendant. This is most likely to be the case in instances where the prosecution has failed to establish a prima facie case against the defendant (see Jackson, 2003). In some circumstances, the acquittee can be committed for treatment, even against his/her wish. Mandatory hospitalisation or detention was held not to be a violation of Hong Kong's Bill of Rights in *R v. Leung Tak-Choi* (1995).

The other approach involves the court making a decision about FTP. This is the responsibility of judges or magistrates, in the case of district and magistrate courts, or jurors, in the case of higher courts. The decision-making regarding FTP will ultimately result in one of two outcomes: a defendant is fit to face the charges or unfit to plead. In the event of the former, the criminal adjudication process will proceed. Interestingly and worthy of note, a defendant may be found fit if even he/she may not be able to participate fully in the trial process. The mere fact that a defendant demonstrates fitness in some aspects of the trial process is presumably enough to warrant the continuation of the process. This was illustrated in *R v. Podola* (1960), where the defendant (Podola) was unable to remember and provide accounts of some events that happened at the time of the alleged offence due to hysterical amnesia. Conversely, where a defendant is found unfit to plead, the court must further decide whether the defendant committed the crime or made the omission in question. This largely depends on the evidence adduced by the prosecution or the person appointed by the court for this purpose (see *R v. Egan*, 1997). Pursuant to section 76(2), the court shall make one of the following orders upon being satisfied that a defendant committed the crime or made the omission charged. The first is an order for hospitalisation or admission to the Correctional Services Department Psychiatric Centre or a mental hospital. This order depends on the seriousness of the crime (e.g., murder) and medical evidence that hospitalisation is necessary both in the best interests of the defendant and for the protection of the public. Once this order is made, it is governed by section 45 of the *Mental Health Ordinance* (MHO), and the provision of care and treatment is subject to the provisions of the MHO. A guardianship order and a supervision and treatment order can also be made on the evidence of two or more registered medical practitioners. These orders are also made with reference to the MHO. The last order, which also depends on the type and nature of the crime and the mental disorder, is absolute discharge: that is, the defendant is acquitted of the charges and subsequently discharged. With the exception of the absolute discharge order, all other orders are made with the view of "restoring" the defendant to fitness. Therefore, where the available medical evidence suggests that the defendant is satisfactorily restored and the court deems it rightly so, he/she may be brought back to face the charges or for the continuation of the trial (for more information, see Jackson, 2003; Roebuck, 1995).

Conclusion and recommendations for research

This chapter provides a review of one of the important criminal procedural issues, fitness to plead, in Hong Kong's judicial system. It is important for defendants to actively participate in their own trial and to understand every stage of the criminal justice process from arrest to sentencing. In an adversarial criminal justice system, such as in Hong Kong, defendants' ability to provide their lawyers with pertinent information, including information relating to the alleged offence and witnesses to testify, will enable the lawyers to develop appropriate legal strategies and consequently mount an effective defence. To this extent, it is argued that the extent of participation or engagement in the process can affect how the proceedings and the final outcome (guilty and sentencing or acquittal) are appraised (i.e., fair and unfair). Jury selection and composition is an essential and crucial aspect of the judicial system in Hong Kong. Understanding the factors impacting on jury decision-making can help in the selection of an impartial jury to make a decision without undue personal biases and influences. Potential research areas include jurors' understanding of FTP as well as the discrete court-related functions that are indicative of FTP, the impacts of judges' instructions on jurors' decision-making process, and the extra-legal factors likely to affect jury decision-making on competency to stand trial. Research into the characteristics of defendants raising fitness issues and those found unfit to plead is equally warranted. To a very large extent, the perceived fairness of the criminal proceedings can impact confidence in and attitudes towards the criminal justice system.

Chapter summary points

- Fitness to plead (FTP) ensures the postponement of criminal proceedings for defendants who are not able to participate in and contribute to their own defence, particularly due to mental disease.
- The FTP legislation in Hong Kong stipulates that a defendant is unfit to plead if he/she labours "under any disability such that apart from this Ordinance it would constitute a bar to his being tried" (Section 75(1) of the *Criminal Procedure Ordinance* (CPO)).
- Issues concerning FTP can be raised by the prosecution, the defence, or the trial judge.

- The CPO specifies two discrete and independent pathways to determine FTP: (a) at the magistrate and district courts, the trial or the sitting judges or magistrates naturally hear and make a finding on FTP; (b) at the high courts, juries are empanelled to ascertain fitness issues.
- The decision-making regarding FTP will ultimately result in one of the two outcomes: a defendant is fit to face the charges or unfit to plead. In the event of the former, the criminal adjudication process will proceed.
- Where a defendant is found unfit to plead, the court must further decide whether the defendant committed the crime or made the omission in question before orders such as a guardianship and hospitalisation orders are made.

References

Adjorlolo, S., & Chan, H. C. O. (2016). Determination of competency to stand trial (fitness to plead): An exploratory study in Hong Kong. *Psychiatry, Psychology and Law*. Advance online publication. 1–18. doi: 10.1080/13218719.2016.1247417

Adjorlolo, S., Chan, H. C. O., & Agboli, J. M. (2016). Adjudicating mentally disordered offenders in Ghana: Criminal and mental health legislations. *International Journal of Psychiatry and Law*, *45*, 1–8. doi: 10.1016/j.ijlp.2016.02.001

Bonnie, R., & Grisso, T. (2000). Adjudicative competence and youthful offenders. In T. Grisso & R. Schwartz (Eds.), *Youth on trial: A developmental perspective on juvenile justice* (pp. 73–103). Chicago, IL: University of Chicago Press.

Breheney, C., Groscup, J., & Galietta, M. (2007). Gender matters in the insanity defense. *Law & Psychology Review*, *31*, 93–123.

Daftary-Kapur, T., Groscup, J. L., O'Connor, M., Coffaro, F., & Galietta, M. (2011). Measuring knowledge of the insanity defense: Scale construction and validation. *Behavioral Sciences & the Law*, *29*(1), 40–63. doi: 10.1002/bsl.938

Dusky v. United States, 362 US, 402 (1960).

Exworthy, T. (2006). Commentary: UK perspective on competency to stand trial. *Journal of the American Academy of Psychiatry and the Law Online*, *34*(4), 466–471.

Finkel, N. J., & Handel, S. F. (1988). Jurors and insanity: Do test instructions instruct? *Forensic Reports*, *1*, 65–79.

Gray, N. S., O'Connor, C., Williams, T., Short, J., & MacCulloch, M. (2001). Fitness to plead: Implications from case-law arising from the Criminal Justice and Public Order Act 1994. *The Journal of Forensic Psychiatry*, *12*(1), 52–62. doi: 10.1080/09585180121865

Grubin, D. (1991). Unfit to plead in England and Wales, 1976–88: A survey. *The British Journal of Psychiatry*, *158*(4), 540–548.

Heilbronner, R. L., & Frumkin, I. B. (2003). Neuropsychology and forensic psychology. *Journal of Forensic Neuropsychology*, *3*(4), 5–12. doi: 10.1300/J151v03n04_02

Jackson, M. (2003). *Criminal law in Hong Kong*. Hong Kong: Hong Kong University Press.

Melton, G. B., Petrila, J., Poythress, N. G., & Slobogin, C. (1997). *Psychological evaluations for the courts: A handbook for mental health professionals and lawyers* (2nd ed.). New York, NY: Guilford.

Narby, D. J., Cutler, B. L., & Moran, G. (1993). A meta-analysis of the association between authoritarianism and jurors' perceptions of defendant culpability. *Journal of Applied Psychology*, *78*(1), 34–42.

Peters, M., & Lecci, L. (2012). Predicting verdicts, adherence to judge's instructions, and assumptions about the disposition of the defendant in a case involving the insanity defense. *Psychology, Crime & Law, 18*(9), 817–831. doi: 10.1080/1068316X.2011.566872

Pirelli, G., Gottdiener, W. H., & Zapf, P. A. (2011). A meta-analytic review of competency to stand trial research. *Psychology, Public Policy, and Law, 17*(1), 1–53. doi: 10.1037/a0021713

R v. Chiu Te-ken, 2 HKCLR, 21 (1993).

R v. Egan, Crim LR, 225 CA (1997).

R v. Keung Sai-chung, HKLR, 838 CA (1986).

R v. Leung Tak-Choi, 2 HKCLR, 32 (1995).

R v. Podola, 1 QB, 325 (1960).

R v. Pritchard, 7 C & P., 303 (1836).

Roebuck, D. (1995). *The criminal law of Hong Kong: A descriptive text.* Beijing: Peking University Press.

Roesch, R., Zapf, P. A., Golding, S. L., & Skeem, J. L. (1999). Defining and assessing competency to stand trial. In A. K. Hess & I. B. Weiner (Eds.), *The handbook of forensic psychology* (2nd ed., pp. 327–349). New York, NY: John Wiley & Sons.

Rogers, T. P., Blackwood, N. J., Farnham, F., Pickup, G. J., & Watts, M. J. (2008). Fitness to plead and competence to stand trial: A systematic review of the constructs and their application. *The Journal of Forensic Psychiatry & Psychology, 19*(4), 576–596. doi: 10.1080/14789940801947909

Rogers, T. P., Blackwood, N. J., Farnham, F., Pickup, G. J., & Watts, M. J. (2009). Reformulating fitness to plead: A qualitative study. *The Journal of Forensic Psychiatry & Psychology, 20*(6), 815–834. doi: 10.1080/14789940903174139

Sakdalan, J. A., & Egan, V. (2014). Fitness to stand trial in New Zealand: Different factors associated with fitness to stand trial between mentally disordered and intellectually disabled defendants in the New Zealand criminal justice system. *Psychiatry, Psychology and Law, 21*(5), 658–668. doi: 10.1080/13218719.2014.910857

Skeem, J. L., Eno Louden, J., & Evans, J. (2004). Venirepersons's attitudes toward the insanity defense: Developing, refining, and validating a scale. *Law and Human Behavior, 28*(6), 623–648. doi: 10.1007/s10979-004-0487-7

White, A. J., Batchelor, J., Pulman, S., & Howard, D. (2012). The role of cognitive assessment in determining fitness to stand trial. *International Journal of Forensic Mental Health, 11*(2), 102–109. doi: 10.1080/14999013.2012.688091

White, A. J., Meares, S., & Batchelor, J. (2014). The role of cognition in fitness to stand trial: A systematic review. *The Journal of Forensic Psychiatry & Psychology, 25*(1), 77–99. doi: 10.1080/14789949.2013.868916

Yourstone, J., Lindholm, T., Grann, M., & Svenson, O. (2008). Evidence of gender bias in legal insanity evaluations: A case vignette study of clinicians, judges and students. *Nordic Journal of Psychiatry, 62*(4), 273–278. doi: 10.1080/08039480801963135

Zapf, P. A., Roesch, R., & Pirelli, G. (2014). Assessing competency to stand trial. In I. B. Weiner & R. K. Otto (Eds.), *The handbook of forensic psychology* (4th ed., pp. 281–314). Hoboken, NJ: John Wiley & Sons.

5 Juries as decision-makers in East Asian judicial systems

Hong Kong, Mainland China, South Korea, and Japan

Cora Y. T. Hui, Samuel Adjorlolo, and Heng Choon (Oliver) Chan

Introduction

One index of socioeconomic development is the legal system. In Western countries like the United States and the United Kingdom, a robust and independent legal system has paralleled socioeconomic developments. Laws are crafted not only to regulate transactions among people but also to promote an atmosphere of transparency and fairness for business to thrive. This observation equally applies to many Asian, particularly East Asian, jurisdictions such as Hong Kong, Mainland China, South Korea, and Japan. The legal systems in these jurisdictions are embodiments of socio-cultural factors as well as foreign influences. Therefore, to appreciate and understand the contemporary architecture of the legal systems in these jurisdictions, one must endeavour to appreciate the inextricable link and interplay of social, cultural, political, and historical factors over the past decades. A nuanced approach to gaining deeper insights into the legal systems in these East Asian countries is via a comparative review.

Indeed, a very interesting development that has taken place across these jurisdictions is the involvement of lay people in the judicial system, often termed as lay participation or the jury system. In other words, people without legal training or background are called upon by the courts to adjudicate and when necessary determine the appropriate and suitable punishment for individuals guilty of a criminal offence. Jury systems have been termed "democratic ideals around the world" (Fukurai, Chan, & Miyazawa, 2010, p. 141). This democratisation of the legal system purportedly brings legitimacy to the criminal justice system as it empowers fellow citizens to decide whether the defendant should be punished. Advocates of jury trials also hope that the use of juries would lead to acquittals in systems that had previously been disposed towards convictions. In cases with political implications, the jury might even act as the "defender of freedom in politically sensitive cases" (Duff, Findlay, Howarth, & Chan, 1992, p. 101).

The practice of a jury system varies across these jurisdictions, especially given the obvious differences in their legal systems. There is no singular idea of a jury system in Asia: each jury system is distinct and reflects the unique history of each country. Fukurai et al. (2010) regarded jury research in East Asia to be "at an early, yet very exciting stage in answering fascinating research questions on the socio-political role of lay participation in legal decision-making" (p. 147). Fukurai and Hans (2012) remarked that jury research in East Asia is able to offer "theoretical insights about the purposes and phenomenon of lay adjudication" (p. 27). Given the limited work on a comparative review of the jury systems in East Asian jurisdictions, this chapter seeks to provide a brief overview of the legal systems in Hong Kong, Mainland China, South Korea, and Japan and to compare the jury systems in these jurisdictions. To proceed, an overview of the legal and jury systems in these jurisdictions is provided. Next, we critically examine factors affecting jury decision-making in the Asian context. Finally, we offer some directions for studies into jury decision-making in these selected Asian jurisdictions.

Overview of the judicial system in Hong Kong

As a former British colony, the legal system in Hong Kong resembles the system in England and Wales to a greater degree than it does the system in Mainland China. However, some changes have been effected to the legal and judicial practices in Hong Kong since the British handed over the territory to the People's Republic of China on 1 July 1997. Notably, the root source of the laws in Hong Kong (e.g., criminal law and the *Basic Law*) is enacted by the National People's Congress of the People's Republic of China (see Ghai, 2001). The principle of "One Country, Two Systems" nevertheless grants Hong Kong a high degree of autonomy and promises little change to its society for 50 years after its return to Chinese sovereignty. Laws that were previously in force in Hong Kong until 1 July 1997 are still enforceable insofar as they have not been amended and do not contravene the *Basic Law* (see Jackson, 2003). There are four levels of courts in Hong Kong: Magistrates' Courts, the District Court, High Courts (Court of First Instance and Court of Appeal), and the Court of Final Appeal. Courts with original criminal jurisdiction (i.e., trial courts) include the Magistrates' Courts, the District Court, and the Court of First Instance. Summary offences are only tried in the Magistrates' Courts. Many offences may be tried either summarily (in the Magistrates' Courts) or on indictment (in the District Court or the Court of First Instance), and the prosecution has the right to determine the venue of the trial. The Court of First Instance has unlimited jurisdiction in both civil and criminal cases, while the District Court deals with relatively minor civil (disputes that involve less than HKD 1 million, or around USD 129,000) and criminal (offences that could lead to a sentence of imprisonment of less than seven years) cases. The *Basic Law* also guarantees that both parties in the proceedings are entitled to the right to appeal against a conviction and/or sentence. Courts with appellate functions include the Court of Appeal and the Court of Final Appeal. The Court of Appeal deals with appeals on cases from the District Court and the Court of First Instance, and the Court of Final Appeal is the highest appellate court (see Figure 5.1 for the appeal process). Additionally, there are courts that can adjudicate on specific issues, such as the Juvenile Court, the Coroner's Court, and the Lands Tribunal (for the functions of the various courts, see Jackson, 2003). An offence may be tried by a jury, a magistrate, or a judge.

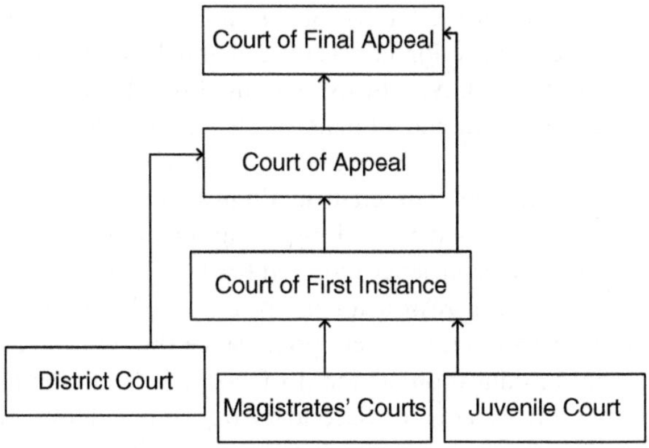

Figure 5.1 The appeal process in Hong Kong

The jury system in Hong Kong

The jury system in Hong Kong has been in operation for over 150 years, the longest-running jury system in East Asia. The system was imported to Hong Kong in 1845, shortly after Hong Kong became a British colony. The importance of the jury is also recognised in Article 86 of the *Basic Law*, which stipulates "the principle of trial by jury previously practised in Hong Kong shall be maintained." As outlined in the *Jury Ordinance*, a person is liable to serve as a juror if he or she meets the following five criteria:

1 Is between 21 to 65 years of age
2 Is a resident of Hong Kong
3 Is of sound mind
4 Is of good character
5 Has sufficient knowledge of the language in which the proceedings are conducted.

The jury system only exists in the Court of First Instance, where a presiding judge tries defendants together with a jury of seven people (or nine people if the judge orders). Should the prosecution select the District Court as the trial venue, the defendant will be tried by a District Court judge and not by a jury. District Court judges, who are empowered to pass a sentence of imprisonment of up to seven years, try defendants in solitary. The most serious criminal offences, including murder, manslaughter, rape, armed robbery, and certain drug offences, can only be tried in the Court of First Instance. It has been held in the case of *Chiang Lily v. Secretary for Justice* that defendants do not have the right to choose the mode of trial. While there is no constitutional right to trial by jury in Hong Kong, trial by jury is one of the most essential features of the legal system in Hong Kong (Judiciary, 2012).

Largely due to Hong Kong's history as a colony, the jury system in Hong Kong differs from the systems in the United States and the United Kingdom (Duff et al., 1992). Firstly, eligibility for jury service is much narrower in Hong Kong than in England and Wales. As a British colony, English was used as the official language in the government and all major trials were conducted in English. The Commissioner of Registrations applied a strict education requirement to ensure that jurors were sufficiently competent in English. English remained as one of the two official languages used after Hong Kong was returned to Chinese sovereignty, and the language proficiency required has been either English or Chinese. Even though the historical reason for imposing an education requirement (to ensure English proficiency) no longer applies since the return, residents are still required to attain an education standard of Form 7 (equivalent to Year 13 in many Commonwealth systems) or Secondary 6 (the new Hong Kong Diploma of Secondary Education Examination system since 2012) to qualify as potential jurors (Juries Sub-Committee of the Law Reform Commission, 2008). It is important to note that the completion of Form 7 or Secondary 6 as a jury requirement means that most potential jurors have satisfied the basic requirement for university entry in Hong Kong. As many common law jurisdictions impose no education requirement on jury eligibility, the education requirement in Hong Kong has been criticised as undermining the representativeness of the jury (Duff et al., 1992; Juries Sub-Committee of the Law Reform Commission, 2008). Second, the jury comprises only seven members (or nine if the judge so orders). Due to the limited number of English speakers in Hong Kong when the *Jury Ordinance* was first enacted, jury size was greatly reduced as compared with the composition in England and Wales. A majority verdict of at least five to two is required, although juries are urged to strive for unanimous verdicts.

Overview of the judicial system of the People's Republic of China (Mainland China)

China undeniably has a rich legal system which, like other Asian countries, is influenced by the famous philosophies of classical China as well as by external factors. When the Communist Party assumed power in 1949, the political philosophies of Marxism-Leninism, Maoism, and the Soviet legal system had a significant influence on the Chinese legal system. The classical philosophies of China include Confucianism, Daoism, and Legalism. Confucius (551–479 BCE) and his disciple Mencius (372–289 BCE) developed and promoted the doctrine and teaching of Confucianism, whose primary tenet is to educate people in ways to behave properly in society. Consequently, Confucianism emphasises *li* (virtue or propriety), construed as positive measures for preventing crime and maintaining social order, rather than *fa* (the law), which is a punitive measure that encourages people to escape being punished rather than doing what is right in the eyes of society (Zhang, Shi, & Lue, 1987). Central to the Confucianism doctrine is a hierarchy of superior-inferior relationships in which the obedience and loyalty of the inferior to the superior is encouraged, while at the same time emphasising the benevolence of the superior to the inferior. Every person must fulfil and play his or her role to ensure and sustain stability, tranquillity, social order, and peace in society.

Unlike Confucianism, Legalism championed the concept of rewards and punishment as the mechanism to keep power in order. This is based on the assumption that man by his nature is evil and needs to be controlled via the promulgation of laws in order to avert social disruption. To the Legalist, nobles and the common people are not different people who should be treated differently insofar as their actions violate or breach laws and rules of society. Yet, Legalism advocated effective governance and the maintenance of institutional continuity by means of strict, explicit, and public laws (Schwartz, 1985). Codification of the law in ancient China, which was primarily penal in nature, was undertaken during the Qin (221–206 BCE), Tang (618–907 CE), Song (960–1279 CE), Ming (1368 1644 CE), and Qing (1644–1912 CE) dynasties (Johnson, 1985). Many Western countries, including the United States, Great Britain, and France, considered the Chinese legal system naturally imperfect and therefore believed that it was inappropriate for their citizens to be tried in Chinese courts. Consequently, these countries established consular courts which had exclusive jurisdiction over their citizens in China, regardless of the crime or civil claim (Willoughby, 1927). The Chinese legal system underwent a massive transformation, as demanded by Western countries in return for relinquishing extraterritorial rights to China. Eventually, China successfully developed a legal framework and drafted the first constitution of the People's Republic of China in 1954. Since then, the legal system has experienced and continues to experience changes in light of societal advancement and in accord with developments across the globe.

Currently, the court system in Mainland China consists of local people's courts, special courts, and the Supreme People's Court (see Figure 5.2). According to the *Constitution of the People's Republic of China*, the Supreme People's Court is the highest court and oversees the people's courts at various local levels and the special courts (Art 132). The Supreme People's Court is also directly responsible to the National People's Congress and its Standing Committee (Art 133). Local

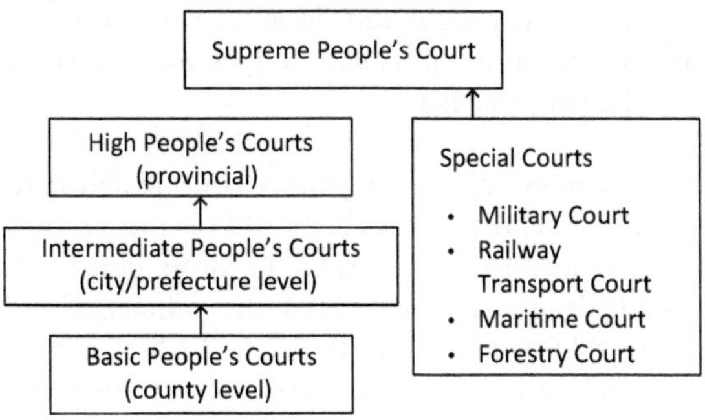

Figure 5.2 The court system in Mainland China

people's courts are divided into three levels. The Basic People's Courts, operating at the level of counties and towns, normally hear civil and criminal cases at the first instance. Basic People's Courts are required to refer more serious cases to higher courts. Immediate People's Courts, operating at the level of prefectures and cities, possess original and appellate jurisdiction. The Higher People's Courts, operating at the provincial level, operate both as trial courts and appellate courts in cases referred by the lower courts. Special courts include the Military Court of China, the Railway Transport Court of China, and the Maritime Court of China; such courts are established to deal with specialised cases.

The jury system in the People's Republic of China

Since the formal establishment of the People's Republic of China in 1949, a series of laws have been written regarding jury trials (Yu & Hu, 2015). However, it was not until approval was given by the 10th National People's Congress (NPC) Standing Committee to improvements of the people's jury system in August 2004 that specific provisions regarding how the jury works were laid down. The introduction of lay participation could be seen as a governmental response to enhance the fairness and transparency of judicial proceedings.

"Jurors" in China, despite the name, are more like lay assessors in the continental mixed tribunal system. The only similarity between Chinese lay assessors and Anglo-American jurors is that neither are required to have legal background. Lay assessors in China sit together with judges in courts and enjoy the same rights as judges (Art 1 in the NPC decision). Both professional and lay assessors deliberate and determine the trial outcome together (Art 11). Three main differences between lay assessors and jurors can be highlighted:

1 The jury consists of 12 members in the US; at least one-third of the collegial panel must be lay assessors in China (Art 3) (as most cases must heard by at least three people under the civil and criminal procedure, the usual panel consists of two lay assessors and one professional judge).
2 The jury is summoned to serve on a case-by-case basis in the US; lay assessors serve five-year terms in China (Art 9).
3 The jury deliberates in private and decides on the verdict in the US; lay assessors only decide on the facts with judges and cannot comment on the application of the law in China.

The lay assessor system in China has expanded considerably in recent years. The Supreme People's Court reported that about 70% of cases at the initial trial stage were tried with jurors in 2014: some 210,000 jurors heard 2.19 million cases ("New rules for China's jury system", 2015); the number of jurors represents a great increase on the 87,000 figure for 2013. The 12th NPC Standing Committee approved the launch of a two-year pilot reform in 10 cities in April 2015. The selection mechanism would be changed from personal applications and institutional recommendations to random selection to enhance the representativeness of jurors. The education requirement would be lowered from college to senior high school level and further lowered for "highly respected people" in villages and remote areas. The number of jurors in the jury pool in each city must be at least three times the number of judges. Jurors will be randomly selected from local residents who meet the following criteria:

1. Aged 28 years or above
2. Completed high school education
3. Do not meet the exclusion and disqualification criteria (mainly based on occupation and personal conduct)

Overview of the judicial system in South Korea

Prior to Japan's occupation and colonialisation of Korea, the Gojoseon Dynasty, which was the first dynasty in Korea, enacted its own statutory law that comprised eight articles – the *Eight-Article Law* (*Pal-jo-geum-beob*). One law stated that any person who kills should be killed (Kim, 2012). The concept of Confucianism, imported from Chinese legal culture, was widely adopted and practised in Korea. During the period of colonialisation, Japan's Western-influenced laws and regulations were imported into Korea, where they functioned as the primary source of law. Korea's independence in 1945 following the Allies' defeat of Japan and the ending of US military rule paved the way for the establishment of a modern legal system. The legal system, which hitherto was influenced by Japanese legislation, is now a mixed system combining Anglo-American laws and European civil laws (Ahn, 1997; Kim, 2012). The prominent and basic codes in South Korean are the Constitution, which was enacted in 1948 and has since undergone nine successful amendments; the civil code; the commercial code; the code of civil procedure; the criminal code; and the code of criminal procedure (Kim, 2012).

The Korean court system includes the Supreme Court, High Courts, District Courts, and specialised courts (e.g., Family Courts, Administrative Courts, Patent Courts) (see Figure 5.3). District Courts are primarily courts of original jurisdiction and try both civil and criminal cases. Cases in District Courts are tried by either a single judge or a panel of three judges for more serious cases. High Courts deal with appeals referred by District Courts (cases tried by a panel of three judges only), Family Courts, and Administrative Courts. The Supreme Court is the highest level of court and hears appeals from District Courts and High Courts.

The jury system in South Korea

Citizen participation in criminal trials was officially introduced by the enforcement of the *Act on Citizen Participation in Criminal Trials* on 1 January 2008. The jury system is completely foreign to Korean legal tradition as South Korea has never had a history of citizen participation (Lee, 2009). It is hoped that this

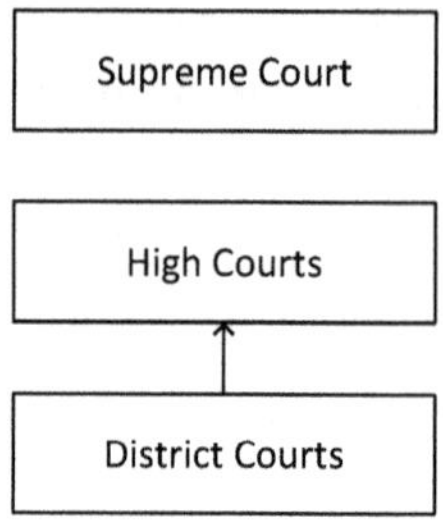

Figure 5.3 The court system in South Korea

fundamental change in judicial decision-making will "raise democratic legitimacy and confidence in the judicial process" in Korea (Art 1). Lee (2009) noted that the right for Koreans to act as legitimate judicial participants seems to be the main driving force behind Korea's adoption of the jury system, whereas the right of the accused to be tried by their peers was not stated explicitly as a reason. The Korean jury system was designed largely on the basis of the American jury system, although the final format and scope of the system will be determined after a five-year experimental phase. Beginning in 2008, ordinary citizens were summoned to adjudicate in serious criminal cases as jurors (*baesimwon*). Jury decisions, however, are not binding during the experimental phase. Judges are instructed to use jury verdicts as important guidance, although they are able to make a contrary decision should they find it appropriate. Presiding judges must notify the defendant of the results of the jury verdict at the time of sentencing; if their judgment differs from the verdict, the judges must explain to the defendant why their verdict is different (Art 48(4)). Judges must also provide written reasons if their judgment differs from that of the jury (Art 49(2)). A person is liable to serve as a juror in Korea if he or she meets the following criteria (Art 16 to 20):

1 Is a Korean citizen
2 Is over the age of 20
3 Does not meet any of the criteria for disqualification, exception (mainly due to occupation), exclusion, or exemption

The jury trial is presided over by a three-judge panel. Five, seven, or nine jurors are summoned depending on the characteristics of the case (Art 13). For serious cases such as murder, where the defendant may receive capital punishment or life imprisonment, a nine-person jury is used. For other less serious crimes such as robbery, assault, and rape, a seven-person jury is used. In cases where the defendant pleads guilty to most of prosecuted facts during the preparatory proceedings, a five-person jury is used. Upon hearing the facts of the case, jurors retreat in private to deliberate and must strive to reach a unanimous verdict. If over half of the jurors agree, the jury may choose to hear the judges' opinion. Yet if jurors fail to reach a unanimous verdict in the first stage, they are required to hear the opinions of the presiding judges. A verdict based on a majority could be accepted in the second stage after consultation with the presiding judges (Art 46(3)). This two-stage practice is designed to reduce the possibility of a hung jury and enhance the accuracy of the verdict (Lee, 2009). One divergence from the American jury model is that Korean jurors participate in sentencing deliberation together with the judges (Article 46(4)).

Overview of the judicial system in Japan

Before the era of Emperor Meiji, a period referred to by many historians as "modern Japan", the legal system of Japan had been based entirely on the elaborate rules of propriety, *Giri*, for nearly three centuries (i.e., 1603–1868) (Hahn, 1984; Parker, 2013; Uchtmann, Blessen, & Maloney, 1988). The then Emperor, Tokugawa Shogunate, promulgated the rules as mechanisms to regulate and enforce appropriate personal conduct as well as relationships with others in society. Thus, the *Giri* were mirrored after traditional social roles such as father and son, husband and wife. Violation or breach of the rules brought disgrace upon the offender. The regime of Emperor Shogunate further adopted the principle of Confucianism and the doctrines of *wa* (harmony), which, together with the existing *Giri,* fostered non-litigious sentiments whereby the people were taught and learnt to resolve and settle disputes amicably without resorting to courts. Emphasis was laid on harmonious living and showing greater respect to superiors. According to Hahn (1983), as a result of the strong and overwhelming emphasis on a non-litigious approach to settling and resolving conflicts, there were no lawyers in Japan, nor were there specialised legal experts to counsel the indigenes or represent them in court.

However, when Emperor Meiji assumed office in 1868 (i.e., the Meija era or "modern Japan"), several reforms, including legal and judicial reforms, were initiated, implemented, and enforced. During this period, Japan renegotiated several treaties that were purportedly hampering Japan's quest for modernisation and rapid socioeconomic development (Uchtmann et al., 1988). As a consequence, Japan adopted new civil and criminal codes that were mirrored on the civil code of Germany and the French criminal code, respectively (Gono et al., 2004). The *Meiji Constitution* adopted in 1889, which was modelled on the Prussian constitution, conferred sovereignty on the Emperor (Uchtmann et al., 1988). After World War II, Japan amended some of its laws to converge with the basic laws in the United States (Gono et al., 2004). Since then, the legal system in Japan has continued to experience changes.

Presently, there is a constitution, statutes, and codes (e.g., the criminal code and the criminal procedure code). There are five types of courts in Japan: the Supreme Court, High Courts, District Courts, Family Courts, and Summary Courts (see Figure 5.4). The Supreme Court is the highest court in Japan and handles appeals referred from the High Courts. High Courts handle appeals filed against judgments rendered by the District Courts, Family Courts, and Summary

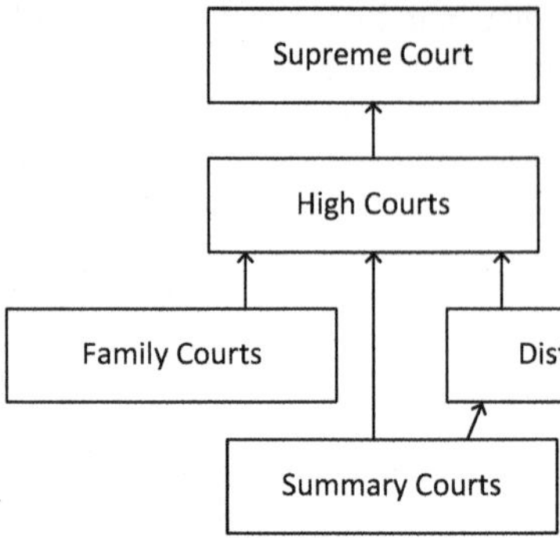

Figure 5.4 The court system in Japan

Courts (criminal cases). Family Courts handle family affairs and juvenile delinquency cases. District Courts handle the first instance of most types of civil and criminal cases. *Saiban-ins* (lay judges) are involved in the adjudication of certain serious cases in District Courts. Summary Courts handle civil cases involving small claims and minor criminal cases.

The jury system in Japan

Unlike Korea, Japan had experienced a limited form of all-citizen criminal jury trial from 1928 to 1943. The jury experiment foundered for a variety of reasons, and the justice system returned to the trajectory of professionalism and elitism (Landsman & Zhang, 2008). The Justice System Reform Committee (JSRC), tasked to examine reforms in the justice system to support Japan in the 21st century, recommended a new participation system in criminal proceedings where judges and *saiban-ins* could decide on verdicts and sentences together (Justice System Reform Council, 2001). The report also recommended that *saiban-ins* possess equivalent authority to that of professional judges to ensure that they have a meaningful and active deliberation in trial decisions. The *Act Concerning Participation of Lay Assessors in Criminal Trials* was enacted in May 2004, and the new *saiban-in* system was introduced in May 2009. The two main stated purposes of the *saiban-in* system are to promote the public's understanding of the judicial system and to raise the public's confidence in the system (Art 1). *Saiban-ins* only try the most serious criminal cases – crimes punishable by death/ indefinite imprisonment or crimes that resulted in the death of the victim (Art 2).

In cases where there are no disputes concerning the admitted facts, a panel of one professional judge and four *saiban-ins* may decide the case. The *saiban-in* system has elements of both the Anglo-American jury system and the German lay assessor system, although it resembles the lay assessor system to a greater degree. Similar to Anglo-American jurors, *saiban-ins* are selected randomly from eligible voters living in the jurisdiction of the given district court on a case-by-case basis. Unlike the all-citizen Anglo-American jury, the judicial panel consists of three professional and six lay judges. The verdict is decided by majority vote, although a conviction requires at least one vote from a professional judge (Art 67). The fact-finding and sentencing stages are not separated in Japanese courts, so *saiban-ins* may question the defendant and witnesses and decide both on fact finding and sentencing.

Factors contributing to jury decision-making

Numerous studies have pointed out that jurors in East Asia are generally competent fact finders. Han and Park (2012) noted that judges agreed with the jury's verdict in 90.6% of all cases in the first four years of citizen participatory trials in South Korea (2008 to 2011). In the 54 inconsistent cases, juries acquitted but the judges convicted in 50 cases; the reverse was true in only four cases. Kim, Park, Park, and Eom (2013) found that judge-jury agreement increased as evidence strength became stronger. When the weakest level of evidence was presented, the judge-jury agreement rate was 84%. The agreement rate increased to 97.9% when the strongest level of evidence was presented. This finding suggests that the accuracy of jury verdicts is strongly related to the strength of the evidence presented. Duff et al. (1992) noted that 72.2% of the barristers they surveyed thought that it was fairly or very unlikely for a person to be wrongly convicted by a jury. When further asked which decision-maker was likely to arrive at a just and fair verdict, the barristers largely believed that a jury was more reliable than a judge sitting alone: 10% of the surveyed barristers thought the judge was more likely to arrive at a just and fair verdict, while around 45% thought the jury was more likely; the remaining barristers thought both the judge and the jury were equally likely to arrive at a just and fair verdict.

A host of factors have been suggested to affect jury decision-making in the last few decades (see Devine, Clayton, Dunford, Seying, & Pryce, 2001 for a comprehensive review). Emerging studies are beginning to show that jury decision-making in East Asia slightly differs from that in the United States. Kim and Penrod (2010), for example, found that Korean lay participants evaluated and weighed evidence differently to their American counterparts. Korean lay participants were more sceptical about the evidence presented in general. They weighed witnesses (both prosecution and defence) more negatively, were more sceptical about the confession being presented, and were less likely to perceive that they had enough evidence to reach a verdict. The present chapter highlights the availability of the defendant's confession to show the slightly different perceptions of confession in another culture.

The availability of a confession

Confession, the defendant's first-hand admission of guilt, has long been considered a "gold standard" of evidence and a "prosecutor's most potent weapon"

(Kassin & Neumann, 1997, p. 221; Kassin, 2012, p. 8). As eyewitnesses could identify the wrong suspect and expert witnesses could reach an incorrect conclusion based on lab misconduct, fact finders would find the defendant's unambiguous admission of guilt to be particularly trustworthy. Although the high reliance placed on confession is not unique to the criminal justice systems in East Asia, not every jurisdiction relies on a defendant's confession as much as the East Asian systems, which see it almost as an essential component of a successful prosecution. Lo (2012) expressed concerns that "the problem in the Chinese criminal justice system is its emphasis on confession as superior to any other kind of evidence" (p. 637), and Hui and Lo (2015) listed a few Chinese slogans to show the historical, cultural, and institutional significance of a defendant's confession (see Table 5.1). The use of torture and coercion to obtain confessions is also quite common in Japan, as even coerced confessions are considered the "queen of evidence" in court (Fukurai & Kurosawa, 2010, p. 2). Approximately 92% of all indicted cases result in confession, and many of these confessions were obtained using coercion.

Table 5.1 Confession-related slogans

Slogans	*Implications*
Only process cases that include the defendant's confession (*wugongbuluan*) Convict the defendant only after he/she confesses (*duanzui biqu shufu gongci*)	Confession has been seen as an essential component of prosecutions throughout Chinese history.
Using the information extracted from testimonial evidence to look for other evidence (*yougongdaozheng*)	The over-reliance on confession evidence is also evident in the modern-day investigation system. The practice of *yougongdaozheng* encourages police officers to interrogate suspects, regardless of the strength of the evidence collected, in the early stages of the investigation and to use the information extracted from the interrogation to look for corroborating evidence.
Leniency for confession and severity for resistance (*tanbaicongkuan kangjucongyan*)	The Chinese criminal justice system has long encouraged defendants to settle court cases through admission of their criminal wrongdoings. At the cultural level, the collectivist Chinese culture interprets confession as a sign of sincere remorse and willingness to repent. At the institutional level, prompt confessions speed up the investigation process. The slogan is therefore often used to threaten suspects into confessing and then to close criminal cases promptly.

The cultural and institutional emphasis on confession has led investigators to use notoriously violent and coercive interrogation techniques to extract confessions. Fukurai and Kurosawa (2010) noted that false confession is the principal cause of wrongful convictions in Japan. The main contributing factors of forced confessions in Japan include the use of physical and psychological torture and violence to obtain confessions and Japanese judges' near-blind acceptance of confession statements as evidence of guilt. Furthermore, the Japanese criminal procedure allows up to 23 days of detention for the police and prosecution to interrogate the suspect, a considerable period of time for defendants to succumb to coercion.

Although the literature suggests that police officers and legal practitioners see the defendant's confession as crucial to a criminal investigation and successful prosecution, could citizen participation protect against this professional tendency? Fukurai and Kurosawa (2010) found that citizens who have served on the Prosecutorial Review Commission (similar to the grand jury system in the US) were willing to question the credibility of confessions and were concerned about the transparency of the investigation process. In cases where there was a discrepancy between the defendant's confession and open-court statement, almost all Prosecutorial Review Commission participants felt the need to understand the circumstances under which the confession was made and three-quarters would choose to believe the defendant's claim of innocence. Around 90% of participants agreed that recording the trial proceedings is important and that jurors should ask the judge to clarify their questions and concerns. The authors were hopeful that the inclusion of ordinary citizens in the deliberative processes might challenge the existing tradition of automatic deference to confession. Hui and Lo (2015) wanted to examine the extent to which jury decisions made by Hong Kong Chinese were shaped by the predominant Chinese criminal justice concept of confession. They found that the Hong Kong Chinese mock jurors in their study placed a high value on confession evidence: 70% of the participants convicted the defendant when presented with a confession. The conviction rate was substantially higher than the 56% conviction rate reported in Kassin and Neumann's (1997) study. Despite the high value placed on confession, the participants were more likely to find the defendant culpable, and to give more guilty verdicts, when presented with DNA evidence (85.3%). The authors interpreted the findings as support for the "one country, two cultures" situation in Hong Kong. Although the mock jurors placed great emphasis on a defendant's confession, their judgment was shaped more by physical and scientific evidence, as commonly advocated in the West. Civic participation is not yet popularised in Mainland China, yet we speculate that the public is growing less and less tolerant of coercive interrogation tactics. Public outcry resulting from the numerous high-profile wrongful conviction cases (e.g., the Zhao Zuohai case) eventually pushed the NPC to amend the *Criminal Procedure Law* (CPL, 2013) in order to reform the collection and use of evidence in criminal cases (see Lewis, 2013 for more details). In particular, CPL 2013 stipulated that oral confessions alone are not sufficient grounds for conviction in the absence of corroborating evidence, and it prohibited the use of torture to extract confessions from defendants.

Conclusion and future directions

Legislation and legal systems are so rooted in a jurisdiction's historical and cultural context that they cannot be completely transplanted from the Anglo-Saxon models. Damaška potently noted that "the score may be the same, so to speak, but if the instruments and players are not, the legal music will sound differently" (in Edwards, 1997). Jury systems in East Asia have appropriately made adjustments to their jury systems to better suit the context in their respective jurisdictions and have not simply transplanted certain procedural rules from one jurisdiction to their own. It must be remembered that the jury system is not a fixed entity: the judicial system needs to constantly evolve according to socio-political changes. A perhaps ironic example to give is that even in the "rigorously adversarial" American system, jury trials are disappearing whereas plea bargaining, settlements, and alternative dispute resolutions are rising (Pizzi, 2008, p. 66). In 2010, 96.8% of cases were settled through plea bargaining (Sourcebook of Criminal Justice Statistics, 2010). Damaška's research in comparative law has shown the three criteria of an effective legal system: careful attention to context, resisting oversimplification, and the ability to adjust to revolutionary changes (Koh, 2008). It is certainly hoped that scholars and practitioners in East Asia will continually monitor and evaluate their hard-earned jury systems.

The classification of a judicial system as either adversarial or inquisitorial has never been as clear-cut as some have imagined (Damaška, 1986). Pizzi (2008) noted that inquisitorial features can be found even in the rigorously adversarial American system. Newly established jury systems in East Asia, which frequently combine features from both adversarial and inquisitorial systems, further challenge scholars to re-examine the adversarial-inquisitorial classification. Research in East Asia offers an interesting platform to explore the universality of legal concepts and theories conceived in the West, and the potential for research is endless. Potential research questions range from mechanisms/processes of jury decision-making to fundamentally embedded legal concepts. How would cultural variations affect one's perception of the evidence presented? How does culture affect jury deliberations? Is the disregarding of legally irrelevant information considered difficult universally? Should juries in adversarial trials be involved in sentencing? Should judges be allowed to summarise the evidence for jurors? One particularly interesting question is whether it is a must to use the dichotomous verdict of guilty/not guilty. Both the Russian and Spanish legislatures rejected the Anglo-American concept of verdict and favoured presenting the jury with a list of questions and propositions (Thaman, 1999). To echo what other jury researchers have noted, now is indeed an exciting time to expand the scope of jury research.

Chapter summary points

- The distinct lay participation systems in Hong Kong, Mainland China, South Korea, and Japan all reflect the unique history and legal system of each country.

- In Hong Kong, a seven-person jury is used to try serious cases. The judge presides over the case and provides judicial guidance.
- "Jurors" in Mainland China are more like lay assessors in the continental mixed tribunal systems and sit together with professional judges in trials.
- In South Korea, jurors are summoned to attend trial upon the request of the defendant. Jurors are required to independently evaluate the evidence presented and provide advisory opinions to judges.
- *Saiban-ins* decide verdicts and sentences together with professional judges in the most serious cases in Japan.
- Early research has shown that jurors in East Asia are generally competent fact finders, although they seem to have an excessively strong focus on the defendant's confession.

References

Ahn, K. W. (1997). The influence of American constitutionalism on South Korea. *Southern Illinois University Law Journal, 22*, 71–115.

Damaška, M. R. (1986). *Faces of justice and state authority: A comparative approach to the legal process.* New Haven, CT: Yale University Press.

Devine, D. J., Clayton, L. D., Dunford, B. B., Seying, R., & Pryce, J. (2001). Jury decision making: 45 years of empirical research on deliberating groups. *Psychology, Public Policy, and Law, 7*, 622–727. doi: 10.1037/1076-8971.7.3.622

Duff, P., Findlay, M., Howarth, C., & Chan, T. (1992). *Juries: A Hong Kong Perspective.* Hong Kong: Hong Kong University Press.

Edwards, H. T. (1997). Comments on Mirjan Damaška's *Of Evidentiary Transplants. American Journal of Comparative Law, 45*, 853–860. doi: 10.1007/978-3-642-40928-8_7

Fukurai, H., Chan, K., & Miyazawa, S. (2010). Introduction to the special issue: The future of lay adjudication and theorizing today's resurgence of civic legal participatory systems in East and Central Asia. *International Journal of Law, Crime and Justice, 38*, 141–148. doi: 10.1016/j.ijlcj.2011.01.001

Fukurai, H., & Hans, V. P. (2012). Special feature: The future of lay adjudication in Korea and Japan. *Yonsei Law Journal, 3*, 25–35.

Fukurai, H., & Kurosawa, K. (2010). Impact of the popular legal participation on forced confessions and wrongful convictions in Japan's bureaucratic courtroom: A cross-national analysis in the U.S. and Japan. *US-China Law Review, 7*, 1–18.

Ghai, Y. (2001). *Hong Kong's new constitutional order.* Hong Kong: Hong Kong University Press.

Gono, J., Hibino, M., Hinokawa, K., Kamiya, S., Maki, H., Nishiyama, S., . . . Yamauchi, Y. (2004). *Overview of legal systems in the Asia-Pacific region: Japan.* Paper 7. Retrieved from http://scholarship.law.cornell.edu/cgi/viewcontent.cgi?article=1007&context=lps_lsapr

Hahn, E. J. (1983). An overview of the Japanese legal system. *Northwestern Journal of International Law & Business, 5*, 517–539.

Han, S. H., & Park, K. (2012). Citizen participation in criminal trials of Korea: A statistical portrait of the first four years. *Yonsei Law Journal, 3*, 55–66.

Hui, C. Y. T., & Lo, T. W. (2015). One country, two cultures: Are Hong Kong mock jurors "mainlandized" by the predominant Chinese criminal justice concept of confession? *International Journal of Offender Therapy and Comparative Criminology, 59*, 1104–1124. doi: 10.1177/0306624X14528463

Jackson, M. (2003). *Criminal law in Hong Kong*. Hong Kong: Hong Kong University Press.

Johnson, W. (1995). Status and liability for punishment in the T'ang code. *Chicago-Kent Law Review, 71*, 217–229.

Judiciary. (2012, 1 February). *Jury*. Retrieved from http://www.judiciary.gov.hk/en/crt_services/pphlt/html/jury.htm

Juries Sub-Committee of the Law Reform Commission. (2008). *Criteria for service as jurors: Consultation paper*. Hong Kong: Law Reform Commission. Retrieved from http://www.hkreform.gov.hk/en/docs/juries_e.pdf

Justice System Reform Council. (2001, 12 June). *Recommendations of the justice system reform council – For a justice system to support Japan in the 21st century*. Retrieved from http://japan.kantei.go.jp/policy/sihou/singikai/990612_e.html

Kassin, S. M. (2012). Why confessions trump innocence. *American Psychologist, 67*, 431–445. doi: 10.1037/a0028212

Kassin, S. M., & Neumann, K. (1997). On the power of confession evidence: An experimental test of the fundamental difference hypothesis. *Law and Human Behavior, 21*, 469–484. doi: 10.1023/a:1024871622490

Kim, K. (2012). *Introduction to Korean Law: Overview*. Berlin: Springer.

Kim, M. C., & Penrod, S. D. (2010). Legal decision making among Korean and American legal professionals and lay people. *International Journal of Law, Crime and Justice, 38*, 175–197. doi: 10.1016/j.ijlcj.2011.01.004

Kim, S., Park, J., Park, K., & Eom, J. (2013). Judge-jury agreement in criminal cases: The first three years of the Korean jury system. *Journal of Empirical Legal Studies, 10*, 35–53. doi: 10.1111/jels.12001

Koh, H. H. (2008). Mirjan Damaška: A bridge between legal cultures. In J. Jackson, M. Langer, & P. Tillers (Eds.), *Crime, procedure and evidence in a comparative and international context: Essays in honour of Professor Mirjan Damaška* (pp. 29–35). Oxford: Hart Publishing.

Landsman, S., & Zhang, J. (2008). A tale of two juries: Lay participation comes to Japanese and Chinese courts. *Pacific Basin Law Journal, 25*, 179–227.

Lee, J. (2009). Getting citizens involved: Civil participation in judicial decision-making in Korea. *East Asia Law Review, 4*, 177–207.

Lewis, K. M. (2013). China's criminal justice system. In L. Cao, I. Sun, & B. Hebenton (Eds.), *The Routledge handbook of Chinese criminology* (pp. 51–63). Oxford: Routledge.

Lo, T. W. (2012). Resistance to the mainlandization of criminal justice practices: A barrier to the development of restorative justice in Hong Kong. *International Journal of Offender Therapy and Comparative Criminology, 56*, 627–645. doi: 10.1177/0306624x11405481

New rules for China's jury system. (2015, 21 May). *Xinhuatnet*. Retrieved from news.xinhuanet.com

Parker, C. L. (2013). *Crime and justice in Japan and China: A comparative view*. Durham, NC: Carolina Academic Press.

Pizzi, W. T. (2008). Sentencing in the US: An inquisitorial soul in an adversarial body? In J. Jackson, M. Langer, & P. Tillers (Eds.), *Crime, procedure and evidence in a comparative and international context: Essays in honour of Professor Mirjan Damaška* (pp. 65–80). Oxford: Hart Publishing.

Schwartz, B. (1985). *The world of thought in ancient China*. Cambridge, MA: Harvard University Belknap Press.

Sourcebook of Criminal Justice Statistics. (2010). *U.S. Sentencing commission guideline cases: Plea versus trial*. Retrieved from http://www.albany.edu/sourcebook/index.html

Thaman, S. C. (1999). Europe's new jury systems: The cases of Spain and Russia. *Law and Contemporary Problems*, *62*, 233–260. doi: 10.2307/1192258

Uchtmann, D. L., Blessen, R. P., & Maloney, V. (1988). The developing Japanese legal system: Growth and change in the modern era. *Gonzaga Law Review*, *23*, 349–359.

Willoughby, W. W. (1927). *Foreign rights and interests in China*. Baltimore, MD: Johns Hopkins Press.

Yu, M., & Hu, X. B. (2015, 17 April). Woguo renminpeishenyuanzhidu de que li (The establishment of the people's jury system in China). *People's Court Daily*. Retrieved from www.chinacourt.org

Zhang, J., Shi, F., & Lue, J. (1987). *A survey of legal history*. Beijing: Mass Publishing House.

Part 2

Offender rehabilitation and treatment

6 Offender rehabilitation

The Hong Kong Correctional Services Department

Samson Chan

Introduction

On 14 January 1998, the Hong Kong Correctional Services Department (CSD) set up a Rehabilitation Division with responsibility for offender rehabilitation in Hong Kong (Hong Kong Correctional Services Department, 1999). This marked the beginning of the provision of specialised and professional offender rehabilitation services within the CSD under one coordinated office and with designated resources, including both manpower and finance, for implementing its various services.

The work on offender rehabilitation in Hong Kong prisons has a long history, with the earliest information recorded in the *Regulations for the Government of the Gaol in Hongkong* under *Ordinance No. 1 of 1853* passed by the Legislature on 20 September of the same year (Norton-Kyshe, 1898). In this first detailed document listing the management and treatment of prisoners in Hong Kong, the only tool mentioned for the rehabilitation of prisoners was religion, in the form of visits by ministers of religion, a practice in line with that in England at the time.[1]

Rehabilitation work for sentenced persons has developed over time in Hong Kong. In the CSD's *Annual Review 2014*, the work on offender rehabilitation was described in great detail, listing the latest in-centre and community support services offered to sentenced persons (Hong Kong Correctional Services Department, 2015). Furthermore, the CSD claimed credit for its offender rehabilitation work, as reflected in the various reintegration programmes it operated showing high success rates of offenders completing their respective supervision programmes without committing further criminal offences.

This chapter analyses in detail the development of offender rehabilitation at different times under the Prisons Department and later the CSD. It is also the intention to identify whether the "nothing works" attitude on offender rehabilitation found in the West in the 1970s (Martinson, 1974) had any impacts in Hong Kong.

Offender rehabilitation in Hong Kong: The early history

The history of Hong Kong's prisons is as old as the history of Hong Kong itself. Victoria Gaol was one of the few earliest secure buildings erected in the colony soon after the British took possession of Hong Kong in 1841 (Chan, 1994). The emphasis inside Victoria Gaol during the formative years of the colony was on custodial discipline and the deterrence of crime through harsh penal practices. At that time, offender rehabilitation was never the priority of penal policy. In line with the pre-war colonial policy, the composition of the prison staff was mainly Indian warders supervised by British prison officers; thus, the language barrier alone for a prison population mainly consisting of Chinese prisoners would have made any counselling or guidance work in offender rehabilitation extremely difficult if not impossible. This situation lasted until the beginning of the Second World War in Asia in 1941.

As reflected in the first gazetted regulations for the operation of Victoria Gaol in 1853, religion, through visits by ministers of religion, was basically the only tool used for the rehabilitation of prisoners. As mentioned in the regulations, "[t]he Chaplain shall read prayers with the Prisoners, and read or preach to them a discourse, and perform all other Offices of religion as often as he may see fit" (CO129/43, p. 244).

Furthermore, religion was not only a rehabilitation tool for prisoners but also a source of spiritual guidance for shaping the behaviour of the prison officials. The gaoler of Victoria Gaol and other officers of the gaol were required to attend divine service. According to the same regulation, the gaoler

> shall attend Divine Service whenever performed in the Gaol, unless unavoidably prevented; if he do not attend he shall record the reasons in his Journal. He shall also enforce the attendance thereat of such of the other Officers of the Gaol, and such of the Prisoners as may not be unavoidably prevented.
> (CO129/43, p. 244)

Hong Kong's penal policies were modelled after England's, which was natural while it was a Crown Colony of Britain. The adoption of the "separate system" and the "silent system" at Hong Kong's Victoria Gaol in the 19th century were examples of the direct importation of British penal policies and practices on prisoner reformation. The main rehabilitative function of the separate system and the silent system was the provision of an isolated environment free from the contamination of criminal elements, that is fellow prisoners, thus allowing individual prisoners to reflect on their wrongdoings while imprisoned (Chan, 1994).

Another rehabilitative move that Hong Kong adopted from British penal practice was the separation of young offenders from adult offenders and the provision of distinctive and more rehabilitation-oriented penal programmes for the former group of offenders. With the setting up of separate juvenile courts to deal with juvenile offenders and the enactment of the 1932 *Ordinance to Provide for and Regulate Industrial and Reformatory Schools*, modelled after the English law of 1910, juvenile offenders aged seven to 16 were provided with industrial and reformatory school programmes. The early reformatory schools were operated by religious organisations such as the Salvation Army and were later taken over by the police.

In 1938, the probation service for offenders was created and placed under the administration of the Prisons Department. The management of the reformatory schools was taken over by the Prisons Department in 1941 under the directive of the Colonial Office in London. The programmes offered in the reformatory schools while under the administration of the Prisons Department were similar to those offered in England. The programmes focused mainly on character training aided by the provision of educational and vocational training so that young offenders upon release from reformatory school could be equipped with basic education and work skills to facilitate their reform and reintegration back into society (Chan, 1994).

Offender rehabilitation after 1945

Hong Kong returned to British administration after the Second World War in 1945. The immediate post-war years saw Hong Kong experiencing some of the its most difficult years: an infrastructure that had been severely damaged during the war years; a poor local and global economy; a shortage of resources; and an influx of refugees from Mainland China as a result of the civil wars. Public order was a major problem in Hong Kong, with large numbers of petty offenders being dealt with by the courts.

Despite the extensive use of fines and corporal punishment as alternatives to imprisonment, the prisons in Hong Kong were so overcrowded that an early release of prisoners had to be arranged in 1948 to relieve the pressures faced by the Prisons Department (Chan, 2012). Rehabilitative programmes for adult prisoners in Hong Kong were basically non-existent in the immediate post-war period as some of the pre-war prison buildings had been damaged during the war and the remaining facilities were only suitable for warehousing those sentenced by the courts. The Hong Kong Government and the Prisons Department were severely handicapped, having neither the physical nor the human resources to provide rehabilitative programmes for offenders.

The Hong Kong Government at the time had to literally rebuild the entire administrative structure from scratch with the assistance of the few remaining British officials who were physically fit enough after spending long and difficult months inside the Stanley internment camp during the Japanese occupation. In the Prisons Department, the middle and senior management ranks were basically filled by British individuals who were recruited either locally or direct from England, and only a very small number of these individuals had any prior experience in prison management. In line with the post-war governmental policy, Chinese people were for the first time recruited to fill rank-and-file posts (Chan, 2012). However, owing to the difficult years Hong Kong experienced immediately after the war, civil servants, in particular junior staff, were poorly paid and therefore civil service posts lacked the attraction to lure high-calibre young people to join the government. The situation was as bad or worse for the law enforcement departments as Chinese families in Hong Kong would in general discourage their offspring from joining the Hong Kong Police Force or the Prisons Department in view of the negative and corruptive image those in uniform had at the time.

As the social and political situation in Hong Kong gradually settled in the 1950s, penal policies in Hong Kong became more progressive and reformative, following the penal welfarism approach adopted in post-war Britain. A long-term sentence prisoner review system was established in Hong Kong in 1950 in which prisoners serving a sentence of more than six years could have their cases reviewed regularly by the Governor. After 1951, prisoners who had no previous history of imprisonment upon admission were classified as "Star Class" prisoners, whereas repeat offenders were classified as "Ordinary Class" prisoners by the Prisons Department. This classification by previous penal history allowed the Prisons Department to separate first-timers from returning prisoners, thus facilitating better penal management as well as preventing first-timers from having undue contact with and being contaminated by habitual offenders. This arrangement also allowed for the better allocation and deployment of tight training and education resources to those with higher priorities.

To comply with the Colonial Office's wish for the colonies to provide aftercare services to prisoners, Hong Kong started a pilot aftercare scheme at Stanley Prison and Lai Chi Kok Female Prison in November 1951. The services were coordinated by the Discharged Prisoners' Aid Sub-Committee of the Hong Kong Council of Social Services, and caseworkers were provided by the Salvation Army and the Family Welfare Society (Chan, 2012).

Some of the senior British prison officers were themselves internees and had personal experience of being locked up inside Stanley Prison during the period of Japanese occupation, making them sympathetic to the lives of persons under custody and more apprehensive of the impact of prison routine on the prisoner population (Chan, 2012). Mr C. J. Norman, one of the former Stanley internees, was Commissioner of the Prisons Department from 1953 to 1968, and during this time, corporal punishment for prisoners in breach of prison rules was discarded. Open visits were introduced at Stanley Prison and Lai Chi Kok Prison to facilitate communication between the prisoners and their families. Earning and canteen schemes were introduced to provide more incentives for prisoners to engage in work during their period of imprisonment. Home leave of up to five days was granted to eligible prisoners in preparation for employment prior to their return to society. In Stanley Prison, a pilot group was set up for 50 long-term Star Class prisoners with less than six months to serve to be accommodated under a more relaxed regime in preparation for their release. Open prisons with minimal security features were set up at Chimawan and Tai Lam Chung in 1957 and 1958, respectively, to accommodate short-sentence prisoners.

In 1957, the Discharged Prisoners' Aid Society (DPAS), a voluntary group, was formed to coordinate rehabilitation work for offenders released from prison, in particular the arrangement of hostel placements for those with urgent accommodation needs upon release. The Commissioner of Prisons was personally involved and was appointed as the Vice-President of the DPAS, with some other senior prison officials acting as advisors to the society. This was the Prisons Department's first direct involvement with a non-governmental organisation (NGO) to fill the service gaps of the department in terms of offender rehabilitation as prison staff were barred under prison rules from having any contact or dealings with discharged prisoners. With support from the Prisons Department, the DPAS started to receive subventions from the Hong Kong Government from 1959 and soon became the main NGO providing welfare and supportive services to both serving and discharged prisoners in Hong Kong.[2]

The training centre programme

Despite the provision of reformative and progressive work for adult prisoners in the 1950s, rehabilitative work continued to focus on young offenders in Hong Kong. The Prisons Department resumed its management of the reformatory for young male offenders under the age of 16 immediately after the Second World War. Young offenders were located in a reformatory in some converted food warehouses in Stanley from 1946 to 1953. After 1953, all the reformatory boys were transferred to Castle Peak and placed under the management of the Social Welfare Officer.

With the removal of the reformatory from the administration of the Prisons Department, the senior administrators of the Prisons Department then decided to set up a similar programme for young offenders aged 14 to 21. The penal elites had taken note of the English Borstal system developed under the *Criminal Justice Act 1948* but decided that there should be local adaptations to fit Hong Kong's unique social and cultural conditions. This vision eventually led to the birth of the training centre programme in Hong Kong.

The *Training Centre Ordinance* was enacted in March 1953 to provide character training for male young offenders aged 14 to 18. Young offenders were detained in a training centre for a period of nine months to three years, and their actual release date was decided by a Review Board composed of members of the Prisons Department. The Review Board was chaired by a senior prison official from the Prisons Headquarters, and members included the officer-in-charge of the training centre and a few prison officers who were in a position to evaluate the in-centre performance of the inmates, including their progress in academic and vocational training. The aftercare officer, who was also a prison officer but had some social work training, was normally included on the Review Board to report on the inmates' response to rehabilitation and other related matters.

The Review Board would look into the progress of the individual inmate in terms of training and rehabilitation in order to decide when he or she should be promoted in grade from beginner to intermediate and finally to leaver. Enhanced privileges were tied to each promotion in grade. When the Review Board considered an inmate ready to leave the training centre, and with employment prearranged, the inmate would be released and would undergo three years' statutory aftercare supervision. A supervision order specified the detailed requirements to be followed while under supervision by Prisons Department aftercare officers, and the supervisee would be recalled if found to be in breach of any of the supervision conditions. Stanley Training Centre (site of the former Stanley Reformatory School) commenced operations in February 1953 (Commissioner of Prisons, 1955). Up to 1970, training centres were basically open institutions where inmates, especially those at the leaver grade, were given a lot more freedom and responsibility in their daily activities. Home leave was regularly approved to strengthen their links with family members and to help them secure a job prior to their release from the centre.

The training centre programme remains in operation today, although changes have taken place over the years. The period of in-centre training was amended to a minimum of six months and a maximum of three years, and in 1970, a separate training centre was established for young girls of the same age group (Commissioner of Prisons, 1972).

The distinctive feature of the training centre programme is the half-day education and the half-day vocational training provided for inmates. The nature and quality of the training has been enhanced greatly over the years by moving away from the provision of elementary academic training in Chinese, English, and Mathematics under the guidance of the Special Education Section of the Education Department to providing a full range of liberal arts subjects in line with normal secondary schools in Hong Kong. Training centres have also acquired registered school status, with qualified teachers providing focused and dedicated academic training for young offenders. The emphasis in the academic education programme is to prepare eligible inmates to sit public examinations so that they can acquire recognised qualifications just like other students in Hong Kong, thus facilitating their eventual reintegration into society. Good public examination results together with their successful stories have been regularly reported in the local newspapers.

The other important tool for offender rehabilitation at the training centres is vocational training. In the early days, only a few basic vocational trades were introduced at the training centres owing to limited resources. The early workshops provided training in carpentry, building maintenance, tool handling, and automobile repair. In addition, some young inmates picked up other vocational skills through their domestic service at the centre as barbers, cooks, cleaners, laundrymen, gardeners, and painters.[3] These early provisions were very different to what is provided nowadays, where the focus is again on providing inmates with accredited vocational qualifications that employers would accept in the open job market.

Character training is another very important element of the training centre programme. Although the maximum period of stay at a training centre could be up to three years, on average, inmates only stay for around 16 months, which allows them sufficient time to take part in other youth programmes such as scouting and marching bands, the Hong Kong Award for Young People (The Duke of Edinburgh's Award prior to 1997), Outward Bound training, and community services for the elderly and the disabled. These types of character-training activities provide opportunities for young offenders to better discover their potential, cultivate team spirit, learn empathy, and gain confidence in reintegrating with the community.

The current philosophy of the training centre programme aims to make use of this comparatively long custodial training period for inmates to develop a positive character and to excel both academically and in terms of employability compared with their situation prior to their admission to a centre. These measures are designed to facilitate inmates to develop an enhanced self-image and hopefully allow them to dissociate themselves from their former undesirable peers. Furthermore, the three-year supervision by rehabilitation officers of the CSD with regular home and workplace visits ensures that supervisees released from the training centres comply with the supervision conditions; if they fail to comply, the supervisees are liable to be recalled back to the training centre by order of the Commissioner of Correctional Services.

Studies on the training centre programme have, in general, found it to be effective (Chan, 2003; Lo et al., 1997; Prisons Department, 1974, 1980; Tam & Heng, 2008). Success rates for training centre supervisees from 1982 to 1997 ranged from 59% to 71% for males and from 86% to 94% for females, and the overall success rate in 2014 was 67% (Hong Kong Correctional Services Department, 1982–97, 2014). The CSD defines the success rate of the training centre programme as supervisees not committing any criminal offences during the three-year aftercare supervision period and fully complying with all supervision requirements. As at 31 December 2015, there were a total of 125 males and 10 female training centre supervisees undergoing supervision by the CSD's rehabilitation officers (Hong Kong Correctional Services Department, 2016a).

The drug addiction treatment centre programmes

The rehabilitative work for adult offenders in Hong Kong provided by the Prisons Department and the Hong Kong Government after the Second World War was, as mentioned earlier, limited in scope and scale. It is argued that for adult offenders in prisons, the rehabilitative focus was on the enforcement of custodial discipline inside the penal institutions, where prisoners had to live under strict and regimented routines. They were expected to obey orders from the authority and to get used to the idea of performing useful tasks in workshops or carrying out domestic assignments. Failing any of these expectations and requirements would result in disciplinary action being taken against the prisoner. The belief was that through this regulated lifestyle and these regulated activities, prisoners would eventually develop the work habit and a respect for the law, which were considered the key resettlement elements for someone who used to stay on the wrong side of the law and lacked the skills and aptitude to acquire gainful employment and self-discipline.

During the 1950s, a high proportion of adult prisoners were either opium or heroin drug addicts as the use of such opiate substances was only considered illegal after the Second World War. The government had at this time started to take law enforcement actions to combat the use of such illicit drugs resulting from the influx of prisoners on drug-related offences, many of whom were drug addicts.

In 1958, over 40% of prisoners admitted that they had committed drug-related offences.

The Prisons Department turned the newly acquired site quarters of Tai Lam Chung into Tai Lam Prison in 1958, the second open prison in Hong Kong after Chimawan Prison. Most of the sentenced drug addicts were assigned to this new prison to undergo an experimental programme designed by the Prisons Department for managing prisoners with a history of addiction. These prisoners were initially located in the prison's sick bay to undergo a short period of detoxification to address their drug withdrawal symptoms. After they had made a full recovery, they were assigned to engage in mainly outdoor work, such as reforestry work around the Tai Lam reservoir area. Upon their discharge, prisoners from Tai Lam were encouraged to take up voluntary aftercare supervision provided by NGOs. The philosophy was that through a period of outdoor work during their period of imprisonment in a drug-free environment, the prisoners could gradually build up a stronger physique and regained a positive personal image. The belief was that this work experience, together with the support provided by social workers while under voluntary aftercare supervision, would give discharged prisoners a better chance to lead a drug- and crime-free life after release. To further support discharged prisoners facing accommodation difficulties, the Prisons Department from August 1968 operated its own half-way house programme providing hostel accommodation for those released from Tai Lam Prison at the New Life House located in the Western district. The aim of the half-way house programme was to provide discharged prisoners with "a bridge between the institution and a return to normal life" (Commissioner of Prisons, 1971).

With the experience gained from the success of working with drug addict prisoners at Tai Lam Prison, the Prisons Department recommended to the Hong Kong Government that a new sentencing option of compulsory drug treatment should be offered for minor offenders with a drug habit rather than sending them to prison. As a result, the *Drug Addiction Treatment Centres Ordinance* was proposed and became law in January 1969; the ordinance authorised the Prisons Department to run these treatment centres.

The ordinance empowers the courts to sentence a confirmed addict, male or female aged 14 years or above and guilty of an offence, to a drug addiction treatment centre for a period of compulsory treatment in lieu of imprisonment. The period of detention can range from six months to a maximum of 18 months, to be followed by 12 months' compulsory aftercare supervision by the Prisons Department. An offender's actual release from a drug treatment centre is determined by a Review Board similar to that used in regard to training centres, with the inmate's progress with regard to treatment, physical health, and likelihood of abstention from drugs upon release being assessed for consideration (*Drug Addiction Treatment Centres Ordinance,* 1997).

The period of treatment was amended to a minimum of four months and a maximum of 12 months in 1976, and in 1986, the minimum period was further reduced to two months, allowing a "greater flexibility within the programme to cater for those addicts who respond well to treatment" (Commissioner of Prisons, 1979; Hong Kong Correctional Services Department, 1987).

The supervision of drug addiction treatment centre (DATC) dischargees by Prisons Department aftercare officers involves regular home and workplace visits and also urine tests to ensure supervisees maintain a drug-free life in addition to maintaining gainful employment and living at agreed locations. Cases found to be in breach of supervision conditions are recalled back to the DATC by order of the Commissioner of Prisons.

The Caritas Lok Heep Club, an NGO with a Catholic Church background, was formed in May 1968. Two drop-in clubhouses for ex-DATC inmates and their family members were established at Caine Road and Tung Tau Estate, respectively; the aim of these drop-in clubhouses was "to assist all persons previously drug dependent to remain abstinent, to foster mutual friendship and co-operative assistance between members and to enable members to assume a responsible role within their families and the community" (Commissioner of Prisons, 1971).

According to CSD statistics, the success rates for supervisees completing the DATC programme and the 12 months' supervision reached 65% in 2008 and 2009 but dropped to 42% in 2011 (Hong Kong Correctional Services Department, 2008–09, 2011). The mechanism for conducting urine tests on DATC supervisees was enhanced following a court case in 2012 (Case No. ESCC 5021/11) where two CSD aftercare officers were found guilty of making false or inaccurate records of urine samples collected from their supervisees in 2009. The success rates of the DATC programme has since improved from 43.6% in 2012 to 46.8% and 51.4% in 2013 and 2014, respectively (Hong Kong Correctional Services Department, 2016c). As at 31 December 2015, there were a total of 531 DATC inmates (male, female, and young addicts) undergoing treatment separately at the CSD's three DATCs (Hong Kong Correctional Services Department, 2016b).

The CSD is proud to take an active role in tackling the drug problem in Hong Kong by providing compulsory drug treatment programmes. Prison commissioners have promoted this model for the treatment and rehabilitation of addict offenders to the international community since the 1970s (Garner, n.d.; Norman, 1971). However, the Asia Pacific region has been more receptive to this compulsory treatment and rehabilitation model than Western countries such as the United Kingdom which maintain the view that drug addiction is more a public health issue than a public order issue (McSweeney & Hough, 2005).

Youth crime in the 1970s and the detention centre programme

In the 1970s, Hong Kong experienced an upsurge in crime rates, in particular violent crimes committed by young offenders. This was not surprising as in 1972 over half of Hong Kong's population was under the age of 25 as the result of baby boom phenomenon of the post-war era (Chan, 2012).

To address the problem of youth crime, the Hong Kong Government introduced the detention centre programme to Hong Kong, a programme imported from Britain that emphasised the 'short, sharp shock' deterrence elements of the programme. Although a detention centre programme was started in Britain in the late 1940s under *Criminal Justice Act 1948*, the Hong Kong penal elites had never felt the need to pick up this practice from Britain during the 1950s and 1960s, believing that the best methods for dealing with the juvenile delinquency problem in Hong Kong should be in the form of character training delivered through the reformatory and training centre programmes; furthermore, Britain had already given up on this sentencing option for young offenders in the 1960s, finding it problematic and ineffective in dealing with these offenders.

With the bitter memories of the 1967 riots and the public's concern, particularly about violent crimes committed by young offenders, the period of reformative penal policy had gradually faded out by the end of the 1960s, and it was followed by a period when penal policies emphasised institutional security, discipline, and control. Apart from the return of corporal punishment as means of judicial punishment by the courts, the legislation for the *Detention Centre Ordinance* was passed in March 1972 and the first detention centre was set up at Sha Tsui on Lantau Island three months later, with corporal punishment included as one of the means used in dealing with indiscipline inside the centre (Chan, 2012).

Only young male offenders with no previous correctional institution experience are admitted into a detention centre. Young males have to be (a) certified fit for the rigorous detention centre programme by the prison medical officer and (b) considered suitable for admission to the detention centre programme by the Commissioner of Prisons before the court can sentence them to this programme. This is the only correctional programme in Hong Kong which excludes female offenders and where the sentencing magistrate/judge needs the consent of the Commissioner of Prisoners before committing a young male to a detention centre under the *Detention Centres Ordinance*.[4] The period of detention was initially between one and six months, and detainees were required to undergo six months' statutory aftercare supervision by Prisons Department aftercare officers on release and were subject to recall if found to be in breach of the supervision requirements.

The short, sharp shock elements of the detention centre programme in Hong Kong aim to deter young offenders "during the earliest stage of their deviation from law and order, from future criminal activity. Emphasis is placed on the strictest discipline and hard work with little or no privileges. Whatever is done must be done well and no excuses from detainees are accepted for failure to maintain a high standard" (Commissioner of Prisons, 1975).

The emphasis of the detention centre programme is more on the deterrence element than the rehabilitative elements during the in-centre period when detainees are given a full day of demanding physical activities. There are remedial education classes organised for the detainees during the evenings. Nevertheless, owing to the short period of stay at a centre, the academic benefit detainees gain at a detention centre are very minimal when compared with the training centre programme; also, no vocational training is included in the detention centre programme.

On the other hand, counselling sessions are available for detainees at a detention centre. These sessions are either conducted by rehabilitation officers or by a clinical psychologist. NGOs are currently also being commissioned to provide specific counselling sessions to address detainees' needs. Some changes have been made over time, including the extension of the admission age group to 25, the extension of the supervision period to one year after release from a centre, and the refinement of the work assigned to detainees, including the removal of rock breaking as physical labour.

Among all the correctional programmes operated by the CSD, the detention centre programme's success rates for the one-year aftercare supervision have always been high, well exceeding 90%. The success rate for the 2014 completed cases was 95% (Hong Kong Correctional Service Department, 2015).

Adult offenders during the 1970s

The treatment approach towards specific groups of adult offenders continued until the early 1970s. In November 1972, the purpose-built psychiatric centre at Siu Lam was completed and provided much needed facilities for the Prisons Department to accommodate remanded and convicted persons with suspected or confirmed mental problems. Diagnosis and treatment was provided by visiting psychiatrists from the Medical and Health Department and supported by prison staff with psychiatric nursing qualifications.

A riot took place at Stanley Prison during Easter 1973 and prison officers were taken hostage by prisoners. Successful negotiation through the personal involvement of the Commissioner of Prisons led to the peaceful resolution of the crisis. The findings from the subsequent enquiries and the recommendations prepared by the advisors from H. M. Prison Service in the United Kingdom prompted the Prisons Department to shift its focus to custodial discipline and security within correctional institutions. The granting of home leave to adult prisoners ceased except for bereavement cases and under escort by prison officers. Open prisons became minimum-security institutions surrounded by tall fences topped with barbwire, and the security standards of dormitory accommodation were upgraded. On the positive side, the aftermath of the Stanley Prison riot brought about the rapid expansion of the Prisons Department through rank restructuring and better remuneration for staff from the end of 1973 onwards. The build-up of better-quality prison staff, including officers with accredited social work qualifications from tertiary institutions, later formed the backbone of prison officers performing aftercare and welfare duties.

In 1973, 17 prisoner welfare officer posts were created, and six of these officers were deployed to work in prisons starting from 1974.[5] The primary tasks of these officers were to attend to prisoners' tangible and welfare needs arising from imprisonment. The most common problems encountered by prisoners were housing-related issues, establishing contacts with family and friends, seeking financial assistance for their families, and marital relationship problems. The prisoner welfare officers, as well as the Prisons Department, only had limited resources at their disposal, and as a result, most of the prisoners' requests were referred to the respective government departments, such as the Social Welfare Department and the Housing Department, for follow-up actions. Assistance from NGOs, in particular the DPAS, was highly sought. In-depth casework or counselling services were rare during these early days, and there were infrequent group sessions, such as the "Never Again Association" involving prisoners and their immediate family members, on topics such as seeking employment and abstaining from drugs. Pre-release workshops were also organised for prisoners approaching their discharge in order to prepare them for employment and other related matters.

At this time, the rehabilitative roles of prison officers performing welfare duties were yet to be appreciated by many line managers at the penal institutions. They liked to consider the prisoner welfare officers part of the custodial team acting as a pressure valve for prisoners to vent their emotional tensions as well as being eyes and ears to forewarn the management of any untoward incidents that might come to their attention through their daily contacts with the prisoners.

In March 1975, Dr Robert G. Andry of London University was attached to the Prisons Department for six months under United Nations' auspices to consider the feasibility of introducing full psychological services to the Prisons Department in Hong Kong. His subsequent recommendations received support from the Hong Kong Government, and the psychological services of the Prisons Department formally started in November 1977 with four clinical psychologist posts (Prisons Department, 1975, 1976, 1979). Details on the development and work of the psychological services in Hong Kong are covered in Chapter 2.

To assist the newly appointed aftercare and welfare officers in performing their rehabilitative duties, the Prisons Department, from 1977 to 1980, arranged related training courses at the University of Hong Kong for them. It was also arranged for assistant officers performing similar duties to receive training in social work at Hong Kong Polytechnic.

The Prisons Department continued to grow in the late 1970s, with new penal institutions completed and staff strength much enhanced. The department was at this stage ready to present its work to counterparts in the region and hosted the first Asia and Pacific Conference of Correctional Administrators in February 1980. This conference has become an annual event and a platform for the correctional heads of the Asia Pacific region to meet annually to share operational experiences and address issues of common concern, which include topics on offender rehabilitation and reintegration.

From prison services to correctional services

The Prisons Department's management of offenders moved into a new era in 1981 with the removal of dietary and corporal punishment for prisoners and inmates found to be in breach of prison discipline. This move was in line with the international trend on how persons under detention ought to be treated, where the physical punishment of offenders was no longer accepted under international human rights standards.

On 1 February 1982, the Prisons Department was renamed the Correctional Services Department or CSD for short. This change was meant to project a more positive image of the department to the public and also reflect the diversity of programmes the CSD was operating and the types of persons under the department's custody. A new post of Assistant Commissioner (Psychological Services and Programme Development) was created and filled in September 1982 by Dr Andry, who had earlier planned psychological services for the CSD.

Programmes for young offenders under the CSD continued to operate with a rehabilitative focus. In July 1983, a purpose-built half-way house for both male and female young offenders, Phoenix House, located at Lung Cheung Road near the Lion Rock tunnel, was put into operation. The residents of Phoenix House were mainly detainees discharged from detention centres, and they were assigned to reside in the house as part of the supervision requirements. A short period of stay at Phoenix House would allow them to gradually tune in to society after a period of highly intensive disciplinary training. Other Phoenix House residents included those training centre dischargees who were unable to return home for various reasons and were unable to find immediate accommodation. A separate half-way house for females, Bauhinia House, was established at the Corner House of Victoria Prison in August 1984 to enhance the management and accommodation arrangements of the female residents.

The internationalisation of the work of Hong Kong correctional services scaled new heights when Hong Kong hosted the first Commonwealth Correctional Administrators Meeting in March 1985, showcasing the Hong Kong experience outside the Asia and Pacific region. On the other hand, overseas experiences in correction, especially those involving offender rehabilitation such as the parole system, were always closely watched and studied by the penal elites in Hong Kong to see if these ideas could be adopted in Hong Kong.

As early as 1972, the then Commissioner of Prisons started to promote the idea of introducing a parole system to Hong Kong and was able to convince the government to study the idea in detail. The Hong Kong Government kept deliberation on this topic secret, fearing that this proposal would send the wrong message to the public and to criminal elements in Hong Kong that it was turning soft on crime during a time when crime rates were on the rise. The proposal was presented to the Executive Council in 1975 and was rejected because of the same fear. It was only in 1985 that the proposal was positively considered by the government again (Chan, 2012).

Hong Kong's version of parole eventually went through the legislation process and became the *Prisoners (Release under Supervision) Ordinance* in July 1988. This ordinance provides two different routes for local adult prisoners to apply for early release: the Release under Supervision Scheme and the Pre-release Employment Scheme. Non-local prisoners were excluded as under immigration requirements, they would normally be deported from Hong Kong after completing their sentences and thus could not benefit from the supervision elements of the schemes. Eligible prisoners need to submit applications and their cases are considered by an external board consisting of no less than five members and chaired by a High Court judge. Members of the board include a medical practitioner in the field of psychiatry as well as those experienced or interested in offender rehabilitation. Prior to the handover of Hong Kong to China, the board chairman and members were appointed by the Governor of Hong Kong on the recommendation of the Security Bureau (*Prisoners Ordinance,* 1997).

Local prisoners were thrilled, and 103 and 174 prisoners applied for release under the Release under Supervision Scheme and the Pre-release Employment Scheme, respectively, in the first 12 months after the two schemes were launched. However, the board adopted a rather cautious approach in assessing the cases and only approved four and 14 cases, respectively. This conservative approach was adopted by successive boards and as a result prisoners lost interest in submitting their applications. From 1988 to the end of 1997, only 309 prisoners applied for release under the Release under Supervision Scheme, with 45, or 14.6%, being successful; for the Pre-release Employment Scheme, there were 1,014 applications, with 170, or 16.8%, being successful (Chan, 2012).

In 1987, when it was busy setting up its version of the parole system, the CSD also prepared a separate proposal on providing a Care and Control Scheme to supervise adult hard-core offenders upon their release from prison after completing their sentence. As the name of the proposed scheme suggests, it was planned not only to provide assistance and support to dischargees but also, more importantly, to protect the public by monitoring the activities and performance of these hard-core dischargees through a period of compulsory aftercare supervision. The original idea was for a CSD aftercare officer to pair up with a police sergeant to form a supervision team, with the aftercare officer focusing more on the caring part and the police sergeant dealing with the controlling and monitoring elements of the supervision (Hong Kong Correctional Services Department, 1987).

After further debate and discussion within the Fight Crime Committee, the government finally agreed to table the proposal to the Legislative Council in 1994. During the Legislative Council debates, the proposal of involving the police in the supervision team was challenged, and it was finally ruled that the team should be composed of a CSD aftercare officer and his or her assistant together with an assistant social welfare officer from the Social Welfare Department.

The *Post-Release Supervision of Prisoners Ordinance* became law in May 1995 and came into operation in November 1996. Similar to the Release under Supervision Scheme, this Post-Release Supervision Scheme only applied to local prisoners, and a board was appointed by the Governor to assess the cases. Unlike the earlier schemes, where prisoners needed to submit their applications, this new scheme would be compulsory for prisoners serving sentences for specific offences or specific length sentences. The board would study each individual case and decide whether supervision after release should be ordered and for how long after taking into consideration representations from the prisoner. In any case, the maximum period of supervision would not exceed the remitted part of the original sentence, which is normally a third of the total sentence (*Post-Release Supervision of Prisoners Ordinance,* 2014).

The CSD recognised that more rehabilitative work needed to be done for prisoners serving long sentences so that they could adopt a more positive and constructive approach towards their sentences. Through the Scottish connections of the then Commissioner of Correctional Services, Mr Eric McCosh, a staff exchange agreement was made between the CSD and the Scottish Prison Service (SPS) in 1994. One of the assignments for the exchange officer was to study the SPS's Sentence Planning Scheme and see if a similar system could be introduced to Hong Kong.[6] In July 1996, the CSD borrowed some concepts from the SPS and launched its own version of the Sentence Planning Scheme for prisoners serving long prison terms. This scheme was basically a tailor-made programme for individual prisoners with suggested educational and vocational pathways. Good conduct and behaviour plus positive progression in the planned pathway would result in a prisoner earning better privileges and accommodation facilities as incentives.

In 1996, the Standing Committee on Young Offenders of the Fight Crime Committee commissioned a research team from the City University of Hong Kong to study the effectiveness of the rehabilitation programmes for young offenders operated by the Correctional Services Department and the Social Welfare Department in Hong Kong. In the subsequent report, the research team recognised the effectiveness of the CSD programmes but also made two very important recommendations based on comments and feedback from CSD officials. One of the recommendations was to fill the service gaps for both male and female young offenders serving custodial sentences by introducing a new short-term rehabilitative programme. At that time, female young offenders requiring a custodial sentence and male young offenders found unfit for the detention centre programme had no alternative custodial options except to be sentenced to a training centre or to prison custody, neither of which served the best interests of these young offenders. The other recommendation made by the research team was to restructure the CSD's organisation and to set up a new Rehabilitation Division to be headed by an Assistant Commissioner. Both recommendations received the support of the government, leading to the establishment of a rehabilitation centre programme and the formation of the Rehabilitation Division in the CSD (Lo, 2008). Details of these two major developments are covered in the next section.

Offender rehabilitation after 1997

Hong Kong ceased to be a British colony on 30 June 1997 and became a Special Administrative Region of the People's Republic of China. One of the most significant events which affected both the community in Hong Kong and in particular the CSD was the successful conclusion of the Vietnamese saga. Since 1978, the CSD had assisted the Hong Kong Government in operating and managing Vietnamese refugees in detention centres and closed camps. A considerable amount of the CSD's resources, in particular staff, were redeployed from normal correctional duties. CSD officers had to assist in this unique role of providing custodial care to detainees, from infants to ailing elderly persons, for whom normal custodial discipline would not apply. At the height of the influx of the Vietnamese boat people in October 1991, Hong Kong was housing around 64,300 Vietnamese refugees and the CSD had to shoulder the bulk of the workload. It was only in 1998 that the last detention centre for Vietnamese migrants, High Island Detention Centre, was closed, with most of the detainees returned to Vietnam under the Orderly Repatriation Scheme.

Following the scaling down of work involving the Vietnamese detainees, the CSD was able to implement the recommendations proposed by the City University research team by reorganising its organisational structure. In January 1998, a much-needed Rehabilitation Division was set up and headed by an Assistant Commissioner redeployed from duties concerning Vietnamese refugees. The rehabilitation of offenders was no longer under the portfolio of the Operations Division, where custodial discipline and institutional security had always enjoyed a higher resource and management priority.

Apart from enhancing the established services for the welfare, aftercare, education, and vocational training of offenders, a number of new rehabilitative initiatives have been introduced since 1998. The Sex Offenders Evaluation and Treatment Unit located at the Siu Lam Psychiatric Centre came into operation in 1998. This unit provides comprehensive psychological services, including thorough assessment and specialised treatment, to eligible sex offenders. In 1999, the first Inmates-Parents Centre was established at the Tai Tam Correctional Institution. The venue provides a more conducive environment for carrying out group activities when inmates' family members are involved. During the same year, a special Rehabilitation Unit was set up at the Pak Sha Wan Correctional Institution for prisoners who had a mental illness but had completed their treatment at the Siu Lam Psychiatric Centre. A transitional period at this unit under the supervision of qualified staff enables this group of prisoners to gradually readjust for their return to normal institutional routine.

With a revised departmental vision "To deliver quality custodial and rehabilitative services recognised internationally for excellence" and the motto of "We Care" (Hong Kong Correctional Services Department, 2000), the CSD in 1999 launched a major publicity campaign aimed at encouraging the community to give rehabilitated offenders a chance to reform. The publicity campaign included television advertisements, exhibitions, a music CD with songs composed and performed by sentenced persons, and a musical variety show on TV.

To secure support and advice from community leaders, academics, and experts in the field of offender rehabilitation, the CSD in the same year set up a Committee on Community Support for Rehabilitated Offenders to provide advice to the department on strategies and programmes for the reintegration of offenders into the community and to promote community support through education, publicity, and public involvement. In 2000, the CSD took the lead by replacing the long-used nomenclature of *discharged prisoners* with *rehabilitated persons* to encourage greater community support and acceptance of discharged offenders.

In May 2001, the *Rehabilitation Centres Bill* was enacted, and the programme commenced in July 2002. The rehabilitation centre programme, as recommended earlier by the City University research team, aims to fill the service gap in the CSD's custodial programmes for young offenders, both male and female. Unlike some earlier correctional programmes which were imported from England to Hong Kong, the rehabilitation centre programme was developed locally by CSD officials by modifying and merging the best elements of the detention centre, training centre, and half-way house programmes together. The rehabilitation centre programme is divided into two phases, with the first phase consisting of one to five months' institutional training focusing on discipline, education, and vocational training. The second phase consists of residential requirement at a CSD-operated half-way house for one to four months, during which residents are required to take part in community service, to attend educational or vocational training, or to take up approved employment. The minimum period of stay for phase one and phase two together is three months and the maximum period is nine months, to be followed by 12 months' compulsory aftercare supervision by CSD supervision teams (*Rehabilitation Centres Ordinance*, 2002).

Another major CSD initiative in offender rehabilitation is the introduction of the Risks and Needs Assessment and Management Protocol for offenders in Hong Kong. This initiative was made by the psychological units of the CSD's Rehabilitation Division with expert assistance from the Correctional Service of Canada and the Chinese University of Hong Kong. Since October 2006, the CSD has started conducting custodial risks assessments for all local inmates. Matching rehabilitative programmes were introduced in January 2007.

Apart from the enhancement of correctional programmes such as the provision of the rehabilitation centre programme to cater for the needs of young offenders in Hong Kong, the CSD has also made much effort to address the needs of adult prisoners in their reintegration process, in particular their ability to secure gainful employment upon release from correctional institutions. In 2004, the CSD started a pilot scheme whereby it was arranged for adult prisoners to undergo a period of full-time vocational training shortly before their release. This pilot scheme was indeed a radical departure from the tradition of engaging adult prisoners only in production works or manual services under direction of Correctional Services Industries, part of the Operations Division of the CSD, whereby adult prisoners are required by law to engage in work for no more than 10 hours a day except on general holidays (Prison Rules, 2015). Vocational training during the earlier days was not considered as work *per se* and this outdated concept has only changed within the last decade.

With the support of the government, the CSD in February 2009 transferred the management and operation of Correctional Services Industries from the Operations Division to the Rehabilitation Division. Combining the vocational training units, a new Industries and Vocational Training Section was established. This new section allows the CSD to focus more on a rehabilitation-oriented approach to enhancing prisoners' capability and capacity by engaging them in gainful and productive work as well as providing them with suitable and accredited vocational training. On top of the technical and commercial vocational training courses, the CSD had collaborated with external authorities such as the Employees Retraining Board, the Clothing Industry Training Authority, and the Construction Industry Council Training Academy in providing accredited training in areas such as the laundry, garment making, and construction work that prisoners currently perform inside the correctional institutions. Prisoners completing this accredited training are issued with certificates from these external organisations to facilitate their future job hunting after discharge.

Apart from providing employable skills to persons in custody, the CSD, realising that gainful employment is a vital factor in enabling offenders to desist from criminal life, has in recent years taken proactive steps to assist offenders to secure employment upon their release from correctional institutions. These steps have been carried out in partnership with NGOs, employers, and trade leaders, and job opportunities for rehabilitated offenders have been provided through employment symposiums and sharing sessions with employers that already have rehabilitated offenders as employees.[7] To take this initiative a step further, the CSD has organised job fairs inside correctional institutions for potential employers to interview job applicants before their release, thus allowing their seamless reintegration into society. The latest job fair was held in September 2014 in collaboration with the Chinese Manufacturers' Association of Hong Kong and the Merchants Support for Rehabilitated Offenders Committee Limited (Hong Kong Correctional Services Department, 2015).

The CSD has recognised the full potential of the services provided by NGOs for offender rehabilitation. Unlike the early days when voluntary work for prisoners and inmates only came from a few religious groups and the DPAS, there are currently over 80 different NGO groups providing a diverse range of services to persons in custody. In 2004, the CSD formed the CSD Rehabilitation Volunteer Group with volunteers recruited and managed directly by the CSD to improve the arrangement and delivery of services to offenders located at different correctional institutions. This group, with around 300 volunteers, organises a diverse range of activities, including language courses, computer studies, and cultural pursuits, to supplement services designed to meet offenders' needs. (Hong Kong Correctional Services Department, 2015).

Conclusion

It has been the mission of the CSD to provide a safe and humane environment for the detention of persons in custody as well as to facilitate the return of sentenced persons to the community as law-abiding citizens through the provision of comprehensive rehabilitation services.

Much has been done since the 1950s in this area through the development of a range of diversified correctional programmes in Hong Kong covering the special rehabilitative needs of young offenders as well as offenders with addiction problems. The penal welfarism approach that followed the British model was no longer popular in the 1970s following the community's panic about the increase in violent crimes and social disorder involving mainly young offenders. However, Hong Kong never discarded the rehabilitative approach, despite the West going through a "nothing works" period in the 1970s (Martinson, 1974). On the other hand, Hong Kong did follow the move towards the "new penology" trend (Feeley & Simon, 1992) and adopt "new punitiveness" as its penal policy (Pratt, Brown,

Brown, Hallsworth, & Morrison, 2005). Punitive sanctions such as the detention centre programme and corporal punishment for young offenders found in breach of detention centre regulations were introduced. The Release under Supervision Scheme in Hong Kong took more than a decade to establish, but there were few successful applicants. From 1974 onwards, security took precedence over other elements in Hong Kong's penal management, with resources being injected continuously to maintain physical security and human intelligence in institutions and to train correctional officers. On the other hand, the renaming of the Prisons Department as the Correctional Services Department in 1982 and the establishment of the Rehabilitation Division in 1998 reaffirmed the department's commitment to the important policy of rehabilitation in the management of offenders. There is no contradiction from the CSD's point of view in having security taking priority over rehabilitation in penal management as it is believed that maintaining custodial discipline is vital in securing a safe and conducive environment for offenders to settle down without fear of being harmed or abused before they are able to benefit from the various rehabilitation programmes provided.

The effectiveness of the CSD's rehabilitation programmes might not sound too impressive, with an overall 67% success rate covering all the respective supervision programmes in 2014 (Hong Kong Correctional Services Department, 2015). However, when looking at the breakdowns, it is apparent that most of the programmes do have a very high success rate of over 90%, the exceptions being the training centre programme (67%) and the DATC programme (51%). The lower success rate of the training centre programme is understandable as the supervision period of this programme is three years, compared to one year for the other programmes. Among the CSD's programmes, the DATC programme has the largest number of supervisees, and it is not difficult to appreciate the challenges of keeping an ex-addict offender crime- and drug-free during the one-year supervision period. Most important of all is that Hong Kong people are in general finding the work of CSD positive and are now more ready to accept rehabilitated offenders. The CSD no longer publishes the recidivism rate for ex-prisoners, but a drop of almost 40% in the average daily population of prisoners, from a height of 10,119 in 2004 to 6,179 in 2014 (Hong Kong Correctional Services Department, 2015), and a continuous decline in reported crime cases in Hong Kong could certainly qualify as robust indicators reflecting the positive impacts of the CSD's rehabilitative work with offenders.

The success of the CSD's rehabilitative work had been closely studied by other Asian and Pacific countries/territories. Rehabilitative activities similar to those implemented in Hong Kong can be found in the region: the separation of drug-addicted offenders into treatment centres rather than prisons in Thailand; the Yellow Ribbon Project launched by the Singapore Prison Service in soliciting community support for rehabilitated offenders; the Correctional Services Bureau of Macau's annual Inmates' Handicraft Exhibition and Loving Employers – Pre-release Employment Scheme, which promote the positive side of offenders and enhance their employability; and Korea's psychological treatment for sex offenders are just a few examples. Table 6.1 presents a chronology of offender rehabilitation activities launched by the Prisons/Correctional Services Department.

Table 6.1 Major offender rehabilitation activities launched by the Prisons/Correctional Services Department (1938–2014)

Year	*Event*
1938	Probation services set up in Hong Kong under the charge of the Prisons Department.
1941	Management of the reformatory for young offenders transferred from the Police to the Prisons Department.
1946	A temporary reformatory for boys aged from 8 to 16 set up near Stanley Prison.
1947	Probation services were transferred to the Social Welfare Office established under the Secretary for Chinese Affairs.
1951	Separation of habitual offenders from first-timers in prison with 'Ordinary' and 'Star' classifications.
1953	Management of the reformatory for young offenders transferred from the Prisons Department to the Social Welfare Office.
1953	The Prisons Department set up the Stanley Training Centre at site of the former reformatory under the newly enacted Training Centre Ordinance. Inmates on release have to undergo three-year supervision by Prisons Department aftercare officers.
1953	The Prisoner Earnings Scheme was set up to provide incentive to prisoners to work whilst in custody.
1954	Special pilot group with more relaxed regime set up at Stanley Prison for long-term prisoners prior to their release.
1955/56	Open visits were introduced at Stanley Prison and Lai Chi Kok Prison replacing the former practice of shouting to each other through separated grills at the prison main gate lodge.
1956	The first open prison was set up at Chi Ma Wan of Lantau Island.
1957	The Discharged Prisoners' Aid Society, an NGO with close involvement of the Prisons Department, was set up to provide assistance to prisoners upon discharge.
1958	The second open prison was set up at Tai Lam. Prisoners with drug history were transferred there to receive the pilot drug treatment programme with voluntary supervision provided by NGO after discharge.
1967	The first intake of recruit prison officers received trainings including social science courses such as 'group counselling' from the University of Hong Kong.
1968	New Life House, the first half-way house under the management of the Prisons Department, was established for the ex-addict prisoners released from prisons.
1969	The Drug Addiction Treatment Centres Ordinance was enacted and Tai Lam Drug Addiction Treatment Centre became operational.
1972	The Detention Centre Ordinance was enacted and Sha Tsui Detention Centre came into operation running the 'Short, Sharp and Shock' regime.
1972	Siu Lam Psychiatric Centre, a purpose-built prison for offenders with psychiatric problems, became operational.
1975	Prisoner Welfare Officer posted was created in all prisons for adult prisoners.
1976	Psychological services were formally provided in the Prisons Department with the establishment of Clinical Psychologist posts.

Year	*Event*
1981	Dietary and corporal punishments for breach of prison discipline were removed from the Prison Rules.
1982	Prisons Department was renamed the Correctional Services Department (CSD) to reflect the modern penal philosophies with emphasis on offender rehabilitation.
1983	Phoenix House, the first purpose-built half-way house for young offenders, was in operation.
1984	Bauhinia House, the first half-way house for female offenders, was opened.
1986	The Hong Kong Examination Authority recognised inmates from Pik Uk Correctional Institution as 'school candidates' to participate in the Hong Kong Certificate of Education Examination inside the prison.
1986	CSD was licensed as an Operating Authority of the Duke of Edinburgh's Award Scheme to organise accredited activities for the training centre inmates.
1986	The 221st Hong Kong Group was inaugurated to provide training centre inmates with scouting activities. (The 141st Island Ranger Guides Service Unit was formed later in April 1987 to provide female training centre inmates with girl guide trainings.)
1988	The Release under Supervision Scheme and the Pre-Release Employment Scheme, the first parole schemes for local prisoners, came into operation.
1995	Pelican House, the first half-way house solely for adult offenders, was opened. The half-way house programme was further extended to young drug offenders.
1996	The Post-Release Supervision of Prisoners Scheme, a compulsory supervision scheme for adult prisoners, came into operation.
1997	The Long-Term Prison Sentences Review Ordinance became operational.
1998	A new Rehabilitation Division, headed by the Assistant Commissioner (Rehabilitation), was set up to co-ordinate and direct rehabilitation services for prisoners and inmates.
1998	The Sex Offenders Evaluation and Treatment Unit located at Siu Lam Psychiatric Centre came into operation.
1999	The first Inmates-Parents Centre was opened at Tai Tam Gap Correctional Institution.
1999	A special Rehabilitation Unit was set up at Pak Sha Wan Correctional Institution to prepare former psychiatric centre prisoners to return to the main prison population.
1999	A new service emblem with the motto of "We Care" was introduced to symbolise CSD's goal of rehabilitating offenders through the process of custody and care.

Sources: Adapted from Chan (2012); Correctional Services Department (2016b)

Chapter summary points

- The colonial penal system in 19th-century Hong Kong adopted the principle of deterrence through corporal punishment and harsh penal treatments as measures to scare off potential offenders. Religion was the only means of offender reformation adopted at the time, but it was ineffective for local prisoners.
- Hong Kong in the early 20th century followed the progressive penal policies of England. Probation services for adult offenders as well as reformatories for young offenders were established in the colony with the assistance of religious groups.
- Administrators in Hong Kong adjusted their colonial mindset after the Second World War. For the first time, Chinese men were allowed to become prison warders, thus facilitating much needed communication between the prison authority and the prisoner community, who were predominately Chinese.
- The post-war penal welfarism approach towards offenders in England was copied by Hong Kong. Prison conditions were enhanced and rehabilitative measures introduced through services provided by designated NGOs with direct involvement from the Prisons Department.
- Specialised custodial programmes addressing different offender groups, such as training centres for young offenders, open prisons for adult offenders, and drug treatment centres for offenders with addiction problems, were developed by the penal elites in Hong Kong.
- Hong Kong became more punitive in the 1970s with the rise in the number of violent crimes committed by young offenders. The outdated and harsh detention centre concept was introduced from England and altered to meet local requirements, including the use of caning to maintain custodial discipline.
- The 1973 Stanley Prison riot focused the Prisons Department's attention on security and discipline. However, modern rehabilitative standards were still being attained through the provision of a psychiatric centre and welfare officers to address prisoners' needs.
- In the early 1980s, Hong Kong removed all draconian penal punishments. With the new title of Correctional Services reflecting the reformative image of the department, offender rehabilitation initiatives were further developed, covering both pre- and post-release programmes.
- The formation of the Rehabilitation Division in 1998 allowed the CSD to develop better rehabilitative programmes and to enhance reintegration opportunities for ex-offenders through successful publicity campaigns designed to get the public to accept rehabilitated offenders.
- Hong Kong is one of the safest cities in Asia, with declining crime and imprisonment rates. There is no doubt that the effective offender rehabilitation activities initiated by the CSD have made a significant contribution to this success.

Notes

1 CO129/43: 241–248.
2 The Discharged Prisoners' Aid Society (DPAS) was renamed The Hong Kong Society for the Rehabilitation of Offenders (SRO) in 1982; the current name, The Society of Rehabilitation and Crime Prevention, Hong Kong (SRACP), was adopted in 2001.
3 Government Information Services. (n.d.). *Training centres.* Hong Kong: Government Printer.
4 S. 4(4) of the *Detention Centres Ordinance*, Cap. 239 states that "[a] court shall not make a detention order against a young offender unless the Commissioner has not earlier than 1 month before the date of the order informed the court that in his opinion the young offender is suitable for detention and that a place is available for him in a detention centre."
5 Before the creation of these posts, the deputy heads of the penal institutions acted as "welfare officers" in addressing prisoners' requests and complaints (Prisons Department, 1952–53, p. 14).
6 The author was attached to the Scottish Prison Services from 20 June to 14 July 1994 and was responsible in drafting the Hong Kong version of the Sentence Planning Scheme.
7 In June 2014, more than 200 representatives from over 100 business organisations, social enterprises, statutory bodies, and social sectors attended the "Unleashing Rehabilitated Offenders' Potential" employment symposium jointly held by the CSD and the Centre for Criminology of the University of Hong Kong.

References

Chan, H. Y. (2003). *The institutional control and care of young people in colonial Hong Kong 1932–1997: A social history* (Unpublished doctoral dissertation). University of Hong Kong, Hong Kong.

Chan, S. (1994). *Development of the Hong Kong penal policy and programme under the British administration (1841–1945)* (Unpublished master's dissertation). University of Leicester, UK.

Chan, S. (2012). *Colonial penality: A case study of Hong Kong's penal policy and programmes under British administration (1945–1997)* (Unpublished doctoral dissertation). University of Hull, UK.

Commissioner of Prisons. (1955). *Hong Kong annual departmental report by the Commissioner of Prisons for the financial year 1954-55.* Hong Kong: Government Printer.

Commissioner of Prisons. (1971). *Hong Kong annual departmental report by the Commissioner of Prisons, G.R. Pickett, for the financial year 1970-71.* Hong Kong: Government Printer.

Commissioner of Prisons. (1972). *Hong Kong annual departmental report by the Commissioner of Prisons, T. G. Garner, J. P. for the financial year 1971-1972.* Hong Kong: Government Printer (Code: 95949-12K-11/72).

Commissioner of Prisons. (1975). *Hong Kong annual departmental report by the Commissioner of Prisons, T. G. Garner, J. P. for the financial year 1974-75.* Hong Kong: Government Printers (Code: 53844-12K-9/75).

Commissioner of Prisons. (1979). *A summary of the work of the Prisons Department by the Commissioner of Prisons, T. G. Garner, C. B. E., J. P. for 1978.* Hong Kong: Government Printer.

Detention Centres Ordinance. Cap. 239 Laws of Hong Kong (1997).

Drug Addiction Treatment Centres Ordinance. Cap. 244 Laws of Hong Kong (1997).

Feeley, M., & Simon, J. (1992). The new penology: Notes on the emerging strategy of corrections and its implications. *Criminology, 30*(4), 449–474. doi: 10.1111/j.1745-9125.1992.tb01112.x

Garner, T. (n.d.). *An authoritative approach to the treatment of drug dependence.* Hong Kong: Prisons Department.

Hong Kong Correctional Services Department. (1982–2013). *Correctional services annual review.* Hong Kong: Correctional Services Department.

Hong Kong Correctional Services Department. (1987). *Care and control for adult prisoners after release from custodial sentences.* Hong Kong: Correctional Services Department.

Hong Kong Correctional Services Department. (2015). *Hong Kong correctional services annual review 2014.* Retrieved from http://www.csd.gov.hk/annualreview/2014/normal/ebook/index_tc.html

Hong Kong Correctional Services Department. (2016a). *A chronology of CSD's development and penal measures of Hong Kong.* Retrieved from http://www.csd.gov.hk/english/about/about_history/abt_his.html

Hong Kong Correctional Services Department. (2016b). *Correctional Services Department.* Retrieved from http://www.csd.gov.hk/english/home/home.html

Hong Kong Correctional Services Department. (2016c). *Hong Kong correctional services 2015 annual review.* Retrieved from http://www.csd.gov.hk/annualreview/2015/htm_en/pdf/full_version.pdf

Hong Kong Government Information Services. (n.d.). *Training centres.* Hong Kong: Government Printer.

Hough, M., & McSweeney, T. (2005). Drugs and alcohol. In N. Tilley (Ed.), *Handbook of crime prevention and community safety* (pp. 563–594). Cullompton, UK: Willan Publishing.

Lo, T. W. (2008). Custodial sentences and correctional services. In H. C. Wong & T. W. Lo (Eds.), *Understanding criminal justice in Hong Kong* (pp. 224–247). Cullompton, UK: Willan Publishing.

Lo, T. W., Wong, S. W., Chan, W. T., Leung, S. K., Yu, C. S., & Chan, C. K. (1997). *Research on the effectiveness of rehabilitation programmes for young offenders: Full report.* Hong Kong: Government Printing Department.

Martinson, R. (1974). What works? – Questions and answers about prison reform. *The Public Interest, 35*(2), 22–54.

Norman, J. (1971). *How to cure drug addicts.* London: Tom Stacy.

Norton-Kyshe, J. (1898). *The history of the laws and courts of Hong Kong, tracing consular jurisdiction in China and Japan and including parliamentary debates, and the rise, progress, and successive changes in the various public institutions of the colony from the earliest period to the present time* (Vol. 1). London: Unwin.

Post-Release Supervision of Prisoners Ordinance. Cap. 475 Laws of Hong Kong (2014).

Pratt, J., Brown, D., Brown, M., Hallsworth, S., & Morrison, W. (Eds.). (2005). *The new punitiveness: Trends, theories, perspectives.* Oxford: Routledge.

Prisoners (Release under Supervision) Ordinance. Cap. 325 Laws of Hong Kong (1997).

Prisons Department. (1952/53–1974/75, 1975–1977). *Annual departmental report.* Hong Kong: Prisons Department.

Prisons Rules. Cap. 234A 38 Laws of Hong Kong (2015).

Rehabilitation Centres Ordinance. Cap. 567 Laws of Hong Kong (2002).

Tam, K. Y., & Heng, M. A. (2008). Rehabilitation for young offenders in Hong Kong correctional institutions. *Journal of Correctional Education*, *59*(1), 49–63.

7 Development of psychological services in the Hong Kong Correctional Services Department

Ching Chuen Lu Chan, Shuk Han Hui, Hung Kei Cheung, and Barbara Ka Yan Pau

Introduction

With their knowledge and expertise in applying psychology to forensic settings, clinical psychologists have a unique role in the promotion of offenders' psychological well-being and the management of custodial and reoffending risks among offenders. In 1976, under the advice of the United Nations advisor Dr Robert Andry, the then Prisons Department of Hong Kong, recognising the need for such expertise in the rehabilitation of offenders, began to set up psychological services within the department, initially with only one clinical psychologist in post. After 40 years of development, the Correctional Services Department (CSD) of the Hong Kong Special Administration Region now has a much bigger professional team of close to 30 clinical psychologists and also close to 30 officers providing services to persons in custody (PIC)[1] as well as to staff in the department. Given the limited labour poweravailable when the services were first introduced, the focus was on crisis intervention and the prevention and management of custodial risks (i.e., self-harm and violent behaviours). Initially, young offenders were identified as the targets for more focused psychological services as it was hoped that early intervention might bring about the necessary changes to curb their criminal development. Over the years, the services have become more specialised in providing necessary interventions for different groups of offenders, such as sex offenders, violent offenders, young offenders, drug abusers, and women offenders. In the last 20 years, with the development of an empirically based framework for risks and needs evaluation and the management of offenders, more locally developed actuarial reoffending risk assessment tools as well as evidence-based treatment programmes have been launched. This chapter first summarises the development of psychological services in four major areas, namely: (a) forensic assessment for the courts and other statutory bodies; (b) psychological treatment programmes; (c) the management of PIC with a custodial risk, mental health problems, and adjustment difficulties; and (d) the provision of consultation services to management and staff. It then discusses essential elements for the development of effective psychological services and future development directions.

Development of psychological services

Forensic assessment

Conducting a forensic assessment has always been a core duty for clinical psychologists at the CSD. As early as in the 1980s, psychologists had already started to offer professional opinions to the courts and other statutory bodies. Clinical psychologists regularly provide psychological assessment reports to the courts at the pre-sentencing stage, particularly for those convicted of violent and sexual offences. In conducting an assessment, consideration has to be given to the offender's psychological profile, risk of reoffending, need for treatment, and readiness for rehabilitation and the factors contributing to his/her offending behaviours, all of which facilitate the sentencing of the offender by the court.

For decades, the Suitability Board had routinely requested assessment reports from psychologists to assist in determining the appropriate management of young offenders. Nowadays, psychologists also regularly provide assessment reports to other statutory review boards such as the Post-Release Supervision Board and the Long-Term Prison Sentence Review Board. Apart from the offender's psychological profile, treatment progress, and risks and needs profile, the submitted assessment report also provides updated psychological opinions about the prisoner's rehabilitation plan during the supervision period to facilitate successful reintegration upon release. For reports on prisoners convicted of a serious offence and serving a life sentence, the psychologist's professional opinion serves as a piece of important information to determine their readiness for conditional release.

In the past, one of the major challenges was the lack of locally developed actuarial assessment tools for the assessment and prediction of offending behaviour. Recognising the need for such tools, an attempt was made in the early 1980s to develop a local norm for an intellectual screening tool, the Ravens Progressive Matrices, which was used to evaluate the intellectual competence of young inmates. Validated local risk assessment tools for sex offenders and violent offenders have also been developed since 2002 to enhance the accuracy of the prediction in forensic assessments. These local actuarial risk assessment tools, namely the Hong Kong Risk Assessment Scale for Sex Offenders and the Hong Kong Risk Assessment Scale for Violent Offenders, are among the first to be developed for an evidence-based assessment of offending risk. Psychological opinions are now more frequently consulted in making important decisions in the criminal justice system.

Psychological treatment programmes

Apart from conducting forensic assessments, the treatment of offending behaviours, with the aim of providing suitable psychological treatment services to prevent reoffending and facilitate eventual reintegration into society, has also been a core duty of clinical psychologists at the CSD. In the 1980s, owing to limited manpower, priority in terms of service provision was given to young offenders, offenders with a long-term sentence, sex offenders, and substance abusers. Working groups were set up for these groups of offenders to develop specialised treatment for them; for instance, the Young Offender Working Group made various attempts to develop a classification system for local young offenders with a view to better matching the treatment programmes to the needs of young offenders. The interpersonal maturity level classification system (I-level) for offenders, which was commonly used in the West in the 1980s, was taken as a reference for such efforts. At the same time, the possibility of developing a psycho-educational programme for young offenders (i.e., the Human Development and Social Adaptation Programme) to facilitate their overall development and adjustment was explored. Apart from services for young offenders, tailor-made programmes were also provided for their parents to enable better support and communication for the reintegration of young offenders. In view of the increasing complexity of the penal population, treatment programmes for offenders with special needs, such as those with intellectual deficiencies and problems with impulse control and anger management, were also developed from the early 1980s onwards. Apart from the ongoing development of services for young offenders, sex offenders, and long-term offenders, inmates at the Drug Addiction Treatment Centre also received additional attention with regards to the development of rehabilitative services.

In general, the treatment programmes were delivered both in a didactic and a self-help manner. Activities such as role play, exercise, discussion, computer-aided games, and interactive learning materials were employed. These interactive approaches have been shown to enhance motivation for learning, particularly among young offenders (Dowden & Andrews, 1999). In order to provide a more comprehensive treatment programme for sex offenders and offenders with special needs, the Psychological Care Unit (PCU) was set up in 1991. Additionally, programmes for substance abusers in the Drug Addiction Treatment Centre were developed on the basis of the motivation enhancement and relapse prevention model (Marlatt & George, 1984) to help inmates to better cope with situations conducive to their cravings and high-risk behaviours. Recognising their need for support and counselling after discharge, attempts were made by working together with other rehabilitation staff to provide substance abusers with relapse prevention follow-up services.

Since 1990, most of the research on offender rehabilitation has primarily focused on identifying treatment programmes which may successfully reduce offending behaviours. The principles of risk, need, and responsivity (RNR) were found to be highly relevant to the service provision of psychological treatment programmes, and thus these principles were adopted after careful consideration (Andrews, Bonta, & Hoge, 1990; Andrews, Bonta, & Wormith, 2006). The RNR model guides the priorities for the delivery of services (i.e., targeting moderate and high risk offenders), the type of services to be provided (i.e., those addressing criminogenic needs), and the manner by which services are delivered (i.e., those with an empirically based framework such as cognitive-behavioural-oriented programmes). As psychological services at the CSD continued to develop, the scope and depth of the treatment programmes also expanded. Treatment programmes responding to the unique needs of each offender group have been developed. These programmes include treatment programmes for sex offenders and violent offenders and, given the government's policy on gender mainstreaming, gender-specific treatment programmes tailor-made for female offenders with serious emotional problems.

In recent years, the concept of the therapeutic community has also been employed in the treatment of offenders to enhance treatment effectiveness. As a result, two therapeutic communities for sex offenders and female offenders, namely the Sex Offenders Evaluation and Treatment Unit (ETU) and the PSY GYM: Personal Growth and Emotion Treatment Centre for Women, were set up in 1998 and 2011, respectively. Within these communities, the therapeutic atmosphere encourages positive change and mutual support. The participants learn and practise the skills introduced during their treatment, such as interpersonal skills, conflict resolution skills, and problem-solving skills, with regular feedback being provided by the well-trained staff. Through living together, participants give constructive feedback among themselves to recognise behavioural improvement and areas for further improvement. Importantly, this method also helps to foster the incentive for change among participants.

Treatments that engender a greater sense of well-being and build on clients' strengths are trends in the emerging field of positive psychology (Linley & Joseph, 2004) and the strength-based approach. With the development of theories, these new treatment approaches were also introduced into treatment programmes in correctional settings on top of the cognitive-behavioural approach. Positive psychology and the strength-based approach were introduced into treatment programmes for female offenders and sex offenders. In recent years, mindfulness therapy and acceptance commitment therapy have also been incorporated into the Violence Prevention Programme, which targets offenders with serious violence problems, to enhance the effectiveness of treatment.

As the repertoire of literature on offender rehabilitation is constantly increasing, the CSD makes efforts to ensure standards of practice are maintained. For instance, an Independent Treatment Advisory Panel composed of international experts and local academics has been set up to benchmark the treatment programmes with internationally recognised standards for best practice. This best practice standard has become a good reference for programme development for other offender groups to enhance treatment effectiveness. Table 7.1 presents an outline of the Correctional Services Accreditation Panel's (CSAP, 2004) accreditation criteria for offending behaviour intervention programmes. These best practice criteria serve as a good reference for the development of treatment programmes for offenders.

Management of persons in custody with a custodial risk, mental health problems, and adjustment difficulties

With maintaining the safe custody of PIC being one of the prime concerns of the CSD of Hong Kong, the clinical psychologist has a unique role in assisting the administration in formulating strategies for improving the management of

Table 7.1 Outline of the Correctional Services Accreditation Panel's (CSAP, 2004) accreditation criteria for offending behaviour intervention programmes

Criteria	*Descriptions*
Criterion 1	There should be an explicit and evidence-based model of how the programme is supposed to work. There should be evidence to justify the assumptions in this model.
Criterion 2	Programme intensity should match participant's risk level according to risk principle. The programme should choose participants with a higher risk level and whose risk is likely to be reduced by the programme.
Criterion 3	Programme should target appropriate criminogenic needs according to need principle. The programme should change factors that have been closely linked to the offending of those taking part.
Criterion 4	According to the responsivity principle, the methods used to target criminogenic factors should be ones to which those participating in the programme are responsive. The conditions necessary for these methods to operate effectively should be specified as part of the programme.
Criterion 5	The amount, strength, sequencing, and spacing of treatment should be related to the seriousness and persistence of offending behaviour, taking into the consideration of the range and seriousness of the criminogenic factors typical of the participants.
Criterion 6	Progress made in the institution should be reinforced and strengthened by rehabilitative services in the community for good continuity of care.
Criterion 7	There should be provision of good training for staff and good documentation of treatment manuals.
Criterion 8	A commitment to the ongoing monitoring of its effects should be built into the programme.
Criterion 9	A commitment to the ongoing evaluation of its effects should be built into the programme.

Source: Adapted from the Correctional Services Accreditation Panel's (CSAP, 2004) accreditation criteria for offending behaviour intervention programmes

custodial risk, such as self-harm prevention for PIC. Research findings support the view that the suicide rate in correctional institutions, especially in the remand population, is significantly higher than that in the general population (Wu, Lu, & Chan, 1996). Clinical psychologists at the CSD have adopted several strategies in managing the self-harm risk in penal institutions, including: (a) surveying the profile of self-harm behaviours in penal institutions, (b) developing empirical tools for the better detection of self-harm ideations and behaviours, (c) providing training for staff to increase their awareness in identifying and working with inmates who are prone to self-harm behaviours, and (d) liaising with the management team in providing an environment that is conducive to the safe custody of inmates.

During the 1980s and 1990s, clinical psychologists at the CSD started to administer a survey on self-harm behaviour to PIC. From the survey, core factors related to self-harm ideation and behaviour were identified and the Emotionality and Suicidal Tendency Scale with a local offenders' norm was developed for use in the initial screening of all persons on remand in correctional institutions before they were sentenced (Wu et al., 1996). In the 2000s, clinical psychologists started to collaborate with other units in developing the Self-Harm Risk Index (SRI) for screening purposes. The SRI is administered by frontline staff to all PIC upon admission to an institution. Frontline staff then makes referrals to clinical psychologists and related personnel when particular PIC show a high level of self-harm risk. There have been regular reviews of the SRI, with clinical psychologists playing a major role. Refinement has been made to enhance consistency in the assessment.

In addition, clinical psychologists provide regular training for frontline staff and take part in institution-based committee meetings on the monitoring of self-harm behaviours among PIC. Through psycho-educational talks, frontline staff's awareness of the identification and management of offenders' self-harm ideation or behaviours can be increased, which in turn would facilitate the necessary psychological intervention for PIC. Moreover, by taking part in regular self-harm meetings with the management team, clinical psychologists can liaise with the team to provide an environment that is conducive to the safe custody of PIC.

Incarceration is a stressful experience for most PIC, especially those who are emotionally vulnerable with mental health problems. A special unit – the Rehabilitation Unit (renamed the Recovery Group in 2014) – was established in 1999. This unit, with the primary aim to assist PIC with mental problems and difficulties in adjusting to ordinary penal institutions, provides a multidisciplinary mental health service staffed by a psychiatrist, a clinical psychologist, and correctional staff with psychiatric nursing training. In fact, the psychological treatment of PIC with serious adjustment problems and various mental disorders continues to be the core duty of the clinical team in the Recovery Group and other correctional institutions.

Provision of consultation services to management and staff

Apart from direct services to the offenders, clinical psychologists at the CSD also play a key role in offering professional advice to the CSD and the management team of different correctional institutions in response to the changing profile of the penal population and the emerging needs of PIC. Clinical psychologists adopted the RNR (Risk-Need-Responsivity) model (Andrews et al., 1990) in the 1990s with a view to facilitating the delivery and development of services. The model provides valuable guidance on the parameters of the services, such as the priority of services and the modes of service delivery. Beginning in the 2000s, with the support of the CSD's senior management, a major consultancy study on the Risks and Needs Assessment and Programme Management Protocol was launched to improve the management of custodial and reoffending risks and to address the rehabilitative needs of offenders. Continual information exchanges and visits by the CSD's consultant, Dr Larry Motiuk of the Correctional Service of Canada, were arranged. The objective of the consultancy was to set up an integrated management system for the identification of custodial and reoffending risk as well as to develop a protocol for the assessment of offenders' rehabilitative needs. The project's aims were as follows: (a) to set up a sentence plan addressing the risk of reoffending and rehabilitation needs, (b) to allocate resources and to assign offenders to different rehabilitative programmes according to their risks and needs profile, (c) to develop rehabilitative programmes by targeting different offenders' criminogenic needs, and (d) to establish post-discharge case management and supervision. As a result of the consultancy, the Risks and Needs Assessment and Management Protocol for Offenders was implemented, and this remains an integral part of the rehabilitation services provided to PIC.

In response to the increase in the number of elderly persons in custody in recent years, clinical psychologists also provide a professional consultation service to the management on handling the rehabilitation needs of this group of offenders. In 2014, Evergreen Garden was set up in the Elderly Unit in Tai Lam Correctional Institution for persons in custody aged over 65. Vocational training, psycho-educational talks, rehabilitation services, and hobby classes suitable for elderly persons are delivered in Evergreen Garden according to their needs to assist their successful reintegration into the community after release.

In addition to the provision of services for offenders, the services provided to correctional staff remain an integral part of psychological services in CSD. In order to provide more systematic and comprehensive services to correctional staff, the Stress Clinic and Resource Centre was set up in 1991. Services to staff include talks on issues such as stress management and healthy lifestyle as well as individual psychological treatment. Regular training on self-harm prevention and handling the violent behaviour of prisoners is also included in the training of new correctional staff.

Key developments in psychological services during the last four decades

The Psychological Unit (later renamed the Psychological Services Section) set up in the CSD in Hong Kong in 1976 was probably among the first of its type in Asia. Its development throughout the years has been impacted by manpower constraints (particularly in the 1980s and early 1990s), the changing profiles and needs of offenders, and the ever-evolving theoretical framework of offender management and rehabilitation in the 1990s and 2000s. Despite being a relatively small unit in the beginning, the emphasis for the services was always on employing evidence-based practices. Therefore, attempts were made in the 1980s to develop actuarial risk assessment tools with norms for local offenders for self-harm identification as well as intellectual screening. Explorations on the classification of young offenders (i.e., interpersonal maturity level classification system) and the development of psycho-educational programmes for young offenders were also conducted.

In the 1990s, more structured programmes based on cognitive-behavioural models were developed for young offenders, sex offenders, and substance abusers. Apart from being didactic and interactive, self-help manuals are used as an adjunct to facilitate learning. With more stable manpower since the mid-1990s, the service has been more able to move towards an empirically based RNR mode of offender rehabilitation.

The year 2000 saw the consolidation of various treatment programmes for young offenders and sex offenders. Recognising the fact that offender rehabilitation in the department formed only part of the effort in reducing recidivism, efforts were also made to solicit support from policymakers and the community to improve the management of offenders, as in the case of sex offenders. It has been proven overseas that concerted efforts from law enforcement, the judiciary, rehabilitative personnel, and the community have to be made for the successful rehabilitation of sex offenders. As such, close dialogue was arranged with the relevant branches and agencies in refining the policies as well as community support for the offenders. The implementation of the Risk and Needs Assessment and Programme Matching Protocol also reflects the wider contribution of an empirically based framework of offender treatment and risk and need principles in guiding the management of offenders as a whole in the department.

Specialised treatment programmes for sex offenders, women offenders, and violent offenders have been actively developed in the 2010s. The introduction of the internationally adopted best practice criteria by overseas advisors further enhances the professional standard of the programmes. The innovative development of PSY GYM for female offenders marked an important step in devising gender-specific treatment programmes.

Essential elements for the development of effective psychological treatments for offenders

The psychological treatment of offenders provided by the CSD in Hong Kong has undergone many changes in last four decades. Lessons were learnt in reviewing the evolution of the services. We conclude this chapter by delineating the essential elements for the development of effective services.

Risk-need-responsivity principles

The RNR principles (Andrews & Bonta, 2010), which are proven to be important for an effective service, have been adopted as the foundation for the psychological treatment programmes in the CSD, as they have in many countries with advanced correctional services such as Canada. The treatment of offenders therefore focuses on offenders with a moderate or high risk of reoffending instead of low-risk offenders *(risk principle)*. The programme targets criminogenic needs, problems that are closely linked to offending behaviour such as pro-criminal attitudes and mood management, instead of non-criminogenic needs *(need principle)*. The design of treatment also takes into consideration offenders' individual characteristics, such as learning style, abilities, motivation, gender, and cultural background, to enhance the responses to treatment *(responsivity principle)*; under this principle, a series of therapeutic exercises tailor-made for different groups of local offenders has been developed. Clinical psychologists use different innovative methods, such as setting up therapeutic communities and using music and art work in treatment, to improve treatment responses.

Supportive work culture in the CSD

The cultivation of a supportive work culture in the CSD over the years has been conducive to the development of the rehabilitation of offenders in Hong Kong. The mindset of the staff changed considerably through regular staff training and internal seminars. Staff at different levels developed more understanding of the importance of the rehabilitation of PIC, especially after the setting up of the Rehabilitation Division in 1998. The supportive work culture is very important for the successful delivery of rehabilitation, including psychological treatment.

Professional specialisation

The psychological assessment and treatment of offenders requires specialised psychological knowledge of offending behaviour and clinical skills. There was a vigorous development of this specialty in Hong Kong through the active development of specialised treatment programmes for offenders and research work. To enhance specialisation, international experts are regularly invited by the CSD to conduct training workshops for psychological staff. Local and overseas academics have been invited to be the advisors to different programmes. They have brought very useful perspectives to the development of services. CSD psychologists also pay visits to effective programmes in other countries. In addition, local universities also contribute to the development of this specialty by enriching the training of clinical psychologists through the incorporation of forensic psychology into their curriculum. The professional specialisation of the CSD not only contributes to the enhancement of the effectiveness of services, it is also very important for building a strong and stable professional clinical team, which is essential for a healthy service.

Evidence-based practice and local research work

In order to be effective, psychological assessment and treatment must be based on an explicit theoretical model of change based on robust empirical evidence. Continuous data collection in actual clinical practice must be carried out to verify the assumptions in the model of change and monitor the effectiveness of treatment. As most of the assessment tools and psychotherapy for offenders have been developed in the West, the cultural background of local offenders in Hong Kong may affect their responses to treatment. Having more local research on assessment tools and treatment programmes in the past decade has helped to adjust clinical practice to improve the effectiveness of treatment programmes.

Multidisciplinary collaboration

The rehabilitation of offenders involves professionals in several disciplines. Apart from psychologists, rehabilitation officers, psychiatrists, teachers, and vocational training staff all play important roles within correctional organisations. Building up effective mechanisms such as case conferences and multidisciplinary committees allows the frequent exchange of opinions among stakeholders. Collaboration with university academics has helped to strengthen evidence-based practice. The successful rehabilitation of offenders does not end with their release. Their adjustment after release is critical for their smooth reintegration into the community. We found networking with service providers in the community over the years to be essential for the provision of good continuity of care to offenders after discharge.

Legislation and policy supporting rehabilitation

Comprehensive legislation and policy on the management of offenders is the cornerstone of the effective rehabilitation of offenders. The *Post-Release Supervision of Prisoners Ordinance* and the *Long-Term Prison Sentences Review Ordinance* in Hong Kong are good examples illustrating how legislation can help to enhance the risk management of offenders. The observations of mental health professionals in forensic settings also provide useful information to policymakers in designing up-to-date, effective policy for the management of offenders.

Conclusion and future directions for development

In last four decades, the psychological services in the Hong Kong CSD have gone through many changes. Rich knowledge and experience of the application of assessment and treatment strategies for local offenders have been accumulated. Through helping offenders to change, the clinical team contributes to the maintenance of public safety. Future directions for development may include the following:

1. Benchmarking the service with reference to the standard of best practice developed in countries with advanced correctional services.
2. Developing innovative assessment strategies and treatment programmes that match the characteristics of offenders in Hong Kong on the basis of local research findings and clinical experiences. The successful experience in setting up PSY GYM, the treatment unit for female offenders in Hong Kong, serves as a good exemplar for local innovation.
3. Conducting continuous local research work to understand the behaviour of offenders in the Chinese culture and validating psychological tests for forensic assessment.
4. Engaging in continuous collaboration with relevant parties in the communities to enhance the overall psychological adjustment and well-being of offenders.

5 Adding more forensic psychology elements to the core curriculum of local clinical psychology training to help develop local practice.
6 Sharing of psychological observations and clinical findings with stakeholders through seminars and publications to strengthen the supportive work culture within the CSD and multidisciplinary collaboration.

Chapter summary points

- The psychological service of the Correctional Services Department (CSD) in Hong Kong was set up in 1976. Since then, there has been much development in terms of its four areas of service: forensic assessment; psychological treatment programmes; the management of PIC with a custodial risk, mental health problems, and adjustment difficulties; and the provision of consultation services to management and staff.
- For decades, the clinical psychologists of the CSD have routinely conducted forensic psychological assessments and offered professional opinions to the courts and other statutory boards. Nowadays, the accuracy of the predictions in the assessments is constantly improving due to the development of local actuarial risk assessment tools.
- The clinical psychologists of the CSD provide suitable psychological treatment to prevent reoffending and to facilitate offenders' eventual reintegration into society. In recent years, the focus has shifted to the development of systematic treatment programmes for specific target groups, namely sex offenders, violent offenders, and women offenders. Therapeutic communities have also been employed to enhance treatment effectiveness.
- With a view to maintaining the safe custody of persons in custody (PIC), clinical psychologists take an active part in formulating self-harm prevention strategies and provide psychological treatment to PIC who experience emotional, mental, or adjustment difficulties in penal institutions.
- Professional consultation is offered to the CSD and the management teams of different correctional institutions. Examples included the consultancy project on the risk-need-responsivity (RNR) model and the development of rehabilitation for elderly PIC. Psychological services are also offered to staff.
- In the last four decades, the psychological services of CSD have overcome many challenges in its development. It upholds evidence-based practice, and its services have been constantly evolving to accommodate the changing needs of the offender population and the CSD.
- After undergoing four decades of transformation, the Psychological Services Section (PSS) has concluded that the essential elements for the development of effective psychological treatment for offenders include: (a) RNR principles, (b) a supportive work culture in the organisation, (c) professional specialisation, (d) evidence-based practice and local research work, (e) multidisciplinary collaboration, and (f) legislation and policy supporting rehabilitation.

Note

1 Persons in custody (PIC) is a term coined by the Correctional Services Department of Hong Kong and refers to individuals on remand, prisoners, or inmates undergoing correctional programmes.

References

Andrews, D. A., & Bonta, J. (2010). Rehabilitating criminal justice policy and practice. *Psychology, Public Policy and Law*, *16*(1), 39–55. doi: 10.1037/a0018362

Andrews, D. A., Bonta, J., & Hoge, R. D. (1990). Classification for effective rehabilitation: Rediscovering psychology. *Criminal Justice and Behavior*, *17*(1), 19–52. doi: 10.1177/0093854890017001004

Andrews, D. A., Bonta, J., & Wormith, J. S. (2006). The recent past and near future of risk and/or need assessment. *Crime & Delinquency*, *52*(7), 7–27. doi: 10.1177/0011128705281756

Dowden, C., & Andrews, D. A. (1999). What works in young offender treatment: A meta-analysis. *Forum on Corrections Research*, *11*, 21–24.

Linley, P. A., & Joseph, S. (Eds.). (2004). *Positive psychology in practice.* Hoboken, NJ: John Wiley & Sons.

Marlatt, G. A., & George, W. H. (1984). Relapse prevention: Introduction and overview of the model. *British Journal of Addiction*, *79*(3), 261–273. doi: 10.1111/j.1360-0443.1984.tb00274.x

Wu, K. K., Lu, C. C., & Chan, C. M. (1996). Development of emotionality and suicidal tendency scale for prisoners in Hong Kong. *Journal of Offender Rehabilitation*, *23*(1–2), 23–36. doi: 10.1300/J076v23n01_03

8 Gender-specific assessment and treatment for female offenders in Hong Kong

Vivian Wai Ming Mak, Regina Wing Yin Kwong, Wing Ling Li, and Barbara Ka Yan Pau

Introduction

Male offenders constitute the majority of the prison population both in Hong Kong and all over the world. In the past, psychological programmes in Hong Kong Correctional Services (HKCS) were developed on the basis of samples of male offenders. Without studying the unique needs of female offenders, assessments and treatments were mirrored from the psychological protocols for male offenders. However, difficulties were encountered when applying those male-oriented practices to women.

To recall the history, several psychological treatment programmes, such as the Violence Prevention Programme (VPP) and the Mental Health Programme (MHP), were delivered to both male and female offenders in Hong Kong for over 10 years. The VPP was developed for and mainly targeted at male offenders. In men's eyes, violence might predominantly refer to physical violence, and the VPP was important for those who had committed violent offences such as murder, manslaughter, and serious wounding. Compared with men, physical violence was relatively uncommon among women. Violence among women was more likely to be exhibited in the form of verbal and relational aggression. Hence, it was not applicable to adopt the males' programmes directly for females. In view of the different manifestations of violence, the VPP was revised to match the needs of female offenders. New programmes were created, including self-help programmes on cognitive restructuring for violence prevention (female version), relapse prevention for violence prevention (female version), and violence against children and conflict resolution (female version), all of which were tailor-made for women. The female versions differed from the male versions by attending to the distinctive targets, pathways, and motives of female violence. Typical cognitive distortions, high-risk situations, crises, and life examples specific to female offenders were also included. As women, instead of turning aggression outwards, have the tendency to turn aggression inwards, which may result in self-harm, programmes on self-harm prevention and emotional regulation were developed to prevent women committing violence against themselves. As for the MHP, a wide range of topics was selected for different mental health concerns at different phases of incarceration in order to improve offenders' mental health and to facilitate their penal adjustment. However, topics suitable for men were uncommon for women. Considering the uniqueness of the two genders, different topics were selected in female institutions. Instead of conducting treatment groups on violent behaviours, sexual problems, pathological gambling, and criminal/subcultural attitudes, groups on kleptomania, emotional problems, and self-harm prevention were developed for female offenders by clinical psychologists in the HKCS to address the unique characteristics of these offenders.

Clinicians' observations of the unique needs of female offenders in Hong Kong concurred with overseas research findings. Researchers have highlighted that women have significantly different pathways to crime (Bloom, Owen, & Covington, 2003). It has also been suggested that concerns regarding women's various risks are different to those regarding men's risks. For women, apart from the reoffending risk, the "risks of harm to the self and immediate family caused by psychological and psychiatric dysfunction" should be considered (Howells, 2000, p. 4). In developing specialised psychological assessment and treatment for adult female offenders, a Women Offender Working Group (WOWG) was established in 2008. To facilitate the professional development of specialist psychological services for women, WOWG had regular meetings to devise specialised assessment tools and treatment programmes. The Women Offender Empowerment Programme (WOEP) was launched afterwards. The treatment modalities of WOEP were in the form of talks, video seminars, self-help programmes, and treatment groups. Under WOEP, pilot studies on treatment groups with different approaches and therapeutic means were conducted to test female offenders' responsivity. For instance, therapeutic groups using art and music were conducted for both local and non-Chinese female offenders. A therapeutic group on positive psychology was also conducted as a pilot scheme. New self-help programmes on the prevention of child abuse and healing from trauma and victimisation were developed. With consideration of the relationship between parental stress and crime (Ferraro & Moe, 2003; Ross, Khashu, & Wamsley, 2004), rehabilitative programmes for enhancing female offenders' parenting skills and reducing their parenting stress were conducted. Albeit offenders responded positively to many programmes, particularly those involving the use of art, music, and positive psychology interventions, systematic planning and a solid theoretical framework were lacking at this stage. There was also room for improvement in the comprehensive evaluation of individual programmes.

In view of the above limitations, WOWG invited professional consultation from both overseas and local experts for programme development in 2009. With reference to overseas programmes in women's prisons, a more systematic and evidence-based gender-specific assessment and treatment package was devised for female offenders.

Gender-specific assessment for female offenders

The risk-need-responsivity principles were adopted in the assessment of female offenders in the HKCS. According to this principle, the "assignment of cases to treatment is based on a reliable and valid assessment of risk" and criminogenic needs (Andrews & Bonta, 2010, p. 45). Thus, resources should be given to offenders at higher risk, with greater needs, and a high responsivity to treatment. However, the development of most risk assessment inventories was based on male samples, and the risk factors involved might be invalid in predicting risk for women. Research has shown that these assessment tools consistently classified women as being at a lower risk level than their male counterparts (Blanchette, 2002). Hence, female offenders' programme needs were overlooked (Blanchette, 2002) when the focus was placed on the generic risk level. Overseas studies indicate that women have their specific risk/need factors. Table 8.1 presents an overview of the gender-specific risk factors.

Emotional/mental problems

Women are more likely to suffer from emotional/mental health problems than men. One study quoted that the rates of depression, anxiety, and co-morbidity for women are nearly four times the rates for men (Blume, 1997). Similarly, female offenders have a higher prevalence of mental health problems compared with male offenders (Gunter, 2004; Plugge & Fitzpatrick, 2005; Young et al., 2005) or with females in general (James & Glaze, 2006). Some researchers have even suggested that stress, depression, and fearfulness are strong predictors of

Table 8.1 Gender-specific risk factors

Risk factors	*Gender differences*
Emotional/mental problems	Female offenders have higher rates of emotional/mental problems than male offenders or females in general (Gunter, 2004; James & Glaze, 2006; Plugge & Fitzpatrick, 2005; Young, Waters, Falconer, & O' Rourke, 2005).
Self-harm behaviours	Self-harm is positively correlated with criminal convictions (Bonta, Pang, & Wallace-Capretta, 1995).
Self-regulation problems	A larger proportion of female offenders have considerable needs in the areas of self-concept, cognitive problems, impulse control, and behavioural problems (Boe, Nefekh, Vuong, Sinclair, & Cousineau, 2003).
Trauma and victimisation	Female offenders are more likely to have experience of victimisation than male offenders (Blanchette, 1996; Bonta et al., 1995; Tien, Lamb, Bond, Gillstom, & Paris, 1993).
Dysfunctional relationship	Establishing a supportive relationship facilitates successful reintegration (O'Brien, 1999).
Parenting stress	Parenting stress is positively related with criminal behaviours (Ferraro & Moe, 2003; Ross et al., 2004).
Violence	Women are more likely to use indirect violent strategies (Bjorkqvist, 1994; Krakowski & Czobor, 2004).

women's recidivism, which is not the case for men (Benda, 2005; Blanchette & Motiuk, 1995; Brown & Motiuk, 2005).

Self-harm behaviours

In relation to their higher frequency of mental health problems, female offenders display more suicidal or self-injurious behaviours. Overseas studies have reported that 40% to 59% of female offenders have engaged in self-injurious behaviour (Correctional Service Canada, 1990; H.M. Chief Inspector of Prisons, 1997). Moreover, it has been found that self-harm is positively correlated with criminal convictions (Bonta et al., 1995) and violence (Blanchette & Motiuk, 1995; Rettinger, 1998).

Self-regulation problems

In the areas of self-concept, cognitive problems, impulse control, mood management, and behavioural problems, a large proportion (over 60%) of female offenders are assessed as having considerable needs (Boe et al., 2003). Brown and Motiuk (2005) demonstrated that weaknesses in the above-mentioned areas as assessed at intake show close correlation with reoffending behaviours.

Trauma and victimisation

Female offenders are more likely to have victimisation experiences than male offenders. Overseas researches showed that 60% to 80% of adult female offenders had suffered from some form (like physical, sexual, or psychological) of abuse in their lives (Blanchette, 1996; Bonta et al., 1995; Tien et al., 1993). As the vast majority of female offenders have been abused and their post-traumatic symptoms may impede progress in addressing their needs in other areas, it is advocated that handling the psychological sequelae of the victimisation experience is an important part of a holistic approach for effective correctional intervention (Blanchette & Brown, 2006).

Dysfunctional relationship

According to Covington (1998), a dysfunctional relationship is identified as one of the gender-specific risk factors for female offenders. She stated that offences committed by women are more likely to involve relationship issues and are less likely to involve antisocial rationalisations than offences committed by men. She also pointed out that while women's capacity for relatedness and connection is a particular source of strength, female offenders' ability in terms of achieving healthy relationships is usually dampened because of the high rate of abuse, trauma, and neglect experienced. A study on released female offenders showed that establishing supportive relationships is one of the crucial elements that facilitate successful reintegration (O'Brien, 1999).

Other factors

Other gender-specific risk/needs factors include parenting stress and violence in women. The relationship between parenting stress and crime has been mentioned previously. Regarding violence, women are more likely to use indirect violent strategies, such as verbal aggression and social aggression, than physical violence (Bjorkqvist, 1994; Krakowski & Czobor, 2004).

In view of this, assessment tools with female normative data were employed to ensure evidence-based practice. Based on extensive research, a gender-specific need assessment protocol for female offenders is also under development, with the personal/emotion domain as one of main focuses. A brief description of the current assessment package is provided in the section below. These inventories are used when a gender-specific assessment is needed for particular female offenders.

Risk assessment tools

Level of service inventory-revised: Screening version (LSI-R:SV)

The LSI-R:SV is derived from the 54-item LSI-R (Andrews & Bonta, 1995). It consists of eight items that reflect the risk factors and criminogenic needs of offenders. In the assessment of female offenders, it is adopted for screening and programme matching purposes by identifying cases that require a higher level of attention and follow-up services.

The depression anxiety stress scale (DASS)

The 21-item DASS (Lovibond & Lovibond, 1995) assesses psychological distress in three seven-item subscales: (a) the depression subscale, (b) the anxiety subscale, and (c) the stress subscale. As personal/emotional need is one of the core gender-specific need domains for females, the Chinese version (Taouk, Lovibond, & Laube, 2001) of DASS-21 is used to assess the emotional states of female offenders in the corresponding areas. Those who fall into the moderate, severe, or extremely severe level will be potential targets for more intensive interventions.

HCR-20

The HCR-20 (Webster, Douglas, Eaves, & Hart, 1997) is the world's most widely used violence risk assessment instrument. It consists of 20 items that assess violence in three respective subscales: historical, clinical, and risk management. It is mainly applied to cases with a history of violence or the potential risk of violence.

Gender-specific risk and needs assessment protocol

The Risk and Needs Assessment Protocol was developed by the WOWG to assess the risk, needs, and responsivity of adult female offenders. It consists of 12 sections. Apart from the generic risk/needs factors such as criminal history, criminal attitude, and drug abuse history, which are applicable to both males and females, factors which are specific to females' risk/needs are also included. These factors are emotional/mental state, psychiatric history, and interpersonal relationship as well as a history of self-harm and past traumatic experience. This protocol was developed for making decisions about the risk and treatment needs of female offenders. Intensive services would be provided to those offenders who are assessed as having a high or moderate risk and a high responsivity to treatment. These offenders would be matched with the programme(s) which are designed to meet their needs. Currently, this protocol is being used on a trial-run basis. Continuous effort will be put into the further refinement of the protocol and its local validation study.

Gender-specific treatment for female offenders

A Working Group on the Gender-Specific Risks and Needs Programme for Women Offenders was set up in 2010. It aims to develop evidence-based treatment programmes for female offenders. As mentioned above, female offenders have unique criminogenic needs. It is important to develop a gender-responsive intervention to address those needs. This echoes the concept of gender mainstreaming advocated by the United Nations (Government of the Hong Kong Special Administrative Region, 2013). Gender mainstreaming is a global strategy which promotes gender equality and women's advancement. The overseas trend also emphasises the specific criminogenic risk/needs of female offenders, and female-oriented treatment programmes have been developed in different countries, such as the United States, Canada, and Australia (Mental Health Coordinating Council, 2010; Morash, Bynum, & Koons, 1998).

Motivational interviewing (MI) and cognitive behavioural therapy (CBT) were adopted as the major theoretical frameworks. Studies have shown that MI yields satisfactory outcomes in the field of offender rehabilitation (Austin, Williams, & Kilgour, 2011; McMurran, 2009). CBT is also proven to be an effective treatment for psychological disorders (Butler, Chapman, Forman, & Beck, 2006) and criminal behaviours (Landenberger & Lipsey, 2005; Pearson, Lipton, Cleland, & Yee, 2002; Wilson, Bouffard, & Mackenzie, 2005). While CBT aims at symptom reduction, mounting evidence suggests that the absence of negative characteristics does not equal the presence of positive ones such as strengths, hope, optimism, and gratitude (Duckworth, Steen, & Seligman, 2005). Thus, in recent years, positive psychotherapy (PPT) has also been employed to complement CBT and to help enhance positive thinking and emotion. Studies show that PPT can significantly reduce distress and promote well-being (Sin & Lyubomirsky, 2009).

On the basis of these theoretical frameworks, different formats of treatment programmes have been developed:

a *Individual treatment or self-help programmes with the following contents:*

i. Prevention of self-harm
ii. Emotional regulation
iii. Healing from trauma

iv. Relationship skills, including conflict resolution and bereavement
v. Prevention of violence against children
vi. Prevention of stealing behaviours
vii. Cognitive restructuring for violence prevention
viii. Relapse prevention for violence

b *Treatment groups*

i. Psychological groups are conducted for long-term offenders with 10 years or more remaining on their sentence. The aim is to address their mood problems, maladaptive thinking, and interpersonal relationship issues. Interactive activities, art, and music as well as personal sharing are used to facilitate skills learning and the expression of thoughts and feelings.
ii. Various treatment groups are also provided to offenders with specific needs, with the aims of crime prevention and the enhancement of penal adjustment. Participants include mother-offenders, repeat thieves, and so on.

c *Psychological Gymnasium (PSY GYM)*

Hong Kong Correctional Services started up an innovative psychological service, namely Psychological Gymnasium (PSY GYM), in 2011 to enhance the specialised services for female offenders.

In PSY GYM, participants can work on their psychological well-being as in an ordinary gymnasium. Clinical psychologists act as coaches who assess and work on participants' emotions and personal growth through identifying their strengths and weaknesses and equipping them with the skills to train their strengths and overcome their weaknesses. It is hoped that after participants pick up the habit and become proficient in using the skills, they will be competent in training themselves whenever needed. With the aim of training participants to acquire crucial skills to alleviate clinical symptoms and promote psychological growth, PSY GYM has developed a rehabilitative model which consists of both recovery-focused and growth-focused interventions, namely CBT and PPT. These therapeutic approaches attempt to address participants' needs systematically through structured programmes. Apart from these approaches, PSY GYM employs three distinctive features to ensure participants develop and polish the skills needed to enhance their mental health.

Features of PSY GYM

Gender-specific programme designs

Firstly, as illustrated earlier, female offenders have distinctive needs, so psychological intervention with gender-responsive designs would best benefit them. PSY GYM has been developed with contents and activities that have been found to be relevant and interesting to female offenders. All PSY GYM programmes are activity-based and some include expressive art and multimedia components. The activities are carefully selected to enhance understanding of the materials and encourage interactive participation. Participants are welcome to contribute to the programme content. Any issues or experiences they share in the group may be used as learning materials and scenarios for their skills practice.

PSY GYM offers programmes of various natures, from psycho-education on handling adjustment issues to intervention in clinical problems and the promotion of personal growth, and different intensities, from one-day programmes to five-month intensive programmes. Participants are invited to join a programme according to their needs. The content of each programme is tailor-made to meet the common needs of participants, while personal coaching and individual counselling by clinical psychologists are also available, contingent on the progress in terms of therapeutic gains and personal needs of each participant.

Therapeutic community

As evidenced in the literature, a therapeutic community is considered effective as treatment intervention with increased improvement in mental health (Magor-Blatch, Bhullar, Thomson, & Thorsteinsson, 2014). PSY GYM includes elements of a therapeutic community which allow participants to form a supportive network. Participants are encouraged to share their thoughts and feelings and to learn from and support one another in group sessions. In addition, participants in intensive programmes are specially arranged to work together and stay in the same dormitory to facilitate the learning and application of skills while getting communal support among themselves. Such an arrangement allows participants to get hands-on experiences of the application of the skills learnt. For instance, participants can take interpersonal issues from daily life to the group to learn about conflict resolution and act accordingly when they return to the dormitory or they can bring up problems they encounter and seek suggestions and feedback from the group on problem solving. Further psychological interventions are provided if needed.

Everyday life habit building

PSY GYM aims at equipping individuals with sustainable skills for self-management in the long run. As such, it introduces skills that can be easily transferred to and applied in daily life activities. For instance, PSY GYM utilises materials from the media, such as the news and songs, to train individuals' awareness of positive elements in their surroundings. Difficult and problematic situations familiar to participants in their daily life are chosen in the group for sharing, discussion, role play, and feedback on the use of skills in real life. Between-session exercises are also designed for participants to practise newly acquired skills in their everyday life and to turn the use of these skills into habits. More often than not, participants experience difficulties in applying the skills at the beginning, but once they start regular practice, an improvement in their use of skills to manage their mood and interpersonal relationships becomes obvious.

Therapeutic approach and treatment model

Apart from the aforementioned features, PSY GYM has introduced a pioneering psychotherapeutic approach in its intensive programme which integrates CBT and PPT. In this way, participants not only find out "what's wrong" about them and their situations but also go further to look for "what's great" to achieve authentic happiness. In other words, through understanding their psychopathology, past relationship issues, and their pathways to criminality, participants learn corresponding skills to "fix the problems" and start on their road to recovery. However, as a "problem-free" life is no promise of happy living, participants continue to attain personal growth by cultivating their psychological resources, such as a mindful awareness of positive experiences, hope for their life, gratitude for their blessings, and use of their strengths. Towards the end of the intensive programme, participants review their life experiences with the knowledge and skills acquired from CBT and PPT, which helps to identify their strengths and weaknesses, and further develop plans to attain their personal goals.

Case illustration: The case of Claire

Claire[1] (an alias is used for the protection of privacy) is a 35-year-old lady, a single mother of a five-year-old girl, who was convicted for fraud and sentenced to four years' imprisonment. Before joining PSY GYM, Claire had a difficult time getting along with peers. She tended to have inappropriate boundaries with others while getting offended easily. She used to lose her temper readily, and she did not know the way to make up with others, despite feeling sorry for her temper outbursts. Her vocational training courses in the institution were never completed because of disciplinary problems related to her anger issues. She was viewed as a ticking time bomb and avoided by others. She was deeply disturbed by her unpopularity and frequent failures to achieve her personal goals. Claire also had constant worries about her romantic relationship, despite repeated reassurance from her partner. She tended to ruminate on suicidal thoughts and self-harm ideation when she felt distressed about the possibility of being abandoned.

As Claire went through psychological assessment, she showed moderate levels of depression and stress symptoms and revealed gender-specific needs in terms of mood problems, difficulties in self-regulation, past dysfunctional relationship, and use of violence. Claire presented moderate to high levels of services needs, and she was invited to join the five-month intensive programme in PSY GYM.

PSY GYM in action

Getting into a PSY GYM programme does not guarantee a magical transformation of an individual. Claire's first few weeks in PSY GYM were uneventful; she met new friends and enjoyed the honeymoon period of bonding with others. However, as time went by, Claire's sense of insecurity emerged gradually. She became overly sensitive to criticism and showed jealousy towards peers who got close to her friends. She had frequent fallings-out with others and soon became out of favour with most other participants. In a PSY GYM session, Claire and other participants in the group were given chances to voice their perspectives of the chaotic situation. After Claire heard from others, she reflected on her typical relationship issues and acknowledged the need to improve her ways of interacting with others. At the same time, her peers got to understand Claire better instead of making random judgments. With mutual understanding, the group, despite sometimes getting distressed as a result of Claire's mood issues, agreed to be very tolerant of the situation while Claire was making active efforts to change. Ways for both sides to cope with the situation were openly discussed among the group and carried out in real life.

While Claire was struggling to find remedies for interpersonal relationships, she had to identify and address the cognitive distortions related to her anger and self-image issues. In addition, she needed to pick up effective behavioural skills to manage her anger and to learn ways to better express herself, including apologies and self-reflection. These essential skills and knowledge were all incorporated into the PSY GYM programme Claire attended, and she received individual coaching alongside the group sessions to monitor her progress and make fine-tuning adjustments. In addition, PSY GYM offered Claire the chance to review her life experiences, which helped her to gain better self-understanding and identify her strengths and weaknesses for further self-management.

Through reviewing her life experiences, Claire recognised how her early experiences had been affecting her, including perceived parental favouritism towards her twin brother and her fear of abandonment, her strong desire for love and dread of rejection, her unstable love life and peer relationships, her inappropriate and ineffective coping with life stressors, her mood problems, her use of alcohol, drugs, and casual sex, and her aggressive behaviour. It became clear to Claire that she had developed maladaptive thinking about herself and others from these experiences. These maladaptive cognitions, such as "I am unlovable and worthless", "People will dump me eventually", and "I do not deserve anything nice", had gradually turned into cognitive traps which haunted her constantly and gave her a feeling of abandonment, emotional deprivation, and personal defectiveness, which in turn contributed to her sense of insecurity towards relationships and hence her lack of appropriate boundaries with others and her excessive defensive attitude against perceived criticism and rejection. She also recognised that her mood management problems had been affecting her parenting of her daughter, whose temper appeared to closely resemble her mother's.

With this new understanding of herself, Claire started to make use of the cognitive skills learnt from group sessions to establish more adaptive ways of seeing herself and the world. For instance, she figured that "despite making wrong decisions in the past, I still deserve love and am loveable" and "I could make continuous efforts to build and maintain relationships if I want to" and stopped readily seeing rejections. On top of fixing the problems, Claire learnt to set goals for her future. She was aware of the importance of family to her and wanted to rebuild her relationship with her parents. She explored her strengths in PSY GYM, such as her enthusiastic attitude in helping out, her love towards her family, and her willingness to self-reflect and make positive changes. Claire found ways to make use of her strengths for self-improvement and the achievement of her personal goals, thus becoming more hopeful for her future. In addition, Claire became more observant of the positive elements in her surroundings and became grateful of them. For instance, she was able to see a challenge in a positive way and encourage herself to try her best. She also showed increased empathy and gratitude to others and improved her social relationships. In this process of reflection on her life, Claire was not on her own. She received suggestions and encouragement from other participants in the group, which she valued a lot.

Upon completion of the PSY GYM programme, Claire was showing significant improvement in her anger management; she got along with peers generally and was grateful for the acceptance and tolerance she received from others. Feedback from Claire highlighted the support she received from the therapeutic community in PSY GYM. She appreciated the programme for giving her chances and ways to understand, reflect, make changes, and have alternative experiences and hopes in life. Her peers also gave positive feedback on Claire's improvement in terms of interpersonal skills and temper control. With follow-up individual counselling, Claire has started to use a new perspective to look at life and to be aware of her negative thoughts. She continues to practise the cognitive skills and behavioural strategies in her daily life for self-management and no longer sees herself as flawed, and she has become more open towards criticism. She is able to self-regulate and has completed a vocational training course of her choice for the first time! She has tasted the sweet satisfaction of achievement and gained more confidence to build up relationships with others. Instead of experiencing anxiety as a result of being deserted, she is ready to take a positive and active approach in maintaining her relationship with her partner and being appreciative. Claire no longer harbours suicidal thoughts or uses self-harm behaviours to deal with stress. She now finds peace in using adaptive ways of thinking and self-expression while learning to be grateful about her life.

Evaluation and development

Positive research findings, feedback, and recognition support the effectiveness of PSY GYM. Participants have been found to have reduced levels of clinical symptoms, including symptoms of depression, anxiety, and stress. Their depression and anxiety related cognitions and their awareness of negative information have decreased. Meanwhile, participants have experienced positive changes. Their awareness of positive information has increased, along with their levels of hope, gratitude, and life satisfaction. Participants have also reported that the PSY GYM intensive programme has helped them to handle negative emotions, learn social skills, be more aware of positive elements in life, learn to achieve goals, and enhance their positive emotions. Apart from participants' feedback, frontline staff have noticed that participants' emotional stability, positive thinking, attitude towards others, work performance, and discipline improve after taking part in the programme. Management staff have also made positive remarks, stating that PSY GYM brought about positive changes in participants which could assist the staff in performing secure custodial duties in the long run. Clinical psychologists who carried out the programmes rated that participants performed well in terms of attitude towards treatment, understanding of concepts in psychotherapy, quality of completed assignments, application of learned skills, and positive changes in emotion, thinking, and behaviour. In addition, the PSY GYM consultant commented that PSY GYM is one of the few forensic settings in the world to have applied PPT systematically and that PSY GYM has played a pioneering role in the development of PPT. The consultant will continue to work with the working group on the future development of PSY GYM.

Besides receiving positive feedback from internal evaluation, the work of PSY GYM has been well recognised by Hong Kong society. PSY GYM has gained media coverage in several local newspapers and television documentaries since it was first established in 2011. In 2013, the Women's Commission presented PSY GYM and Lo Wu Correctional Institution with the Gender Mainstreaming Award in recognition of HKCS's efforts to design gender-specific services for women. In 2015, PSY GYM received two more awards in recognition of its outstanding programmes, namely the Meritorious Award and a Special Citation for Responsiveness to Customer Needs Award under the Civil Service Outstanding Service Award Scheme organised by the Civil Service Bureau.

As PSY GYM is still in the development stage, there are limitations to its findings. Given that PSY GYM only started since 2011, its research findings are limited. By modifying PSY GYM programmes according to continuous research findings and feedback from participants, staff, and the consultant, it is hoped that the effectiveness of PSY GYM can be further enhanced. Initial feedback from participants and staff suggested an adjustment to lengthen the intensive programmes of PSY GYM so as to facilitate more skills practice and in-depth sharing. While attempting to create a balance between available resources and service effectiveness, not all female offenders with matching risks and needs have been covered by PSY GYM programmes. Considering the promising results of PSY GYM, female offenders' risks and needs levels and their enthusiasm to join PSY GYM, it would be more beneficial if service coverage could be expanded.

Conclusion and future directions

The provision of psychological assessment and treatment for female offenders in Hong Kong has expanded and become more tailored and gender-specific over the years. The working group has developed an assessment to detect the risks and needs of female offenders and has tailored treatment programmes for female offenders via various modalities (self-help, individual, group). As a result of efforts to study experiences from overseas and research on local practices, current evidence-based treatment programmes are not only tailored to the needs of female offenders but also adopt pioneering psychotherapeutic approaches.

Continuous research is undertaken to fine-tune and further develop psychological assessments and treatment programmes for female offenders. By incorporating the latest research findings, the working group endeavours to provide effective and innovative gender-specific assessment and treatment for female offenders.

Chapter summary points

- Female offenders' specific risk and need factors include emotional/mental problems, self-harm behaviours, self-regulation problems, trauma and victimisation, dysfunctional relationships, and parenting stress.
- A gender-specific assessment protocol has been developed and is currently in a trial run. The protocol assesses the risks, needs, and responsivity of adult female offenders.
- In response to gender-specific needs, individual treatment, group treatment, and self-help programmes designed for female offenders have been established.
- Specifically, PSY GYM, which provides gender-specific group-based treatment programmes, has been launched. It provides a therapeutic community for the formation of a supportive network, introduces and encourages the practice of self-management skills in everyday life, and adopts an innovative treatment approach which integrates cognitive behavioural therapy and positive psychotherapy.
- The effectiveness of PSY GYM is not only supported by research findings but is also recognised by participants, staff, the government, and the community.

Note

1 Consent was obtained from the client to share her case in anonymity. Modifications have been made to protect her identity.

References

Andrews, D. A., & Bonta, J. (1995). *The level of service inventory-revised.* Toronto, ON: Multi-Health Systems Inc.

Andrews, D. A., & Bonta, J. (2010). Rehabilitating criminal justice policy and practice. *Psychology, Public Policy and Law, 16*(1), 39–55. doi: 10.1037/a0018362

Austin, K. P., Williams, M. W. M., & Kilgour, G. (2011). The effectiveness of motivational interviewing with offenders: An outcome evaluation. *New Zealand Journal of Psychology, 40*(1), 55–67.

Benda, B. B. (2005). Gender difference in life-course theory of recidivism: A survival analysis. *International Journal of Offender Therapy and Comparative Criminology, 49*, 325–342. doi: 10.1177/0306624X04271194

Bjorkqvist, K. (1994). Sex differences in physical, verbal and indirect aggression: A review of recent research. *Sex Roles*, *30*(3–4), 177–188. doi: 10.1007/BF01420988

Blanchette, K. (1996). The relationship between criminal history, mental disorder, and recidivism among federally sentenced female offenders. (Unpublished master's thesis). Carleton University, Ottawa, ON.

Blanchette, K. (2002). Classifying female offenders for effective intervention: Application of the case-based principles of risk and need. *Forum on Correctional Research*, *14*, 31–35.

Blanchette, K., & Brown, S. L. (2006). *The assessment and treatment of women offenders: An integrative perspective*. Chichester, UK: John Wiley & Sons.

Blanchette, K., & Motiuk, L. L. (1995, June). *Female offender risk assessment: The case management strategies approach*. Poster session presented at the Annual Convention of the Canadian Psychological Association, Charlottetown, Prince Edward Island.

Bloom, B., Owen, B., & Covington, S. (2003). *Gender-responsive strategies: Research practice and guiding principles for women offenders*. Washington, DC: National Institute of Corrections.

Blume, S. (1997). Women: Clinical aspects. In J. Lowinson, P. Ruiz., A. Milkman, & J. Langrod (Eds.), *Substance abuse: A comprehensive textbook* (pp. 645–654). Baltimore, MD: Williams and Wilkins.

Boe, R., Nefekh, M., Vuong, B., Sinclair, R., & Cousineau, C. (2003). *The changing profile of the federal inmate population: 1997 and 2002* (Research Report R-132). Ottawa, ON: Research Branch, Correctional Service Canada.

Bonta, J., Pang, B., & Wallace-Capretta, S. (1995). Predictors of recidivism among incarcerated female offenders. *The Prison Journal*, *75*, 277–294. doi: 10.1177/0032855595075003002

Brown, S. L., & Motiuk, L. L. (2005). *The dynamic factor identification and analysis (DFIA) component of the Offender Intake Assessment (OIA) process: A meta-analytic, psychometric and consultative review* (Research report R-164). Ottawa, ON: Research Branch, Correctional Service Canada.

Butler, A. C., Chapman, J. E., Forman, E. M., & Beck, A. T. (2006). The empirical status of cognitive-behavioral therapy: A review of meta-analyses. *Clinical Psychology Review*, *26*(1), 17–31. doi: 10.1016/j.cpr.2005.07.003

Correctional Service Canada. (1990). *Reduction of self-injury: A mental health priority*. Ottawa, ON: Forum on Corrections Research.

Covington, S. (1998). The relational theory of women's psychological development: Implications for the criminal justice system. In R. T. Zaplin (Ed.), *Female offenders: Critical perspectives and effective interventions* (pp. 113–128). Gaithersburg, MD: Aspen Publishing.

Duckworth, A. L., Steen, T. A., & Seligman, M. E. P. (2005). Positive psychology in clinical practice. *Annual Review of Clinical Psychology*, *1*(1), 629–651. doi: 10.1146/annurev.clinpsy.1.102803.144154

Ferraro, K., & Moe, A. (2003). Mothering, crime, and incarceration. *Journal of Contemporary Ethnography*, *32*, 9–40. doi: 10.1177/0891241602238937

Government of the Hong Kong Special Administrative Region. (2013). *Gender mainstreaming*. Retrieved from http://www.lwb.gov.hk/Gender_Mainstreaming/eng/introduction.html

Gunter, T. D. (2004). Incarcerated women and depression: A primer for the primary care provider. *Journal of the American Medical Women's Association, 59*(2), 107–112.

H. M. Chief Inspector of Prisons. (1997). *Women in prisons: A thematic review.* England: Home Office.

Howells, K. (2000, October-November). *Treatment, management and rehabilitation of women in prison: Relevance of rehabilitation principles.* Paper presented at the Women in Corrections: Staff and Clients Conference convened by the Australian Institute of Criminology in conjunction with the Department for Correctional Services South Australia.

James. D., & Glaze, L. (2006). *Mental health problems of prison and jail inmates (NCJ 213600).* Washington, DC: Bureau of Justice Statistics.

Krakowski, M., & Czobor, P. (2004). Gender differences in violent behaviors: Relationship to clinical symptoms and psychosocial factors. *American Journal of Psychiatry, 161*(3), 459–465. doi: 10.1176/appi.ajp.161.3.459

Landenberger, N. A., & Lipsey, M. W. (2005). The positive effects of cognitive-behavioral programs for offenders: A meta-analysis of factors associated with effective treatment. *Journal of Experimental Criminology, 1*(4), 451–476. doi: 10.1007/s11292-005-3541-7

Lovibond, P. F., & Lovibond, S. H. (1995). The structure of negative emotional states: Comparison of the Depression Anxiety Stress Scales (DASS) with the Beck Depression and Anxiety Inventories. *Behaviour Research and Therapy, 33*(3), 335–343. doi: 10.1016/0005-7967(94)00075-U

Magor-Blatch, L., Bhullar, N., Thomson, B., & Thorsteinsson, E. (2014). A systematic review of studies examining effectiveness of therapeutic communities. *The International Journal of Therapeutic Communities, 35*(4), 168–184. doi: 10.1108/TC-07-2013-0024

McMurran, M. (2009). Motivational interviewing with offenders: A systematic review. *Legal and Criminological Psychology, 14*, 83–100. doi: 10.1348/135532508X278326

Mental Health Coordinating Council. (2010). *The psychological needs of women in the criminal justice system: Considerations for management and rehabilitation.* New South Wales: Mental Health Coordinating Council.

Morash, M., Bynum, T. S., & Koons, B. A. (1998). *Women offenders: Programming needs and promising approaches.* National Institute of Justice Research in Brief. Washington, DC: United States Department of Justice, National Institute of Justice.

O'Brien, P. (1999). *Making it in the "free world" – Women in transition from prison.* New York, NY: State University of New York Press.

Pearson, F. S., Lipton, D. S., Cleland, C. M., & Yee, D. S. (2002). The effects of behavioral/cognitive-behavioral programs on recidivism. *Crime and Delinquency, 48*(3), 476–496. doi: 10.1177/001112870204800306

Plugge, E., & Fitzpatrick, R. (2005). Assessing the health of women in prison: A study from the United Kingdom. *Health Care for Women International, 26*(1), 62–68. doi: 10.1080/07399330590885768

Rettinger, J. L. (1998). *A recidivism follow-up study investigating risk and need within a sample of provincially sentenced women* (Unpublished doctoral dissertation). Carleton University, Ottawa, ON.

Ross, T., Khashu, A., & Wamsley, M. (2004). *Hard data on hard times: An empirical analysis of maternal incarceration, foster care, and visitation*. New York, NY: Vera Institute of Justice.

Sin, N. L., & Lyubomirsky, S. (2009). Enhancing well-being and alleviating depressive symptoms with positive psychology interventions: A practice-friendly meta-analysis. *Journal of Clinical Psychology*, *65*(5), 467–487. doi: 10.1002/jclp.20593

Taouk, M., Lovibond, P., & Laube, R. (2001). *Psychometric properties of a Chinese version of the 21-item Depression Anxiety Stress Scales (DASS21)*. Sydney: Report for New South Wales Transcultural Mental Health Centre, Cumberland Hospital.

Tien, G., Lamb, D., Bond, L., Gillstom, B., & Paris, F. (1993). *Report on the needs assessment of women at the Burnaby Correctional Centre for Women*. Burnaby, BC: BC Institute on Family Violence.

Webster, C. D., Douglas, K. S., Eaves, D., & Hart, S. D. (1997). *HCR-20 assessing risk for violence: Version 2*. Canada: Mental Health, Law & Policy Institute.

Wilson, D. B., Bouffard, L. A., & Mackenzie, D. L. (2005). A quantitative review of structured, group-oriented, cognitive-behavioral programs for offenders. *Criminal Justice and Behavior*, *32*(2), 172–204. doi: 10.1177/0093854804272889

Young, M., Waters, B., Falconer, T., & O'Rourke, P. (2005). Opportunities for health promotion in the Queensland women's prison system. *Australian and New Zealand Journal of Public Health*, *29*(4), 324–327. doi: 10.1111/j.1467-842X.2005.tb00201.x

9 Towards a safer society

Psychological assessment and treatment of serious violent offenders in Hong Kong

Kit Shan Yvonne Lee, Wing Ki Winnie Wong, and Wing Yan Kung

Introduction

Violence is a global public health issue, and it has recently been listed by the United Nations as a priority for the post-2015 international development agenda. Homicide, which refers to murder and manslaughter and represents serious violence that claims people's lives, is the third leading cause of death globally for males aged 15 to 44 years (World Health Organization, 2014). In Hong Kong, the number of homicides reported to the police each year ranged from 17 to 62 between 2005 and 2015, that is, 0.2 to 0.9 homicides per 100,000 people (Hong Kong Police Force, 2016). In 2015, there were approximately 270 male persons in custody convicted of murder or manslaughter, with an annual admission of 10 to 15 over the past three years. At first glance, the local figures may look small. Homicide, however, is always of great public concern due to the seriousness of the offence and the irreversible harm done to the affected families as well as to society. Its gravity is also reflected in the sentencing of homicide offenders. Those convicted of murder are given a mandatory life sentence, while the conviction of manslaughter results in a determinate sentence or a life sentence at maximum.

To safeguard public safety in Hong Kong, the Long-Term Prison Sentence Review Board reviews life-sentenced homicide offenders at regular intervals and will not recommend a determinate sentence for their release until the purposes of incarceration, namely punishment, deterrence, and rehabilitation, have been satisfied. The Long-Term Prison Sentence Review Board considers a series of relevant factors in making a release decision, including the nature of the offence, the length of sentence served, the rehabilitation of the person in custody, and public safety. The psychological evaluation of the risk of violent reoffending will also be called upon to facilitate the decision-making. Therefore, under the local system, clinical psychologists have a unique statutory duty to conduct violence risk assessments for life-sentenced homicide offenders and to foster their rehabilitation through ameliorating their violent tendencies. After release, these homicide offenders with a sentence of two years or above will be subject to statutory community supervision under the Post-Release Supervision Scheme, the aim of which is to provide guidance and assistance to facilitate their reintegration into the community and to enable them to lead a law-abiding life after a long period of incarceration, thereby reducing the chances of reoffending. For continuity of care, psychological follow-up will be arranged for discharged homicide offenders on a needs basis.

In fact, the integral role played by clinical psychologists in both the assessment and treatment of this group of serious violent offenders in Hong Kong underscores the continuing endeavours in advancing evidence-based violence risk assessment procedures and developing effective treatment programmes for violence reduction for the ultimate goal of protecting the public. A similar emphasis on the risk/needs assessment, treatment, and management of violent offenders has also been witnessed in overseas jurisdictions over the past few decades (Gilbert & Daffern, 2010; Polaschek & Reynolds, 2004; Serin & Preston, 2000; Ware, Cieplucha, & Matsuo, 2011).

The heterogeneity of violent offending

Violence is a heterogeneous construct with wide variations in form, frequency, seriousness, lethality, and motive as well as whom the violence is directed against. It can range from minor purposeful embarrassment to actual physical assault. Victims of violence could be family members, acquaintances, or strangers to the perpetrator. Certainly, the motive for using violence could be different from one individual to another even if they perform the same violent act. There were two local homicide studies that provided an objective summary of the diverse forms, motives, and target victims of local homicides, although these early attempts were not up to date and had a portion of missing data. According to the police classification of homicide motives for 1,460 reported cases between 1976 and 1992 in Hong Kong, robbery stood out as the main motive underlying local homicides, followed by disputes involving different parties such as family members, lovers, and gang members. The overlap of these motives was not clear. The motive for about a quarter of the homicide cases remained unknown due to failure to access the records (Gaylord & Galligher, 1994; see Figure 9.1). Another local homicide study with data collected from the Coroner's case files 1989–1999 investigated the relationship between the victim and the homicide offender (Broadhurst, 1999). Among 532 homicide cases, there was an apparently high level of stranger homicide (35%), followed by varying kinds of acquaintances and family members. The relationship between the homicide offender and the victim was unknown for one-fifth of the cases (see Figure 9.2).

At the theoretical level, there are different typologies of violence. Berkowitz (1993) proposed classifying violence as either "expressive" or "instrumental". Expressive violence is known to be emotionally driven; that is, an individual performs a violent act in an attempt to decrease his or her anger or other physiological responses, while instrumental violence refers to violence used as a means to achieve a goal which is purposeful and involves little or no unpleasant internal states. Studies with forensic populations and psychiatric inpatients suggest that violent behaviours commonly serve more than one function (Daffern, Howells, & Ogloff, 2007; Tapscott, Hancock, & Hoaken, 2012). A similar finding

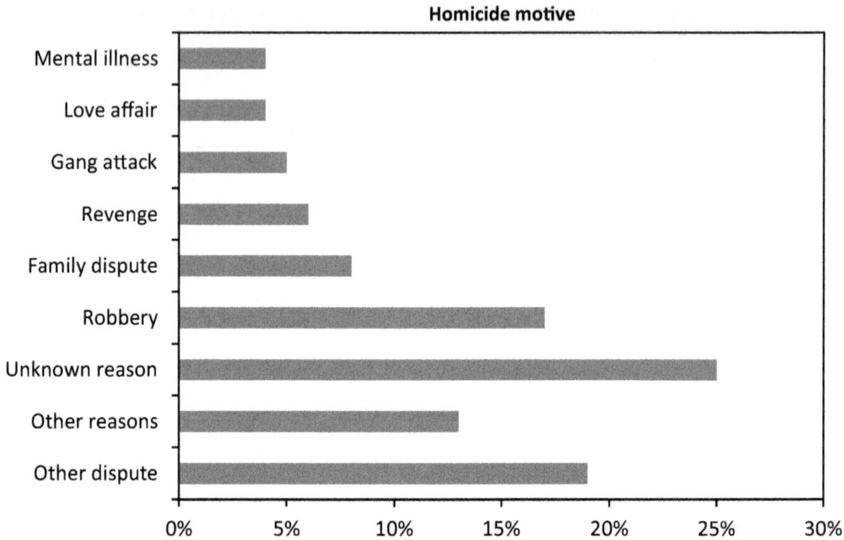

Figure 9.1 Motives for homicide in Hong Kong

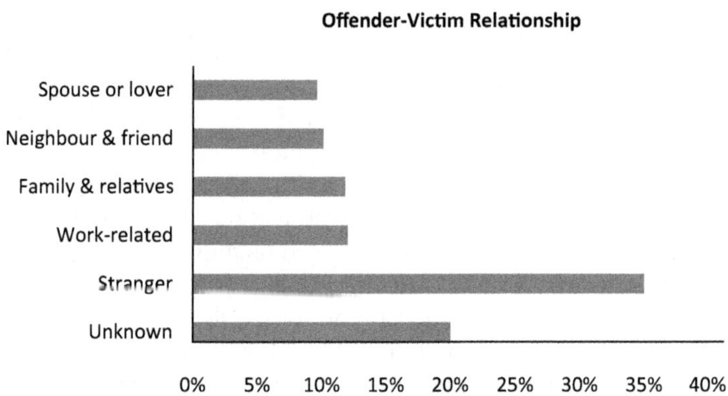

Figure 9.2 Homicide victim-offender relationships in Hong Kong

was revealed in a local study investigating 104 adult male violent offenders serving sentences in Hong Kong (Kong, Leung, Kwong, & Wong, 2009). Principal component analysis of the Impulsive/Premeditated Aggression Scale (IPAS; Stanford et al., 2003) revealed three factors that accounted for 31.1% of the total variance of violent behaviour: impulsive (expressive) aggression, premeditated (instrumental) aggression, and combined aggression, which characterises both expressive and premeditated aggression. The three-factor solution, and in particular the combined aggression factor, suggests local violent offenders tend to show both expressive and premeditated acts. For example, a robber may use force to subdue the bank staff as planned yet could still experience a high level of anger in response to any resistance from the victim.

Violence risk assessment

The individual differences and heterogeneity inherent in the violent offender population suggest that the assessment of the risk for future violence is no simple task. The risk factors contributing to the violent offending of one offender may not be the same for another offender. Also, the weight of an individual risk factor may be different for each violent offender. Fortunately, the considerable advances in risk assessment for violent offenders witnessed in the forensic literature offer sound empirical and theoretical support to guide violence risk assessment procedure and enhance risk prediction accuracy for various usages in the local jurisdiction. Apart from the aforementioned release decision and supervision recommendations made by the statutory review boards, psychological evaluations of future violence risk also help the courts make sentencing decisions.

Empirical research evidence has prompted a shift of assessment procedures from professional judgment alone to a reliance on objective, empirical approaches to offender assessment (Borum, 1996). Meta-analytic reviews of the violent recidivism prediction literature helped identify risk factors which are associated with criminal violence. Empirical research was also able to identify the risk factors which are more critical and may guide us towards focusing on the assessment of those offender characteristics. The general personality and social psychological perspective of criminal behaviour has also received significant empirical support and has practical implications for the identification of risk factors. The Violence Risk Appraisal Guide (VRAG) for violence risk prediction among mentally disordered offenders (Quinsey, Harris, Rice, & Cormier, 2006), the Historical, Clinical and Risk Management-20 Version 3 (HCR-20^{V3}; Douglas, Hart, Webster, & Belfrage, 2013), and the Violence Risk Scale (VRS; Wong & Gordon, 2006) for assessing risks of future violence are among some of the better researched, standardised risk assessment tools with good predictive accuracy (Singh, Grann, & Fazel, 2011; Yang, Wong, & Coid, 2010). The applicability of these assessment tools was later extended to violent offenders with no mental disorder, women offenders, and adolescent offenders after empirical validation beyond the original development samples (Douglas, Yeomans, & Boer, 2005; Strand & Belfrage, 2001). At the practical level, mental health professionals have also recognised that predictions of violent recidivism are enhanced by the use of these objective assessment instruments (National Institute for Health and Clinical Excellence, 2009). A significant development was shown in some of the aforementioned risk assessment tools by combining the use of static and dynamic risk factors in predicting recidivism risks. Static risks factors are offending-related background variables that are not readily subjected to changes through planned intervention. Dynamic risk factors are those psychological attributes that can be more readily changed with rehabilitation efforts, thereby modifying the odds of reoffending. Restricting offender risk assessments to static factors may limit our efforts in effective offending rehabilitation programming and management. Assessment for dynamic risk factors allows us to make room for the implementation of specific treatment programmes for criminogenic needs. Appropriate treatment evaluation could also be arranged. Knowledge of these theoretically changeable risk factors could also improve the multi-professional management and supervision of offenders. Through the evaluation of dynamic risks in addition to static risks in clinical risk assessment instruments and procedures, psychologists are no longer solely performing risk prediction or classification based on the static assessment instruments. The combination of static and dynamic factors in risk-need instruments has been found to maintain predictive accuracy and to allow for treatment planning and the assessment of offender change.

Having received professional training in the use of VRAG and HCR-20^{V3} from the test developers, local clinical psychologists conduct violence risk assessments on the basis of empirically supported static and dynamic risk factors predictive of future violence with reference to these two prominent violence risk assessment scales and with regard to the idiosyncratic characteristics of an individual violent offender. To achieve higher inter-rater reliability in the use of the risk assessment tools and to continue to nurture professional expertise in violence risk assessment, there is case conference among local clinical psychologists for professional sharing on the scoring of risk assessment tools, the classification of risk level, risk assessment issues, risk communication, and the formulation of violence risk management and treatment strategies.

Due to cultural differences and the need to adapt or validate Western risk assessment scales in the Chinese prison population, the best strategy to enhance the predictive accuracy of future reoffending risk in violent offenders in Hong Kong is to develop a local risk assessment scale on the basis of Western research and experience. As such, The Chinese University of Hong Kong was commissioned to conduct a consultancy study to construct and validate clinical risk assessment scales for predicting violent recidivism among incarcerated offenders with a history of convictions for violent crimes (Hong Kong Correctional Services Department, 2005). A release cohort of 168 adult male violent offenders released from correctional institutions in 2003 was recruited for this recidivism research. A set of static and dynamic risk factors based on multi-method measurement, namely clinical interview, self-report questionnaire, and record review, were used as predictors. The resulting intra-class correlation (ICC) showed the good to excellent inter-rater (ICC = 0.59–0.84) as well as test-retest (ICC = 0.65–0.94) reliability of most clinical ratings. The internal consistency (α = 0.59–0.95) and test-retest reliability (ICC = 0.61–0.89) of the self-report questionnaires also reached a good to excellent level. Local norms for violent offenders and non-offenders were developed for these questionnaires to assess dynamic risk factors and measure treatment changes. Nevertheless, the prediction analysis of violent reoffending for a follow-up period of seven years in the community is still under way. Upon completion of the prediction analysis, this recidivism research will identify empirically derived risk factors predictive of violent recidivism in local offenders and validate a local violence risk-need assessment scale with a good evidence base.

Multi-modal violence prevention programme (VPP)

Consistent with the Hong Kong Correctional Services Department's mission of crime prevention, the stress on offender rehabilitation by the Long-Term Prison Sentences Review Board, and the international recognition of the need for violent offender treatment, clinical psychologists in Hong Kong developed a Violence Prevention Programme (VPP) in early 2000, targeting adult male persons in custody with a history of violent offending, although homicide offenders have always been given priority for participation. Much reference has been made to the Violence Prevention Programme of the Correctional Service of Canada (Bettman, Yazar, & Rowe, 1998), the Persistently Violent Offenders Programme (Preston, Murphy, Serin, & Bettman, 1999), Aggression Replacement Training (Goldstein, Glick, & Gibbs, 1998), the Cognitive Self-Change Programme in the Vermont Department of Corrections (Bush, 1995a), and the Rimutaka Violence Prevention Unit (RVPU) in New Zealand (Polaschek, 2011; Polaschek, Wilson, Townsend, & Daly, 2005) in developing the local programme.

Programme description

The VPP is grounded in theories of violent behaviour and empirically informed risk factors associated with aggressive individuals. As mentioned above, there are multiple determinants of violent behaviour and violent offenders are a heterogeneous offender group; therefore, each violent offender should have idiosyncratic criminogenic needs or deficits contributing to his or her aggressive act. Literature reviews suggest that anger is often an important proximal risk factor for violence (Rice, Harris, Quinsey, & Cyr, 1990; Zamble & Quinsey, 1997), but it is neither a necessary nor sufficient antecedent to aggressive behaviours (Serin & Preston, 2000). Other risk factors for violence identified from the literature include impulsivity (Henry & Moffitt, 1997; Nussbaum et al., 2002), substance abuse (Boles & Miotto, 2003; Pihl & Peterson, 1993), hostility (Megargee, 1976), cognitive or information-processing biases (Beck, 1999; Copello & Tata, 1990; Dodge & Schwartz, 1997), violence-related cognition (Collie, Vess, & Murdoch, 2007), social support for violence (Polaschek & Reynolds, 2004), and empathy deficit (Jolliffe & Farrington, 2004). In addition, 168 local violent offenders exhibited significantly more impulsivity, anger, antisocial attitudes, and aggressive thoughts than 300 members of a non-criminal community sample, with the effect size ranging from moderate to large (Cohen's d = .57 – .96; Hong Kong Correctional Services Department, 2005). In their paper, Serin and Preston (2000) stressed the importance of considering the complexity of risk factors when developing a general theory of violent offending, formulating a theory about individual cases, and responding to violence through intervention.

The VPP in Hong Kong thus adopts a multi-modal treatment approach to target the above-mentioned risk factors and aims to reduce the likelihood of post-treatment violent offending in adult male persons in custody. The programme contains 10 modules (see Table 9.1). It is a cognitive-behavioural programme whose treatment orientation constitutes an empirically proven principle of effective offender rehabilitation (Gendreau, 1995). The Understanding Violence, Cognitive Restructuring, Combating Domestic Violence, and Reducing Violence against Children modules are designed to address violent offenders' cognitions, thinking patterns, attitudes, or beliefs which support, condone, and promote violent behaviours. Participants learn to identify their cognitive distortions (e.g., "Violence is the most effective means to solve a problem"; "It is okay to take revenge on people who have offended me") and to respond to events/people in non-violent ways (e.g., "Conflicts can be handled with open communication which brings fewer adverse impacts"; "He is in a bad mood and has no intention of being hostile to me"). Such a cognitive approach has been explicitly used in the treatment of violent offenders and found to be effective in reducing violent recidivism (Antonowicz, 2005; Bush, 1995b; McGuire, 2005; Robinson, 1995). Other modules target the outstanding criminogenic needs related to violent offending, with an emphasis on behavioural skills building. Participants learn to develop non-violent skills to manage interpersonal relationships, handle stresses, address unpleasant internal states (such as anger, sadness, and jealousy), and generate alternative and prosocial life maps through relapse prevention planning and goal setting. For example, participants are equipped with skills to refuse an invitation to a gang fight from subcultural associates, to divert attention to work or another person when becoming enraged in a social conflict, and to resolve conflicts with an intimate partner with the assistance of a counsellor or a trustworthy friend.

Programme delivery

The VPP is delivered in the format of group therapy or as individual treatment. As in most correctional programmes, group therapy is preferred, as it is known to be cost-effective in offender rehabilitation (Gendreau, 1995). Individual intervention will be particularly rendered to violent offenders whose responsivity factors, such as psychopathic tendency, intellectual problem, and literacy level, require special attention. Homework assignments are an important component in both

Table 9.1 Summary of the 10 modules of the Violence Prevention Programme

Violence Prevention Programme (VPP)			
Core modules	*Elective modules*		
Cognitive Restructuring	Anger Management	Conflict Resolution	Reducing Violence against Children
Relapse Prevention	Assertiveness Training	Empathy Training	Understanding Violence
	Combating Domestic Violence	Problem-Solving Training	

treatment modalities. There is a group manual and a self-help homework manual for each treatment module. For each module, the treatment group consists of 8 to 10 sessions, each approximately three hours in duration and occurring once a week. Homework sessions are on a biweekly basis, and each session lasts three hours. The group size is usually no more than 10 participants, which allows for a more personal and dedicated environment for discussion and sharing. To better manage this specialised offender group, the treatment group is now run by two clinical psychologists.

Of the 10 modules, Cognitive Restructuring and Relapse Prevention are the core modules. Other modules will be added on according to the reoffending risk and idiosyncratic treatment needs of the participants. In other words, treatment intensity or the number of modules required for an individual participant will be determined according to the risk-need-responsivity (RNR) principles of effective correctional rehabilitation (Andrews & Bonta, 2003). Often, higher treatment intensity is needed for those offenders with a high risk of violent reoffending (Serin & Preston, 2000; Ware et al., 2011). A meta-analysis of 154 controlled outcome studies demonstrated that correctional programmes adhering to all RNR principles yield an average 30% reduction in the recidivism rate (Andrews & Bonta, 2010). Lösel (2014) stressed that the effectiveness of these correctional programmes was remarkable, as well-accepted medical treatments such as radiation and chemotherapy for brain tumours achieve only a 10% decline in mortality rate. In fact, the VPP is arranged when homicide offenders show good acceptance of their long or life sentence. Participation in the VPP is voluntary. The life-sentenced homicide offenders are generally motivated to undertake psychological treatment. As successful rehabilitation is one of the factors considered by the Long-Term Prison Sentences Review Board in granting them a determinate sentence, there is a built-in incentive for positive change in this offender group.

Preliminary programme evaluation

Participants were administered the self-report Relapse Prevention Questionnaire (Beckett, Beech, Fisher, & Fordham, 1994), which was adapted to the violent offender population, both before and after completion of the core modules of the VPP. They showed significantly increased awareness of the risk factors and risky situations that lead to the violence cycle as well as reporting more appropriate coping strategies ($t = 6.13$, $p < .001$). On the Aggression Questionnaire, which measures hostility, anger, verbal aggression, and physical aggression, there were significant decreases after completion of the VPP ($t = 2.23$, $p < .05$). The significant differences of these two psychological measures ranged from a small (Cohen's $d = .28$) to a moderate (Cohen's $d = .64$) effect size.

Response from the participants' feedback reflected a general satisfaction with the programme. The programme contents they found particularly helpful were learning the consequences of a pattern of violence, the means to reduce anger arousal, the strategies to modify distorted attitudes, and the effective ways to prevent violent relapse. Their average rating of the VPP was 86.2 out of 100, and

87% of the participants reported that they would recommend the programme to other persons in custody.

New initiatives

Striving for a more effective treatment programme for violent offenders, new concepts advocated in the third wave of cognitive behavioural treatments, namely mindfulness, acceptance, and healthy behavioural skills building (Hoffman, Sawyer, & Fang, 2010), have been piloted in the recent implementation of the VPP.

(1) Incorporating mindfulness training into the VPP

Kabat-Zinn (2013) defines mindfulness as "paying attention in a particular way, on purpose, in the present moment, and nonjudgmentally." It is proposed that through the regular practice of meditation, practitioners can enhance the moment-by-moment awareness of internal states such as physical sensations, emotions, and thoughts and hence cultivate deep and long-lasting experiences of inner calm, well-being, and self-respect (Kabat-Zinn, 1993).

Recent empirical research on mindfulness has extended the interest from patients with chronic pain (Kabat-Zinn, 1982; Kabat-Zinn, Lipworth, & Burney, 1985), anxiety, and depression (Kabat-Zinn, 1993; Teasdale et al., 2000) to incarcerated populations (Himelstein, Hastings, Shapiro, & Heery, 2011; Samuelson, Carmody, Kabat-Zinn, & Bratt, 2007). The study results show that meditation-based interventions are rehabilitative to incarcerated populations; there are improvements in self-reported anger, self-compassion (Suarez et al., 2014), hostility, self-esteem, and mood disturbance (Samuelson et al., 2007) and decreases in perceived stress (Himelstein et al., 2011), substance use, and recidivism (Alexander et al., 2003; Himelstein, 2011; Rainforth, Alexander, & Cavanaugh, 2003).

By cultivating their inner strengths, inmates are believed to become less reactive to stress/intense emotional states or to respond reflectively to situations instead of reacting to them on the basis of habitual coping strategies, which should decrease the chance of continuing criminal behaviour and recidivism. For this reason, the clinical psychologists of the Hong Kong Correctional Services Department started incorporating mindfulness training into VPP modules in 2014 as pilot exercises. The skills taught are adopted from the mindfulness-based stress reduction (MBSR) course, which includes tuning into one's breathing during sitting meditation, eating meditation, body scan meditation, and walking meditation (Kabat-Zinn, 1990, 2013). Participants were introduced to and instructed to practise one form of meditation for approximately 25 minutes; this was followed by discussion and sharing in each group session. They were also encouraged to do formal meditation practice with audio guidance for 45 minutes every day.

Some modifications of mindfulness exercises were allowed to fit into the correctional setting. For example, participants were instructed to practice body scan meditation while sitting, as yoga mattresses were not available in adult prisons. Tentatively, group members reported a decrease in subjective stress and an increase in inner calm after several weeks of practising meditation. It is anticipated that Hatha yoga postures, another form of meditation, will be introduced to persons in custody when more resources and safety measures are allocated.

(2) Maintenance programme after completion of the VPP

The Maintenance Programme was newly developed for the homicide offenders who had completed the Violence Prevention Programme but were waiting for the recommendation of a determinate sentence for their life imprisonment term. This programme has the dual purpose of sustaining their motivation for positive change as well as maintaining treatment gain. It is a biannual group-based programme which involves a large group of about 25 VPP completers and relies heavily on a variety of innovative activities with the use of multimedia. Group facilitators include both clinical psychologists and psychologists' assistants. It is interesting to note that 95% of the participants of the Maintenance Programme are located in the units assigned for final-stage life imprisonment, a built-in therapeutic environment in the penal system where persons in custody are geared towards positive change and provided with more incentives for positive behaviour, such as opportunities for more rehabilitative activities and more social time instead of being confined to a cell, and are purposefully well behaved to remain in these units. The therapeutic environment in turn helps reinforce the objectives of the programme.

The following will illustrate the Maintenance Programme with activities in line with the theme of "Striving for the New Me" in 2014. First, the programme completers, divided into small groups, were asked to present the theme in an activity called "The Talent Quest". The ultimate group-singing, self-created drama and talk show performed in "The Talent Quest" presented the defeat of the violent, antisocial and egocentric "old me" by the empathetic, rational, even-tempered and prosocial "new me". To facilitate goal-setting for the "new me", the programme completers were trained to use the Bull's Eye dartboard to set valued life goals in accordance with acceptance and commitment therapy (ACT) (Luoma, Hayes, & Walser, 2007). Through announcing their valued life goals and the concomitant action plan during the groundbreaking ceremony for potting "The Plant of the Maintenance Programme", they made public commitments to accomplish the goals (Hayes et al., 1985). In addition, a group activity "obstacle race", an angel vs. devil role play, and "The Fly and Samurai" animation were arranged to help them keep their commitments in the face of barriers. By keeping their own Bull's Eye dartboard either on the desk inside their cells or on the table in the workshop, they had a physical reminder to prompt their committed action and to keep track of their progress. Voting for the top three goal-setting participants and the subsequent public interviews of these role models also reinforced effective goal setting towards valued living. Overall, these programme activities aim to promote behavioural change in the rehabilitation of homicide offenders.

It was observed that the participants demonstrated active participation in the various group activities throughout the Maintenance Programme. The participants could also report progress while implementing their committed action in achieving the goals, such as more self-disclosure when writing letters to family members to improve relationships and more running exercise to maintain their physical health. Seemingly, an activity-based approach and behavioural skills building form the right track for the Maintenance Programme.

A case illustration: Alan

Having worked hard to turn over a new leaf for many years, Alan[1] (an alias) received a handshake and congratulations from the Senior Superintendent of Stanley Prison on 1 May 2014. The Long-Term Prison Sentences Review Board finally recommended commuting his life sentence for a murder conviction to a 25-year sentence after considering the prison report, the psychologist's violence risk assessment, and a psychiatric examination. On 7 February 2015, he was released to the community in his early 40s.

Tracing back, Alan's parents divorced when he was three years old. Together with his younger brother, he resided with their stepmother after their father remarried. The two brothers were said to have been always close and loving. Alan also related well to his father, but his father seldom stayed at home for work reasons. However, Alan was on bad terms with his stepmother, who was described as demeaning and punitive. He recalled that his stepmother arranged for the two brothers to eat in the kitchen with the maid when his father was away from home. Feeling no warmth at home, he began hanging around with subcultural peers in early adolescence. He enjoyed the support and acceptance he gained in this peer group, something which was not available at home. His peers also protected him from bullying at school. Because of this brotherhood, he joined them in illegal activities such as opening a vice establishment and collecting debts for loan sharks. Gang fights were not uncommon in those days. From movies, he learned about criminal gangs, that violence was the quickest means to stop attacks by others, and how to take away others' possessions. On one hand, he gained status and recognition among his peers; on the other hand, he was subject to a superintendent's caution and later sentenced to a detention centre after being convicted of conspiracy to rob at the age of 16. He continued to mingle with these subcultural peers after his discharge from the detention centre. A year later, one of his subcultural peers was attacked by another gang. Having the culture of an eye for an eye, his gang went for a revenge attack against the gang who beat up his peer. As a fighter in the gang, Alan joined the knife attack. They planned to make stab wounds to the limbs only, but one of the gang members was ultimately stabbed to death in the violent attack. Alan was therefore sentenced to life for murder at the age of 18. Three other gang members received the same life sentence, but the gang leader who initiated the revenge attack was not arrested.

Alan felt hopeless and frustrated at the start of his life sentence. Although he was told a determinate sentence would be granted when he was reformed, he could not imagine living behind bars for decades at the young age of 18. His biological mother, who visited him every other week, encouraged him to behave well in prison. She promised not to leave him behind while he was in custody. Her unfailing love, support, and guidance made him feel less confused and lonely. Two years after his conviction, he obtained a pass in English Language from the OUHK in 1995, and then a pass in Putonghua and Translation. He also joined the Christian group and the music interest group with fellow prisoners. Psychological services at the time focused on reinforcing his constructive use of prison time, enhancing harmonious interpersonal relationships, and strengthening his ties with his supportive mother.

To facilitate his positive change, a clinical psychologist first conducted a comprehensive violence risk-need assessment. He was assessed as having a high risk of future violence due to the adolescence onset of his behavioural problem and his young age, subcultural affiliation, violent and antisocial attitude, inadequate anger management, and impulsivity. Given his high risk profile, it was arranged for him to participate in a treatment group covering three modules of the VPP, namely Understanding Violence, Cognitive Restructuring, and Relapse Prevention, from 2002 to 2003. Anger management training was additionally done in individual sessions. He learned that violence multiplies but does not solve problems and that bullying does not bring true respect. Thinking through all sorts of consequences of violence was important. Subcultural affiliation was a kind of instrumental relationship. He practised assertive skills to resist temptation from subcultural friends through role play. He gradually used time out and positive self-talk, such as "no fighting in prison in order to give mom some relief", to reduce anger arousal. To prevent violent relapse, he refrained from contact with subcultural peers and connected with religious groups. He reported very high self-efficacy to stop violence at the end of the treatment programme.

On 16 June 2014, Alan attended his last session of the Maintenance Programme with other programme completers at Stanley Prison. He shared his reflections about his life sentence:

> I can sum up my 25-year imprisonment in four stages. First, I felt like I was floating aimlessly with a life buoy in the endless sea after the High Court Judge sentenced me to life for murder. There was only fear, loneliness, and helplessness. Later, I saw some light at the far end and I swam toward the light source with the support of the life buoy. It was the time when I received support from my family, the clinical psychologist, the pastor, and the correctional staff. They gave me reasons and guidance to start anew. In the third stage, the sea was rough with thunderstorms and sharks. I had to swim nonstop for survival. Amid life crises such as my mother's cancer, my younger brother's migration to the US, and interpersonal conflicts in the music interest group, I urged myself to stay the course on the road to rehabilitation: day after day, year after year, until I saw the shore where my family were waving to me. In the final stage, my family was waiting for my release to have a family reunion in the community. "The early bird catches the worm" has always been my motto.

At Alan's request, the provision of psychological services for him was also arranged in the community while he was undergoing statutory supervision. Socially, he had a daily phone call with his mother and a weekly gathering with his mother and other family members. While sustaining this positive social network, he reported no single attempt to resume contact with previous subcultural associates. He proudly said that he had successfully applied the assertive skills he had learned to refrain from engaging with the subcultural associates he met in the street. He told them that he had promised his mother not to reoffend but to engage in gainful employment and embark on academic study. He did not give them his phone number for further contact. What was most gratifying was that he had started a religious course in September 2015 as the first step to executing his release plan of becoming a preacher one day.

Conclusion and future directions

Clinical psychologists of the Hong Kong Correctional Services are committed to evidence-based practice in working with serious violent offenders. While empirical validation of the local violence risk-need assessment scale is still in progress, further efforts to increase the predictive validity of this scale have been made. A replication study to test the locally developed violence risk-need assessment scale on an independent sample of about 200 local adult male violent offenders has begun. Data collection was completed in 2009. Data analysis will be commenced when the replication sample has undergone a sufficient follow-up period in the community.

With regard to treatment services for violent offenders, refinement of the programme content with the latest research in forensic literature will be continued. The role of mindfulness training in violence reduction and the delivery of the VPP for life-sentenced homicide offenders will be studied, whether delivering the whole programme at an early or later stage of the life sentence or spacing out the various modules of the programme over the life sentence. As the VPP targets problems relating to violent behaviour for the purpose of violence reduction, the incorporation of the Good Lives Model of offender rehabilitation (Fortune & Ward, 2014), which emphasises strengths and resources for a prosocial good life, into the Maintenance Programme for the successful completers of the VPP as a step-up phase in the ongoing rehabilitation process will be a future development. Lastly, an Orientation Programme is now on a pilot run for homicide offenders who have just received a life sentence. Based on Snyder's (1994) cognitive theory of hope and Miller and Rollnick's (2013) motivational interviewing, the Orientation Programme aims at fostering adaptive coping with the life sentence, facilitating the rehabilitation process, enhancing personal insight and readiness to receive psychological services, and conducting evidence-based violence risk-need assessment to devise a tailor-made treatment plan for individual homicide offenders. Efforts will also be made to identify more psychological measures and other outcome measures in order to have a comprehensive evaluation of the programme's effectiveness.

Chapter summary points

- Clinical psychologists in the Hong Kong Correctional Services have a statutory duty to provide a violence risk assessment and to facilitate the rehabilitation of homicide offenders, both of which contribute to the judicial decision to release homicide offenders into the community while protecting public safety.
- Homicide represents a serious violent offence which causes irreversible harm to the victims. Violent offences are heterogeneous in terms of form, frequency, seriousness, lethality, motive, and relationship with the victim.
- To enhance the accuracy of violence risk prediction, a local violence risk-need assessment scale has been constructed. Inter-rater and test-retest reliabilities were found to be satisfactory. A statistical analysis of its predictive validity for local violent offenders within seven years of release is in progress. A replication study with a separate sample of violent offenders has also been started.
- The Violence Prevention Programme (VPP) in Hong Kong is specifically designed for violent offenders and homicide offenders with a view to promoting their skills to lead a non-violent lifestyle. The 10 modules grounded in cognitive-behavioural therapy are assigned according to the assessed risk and needs. The preliminary findings on the programme's effectiveness are positive.
- Two new initiatives for the treatment programmes for violent offenders are (1) incorporating mindfulness training into the VPP to enhance programme effectiveness and (2) introducing the Maintenance Programme to sustain treatment gains and motivation for positive change among homicide offenders who have completed the VPP but are still serving their sentence in prison.
- Based on the cognitive theory of hope, an Orientation Programme is undergoing a pilot run with newly sentenced homicide offenders to foster their adaptive coping with the life sentence and to increase their readiness for psychological treatment.

Note

1 Written consent was obtained from Alan to share his road to rehabilitation.

References

Alexander, C. N., Rainforth, M. V., Frank, P. R., Grant, J. D., Stade, C. V., & Walton, K. G. (2003). Walpole study of the transcendental meditation program in maximum security prisoners III: Reduced recidivism. *Journal of Offender Rehabilitation, 36*(1–4), 161–180. doi: 10.1300/J076v36n01_08

Andrews, D. A., & Bonta, J. L. (2003). *The psychology of criminal conduct* (3rd ed.). Cincinnati, OH: Anderson Publishing.

Andrews, D. A., & Bonta, J. L. (2010). *The psychology of criminal conduct* (5th ed.). Newark, NJ: LexisNexis.

Antonowicz, D. H. (2005). The reasoning and rehabilitation program: Outcome evaluations with offenders. In M. McMurran & J. McGuire (Eds.), *Social problem solving and offending: Evidence, evaluation and evolution* (pp. 163–182). Chichester, UK: John Wiley & Sons.

Beck, A. T. (1999). *Prisoners of hate: The cognitive basis of anger, hostility, and violence.* New York, NY: HarperCollins Publishers.

Beckett, R., Beech, A., Fisher, D., & Fordham, A. S. (1994). *Community-based treatment for sex offenders: An evaluation of seven treatment programmes.* London: Home Office.

Berkowitz, L. (1993). *Aggression: Its causes, consequences, and control.* New York, NY: McGraw-Hill.

Bettman, M. D., Yazar, R., & Rowe, R. (1998). *Violence prevention program manual.* Ottawa, ON: Correctional Services of Canada.

Boles, S. M., & Miotto, K. (2003). Substance abuse and violence: A review of the literature. *Aggression and Violent Behavior, 8*(2), 155–174. doi: 10.1016/S1359-1789(01)00057-X

Borum, R. (1996). Improving the clinical practice of violence risk assessment: Technology, guidelines, and training. *American Psychologist, 51*(9), 945–956. doi: 10.1037/0003-066X.51.9.945

Broadhurst, R. G. (1999). *Homicide in Hong Kong: The homicide monitoring database (1989–1997).* Proceedings of the First Annual of the Hong Kong Sociology Conference, Hong Kong University.

Bush, J. (1995a). *Cognitive self-change: A program manual.* Burlington, VT: Vermont Department of Corrections.

Bush, J. (1995b). Teaching self-risk management to violent offenders. In J. McGuire (Ed.), *What works: Reducing re-offending: Guidelines from research and practice* (pp. 139–154). Chichester, UK: John Wiley & Sons.

Collie, R. M., Vess, J., & Murdoch, S. (2007). Violence-related cognition: Current research. In T. A. Gannon, T. Ward, A. R. Beech, & D. Fisher (Eds.), *Aggressive offenders' cognition: Theory, research & practice* (pp. 179–197). Chichester, UK: John Wiley & Sons.

Copello, A. G., & Tata, P. R. (1990). Violent behaviour and interpretative bias: An experimental study of the resolution of ambiguity in violent offenders. *British Journal of Clinical Psychology, 29*(4), 417–428. doi: 10.1111/j.2044-8260.1990.tb00905.x

Daffern, M., Howells, K., & Ogloff, J. (2007). What's the point? Towards a methodology for assessing the function of psychiatric inpatient aggression. *Behaviour Research and Therapy, 45*(1), 101–111. doi: 10.1016/j.brat.2006.01.011

Dodge, K. A., & Schwartz, D. (1997). Social information processing mechanisms in aggressive behavior. In D. M. Stoff, J. Breiling, & J. D. Maser (Eds.), *Handbook of antisocial behavior* (pp. 171–180). Hoboken, NJ: John Wiley & Sons.

Douglas, K. S., Hart, S. D., Webster, C. D., & Belfrage, H. (2013). *HCR-20: Assessing risk for violence* (Version 3). Burnaby, BC: Mental Health, Law, and Policy Institute, Simon Fraser University.

Douglas, K. S., Yeomans, M., & Boer, D. P. (2005). Comparative validity analysis of multiple measures of violence risk in a sample of criminal offenders. *Criminal Justice and Behavior, 32*(5), 479–510. doi: 10.1177/0093854805278411

Fortune, C., & Ward, T. (2014). Integrating strength-based practice with forensic CBT: The Good Lives Model of offender rehabilitation. In R. C. Tafrate & D.

Mitchell (Eds.), *Forensic CBT: A handbook for clinical practice* (pp. 436–452). Chichester, UK: Wiley-Blackwell.

Gaylord, M. S., & Galligher, J. F. (1994). Death penalty politics and symbolic law in Hong Kong. *International Journal of the Sociology of Law*, *22*, 19–37.

Gendreau, P. (1995). The principles of effective interventions with offenders. In A. T. Harland (Ed.), *Choosing correctional options that work: Defining the demand and evaluating the supply* (pp. 117–130). Thousand Oaks, CA: Sage.

Gilbert, F., & Daffern, M. (2010). Integrating contemporary aggression theory with violent offender treatment: How thoroughly do interventions target violent behaviour? *Aggression and Violent Behavior*, *15*, 167–180. doi: 10.1016/j.avb.2009.11.003

Goldstein, A. P., Glick, B., & Gibbs, J. C. (1998). *Aggression replacement training: A comprehensive intervention for aggressive youth.* Champaign, IL: Research Press.

Hayes, S. C., Rosenfarb, I.,Wulfert, E., Munt, E., Zettle, R. D., & Korn, Z. (1985). Self-reinforcement effects: An artifact of social standard setting? *Journal of Applied Behavior Analysis*, *18*(3), 210–214. doi: 10.1901/jaba.1985.18-201

Henry, B., & Moffitt, T. E. (1997). Neuropsychological and neuroimaging studies of juvenile delinquency and adult criminal behavior. In D. M. Stoff, J. Breiling, & J. D. Maser (Eds.), *Handbook of anti-social behavior* (pp. 280–288). New York, NY: John Wiley & Sons.

Himelstein, S. (2011). Meditation research: The state of art in correctional settings. *International Journal of Offender Therapy and Comparative Criminology*, *55*(4), 646–661. doi: 10.1177/0306624X10364485

Himelstein, S., Hastings, A., Shapiro, S., & Heery, M. (2011). Mindfulness training for self-regulation and stress with incarcerated youth: A pilot study. *Probation Journal*, *59*(2), 151–165. doi: 10.1177/0264550512438256

Hoffman, S. G., Sawyer, A. T., & Fang, A. (2010). The empirical status of the 'new wave' of CBT. *Psychiatric Clinics of North America*, *33*(3), 701–710. doi: 10.16/j.psc.2010.04.006

Hong Kong Correctional Services Department. (2005). *Hong Kong – Risk Assessment Scale for Violent Offenders (HK-RASvo).* Hong Kong: Correctional Services Department.

Hong Kong Police Force. (2016). *Crime statistics in detail: Homicide.* Retrieved from http://www.police.gov.hk/ppp_en/09_statistics/csd.html

Jolliffe, D., & Farrington, D. F. (2004). Empathy and offending: A systematic review and meta-analysis. *Aggression and Violent Behavior*, *9*(5), 441–476. doi: 10.1016/j.avb.2003.03.001

Kabat-Zinn, J. (1982). An outpatient program in behavioral medicine for chronic pain patients based on the practice of mindfulness meditation: Theoretical considerations and preliminary results. *General Hospital Psychiatry*, *4*, 33–47. doi: 10.1016/0163-8343(82)9026-3

Kabat-Zinn, J. (1990). *Full catastrophe living: Using the wisdom of your body and mind to face stress, pain and illness.* New York, NY: Delacorte.

Kabat-Zinn, J. (1993). Mindfulness meditation: Health benefits of an ancient Buddhist practice. In D. Goleman & J. Gurin (Eds.), *Mind/body medicine* (pp. 259–275). Yonkers, NY: Consumer Reports Books.

Kabat-Zinn, J. (2013). *Full catastrophe living: How to cope with stress, pain and illness using mindfulness meditation. Using the wisdom of your body and mind to face stress, pain and illness.* Revised and updated edition. London: Piatkus.

Kabat-Zinn, J., Lipworth, L., & Burney, R. (1985). The clinical use of mindfulness meditation for the self-regulation of chronic pain. *Journal of Behavioral Medicine*, *8*, 163–190. doi: 10.1007/BF00845519

Kong, V. C. C., Leung, P. W. L., Kwong, E., & Wong, W. (2009). *Characterizing aggressive behaviour in Hong Kong adult violent offenders* (Unpublished thesis). The Chinese University of Hong Kong, Hong Kong.

Lösel, F. (2014, September). *Treating violent offenders more effectively: Alternatives to punishment.* Paper presented at the World Health Organization and the University of Cambridge Global Violence Reduction Conference, King's College, Cambridge, UK.

Luoma, J. B., Hayes, S. C., & Walser, R. D. (2007). *Learning ACT: An acceptance and commitment therapy skills-training manual for therapists.* Oakland, CA: New Harbigner.

McGuire, J. (2005). Social problem solving: Basic concepts, research and applications. In M. McMurran & J. McGuire (Eds.), *Social problem-solving and offending: Evidence, evaluation and evolution* (pp. 3–29). Chichester, UK: John Wiley & Sons.

Megargee, E. I. (1976). The prediction of dangerous behavior. *Criminal Justice and Behavior*, *3*(1), 3–21. doi: 10.1177/009385487600300101

Miller, W. R., & Rollnick, S. (2013). *Motivational interviewing: Helping people change* (3rd ed.). New York, NY: Guilford Press.

National Institute for Health and Care Excellence. (2009). *NICE Clinical Guideline 77. Antisocial personality disorder: Prevention and management.* Manchester: National Institute for Health and Clinical Excellence.

Nussbaum, D., Collins, M., Cutler, J., Zimmerman, W., Farguson, B., & Jacques, I. (2002). Crime type and specific personality indicia: Cloninger's TCI impulsivity, empathy and attachment subscales in non-violent, violent and sexual offenders. *American Journal of Forensic Psychology*, *20*(1), 23–56.

Pihl, R. O., & Peterson, J. B. (1993). Alcohol/drug use and aggressive. In S. Hodgins (Ed.), *Mental disorder and crime* (pp. 263–283). Newbury Park, CA: Sage.

Polaschek, D. L. L. (2011). High-intensity rehabilitation for violent offenders in New Zealand: Reconviction outcomes for high and medium-risk prisoners. *Journal of Interpersonal Violence*, *26*(4), 664–682. doi: 10.1177/0886260510365854

Polaschek, D. L. L., & Reynolds, N. (2004). Assessment and treatment: Violent offenders. In C. Hollin (Ed.), *The essential handbook of offender assessment and treatment* (pp. 201–218). Chichester, UK: John Wiley & Sons.

Polaschek, D. L. L., Wilson, N. J., Townsend, M. R., & Daly, L. R. (2005). Cognitive-behavioral rehabilitation for high-risk violent offenders: An outcome evaluation of the violence prevention unit. *Journal of Interpersonal Violence*, *20*, 1611–1627. doi: 10.1177/0886260505280507

Preston, D. L., Murphy, S., Serin, R. C., & Bettman, M. (1999). *Persistently violent offender program: A treatment manual.* Ottawa, ON: Correctional Service Canada.

Quinsey, V. L., Harris, G. T., Rice, M. E., & Cormier, C. (2006). *Violent offenders: Appraising and managing risk* (2nd ed.). Washington, DC: American Psychological Association.

Rainforth, M. V., Alexander, C. N., & Cavanaugh, K. L. (2003). Effects of the transcendental meditation program on recidivism among former inmates of Folsom Prison: Survival analysis of 15-year follow-up data. *Journal of Offender Rehabilitation*, *36*(1–4), 181–203. doi: 10.1300/J076v36n01_09

Rice, M. E., Harris, G. T., Quinsey, V. L., & Cyr, M. (1990). Planning treatment programs in secure psychiatric facilities. In D. N. Weisstub (Ed.), *Law and mental health: International perspectives* (Vol. 5, pp. 162–230). New York, NY: Pergamon Press.

Robinson, D. (1995). *The impact of cognitive skills reasoning on post-release recidivism among Canadian federal offenders*. No. R-41 Research Branch. Ottawa, ON: The Correctional Services.

Samuelson, M., Carmody, J., Kabat-Zinn, J., & Bratt, M. A. (2007). Mindfulness-based stress reduction in Massachusetts correctional facilities. *The Prison Journal, 87*(2), 254–268. doi: 10.1177/0032885507303753

Serin, R. C., & Preston, D. L. (2000). *Violent offender programming*. Retrieved from http://www.csc-scc.gc.ca/research/com2000-chap_18-eng.shtml

Singh, J. P., Grann, M., & Fazel, S. (2011). A comparative study of violence risk assessment tools: A systematic review and metaregression analysis of 68 studies involving 25,980 participants. *Clinical Psychology Review, 31*(3), 499–513. doi: 10.1016/j.cpr.2010.11.009

Snyder, C. R. (1994). *The psychology of hope: You can get there from here*. New York, NY: Free Press.

Stanford, M. S., Houston, R. J., Mathias, C. W., Villemarette-Pittman, N. R., Helfritz, L. E., & Conklin, S. M. (2003). Characterizing aggressive behaviour. *Assessment, 10*(2), 183–190. doi: 10.1177/1073191103010002009

Strand, S., & Belfrage, H. (2001). Comparison of hcr-20 scores in violent mentally disordered men and women: Gender differences and similarities. *Psychology, Crime & Law, 7*(1–4), 71–79. doi: 10.1080/10683160108401784

Suarez, A., Lee, D. Y., Rowe, C., Gomez, A. A., Murowchick, E., & Linn, P. L. (2014). Freedom project: Nonviolent communication and mindfulness training in prison. *Sage Open, 4*(1), 1–10. doi: 10.1177/2158244013516154

Tapscott, J. L., Hancock, M., & Hoaken, P. N. S. (2012). Severity and frequency of reactive and instrumental violent offending divergent validity of subtypes of violence in an adult forensic sample. *Criminal Justice and Behavior, 39*(2), 202–219. doi: 10.1177/0093854811429647

Teasdale, J. D., Segal, Z. V., Williams, J. M. G., Ridgeway, V. A., Soulsby, J. M., & Lau, M. A. (2000). Prevention of relapse/ recurrence in major depression by mindfulness-based cognitive therapy. *Journal of Consulting and Clinical Psychology, 68*(4), 615–623. doi: 10.1037//0022-006X.68.4.615

Ware, J., Cieplucha, C., & Matsuo, D. (2011). The Violent Offenders Therapeutic Programme (VOTP) – Rationale and effectiveness. *Australasian Journal of Correctional Staff Development, 6*, 1–12.

Wong, S. C., & Gordon, A. (2006). The validity and reliability of the Violence Risk Scale: A treatment-friendly violence risk assessment tool. *Psychology, Public Policy, and Law, 12*(3), 279–309. doi: 10.1037/1076-8971.12.3.279

World Health Organization. (2014). *Global status report on violence prevention*. Geneva: World Health Organization.

Yang, M., Wong, S. C., & Coid, J. (2010). The efficacy of violence prediction: A meta-analytic comparison of nine risk assessment tools. *Psychological Bulletin, 136*(5), 740–767. doi: 10.1037/a0020473

Zamble, E., & Quinsey, V. L. (1997). *The criminal recidivism process*. New York, NY: Cambridge University Press.

10 The development of psychological treatment programmes for incarcerated sex offenders in Hong Kong

From relapse prevention to a positive treatment approach

Ka Po Jessica Chan and Chin Pang Woo

Introduction

The psychological treatment of incarcerated sexual offenders in Hong Kong has been developing since 1998. Over time, various types of interventions, ranging from pharmacological to behavioural approaches, have been applied to this group of clients (Yates, 2002). Although there is a debate pertaining to the demonstration of the effectiveness of various treatment, current research seems to support cognitive behavioural treatment (CBT) as having the greatest impact on reducing recidivism (Hanson et al., 2002). A common component of CBT, relapse prevention (RP), has been described as the "treatment of choice" for sexual offenders (Laws, Hudson, & Ward, 2000). This chapter will discuss how the Sex Offenders' Evaluation and Treatment Unit (ETU) adopted different approaches when developing its treatment programmes.

Relapse prevention model

The ETU's programmes are heavily based on the RP model, which originated in the substance abuse literature in the early 1980s when Alan Marlatt began to disseminate research into the determinants of relapse, particularly for alcoholics (Marlatt, 1985), according to the risk, need, and responsivity (RNR) principles and the principle of professional discretion (Andrews & Bonta, 2010a, 2010b). The RP model assumes that at the outset, the client is committed to avoiding the prohibited behaviour and believes that he can do so. However, on encountering a negative emotional state or interpersonal conflict, a relapsing offender's sense of control is threatened and the offender begins to fantasise about sexual offending. Fantasising about sexual crimes can produce a sense of failure and distress. At the same time, the offender begins to anticipate the short-term rewards of sexual offending. Together, these two phenomena drive him to commit sexual offending behaviours (Polaschek, 2003).

The risk principle is that more extensive and intensive treatment and resources should be allocated to higher risk offenders whose risk levels are derived from actuarial measures based on static risk factors that are basically unchangeable. The need principle means that the treatment should be focused on modifying those changeable (dynamic) features shown to be criminogenic in predicting future sexual reoffending. The responsivity principle is that therapists should be flexible in adjusting their treatment approach and content according to the characteristics of each client (e.g., intellectual level, treatment readiness, literacy level, etc.). The principle of professional discretion simply means that the therapists can override the other three principles in justifiable situations.

RP and RNR are concerned with risk management, where the primary aim of treating offenders is to avoid harm to the community rather than to improve their quality of life (Andrews & Bonta, 2010a, 2010b; Gendreau, 1996). The hope is that by identifying and managing dynamic risk factors (criminogenic needs: e.g., poor problem-solving skills, negative emotionality, and deviant sexual arousal), offending rates will be reduced. From the perspective of these models, the enhancement of offenders' functioning is not a primary objective of therapeutic intervention. The relationship between offenders' level of well-being and recidivism is an instrumental one; it is a means to the end of reduced risk to the community.

Strength-based approach

The application of the RP and RNR probably does represent a significant advancement in the treatment of sexual offenders (Looman & Abracen, 2013; Polaschek, 2003), but these offenders suffer from a variety of problems. However, researchers have provided a detailed theoretical critique of the RP model (e.g., Hudson, Ward, & Marshall, 1992; Ward & Hudson, 1996; Ward, 2000) and RNR principles (e.g., Laws & Ward, 2011; Ward & Stewarts, 2003; Ward, Mann, & Gannon, 2007).

Instead of focusing treatment exclusively on negative terms (i.e., focusing on the elimination of negative attitudes, the reduction of cognitive distortions, and the extinction of sexual deviancy), Ward and Stewart (2003) proposed a strength-based approach, namely the Good Lives Model (GLM), which promotes the enhancement of strengths, skills, and abilities rather than the suppression of negative behaviour in an attempt to promote a "good life." They asserted that enhancing sexual offenders' overall functioning will lead them to attain the goals of a good life, which in turn will reduce their need to offend. It aims at equipping individuals with the necessary internal and external conditions to secure primary human goods in socially acceptable and personally meaningful ways. The underlying notion of the model is that all meaningful human actions reflect attempts to achieve primary human goods (Emmons, 1999; Ward, 2002). Primary goods are actions, states of affairs, characteristics, experiences, and states of mind that are viewed as intrinsically beneficial to human beings and are therefore sought for their own sake rather than as a means to some more fundamental ends (Deci & Ryan, 2000). Primary goods are viewed as objectives and as tied to certain ways of living that, if followed, involve the actualisation of potentialities that are distinctively human. These ideas are actually similar to Maslow's (1954) earlier notion that people strive for self-actualisation and that achieving this state will result in a satisfied and happy person. Ward and Stewart (2003) proposed that individuals can, however, be mistaken about what is really of value and what is in their best interests; human goods are not simply individual preferences or desires. Primary goods emerge out of basic needs, whereas instrumental or secondary goods provide concrete ways of securing these goods (e.g., certain types of work, relationships, or language ability). The nature of the primary goods sought by individuals and the weightings assigned to these goods are formed in specific cultural contexts and represent individuals' interpretations of interpersonal and social events. According to Ward and Stewart (2003), the problem of criminal behaviour exists in the means used to secure goods, the lack of scope within a good life plan, or the presence of conflict among goals. A primary aim of therapy would be to identify the types of relationships an offender finds satisfying and socially acceptable and to equip him with the necessary internal and external conditions to increase his chances of establishing these relationships. Secondary goods provide concrete ways of achieving primary human goods within a particular context, typically offering a range of possible models and opportunities. The choice to seek a particular cluster of secondary goods will be determined by an offender's preferences, strengths, and opportunities (Ward & Stewart, 2003).

Ward and Stewart (2003) proposed that there are nine primary human goods that every person is pursuing: life (including healthy living and functioning), knowledge, excellence in play and work (including mastery experiences), excellence in agency (i.e., autonomy and self-directedness), inner peace (i.e., freedom from emotional turmoil and stress), friendship/relatedness (including intimate, romantic, and family relationships), community, spirituality (in the broad sense of finding meaning and purpose in life), happiness, and creativity. It is the job of therapists to help their clients to identify some (if not all) of these human goods (inner needs) and secure ways to fulfil them incrementally. In fact, Ward and Marshall (2004) provided a detailed account of how a therapist can implement a good lives approach with clients. In this approach, the therapist works collaboratively with clients. First, it is necessary to help them to identify an individualised set of goals (inner needs that they are pursuing) that are consistent with their interests and abilities and that would lead to the attainment of a more satisfying life (e.g., inner peace and friendship). Then, the therapist helps them identify both the skills that need to be enhanced and the attitudes that need to be changed in order to achieve these goals (e.g., proper anger management and heterosexual relationship skills). Next, the clients are required to apply the new knowledge, skills, and attitudes in their daily life. As these phases evolve, the clients and the therapist work together to re-examine and modify these goals if necessary.

Integration of models

Even though the GLM sounds very promising and comprehensive, ETU staff do not believe that it should completely replace the RP model and the RNR principles as sexual offenders do vary in their precipitating factors, risk levels, criminogenic needs, and reasons for sexual offending and there are situations that they should avoid from time to time in order to reduce the risk of reoffending and facilitate case management. For instance, while the GLM suggests that solely enhancing the sexual offenders' capacity to meet their needs properly and prosocially should lead to extinction of their sexual deviancy, we believe with the limited evidence available at this stage that it is still essential to target deviant sexual interests in a successful sexual offender treatment programme (Marshall, 1997). Indeed, we even suggest that the two should actually be complementing rather than conflicting with each other. In fact, our notion is shared by Ward and Stewart (2003), who agreed that the RNR model should be used in conjunction with the good lives framework, which essentially grounds the RNR model and deals more systematically with the issue of offender motivation and responsivity. They even contend that using both models will help therapists understand more clearly the role of motivation in offending and also maximise the chances of creating a sound therapeutic alliance, thereby improving treatment outcome. ETU psychologists have begun to incorporate the strength-based approach into their treatment work with sexual offenders.

One step forward: Positive interventions

Given the recent contemporary positive psychology movement led by Dr Martin Seligman and Dr Mihaly Csikszentmihalyi, researchers have demonstrated the effectiveness and contribution of the positive interventions being used in the field of addictive behaviours (e.g., Akhtar & Boniwell, 2010; Lindgren, Mullins, Neighbors, & Blayney, 2010; Logan, Kilmer, & Marlatt, 2010). A positive intervention is defined as "an intervention, therapy, or activity primarily aimed at increasing positive feelings, positive behaviors, or positive cognitions, as opposed to ameliorating pathology or fixing negative thoughts or maladaptive behavior patterns" (Sin & Lyubomirsky, 2009). Positive interventions can take various different forms. Practices shown to successfully enhance well-being include writing letters of gratitude (e.g., Boehm, Lyubomirsky, & Sheldon, 2011; Layous, Lee, Choi, & Lyubomirsky, 2013), counting one's blessings (e.g., Froh, Sefick, & Emmons, 2008), being practising optimistic acts (e.g., Layous, Nelson, & Lyubomirsky, 2013), performing acts of kindness (e.g., Sheldon, Boehm, & Lyubomirsky, 2012), and using one's strengths in new ways (Seligman, Steen, Park, & Peterson, 2005). Positive interventions such as these, along with other exercises designed to promote kindness, generosity, and mindfulness (Layous, Chancellor, Lyubomirsky, Wang, & Doraiswamy, 2011), have been shown to increase positive emotions, which have in turn been predicted to lead to increases in psychological, cognitive, social, and physical resources; increased life satisfaction; and decreased depression (Fredrickson, Cohn, Coffey, Pek, & Finkel, 2008). All of these findings are indeed consistent with our notion of pursuing "a good life" in the work of the ETU. Over the last few years, the ETU has tried to incorporate these interventions into its treatment programmes and therapeutic community – "The Positive Intervention Campaign" – in order to enhance the well-being of its clients.

From theory to practice in Hong Kong

Having discussed how the most influential theories have affected the ETU's programmes, we will now discuss how its programmes have evolved over the years. Before the 1990s, convicted sexual offenders were sentenced to one of three different categories of prisons according to the length of their sentence. Upon admission, sexual offenders were assessed by an institution-based psychologist and services were rendered according to their needs, mainly their problems adjusting to the penal setting. In 1998, the Correctional Services Department (CSD) devoted itself to developing and implementing more specialised psychological services and programmes for sexual offenders with a view to reducing their reoffending behaviours in order to create a safer society and to help them reintegrate into the community after release.

The setting up of the ETU

The CSD took the initiative to set up the first residential treatment unit for sexual offenders in East Asia in 1998. The ETU was established to develop systematic and comprehensive psychological services for adult sexual offenders. The unit is designed to provide a special therapeutic environment within a discrete unit that promotes mutual care and support among sexual offenders so as to facilitate behavioural change. The unit applies the concept of the "therapeutic community" (TC), which is a widely used approach in prison-based sexual offender treatment that provides more opportunities to increase the intensity of the treatment experience beyond group therapy sessions and is regarded as an extension of the group therapy process (Ware, Frost, & Hoy, 2015). All relationships are considered potentially therapeutic, and attention is directed towards all social experiences, interactions, and activities in pursuit of therapeutic goals. Sexual offenders are also encouraged to practice their newly acquired personal and interpersonal skills; this helps both the generalisation and maintenance of the treatment outside treatment room and over time.

Focused development of the ETU

For quality assurance, the CSD launched the project of "Focused Development of the ETU" in 2008. A treatment advisory panel was formed which comprised of some renowned experts in the field, including Dr William Marshall from Rockwood Psychological Services of Canada; Mr Robert McGrath, who previously worked as a Clinical Director of the Vermont Treatment Program for Sexual Aggressors at the Vermont Department of Corrections, USA; and a distinguished local scholar, Professor Fanny M.C. Cheung, from the Chinese University of Hong Kong (CUHK). The aim of the panel is to enhance the services provided in the ETU towards international standards using an incremental approach. As part of the project of Focused Development of the ETU, the treatment advisory panel conducted two service reviews of the rehabilitative services for sexual offenders in 2009 and 2013. These periodic reviews led to the adoption of the best practices of countries with well-developed programmes for sexual offenders. Special consideration was also given to the unique characteristics of local offenders, the criminal justice system, and the cultural background of Hong Kong. Recommendations were made pointing to future service enhancement. The panel recognised that local rehabilitative services for sexual offenders were of a high standard and generally in line with international practice. The recommendations helped the ETU to set up standards for best practices in the treatment of sexual offenders in Hong Kong, and these standards serve as useful guidelines for future service development and quality assurance. The following sections cover how, using the risk management approach, the ETU's services, namely assessment, treatment during incarceration, and post-release supervision, are provided to sexual offenders at different stages.

Stage 1: Assessment

Psychologists carry out an in-depth assessment of the risk-need profile of each offender upon their admission to correctional institutions. If the sexual offender is assessed as being in need of treatment, he will be encouraged to voluntarily participate in ETU treatment programmes.

The use of actuarial assessment

It has been suggested that actuarially assessed risk is always better than unstructured clinical judgment when assessing sexual offenders (Hanson & Morton-Bourgon, 2005). After studying some commonly used actuarial risk assessment tools from overseas, ETU psychologists adopted STATIC-99R (Hanson & Thornton, 2000; Helmus, Hanson, & Morton-Bourgon, 2011) and STABLE-2006 (Hanson, Harris, Scott, & Helmus, 2007; Harris & Hanson, 2010) as useful tools to assess both the reoffending risk and treatment needs of sexual offenders. The STATIC-99R covers some non-changeable life factors related to risk of sexual recidivism which are generally historical in nature, whereas STABLE-2006 covers dynamic risk factors such as the personality characteristics, skill deficits, and learned behaviours related to the risk of sexual recidivism which are usually regarded to be enduring traits but more amendable to intervention. Static factors include age, history of intimate relationships, offending history (both violent and sexual), and some characteristics of the victim. Stable factors cover 13 factors under five clusters, namely significant social influence, intimacy deficits, general self-regulation, sexual self-regulation, and cooperation with supervision. These factors are also called an individual's criminogenic needs, and these needs become the treatment target and have to be addressed by the offender to reduce his reoffending risk. With the combined risk-need profile, psychologists gain more understanding of a sexual offender's relative risk of sexual recidivism and can prioritise treatment to those with relatively higher risk and need and assign a sufficient length of treatment for them.

Localisation of risk assessment tools

When assessment tools from Western countries have been adopted in Hong Kong, their applicability to the local population has been questioned, as only Western subject samples were used in their development. In 2005, the Hong Kong Risk Assessment Scale for Sexual Offenders (HK-RASSO), a localised actuarial assessment tool for adult sex offenders in Hong Kong, was jointly developed by the CSD and the CUHK (see Table 10.1). This scale predicts sexual offenders' probability of recidivism using a set of static predictors, including an individual's social history and offence-related information. The HK-RASSO is based on actuarial risk assessment using statistically significant predictors derived from the case records of a sample of sexual offenders in Hong Kong. It has been found to have satisfactory inter-rater reliability. The HK-RASSO has a significant positive association with Static-99. There are three sets of scales in the HK-RASSO for predicting different kinds of sexual offender's recidivism, namely, general recidivism, sexual recidivism, and violent recidivism.

In order to further polish the ETU's risk assessment tools, another five-year Risk-Needs Assessment Tool Research Project with the CUHK was launched in 2011. Psychologists are aiming to construct and validate four assessment tools for adult and young sexual offenders, which include both static and dynamic risk factors. ETU psychologists will also increase the sample size and extend the follow-up period based on previous version of the HK-RASSO.

Stage 2: Treatment programmes during incarceration

Over the years, the treatment programmes at the ETU have been evolving. ETU psychologists have adopted the open group format since 2008, having used the closed group format for many years. The use of the open group format allows each sexual offender to progress at his own pace and involves repetitive learning throughout the group process (Ware et al., 2009). In some difficult cases, offenders may be temporarily suspended from the group treatment, but they can

Table 10.1 Some sample items from the HK-RASSO (2005)

General recidivism	Age of current offence, number of previous convictions, employment
Sexual recidivism	Number of minor sex offences, deviant sexual interest, negative relationship with caretakers in childhood
Violent recidivism	Age of first offence, failure during community supervision period

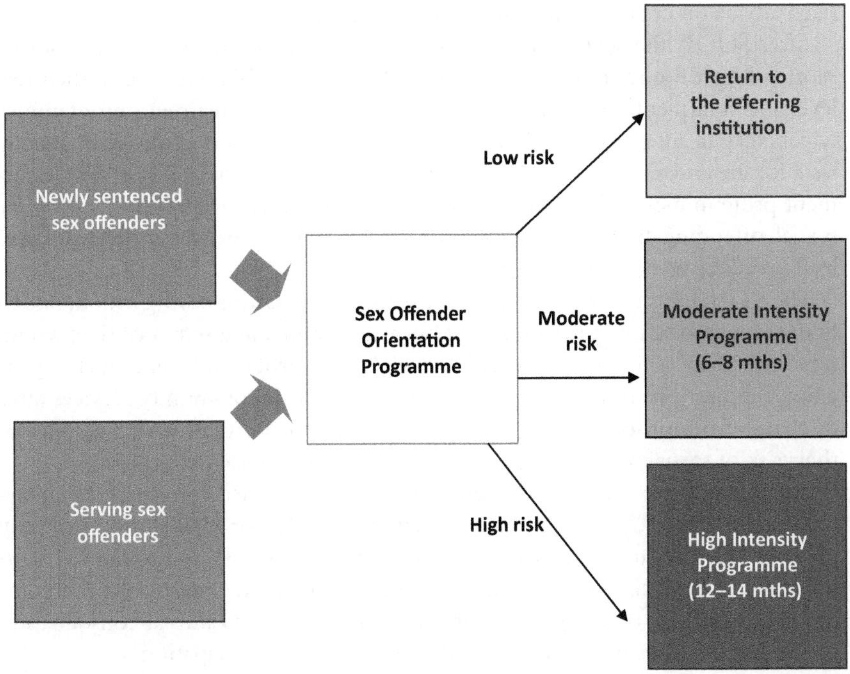

Figure 10.1 The admission flow to the ETU

re-join it without interrupting the group flow. We now summarise how the sexual offender treatment programme at the ETU is implemented (see Figure 10.1).

Programme type and matching

A range of specialised treatment programmes – Sexual Offender Orientation Programme (SOOP), Moderate Intensity Programme (MIP), High Intensity Programme (HIP), Short-Termer Programme (STP), and Booster Programme (BP) – have been designed to match sexual offenders' risk levels and treatment needs. To enhance treatment effectiveness and to maximise the use of resources on various types of programme, a systematic and evidence-based programme matching procedure has been adopted in the ETU. Treatment intensity for a particular sexual offender rests on his reoffending risk, dynamic criminogenic needs, and responsivity, as assessed by a psychologist.

The SOOP is the first direct service offered to sexual offenders during their stay in the ETU, which usually lasts for a month. It is a structured programme for staff from the ETU to evaluate a sexual offender, enhance his readiness and motivation for treatment, and introduce him to the range of psychological services available during and after incarceration. It also helps those sexual offenders who need advice on coping with adjustment to prison.

After SOOP, the sexual offenders who are considered to be at risk of sexual reoffending are admitted onto either the MIP or the HIP according to their risk level and treatment needs. The MIP and HIP are group treatment programmes which vary in intensity and coverage. The treatment period of the MIP usually lasts for around six months, whereas the HIP lasts more than a year. The treatment programmes aim at helping sexual offenders to take responsibility for their sexual offending behaviours, develop skills to prevent sexual reoffending, and lead productive and law-abiding lives.

The STP targets those sexual offenders who are assessed as having a moderate to high sexual reoffending risk and need but whose remaining sentence time would not allow them to complete the MIP or HIP. This programme aims at strengthening the motivation for change and networking with community services after discharge from prison. Some brief treatment to enhance their understanding of their risk of sexual reoffending and increase their self-efficacy is provided.

The BP is a pre-release treatment programme designed for sexual offenders before discharge. Upon completion of either the MIP or HIP during the early phase of their sentence, sexual offenders will enter the BP programme 4 to 6 months before their discharge to prepare for their reintegration into the community by revising their self-management plan. The BP also aims at consolidating the treatment gains obtained from earlier programme participation.

Treatment content

Treatment at the ETU is conducted through group therapy and is based on CBT. Group treatment is supplemented by homework assignments, individual treatment, skills training, and skills practice. Over years of service development, the treatment content has been revised several times using different major theories from the field. The treatment modules are summarised in Table 10.2, and an overview of the all-staff approach and the positive intervention campaign is presented in Table 10.3.

Stage 3: Post-release supervision

Pre-release review

Sexual offenders go through a pre-release assessment before their discharge (see Figure 10.2). In the local Hong Kong context, sexual offenders whose sentences are two years or above are subject to a period of compulsory supervision and rehabilitation provided jointly by the CSD and the Social Welfare Department under the Post-Release Supervision Scheme (PRSS). Psychological follow-up in the community may be recommended as part of the consideration of their risk management plan. Similar to the situation in other countries, sexual offenders, especially those with chronic psychosexual problems, still have the risk of

Table 10.2 Summary of treatment content by module

Module	*Treatment content*	*Authors' observations*
1 Understanding Offending Behaviour	• This module is composed of two parts: autobiography and the offence chain. • The autobiography includes the individual's family relationships, courtship experiences, marital relationship, work, social life, and other major life events or crises. It helps the offender to understand his primary human good/inner needs, previous life goals, and previous ways of achieving his goals and to improve awareness of personal characteristics, with more emphasis on identifying personal needs and strengths in the process. It focuses on the individual sexual offender as a person instead of solely focusing on his sexual offending behaviours. It highlights the positive life cycle and protective factors which can instil the hope for change in an individual. • The offence chain is briefly discussed to identify key risk factors that contribute to an individual's offending behaviours. Psycho-education is given on the formation of offending behaviour and the "offence pathway" according to the self-regulation model, such as the major components of the offence pathway and offending behaviour as an inappropriate means to use in striving to achieve personal goals.	Most sexual offenders are willing to reveal their personal history. Some difficulties in expressing the impact of having an absent father and relationship problems.
2 Self-esteem Enhancement	• Although self-esteem is not found to be a predictor of recidivism, a lower level of self-esteem is associated with higher sexual recidivism rates (Thornton, Beech, & Marshall, 2004). • The mediating role of self-esteem is discussed (Marshall, Marshall, Serran, & O'Brien, 2003). Sexual offenders with low self-esteem are more likely to respond to the stress and problems of life by generating an acute negative mood that puts them at risk of reoffending (Serran & Marshall, 2006), and they are also found to have more cognitive distortions about victims and offending behaviours because cognitive distortions help in bolstering their self-esteem in the face of this deviant behaviour (Pervan & Hunter, 2007). • After considering all these issues, this module focuses on the positive features of the offender rather than exclusively on his past aberrant behaviour. By enhancing offenders' self-esteem, it is expected that they will have increased motivation to effectively participate in treatment, to put the skills they learn into practice, and to attain a secure sense of self-worth by the end of their treatment.	Most sexual offenders respond quite well to this module as it helps to boost their self-esteem by using their strengths in daily life.

(*Continued*)

Table 10.2 (Continued)

Module	*Treatment content*	*Authors' observations*
3 Cognitive Restructuring (CR)	• It has been pointed out in the literature that sexual offenders usually tend to shift blame, deny responsibility, and rationalise and minimise their offence (Happel & Auffrey, 1995; Levenson & Macgowan, 2004; Mann, 2000). These excuses and justifications produced at the time of offending are products of the underlying schemas, thereby forming targets for treatment. • It is emphasised that different underlying schemas point to different interpretations of the same situation. The treatment process helps sexual offenders to identify maladaptive cognitions related to their sexual offending and problematic lifestyle. • Sexual offenders identify and label their own schema as well as generate different hypotheses which can develop and strength alternative self-talk. Developing more adaptive cognitions can facilitate an adaptive and prosocial lifestyle and hence reduce sexual offences.	CR skills are more useful when diffused into other modules to allow more detailed discussion than when focused on in isolation.
4 Mood Management	• Both negative mood regulation and positive mood regulation are discussed in this module. • Three coping styles, namely problem-focused, emotion-focused, and avoidance-focused coping, and their relationship to sexual reoffending are explored for each sexual offender. • Participants also learn and practise effective cognitive and behavioural strategies to better manage their emotions. • Role play is one of the skills used to rehearse effective coping and practise the necessary skills. On the other hand, participants learn how to enhance their positive emotions. • It has been found that positive intervention lastingly increases happiness while reducing depressive symptoms (Seligman, Rashid, & Park, 2006). Participants will count their blessings, perform acts of kindness, appreciate others, etc.	Frontline staff help a lot in assessing offenders' behavioural changes in their daily life.
5 Relationship Skill Building	• Although most sexual offender treatment programmes cover the deficits in a broad range of social skills, more solid evidence points to the intimacy and attachment deficits of this group of offenders (Marshall, Marshall, Serran, & Fernandez, 2006; Ward, Polaschek, & Beech, 2006). • Treatment is tailor-made for an offender's dysfunctional attachment style and aims to increase intimacy skills. • Instead of teaching a broad range of social skills, each offender's social skills deficits are targeted and trained in a step-by-step manner, including initiating a conversation, maintaining a conversation, expressing opinions assertively, and conflict resolution.	Locally, sexual offenders display a spectrum of relationship problems ranging from social alienation, interpersonal

	• Homework assignments are given during their stay at ETU to help generalise the skills learnt to daily life. • All ETU staff are informed of inmates' respective treatment targets and play a role in observing and training the inmates.	mistrust, and sexual promiscuity to deficits in basic social skills.
6 Developing Healthy Sexuality	• This module aims at promoting healthy sexuality. For some offenders, the focus will be on managing their deviant sexual interest, whereas most of them will be managing their sexual preoccupation. • The role of either deviant sexual interest or sexual preoccupation in contributing to sexual offending behaviours is also discussed. • The treatment of sexual preoccupation focuses on controlling the addictive behaviour and helping the person develop a healthy sexuality (Schneider & Irons, 2001). • Helping sexual offenders to successfully handle their sexual preoccupation problems is believed to be useful in reducing their risk of reoffending and helping their subsequent development of stable and fulfilling intimate relationships.	Most sexual offenders have more problems concerning sexual preoccupation than problems concerning deviant sexual interest.
7 Self-management Plan	• By devising their own good life plan, sexual offenders can develop more adaptive identities with personal primary goods and establish more concrete ways to secure these goods. • They integrate their learnt skills and concepts into their release plan, and this helps them in achieving their personal life goals, such as accommodation, employment, use of leisure time, mood management, handling of sexual needs, and strengthening their social relationships with family and friends. Ways to manage high-risk situations in the future are also explored.	Most sexual offenders are more forward-looking when discharged from prison with their plan.

Table 10.3 An overview of the all-staff approach and the positive intervention campaign

All-staff approach
The ETU adopts an all-staff approach as frontline correctional staff usually play a significant role in fostering the therapeutic environment and monitoring skills practice in daily prison life. Regular staff meetings are held to improve communication and cooperation between treatment providers and frontline correctional staff. This approach further enhances the skills monitoring, skills practice, and skills consolidation necessary for sexual offenders to develop a satisfying and law-abiding life after release.
The Positive Intervention Campaign
Several topics based on positive psychology, namely, optimism, appreciation of others and self, blessings, gratitude, and savouring, are included in this campaign. Each topic usually lasts for two to three months, during which time every ETU participant is encouraged to participate. For example, during the savouring section of the campaign, participants have to experience a positive life event slowly and in detail. In the first two weeks, they have to write about a positive life event and share it with others. Then, in the third and fourth weeks, they write about a positive event that happened at the ETU and share it with others. Their sharing is posted on the ETU Facebook page, where they can share with everyone in the therapeutic community. Lastly, every participant gives their comments on the ETU Facebook page. It is hoped that these exercises will continue to enhance their attention to positive events and increase their positive emotions.

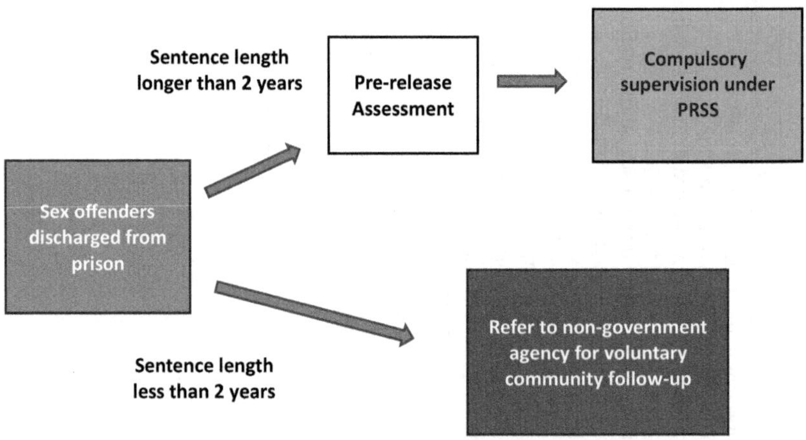

Figure 10.2 Post-release arrangements

reoffending at the time of discharge. Risk assessment at this stage focuses on the extent of change in the dynamic risk factors after treatment that might moderate the risk level measured in the early stage of imprisonment. With a proper pre-release review and a more detailed risk management plan, specialised supervision conditions can be devised for high-risk sexual offenders prior to release. Proper risk management through intensive supervision and rehabilitation after discharge is therefore very important to reduce the reoffending risk.

Community supervision and support

For those sexual offenders under statutory supervision, various disciplines, including supervision staff, social workers, psychologists, and psychiatrists, will be involved in community follow-up when deemed beneficial. Sexual offenders will be regularly followed up by a specialised supervision team. Multidisciplinary case conferences are also held regularly for high-risk sex offenders in order to monitor and better manage their risk in the community. During regular meetings with the offenders, a psychologist will also use some actuarial measures, namely ACUTE (Hanson et al., 2007), in clinical practice. ACUTE covers risk factors with a short or unstable temporal duration that can change rapidly due to environmental or intrapersonal conditions such as victim access, sexual preoccupation, hostility, rejection of supervision, emotional collapse, collapse of social supports, and substance abuse. The last three factors are also related to general recidivism. As this measure compares offenders who recidivate soon after release with those who do not reoffend, ETU staff become more alert to some imminent risk factors which might lead to reoffending in the community.

For those sexual offenders not under statutory supervision but in need of community support, the CSD took the lead in assisting the setting up of voluntary rehabilitation services with a non-government agency. The Caritas Community Support Project on Development of Sexual Health was launched in 2008. This project assists discharged sexual offenders in their reintegration into the community, particularly those who are not subject to compulsory supervision after discharge. Its services include individual counselling, a peer support group, lifestyle restructuring activities, and public education.

A case illustration: Ben

Pre-sentencing assessment

Ben (a pseudo case), a 29-year-old male, attended the SOOP at the ETU after being sentenced to six years for rape. During the assessment, he was found to have had a drinking problem since he was a teenager. His father was also addicted to alcohol and often got drunk. Some domestic violence was reported when he was little. His father passed away when Ben was in his early twenties. Ben lived with his mother, who, although said to be rather submissive, gave him affection. His mother visited him regularly during his imprisonment.

His childhood was generally unremarkable. At school, he described himself as being a quiet student without any conduct problems. Some experiences of being bullied by his classmates were noted. He sometimes engaged in playing the guitar. He started working after graduating from Form Five and was a waiter for more than 10 years. He changed jobs frequently as he always complained about the working hours being too long and the poor career prospects. His social network was limited to his colleagues and the relationships were rather shallow. He had developed one or two brief courtships since his early adulthood. However, these did not last longer than a year. He expressed difficulties in resolving conflicts with his girlfriends once the passionate love faded over time. He admitted indulging in Internet pornography and increasing his alcohol use, especially when he was faced with work stress or conflicts with a girlfriend. He would spend a few hours a day viewing pornography. He also reported frequent visits to prostitutes.

With regard to his index offence, he alleged that on the day of the offence, he was distressed by the conflicts he was experiencing with his girlfriend. After work, he drank a few cans of beer before returning home, where he met his victim, a 23-year-old girl who was his neighbour, although he did not know her personally. He talked with her for a while and then had sexual intercourse with her on the staircase. He attributed his offending behaviours to the influence of alcohol and believed that the victim had flirted with him first. The assessment result of his risk-need profile is presented in Table 10.4 below.

He was scored on the Static-99R, Stable-2007, and HK-RASSO. His static-99R score of 4 was in the medium to high category, and his Stable-2007 score of 11 was in the medium category. His combined risk category score placed him in the medium to high category. His HK-RASSO score was 6. Considering his current scores on these static and dynamic risk measures, his overall risk of sexually reoffending was considered to be in the medium to high category.

During his first week, he appeared to be rather reserved and quiet. After attending the group sessions of the SOOP, he understood that his psychosexual problems were quite common among other sexual offenders. He became more forthcoming and less shameful in the therapeutic community. As reported by the frontline staff, his participation was said to be satisfactory as he became more open in discussing his problems. In his homework assignments, he showed some readiness to understand more about his problems that had contributed to his index offence. He appeared to be more ready for change and indicated some genuine motivation. With his medium to high risk-need profile, he was recommended for the MIP.

MIP treatment progress

After dwelling in the therapeutic community of the ETU for a while, Ben became gradually accustomed to talking, living, and working with other ETU group members. Being nurtured by the atmosphere of group cohesion and self-disclosure, he began to develop a sense of belonging and to perceive himself as one of the members of the ETU community. He also developed more confidence in disclosing himself to others. The ongoing Positive Intervention Campaign also helped him to learn to appreciate himself and others, count his own blessings, think optimistically, and experience pleasures in his daily life, which in turn enhanced his positive cognitions, emotions, and helping behaviours.

Throughout the MIP, Ben underwent many different treatment modules and was noticed to have made significant changes, but only a brief description of some of the relevant core components are provided here as detailed descriptions of the ETU's approach to modifying offence-specific targets are documented elsewhere (e.g., Marshall et al., 2006; Marshall, Marshall, Serran, & O'Brien, 2011).

Results on STATIC-99 and STABLE-2007

Name of Inmate: ________Ben________ Reg. No.: __________________

Sex Offender Evaluation and Treatment Unit

Risks and Needs Evaluation Form

(Revised on 20 July 2012)

Part I: Risks Assessment Battery

Date of Assessment: __________________

Responsible Clinical Psychologist: __________________

A. Hong Kong - Risk Assessment Scale for Sex Offenders on Sexual Recidivism

HK-RASSO-S Coding Form

Predictors		Weighting
1.	Age of first sexual offence	
a	21 or younger	+1
b	22 – 26	+2
c	27 – 42	(+1)
d	43 or older	0
2.	Number of previous minor sexual offence (excluding current)	
a	0	(0)
b	1 – 3	+1
c	4 or more	+7
3.	Deviant sexual interest	
a	Absent	(0)
b	Suspected to be present	+2
c	Present	+3
4.	Negative relationship with caretakers in childhood	
a	Yes	(+2)
b	No	0
5.	Employment	
a	Stable employment	0
b	Unstable employment or unemployment	(+3)
c	Unemployed due to special reasons	+1
6.	Actual sentence length of current offence	
a	Less than or equal to 4 months	(0)
b	More than 4 months	+3

Total: 6

If no information is available in one item, it will be scored as a "0" (zero) and the total score will be prorated as follows: = Total x 20 / (20 – max. possible score of the missing item)

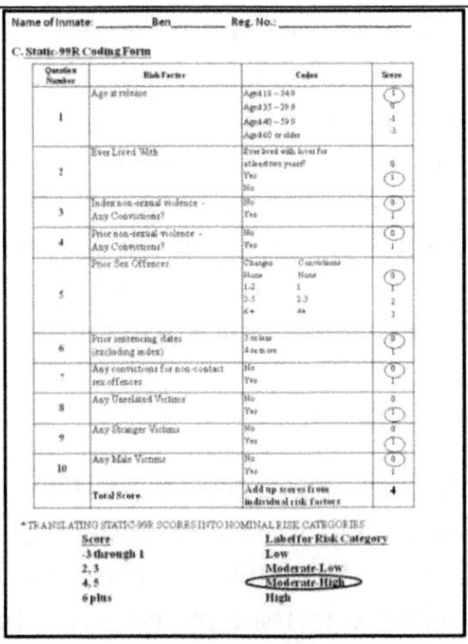

Name of Inmate: ________Ben________ Reg. No.: __________________

C. Static-99R Coding Form

Question Number	Risk Factor	Codes	Score
1	Age at release	Aged 18 – 34.9 Aged 35 – 39.9 Aged 40 – 59.9 Aged 60 or older	(1) 0 -1 -3
2	Ever Lived With	Ever lived with lover for at least two years? Yes No	0 (1)
3	Index non-sexual violence - Any Convictions?	No Yes	(0) 1
4	Prior non-sexual violence - Any Convictions?	No Yes	(0) 1
5	Prior Sex Offences	Charges / Convictions None / None 1-2 / 1 3-5 / 2-3 6+ / 4+	(0) 1 2 3
6	Prior sentencing dates (excluding index)	3 or less 4 or more	(0) 1
7	Any convictions for non-contact sex offences	No Yes	(0) 1
8	Any Unrelated Victims	No Yes	0 (1)
9	Any Stranger Victims	No Yes	0 (1)
10	Any Male Victims	No Yes	(0) 1
	Total Score	Add up scores from individual risk factors	4

*TRANSLATING STATIC-99R SCORES INTO NOMINAL RISK CATEGORIES

Score	Label for Risk Category
-3 through 1	Low
2, 3	Moderate-Low
4, 5	(Moderate-High)
6 plus	High

Results on HK-RASSO

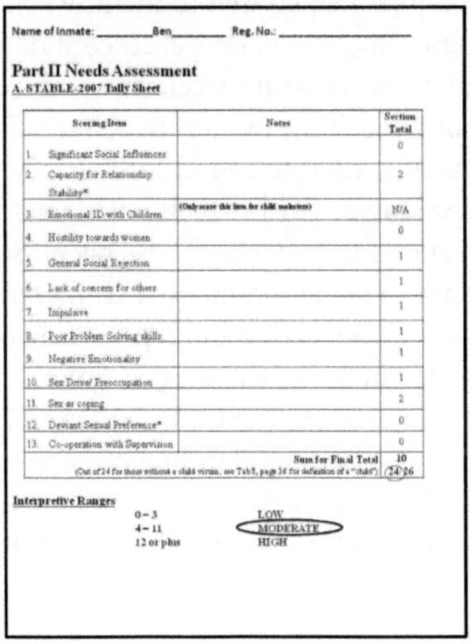

Name of Inmate: ________Ben________ Reg. No.: __________________

Part II Needs Assessment

A. STABLE-2007 Tally Sheet

Scoring Item	Notes	Section Total
1. Significant Social Influences		0
2. Capacity for Relationship Stability*		2
3. Emotional ID with Children	(Only score this item for child molesters)	N/A
4. Hostility towards women		0
5. General Social Rejection		1
6. Lack of concern for others		1
7. Impulsive		1
8. Poor Problem Solving skills		1
9. Negative Emotionality		1
10. Sex Drive/ Preoccupation		1
11. Sex as coping		2
12. Deviant Sexual Preference*		0
13. Co-operation with Supervision		0
	Sum for Final Total	10
	(Out of 24 for those without a child victim, see Tab 8, page 36 for definition of a "child")	(24)/26

Interpretive Ranges

0 – 3	LOW
4 – 11	(MODERATE)
12 or plus	HIGH

Programme Matching

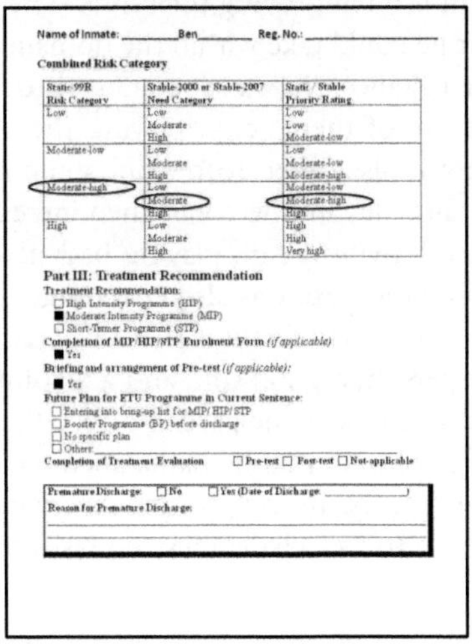

Name of Inmate: ________Ben________ Reg. No.: __________________

Combined Risk Category

Static-99R Risk Category	Stable-2000 or Stable-2007 Need Category	Static / Stable Priority Rating
Low	Low Moderate High	Low Low Moderate-low
Moderate-low	Low Moderate High	Low Moderate-low Moderate-high
(Moderate-high)	Low (Moderate) High	Moderate-low (Moderate-high) High
High	Low Moderate High	High High Very high

Part III: Treatment Recommendation

Treatment Recommendation:

- ☐ High Intensity Programme (HIP)
- ■ Moderate Intensity Programme (MIP)
- ☐ Short-Termer Programme (STP)

Completion of MIP/HIP/STP Enrolment Form *(if applicable)*

- ■ Yes

Briefing and arrangement of Pre-test *(if applicable):*

- ■ Yes

Future Plan for ETU Programme in Current Sentence:

- ☐ Entering into bring-up list for MIP/ HIP/ STP
- ☐ Booster Programme (BP) before discharge
- ☐ No specific plan
- ☐ Others: __________________

Completion of Treatment Evaluation ☐ Pre-test ☐ Post-test ☐ Not-applicable

Premature Discharge: ☐ No ☐ Yes (Date of Discharge: ____________)

Reason for Premature Discharge:

Table 10.4 The assessment result of risk-need profile

Autobiography

After Ben prepared and presented his life history, which covered his relevant and important experiences throughout his life, both Ben and the psychologists gained a deeper understanding of his unhappy childhood experiences and the reasons for his low self-esteem, distorted beliefs about sex, preoccupation with sex, frequent anger outbursts, alcohol abuse issue, and interpersonal relationship and intimacy problems. It also helped him to identify his persistent behavioural, cognitive, and emotional difficulties that could be addressed and managed in treatment later on. Through the process of writing and revealing his life history, the psychologists, group members, and Ben himself were able to identify his primary human goods (e.g., excellence in work and play, inner peace, and friendship and relatedness) and strengths (e.g., helpful, generous, and good at playing the guitar), which were helpful in developing an effective self-management plan that included relevant aspects of the Good Lives Model. The psychologists did not mention anything about his offending history at this stage because they wanted to convince him that their aim, and that of the ETU programme, was to make positive changes rather than find faults.

Self-esteem

Ben's self-esteem module started early in the course of his treatment as he had rather low self-worth. He always held the strong belief that he was "an unlovable person" and "a failure". The ETU psychologists purposefully want to address the self-esteem issue in the early phase of the treatment programme because it serves to persuade clients that the psychologists are concerned not only with their offences but also with their welfare and well-being and that the focus of the treatment is on improving their lives. The psychologists helped Ben to identify actions that he could take within the domain of functioning, where he lacked confidence. For instance, he was encouraged to recognise his signature strengths and make full use of them (e.g., playing the guitar and coaching others in guitar skills). He was also asked to try out some new activities that he found interesting and pleasurable, and he could then increase the frequency with which he engaged in these activities (e.g., playing basketball and chess) in order to boost his sense of self-efficacy. He was also encouraged to prepare a pocket-sized card containing a list of personal features that reflected his good qualities (e.g., being a hardworking person, a good son, and a helpful person), which he read several times every day. Eventually, the psychologists, the supervising staff of the ETU, and even Ben himself found that he had gained more confidence in himself as he began to have more successful and positive experiences. He also became confident that he would be able to face challenges and tasks that were increasingly difficult in the future.

Stress coping, mood management, and social skills

Ben had rather serious anger, mood, and stress management problems, but he often used ineffective and problematic ways to handle his negative moods (e.g., drinking, watching Internet pornography, and sexual indulgence) which often led to a sense of frustration (Cortoni & Marshall, 2001; Marshall, Marshall, & Serran, 2006) and an increased likelihood of committing sexual offending behaviours. He was reported to have lost his temper frequently in prison, especially when he was frustrated by the institutional job arrangements and his negative feelings about being dumped by his ex-girlfriend. The psychologists helped him by identifying and summarising different types of mood as well as effective and ineffective coping styles. The psychologists also assisted him to recognise his maladaptive coping skills and the problems associated with them. As most of his anger and frustration was related to his work stress and relationship problem with his ex-girlfriend, proper stress coping tactics, training on social skills and especially communication skills, intimate relationship skills, proper assertiveness, conflict resolution skills, and effective problem-solving tactics were discussed and rehearsed. In order to provide more opportunities to practise the skills he learned, the psychologists also encouraged him to start using them in his daily life while he was still in custody. While he was asked to report his progress on a regular basis, his learning process was facilitated by fully utilising the ETU's therapeutic community; all the staff and members of ETU were encouraged to practise with him and to provide feedback to him whenever necessary in a supportive manner. Throughout the treatment period, he was observed to have better stress management and anger control and less interpersonal conflicts.

Sexual preoccupation

Although Ben was not suffering from deviant sexual interest, he did have the problem of being preoccupied by sex. The ETU has developed its own protocol for enhancing healthy sexuality and managing sexual preoccupation (see Marshall, Hall, & Woo, in press) for more information on the enhancement of healthy sexuality and the management of sexual preoccupation). The psychologists instructed Ben to use a log to record the time he spent on sexual activities (e.g., masturbation and use of pornography) and then gradually substitute these activities with some healthy and pleasurable activities (e.g., reading books and doing physical exercises). The psychologists also encouraged him to lessen his sexual preoccupation by using the delay and distraction technique and reminder cards. It should be highlighted that the ETU's therapeutic community also played a crucial role in Ben's rehabilitation process. Although Ben reported that he complied very well with the treatment and had made progress in managing his sexual preoccupation, the staff and group members of the ETU revealed that he often masturbated to magazines portraying girls in swimming suits. Eventually, he admitted that he could not focus on these treatment methods because he was so overwhelmed by his sexual fantasies and was sexually preoccupied. The psychologists then motivated him and referred him to see the ETU psychiatrist to consider the option of pharmacological interventions. Such medical interventions are actually considered part of the holistic treatment approach. Winder et al. (2014) and Lievesley, Elliott, Winder, and Norman (2014) have studied and documented pharmacological interventions and their effects. Ben consented to receive pharmacological interventions alongside his ongoing psychological treatment in order to control his sexual preoccupation, and this approach was found to be more effective.

Self-management plan

Apart from assisting Ben to prepare a comprehensive plan on different aspects of his life after release (e.g., family reunion, social support network, intimate relationships, employment, hobbies and interests, management of sexual needs), the psychologists also helped him to list the high-risk situations and conditions that he had to avoid. Unlike the conventional relapse prevention approach to the treatment of sexual offenders that requires clients to generate a long list of avoidance goals, the ETU treatment programme required him to come up with only a very limited number of avoidance goals for a period of time in order to reduce his recidivism risk. In his case, he was required to limit his alcohol consumption in his daily life and avoid jobs where he could have easy access to alcoholic beverages (e.g., working in bars). The psychologists also persuaded him to seek continuous pharmacological treatment after release. In order to increase the likelihood that Ben could adhere to the plan, the psychologists purposely helped him to develop a self-management plan that was easy to attain and practicable by incorporating the elements of the strength-based approach. Ben believed that he could succeed in carrying out the plan because he was convinced that the plan was desirable to him and that it would be personally rewarding if he put his plan into action.

Post-release supervision

As soon as Ben was released into the community, he was closely followed up by his case psychologist and the multidisciplinary team. Not surprisingly, things did not go smoothly as planned. Although he was accepted by his mother, he was afraid of reaching out and reconnecting with his friends as he was worried about being rejected given his subjective stigmatisation as an ex prisoner and a sexual offender. He dared not contact his ex-girlfriend despite the fact that he missed her very much. He also failed to secure a stable job as his work experience was rather limited.

When Ben was interviewed by the psychologist, he was rather upset and frustrated. He admitted to having lapsed into resuming his alcohol and Internet pornography habits for a short while when he was very frustrated, but then he could still remember and implement some of the skills he had learned at the ETU. The psychologist reassured him that a lapse did not necessarily lead to relapse and reminded him of his positive experience in the ETU. The psychologist acknowledged the difficulties that he had encountered since his release and encouraged him to seek tangible support from the social worker and post-release supervision staff of the CSD. The psychologist also revisited the knowledge and skills that he had learned at the ETU and reminded him to adhere to the self-management plan that he had come up with before. In addition, he was reminded of his high-risk situations and ways that he could manage them properly. He reported better adjustment when he was interviewed a few weeks later. Collateral information from the staff of the supervision team also indicated that he was more settled as he was able to find a more stable job and eventually became willing to communicate with his peers.

Evaluation and future directions

Constant evaluation is part of the ETU programme. Several self-report psychometric tests are used to compare the change in offenders after completion of the treatment programme. The results of evaluations suggest that the programme effectively rectifies the participants' criminal thinking and enhances their understanding of their relapse prevention skills, as indicated by the pre- and post-treatment results. The change in these criminogenic factors in a positive direction suggests that the psychological treatment programme is geared towards reducing the recidivism of sexual offenders.

To conclude, psychological treatment for sexual offenders in Hong Kong has been evolving for more than 15 years in an incremental manner. On the basis of many hands-on experiences, the ETU has adapted the mode and content of its programme many times to fit the local context and criminal justice system. The ETU's treatment materials are all localised to be in line with Hong Kong culture. Nevertheless, the road to providing quality services for the treatment of sexual offenders is never ending, and the ETU promotes a multidisciplinary risk management approach to sexual offenders in the field with the aim of providing a good life for sexual offenders as well as a safer society for the public.

Chapter summary points

- The integration of relapse prevention, the Good Lives Model, and positive interventions helps these methods to complement each other and improves the treatment of sexual offenders by managing their risks and needs, enhancing their strengths, and promoting positive emotions at the same time.
- The Evaluation and Treatment Unit (ETU), a residential treatment unit for sexual offenders, has been developed in Hong Kong since 1998, and the concept of the therapeutic community was adopted to improve the effectiveness of treatment.
- Efforts have been made to ensure the standard of best practices in the treatment of sexual offenders through the project of the focused development of the ETU.
- The three stages of services given to a sexual offender under Hong Kong's penal system, namely assessment, treatment during incarceration, and post-release supervision, are highlighted.
- The treatment content has been revised several times, influenced by different major theories from the field, to fit the local context.
- A case illustration is described to enhance understanding of the ETU's treatment approach and delivery.

References

Adjorlolo, S., & Chan, H. C. O. (2016). Determination of competency to stand trial (fitness to plead): An exploratory study in Hong Kong. *Psychiatry, Psychology and Law*. Advance online publication. 1–18. doi: 10.1080/13218719.2016.1247417

Akhtar, M., & Boniwell, I. (2010). Applying positive psychology to alcohol-misusing adolescents: A group intervention. *Groupwork*, *20*(3), 6–31. doi: 10.1921/gpwk.v20i3.707

Andrews, D. A., & Bonta, J. (2010a). *The psychology of criminal conduct* (5th ed.). New Providence, NJ: LexisNexis Matthew Bender.

Andrews, D. A., & Bonta, J. (2010b). Rehabilitating criminal justice policy and practice. *Psychology, Public Policy and Law*, *16*(1), 39–55. doi: 10.1037/a0018362

Boehm, J. K., Lyubomirsky, S., & Sheldon, K. M. (2011). A longitudinal experimental study comparing the effectiveness of happiness-enhancing strategies in Anglo Americans and Asian Americans. *Cognition & Emotion*, *25*, 1263–1272.

Cortoni, F. A., & Marshall, W. L. (2001). Sex as a coping strategy and its relationship to juvenile sexual history and intimacy in sexual offenders. *Sexual Abuse: A Journal of Research and Treatment*, *13*(1), 27–43. doi: 10.1023/A:1009562312658

Deci, E. L., & Ryan, R. M. (2000). The "what" and "why" of goal pursuits: Human needs and the self-determination of behavior. *Psychological Inquiry*, *11*(4), 227–268. doi: 10.1207/S15327965PLI1104_01

Emmons, R. A. (1999). *The psychology of ultimate concerns*. New York, NY: Guilford Press.

Fredrickson, B. L., Cohn, M. A., Coffey, K. A., Pek, J., & Finkel, S. M. (2008). Open hearts build lives: Positive emotions, induced through loving-kindness meditation, build consequential personal resources. *Journal of Personality and Social Psychology*, *95*(5), 1045–1062. doi: 10.1037/a0013262

Froh, J. J., Sefick, W. J., & Emmons, R. A. (2008). Counting blessings in early adolescents: An experimental study of gratitude and subjective well-being. *Journal of School Psychology*, *46*(2), 213–233. doi: 10.1016/j.jsp.2007.03.005

Gendreau, P. (1996). Offender rehabilitation: What we know and what needs to be done. *Criminal Justice and Behavior*, *23*(1), 144–161. doi: 10.1177/0093854896023001010

Hanson, R. K., Gordon, A., Harris, A. J. R., Marques, J. K., Murphy, W., Quinsey, V. L., & Seto, M. C. (2002). First report of the collaborative outcome data project on the effectiveness of psychological treatment for sexual offenders. *Sexual Abuse: A Journal of Research and Treatment*, *14*(2), 169–194. doi: 10.1023/A:1014624315814

Hanson, R. K., Harris, A. J. R., Scott, T.-L., & Helmus, L. (2007). *Assessing the risk of sexual offenders on community supervision: The dynamic supervision project*. User Report, Corrections Research. Ottawa, ON: Public Safety Canada.

Hanson, R. K., & Morton-Bourgon, K. E. (2005). The characteristics of persistent sexual offenders: A meta-analysis of recidivism studies. *Journal of Consulting and Clinical Psychology*, *73*(6), 1154–1163. doi: 10.1037/0022-006X.73.6.1154

Hanson, R. K., & Thornton, D. (2000). Improving risk assessments for sexual offenders: A comparison of three actuarial scales. *Law and Human Behavior*, *24*(1), 119–136. doi: 10.1023/A:1005482921333

Happel, R. M., & Auffrey, J. J. (1995). Sexual offender assessment: Interrupting the dance of denial. *American Journal of Forensic Psychology*, *13*(2), 5–22.

Harris, A., & Hanson, R. K. (2010). Clinical, actuarial and dynamic risk assessment of sexual offenders: Why do things keep changing? *Journal of Sexual Aggression, 16*(3), 296–310. doi: 10.1080/13552600.2010.494772

Helmus, L., Hanson, R. K., & Morton-Bourgon, K. E. (2011). International comparisons of the validity of actuarial risk tools for sexual offenders, with a focus on Static-99. In D. P. Boer, L. A. Craig, R. Eher, M. H. Miner, & F. Pfafflin (Eds.), *International perspectives on the assessment and treatment of sexual offenders: Theory, practice, and research* (pp. 57–83). Chichester, UK: Wiley-Blackwell.

Hudson, S. M., Ward, T., & Marshall, W. L. (1992). The abstinence violation effect in sex offenders: A reformulation. *Behaviour Research and Therapy, 30*(5), 435–441. doi: 10.1016/0005-7967(92)90027-E

Laws, D. R., Hudson, S. M., & Ward, T. (2000). *Remaking relapse prevention with sexual offenders: A sourcebook.* Thousand Oaks, CA: Sage.

Laws, D. R., & Ward, T. (2011). *Desistance and sexual offending: Alternatives to throwing away the keys.* New York, NY: Guilford Press.

Layous, K., Chancellor, J., Lyubomirsky, S., Wang, L. H., & Doraiswamy, P. M. (2011). Delivering happiness: Translating positive psychology intervention research for treating major and minor depressive disorders. *Journal of Alternative and Complementary Medicine, 17*(8), 675–683. doi: 10.1089/acm.2011.0139

Layous, K., Lee, H. C., Choi, I., & Lyubomirsky, S. (2013). Culture matters when designing a successful positive activity: A comparison of the United States and South Korea. *Journal of Cross-Cultural Psychology, 44*(8), 1294–1303. doi: 10.1177/0022022113487591

Layous, K., Nelson, S. K., & Lyubomirsky, S. (2013). What is the optimal way to deliver a positive activity intervention? The case of writing about one's best possible selves. *Journal of Happiness Studies, 14*(2), 635–654. doi: 10.1007/s10902-012-9346-2

Levenson, J. S., & Macgowan, M. J. (2004). Engagement, denial, and treatment progress among sexual offenders in group therapy. *Sexual Abuse: A Journal of Research and Treatment, 16*(1), 49–63. doi: 10.1023/B:SEBU.0000006284.33837.d7

Lievesley, R., Elliott, H. J., Winder, B., & Norman, C. (2014). Understanding service users' and therapists' experiences of pharmacological treatment for sexual preoccupation and/or hypersexuality in incarcerated sexual offenders. *Journal of Forensic Psychiatry & Psychology, 25*(3), 262–287. doi: 10.1080/14789949.2014.909867

Lindgren, K. P., Mullins, P. M., Neighbors, C., & Blayney, J. A. (2010). Curiosity killed the cocktail? Curiosity, sensation seeking, and alcohol related problems in college women. *Addictive Behaviors, 35*(5), 513–516. doi: 10.1016/j.addbeh.2009.12.024

Logan, D. E., Kilmer, J. R., & Marlatt, G. A. (2010). The virtuous drinker: Character virtues as correlates and moderators of college student drinking and consequences. *Journal of American College Health, 58*(4), 317–324. doi: 10.1080/07448480903380326

Looman, J., & Abracen, J. (2013). The risk need responsivity model of offender rehabilitation: Is there really a need for a paradigm shift? *International Journal of Behavioral Consultation and Therapy, 8*(3–4), 30–36. doi: 10.1037/h0100980

Mann, R. E. (2000). Managing resistance and rebellion in relapse prevention intervention. In D. R. Laws, S. M. Hudson, & T. Tony (Eds.), *Remaking relapse prevention with sexual offenders* (pp. 187–200). Newbury Park, CA: Sage.

Marlatt, G. A. (1985). Situational determinants of relapse and skill-training interventions. In G. A. Marlatt & J. R. Gordon (Eds.), *Relapse prevention: Maintenance strategies in the treatment of addictive behaviors* (pp. 71–127). New York, NY: Guilford Press.

Marshall, W. L. (1997). Pedophilia: Psychopathology and theory. In D. R. Laws & W. O'Donohue (Eds.), *Handbook of sexual deviance: Theory and application* (pp. 152–174). New York, NY: Guilford.

Marshall, W. L., Hall, K., & Woo, C. P. (2016). Sexual functioning in the treatment of sexual offenders. In D. Boer (ed.) *The Wiley Handbook of on the Theories,Assessment and Treatment of Sexual Offending, Volume III: Treatment.* Oxford: Wiley-Blackwell.

Marshall, W. L., Marshall, L. E., & Serran, G. A. (2006). Strategies in the treatment of paraphilias: A critical review. *Annual Review of Sexual Research, 17*(1), 162–182. doi: 10.1080/10532528.2006.10559841

Marshall, W. L., Marshall, L. E., Serran, G. A., & Fernandez, Y. M. (2006). *Treating sexual offenders: An integrated approach.* New York, NY: Routledge.

Marshall, W. L., Marshall, L. E., Serran, G. A., & O'Brien, M. D. (2003). Distorted attitudes and perceptions and their relationship with self-esteem and coping in child molesters. *Sexual Abuse: A Journal of Research and Treatment, 15*(3), 171–181. doi: 10.1023/A:1023547316429

Marshall, W. L., Marshall, L. E., Serran, G. A., & O'Brien, M. D. (2011). *Rehabilitating sexual offenders: A strength-based approach.* Washington, DC: American Psychological Association.

Maslow, A. H. (1954). *Motivation and personality.* New York, NY: Harper & Row.

Pervan, S., & Hunter, M. (2007). Cognitive distortions and social self-esteem in sexual offenders. *Applied Psychology in Criminal Justice, 3*(1), 76–90.

Polaschek, D. L. L. (2003). Relapse prevention, offense process models, and the treatment of sexual offenders. *Professional Psychology: Research and Practice, 34*(4), 361–367. doi: 10.1037/0735-7028.34.4.361

Schneider, J. P., & Irons, R. R. (2001). Assessment and treatment of addictive sexual disorders: Relevance for chemical dependency relapse. *Substance Use & Misuse, 36*(13), 1795–1820. doi: 10.1081/JA-100108428

Seligman, M. E. P., Rashid, T., & Park, A. C. (2006). Positive psychotherapy. *American Psychologist, 61*(8), 774–788. doi: 10.1037/0003-066X.61.8.774

Seligman, M. E. P., Steen, T. A., Park, N., & Peterson, C. (2005). Positive psychology progress: Empirical validation of interventions. *American Psychologist, 60*(5), 410–421. doi: 10.1037/0003-066X.60.5.410

Serran, G. A., & Marshall, L. E. (2006). Coping and mood in sexual offending. In W. L. Marshall, Y. M. Fernandez, L. E. Marshall, & G. A. Serran (Eds.), *Sexual offender treatment: Controversial issues* (pp. 109–124). Chichester, UK: John Wiley.

Sheldon, K. M., Boehm, J. K., & Lyubomirsky, S. (2012). Variety is the spice of happiness: The hedonic adaptation prevention (HAP) model. In I. Boniwell & S. David (Eds.), *Oxford handbook of happiness* (pp. 901–914). Oxford, UK: Oxford University Press.

Sin, N. L., & Lyubomirsky, S. (2009). Enhancing well-being and alleviating depressive symptoms with positive psychology interventions: A practice-friendly meta-analysis. *Journal of Clinical Psychology, 65*(5), 467–487. doi: 10.1002/jclp.20593

Thornton, D., Beech, A., & Marshall, W. L. (2004). Pre-treatment self-esteem and post-treatment sexual recidivism. *International Journal of Offender Therapy and Comparative Criminology, 48*(5), 587–599. doi: 10.1177/0306624X04265286

Ward, T. (2000). Relapse prevention: Critique and reformulation. *Journal of Sexual Aggression*, *5*(2), 118–133. doi: 10.1080/13552600008413303

Ward, T. (2002). Good lives and the rehabilitation of offenders: Promises and problems. *Aggression and Violent Behavior*, *7*(5), 513–528. doi: 10.1016/S1359-1789(01)00076-3

Ward, T., & Hudson, S. M. (1996). Relapse prevention: A critical analysis. *Sexual Abuse: A Journal of Research and Treatment*, *8*(3), 177–200. doi: 10.1177/107906329600800303

Ward, T., Mann, R. E., & Gannon, T. A. (2007). The good lives model of offender rehabilitation: Clinical implications. *Aggression and Violent Behavior*, *12*(1), 87–107. doi: 10.1016/j.avb.2006.03.004

Ward, T., & Marshall, W. L. (2004). Good lives, aetiology and the rehabilitation of sexual offenders: A bridging theory. *Journal of Sexual Aggression*, *10*(2), 153–169. doi: 10.1080/13552600412331290102

Ward, T., Polaschek, D. L. L., & Beech, A. R. (2006). *Theories of sexual offending*. Chichester, UK: John Wiley & Sons.

Ward, T., & Stewarts, C. A. (2003). The treatment of sexual offenders: Risk management and good lives. *Professional Psychology: Research and Practices*, *34*(4), 353–360. doi: 10.1037/0735-7028.34.4.353

Ware, J., Frost, A., & Hoy, A. (2015). A review of the use of therapeutic communities with sexual offenders. *International Journal of Offender Therapy and Comparative Criminology*, *54*(5), 721–742. doi: 10.1177/0306624X09343169

Ware, J., Mann, R. E., & Wakeling, H. C. (2009). Group versus individual treatment: What is the best modality for treating sexual offenders? *Sexual Abuse in Australia and New Zealand*, *2*(1), 2–13.

Winder, B., Lievesley, R., Kaul, A., Elliott, H. J., Thorne, K., & Hocken, K. (2014). Preliminary evaluation of the use of pharmacological treatment with convicted sexual offenders experiencing high levels of sexual preoccupation, hypersexuality and/or sexual compulsivity. *Journal of Forensic Psychiatry & Psychology*, *25*(2), 176–194. doi: 10.1080/14789949.2014.903504

Yates, P. M. (2002). What works: Effective intervention with sexual offenders. In H. E. Allen (Ed.), *What works: Risk reduction: Interventions for special needs offenders* (pp. 115–163). Lanham, MD: American Correctional Association.

11 The application of psychology to the Singapore Prison Service

Timothy Hee Sun Leo

Introduction

Over the past decade and the half, the Singapore Prison Service (SPS) has gained an international reputation for offender rehabilitation. With the development of evidence-based offender rehabilitation in Singapore, there has been a substantial decrease in the two-year recidivism rate of prisoners from 44.4% in 1998 to 27.6% for the 2012 release cohort (Singapore Prison Service, 2015). The Yellow Ribbon Project (YRP), a nationwide effort aimed at increasing public awareness and acceptance of ex-offenders, has also received international attention; as an exemplar of innovation in the correctional field, the YRP has inspired similar approaches in other correctional jurisdictions (Graham & White, 2014; Leong, 2015).

This chapter focuses on how psychology has played a game-changing role for the SPS in its transformation from a largely custodial prison service to a progressive correctional service employing the use of cutting-edge psychological practice methods. The chapter will also describe the key elements of psychological work within the SPS.

The historical context

Before the year 2000, the SPS was faced with a huge challenge and threat: prison overcrowding. The system was overstressed and security was threatened. The prisoner to staff ratio was high (7.9:1 in 1983). Staff attrition was high, with a significant number of officers having limited educational qualifications. In such a climate, resources were mainly focused on maintaining security, good order, and discipline. The combination of prison overcrowding and high offender recidivism did not bode well for the SPS.

While short-term measures could be employed to curb the growing prisoner population, the longer-term solution was to cease the "revolving door" effect of released offenders returning to prison, in short, to stem the tide of high recidivism rates. Realising such a goal required the implementation of an effective rehabilitation strategy that would deliver results in time. Although rehabilitative activities were being conducted in prison, these were limited to small groups of offenders and based on the current knowledge of the day. There was a need for utilising methods that had an evidential basis for recidivism reduction.

A review of the scientific literature, or what is commonly known as the "what works" literature, revealed that the application of rehabilitation principles derived from the psychology of criminal conduct (PCC) offered the best means of achieving a significant reduction in recidivism (Andrews & Bonta, 1998, 2010; Gendreau, Little, & Goggin, 1996). The principles found in the PCC are better known as the risk, need, and responsivity (RNR) model of offender rehabilitation; this model is supported by a large number of well-conducted studies and meta-analyses (Andrews & Dowden, 2006; Andrews et al., 1990).

Psychology's contribution to correctional policy and practice

Risk assessment

The adoption of a psychological model of rehabilitation led to the incorporation of psychological principles into the organisational structure of the SPS. Initial efforts to apply psychology in the SPS included the development and implementation of an assessment and intervention framework informed by theory and research evidence. The SPS adopted the Level of Service Inventory – Revised (LSI-R) as the primary offender assessment instrument (Andrews & Bonta, 1995; Leong, 2015). The LSI-R is an empirically validated risk assessment instrument developed in Canada and used in many correctional jurisdictions. To engender confidence in using this instrument within the Singapore context, a large-scale validation research study was conducted to examine the psychometric properties of the LSI-R and to derive local predictive norms. The study found that the instrument met the required psychometric properties, with good predictive validity with regard to reoffending risk (Neo, 2003).

While statistical methods of prediction allow for accurate, quicker, and more efficient methods of estimating risk, psychological risk assessments provide a more individualised and contextually rich formulation of risk that is often required when important decisions are needed: examples include decision-making for the release or sentencing of offenders. In the SPS, psychologists and correctional rehabilitation specialists provide a range of offender risk assessments, ranging from assessing the general risk of committing a criminal offence to specific risk assessments for violent and/or sex reoffending. Assessments are also offered for a variety of purposes, such as helping to place offenders into the appropriate type and level of interventions and providing psychologically relevant information to the state courts for the purpose of sentencing and to specialised boards to assist them in their release decision-making process.

In providing such risk assessment reports, psychologists and correctional rehabilitation specialists use structured professional judgement (SPJ) methods (Douglas & Kropp, 2002; Hart, 1998; Kropp & Hart, 2000). Training in SPJ methods allows the staff to balance complex interactions of factors in assessing offender risk according to sound psychological principles and evidence.

SPS psychologists have also developed a number of evidence-informed SPJ instruments for non-psychologists. The Structured Assessment for Emplacement (SAFE) instrument is currently used by the heads of prison institutions to aid them in their decisions to place the right offenders into community-based programmes. The use of a structured decision-making protocol underpinned by research evidence provides greater consistency and defensibility to the decision-making process and helps to safeguard the credibility and integrity of the SPS.

Rehabilitation and intervention

Since 2001, higher risk offenders have been provided with risk reduction intervention programmes. According to the risk principle in the RNR model, higher risk offenders should receive intensive psychological interventions aimed at changing antisocial attitudes and behaviour by providing them with cognitive and practical problem-solving skills. Such intensive programmes should not be given to low-risk offenders. On the basis of research evidence, the recommended mode of intervention to reduce offender risk is to use cognitive behavioural approaches in working with offenders, with attention given to skills practice and role plays. The need principle focuses the attention of rehabilitation on the targets that would have the greatest impact on reducing offender risk. These targets are referred to as "criminogenic needs". There are eight criminogenic needs, commonly referred to as the Central Eight: History of Antisocial Behaviour, Antisocial Personality Pattern, Antisocial Cognition, Antisocial Associates, Family/Marital Situation, Education Level/Work, Leisure/Recreation and Substance Abuse (Andrews & Bonta, 2010).

Specific prison institutions were selected and reorganised to house prisoners undergoing intensive psychological rehabilitation more efficiently. Psychological programmes were initially developed for general offending. Higher-risk adult offenders were provided with criminogenic programmes conducted by correctional rehabilitation specialists. Specialised assessments and interventions for violent and sexual offending were developed, and these were delivered by SPS psychologists. Offender programmes were also offered to young offenders undergoing court-sentenced reformative training.

Organisational and system change

In the early years of embarking on the rehabilitation journey, the introduction of a psychological model of rehabilitation into a prison system requires leadership commitment and organisational change (Leo, 2012; Leong, 2015). Prison systems have traditionally focused on maintaining order, discipline, and security. One of the major challenges of trying to introduce evidence-based rehabilitation to the SPS was the need to move to a new paradigm and to introduce a new "language" to the prison system while also preserving the excellent work done in providing secure custody to inmates that had allowed the SPS to have the public's confidence over many years. This called for a strategy to engage staff to move from a largely custodial organisation to one that would also offer effective rehabilitation programmes on a large scale. In a system that was already undergoing a high level of stress from prison overcrowding, the impetus needed to go the extra mile had to be sufficiently engaging and compelling.

The SPS also expanded its pool of psychologists and prison counsellors to undertake the required assessments and interventions. The title of *prison counsellors* was eventually changed to *correctional rehabilitation specialists* (CRS) in 2012 to more aptly reflect the specialised intervention work involved in rehabilitating prisoners. It also differentiated them from prison volunteers who offer religious counselling to inmates. CRS would have a basic or postgraduate degree in the fields of counselling, psychology, or social work. In-house training in correctional psychology, such as offender risk assessment, motivational interviewing, and cognitive behavioural therapy, was provided to equip them for working with prisoners (Andrews, 2001; McMurran, 2009).

Towards this end, the leadership engaged staff in developing a compelling shared vision that would motivate staff to make the shift. The conviction held by the leaders was that without capturing the minds and hearts of staff in support of the mission of rehabilitation, it would be extremely difficult to make a significant dent in the recidivism rate of incarcerated offenders. The transformational change process played a pivotal role in enabling the transformation of the SPS into a world-class correctional system.

One of the game-changing outcomes of the change process has been the creation of an inspiring new vision and mission statement calling for all prison staff to be "Captains in the Lives of Offenders" or, in short, "Captains of Lives". Implicit in this title is a noble calling for all officers and staff to lead and inspire offenders to change from a life of crime to become responsible citizens. The notion of 'Captains of Lives' (COL) brought about a great sense of pride and new zeal. It also imbued new purpose into the already strong esprit de corps among prison officers (Chua, 2012; Helliwell, 2011; Leong, 2010, Manfred & Hellwig, 2011). Over the years, the concept of COL has continued to inspire staff, and it has heightened public awareness of the role of SPS beyond secure custody and increased the SPS's ability to recruit good men and women.

Community engagement

On the public front, the SPS strategically engaged and educated the public about the vision and mission of prison. Public engagement was one of the key strategies employed to increase public support for employing ex-offenders and to gain a greater acceptance of ex-offenders in society. In 2004, the YRP was created, and it has become an annual event in September, comprising a set of organised activities conducted nationwide to raise awareness of the need for prisoners to be given a second chance to return to society (Singapore Prison Service, 2013). Without the support of its community partners and the support of the community, the SPS would not have been able to achieve the rehabilitative outcomes for prisoners.

The whole process of organisational change in the SPS involved psychological change, influencing first the mindset of staff, followed by strengthening the relationship with its community partners and creating public awareness of the fact that ex-offenders need help and assistance after they have served their prison term. The process of change drew heavily from concepts of the learning organisation (Senge, 1990; Senge et al., 1999), providing the SPS with useful principles and methods for facilitating organisational learning and change.

Recent developments

During the period 2001 to 2008, much of the effort was focused on building the internal capacity of the prison system to provide rehabilitation services, public engagement, and developing a network (the CARE Network) with both government and non-government bodies in support of the rehabilitation and reintegration of offenders. There were limited offerings of community-based programmes given to a small group of prisoners. The SPS largely relied on community partners from voluntary organisations to provide post-prison follow-up. There was an absence of a "through-care" system that could ensure continuity of rehabilitation efforts for offenders requiring prison support and intervention.

Moving from a prison to a correctional system

In 2009, the Singapore Government formed an Inter-Ministry Committee on the Prevention of Reoffending (CPR) to study and propose recommendations to lower recidivism (Tan, 2012). This committee comprised senior members of the government and community leaders. During this process, the CPR welcomed and incorporated recommendations that were evidence informed: examples included policies that took account of the risk of reoffending (risk principle) and the need to provide evidence-based rehabilitation to offenders. For incarcerated offenders, the CPR recognised the need for rehabilitation to be expanded beyond prison to include services to ex-offenders during their reintegration into society phase. Psychology was able to play an influential role in the development of new policies for effective rehabilitation.

The CPR recommendations set in motion the development of a through-care system of rehabilitation. To take on this new challenge, to expand rehabilitation services beyond the prison walls, and to provide offenders released into community with the needed scaffolding required new thinking, new processes, new capabilities, new policies, and new legislation. The preceding decade of applying evidence-based principles from the field of correctional psychology laid the basic foundation for the next wave of development. The past provided the background for the SPS to move to its next "S" curve in the organisation's development and transformation (Sim, 2015).

New thinking involves moving beyond the known to also explore the emerging knowledge that is relevant to the task or mission of an organisation. The emergence of desistance research in criminology and the Good Lives Model during the past decade was timely in informing the development of a through-care system (Maruna, 2001, Ward & Brown, 2004). Adding to the established evidence from the PCC, desistance thinking and aspects of the Good Lives Model provided useful concepts to further enhance the rehabilitation of offenders within Singapore.

Desistance research attempts to elucidate the factors underpinning the why, when, and how offenders desist from crime. It includes descriptive, subjective accounts from offenders of the factors and experiences that characterised their journey out of offending. McNeill and Weaver (2010) identified some of essential elements offenders may need in desisting from further offending (see Figure 11.1).

Desistance from reoffending has been described not as a "one-off" event in time, though it may be so for some. For many offenders, it may resemble a messy "zigzag" process, with the offender drifting in and eventually out of crime (McNeill & Weaver, 2010). Such findings have significant implications for rehabilitative practice. Knowledge of these processes allows correctional staff and volunteers engaged in rehabilitation to have a better understanding of the challenges of going straight. This potentially enhances their capacity for empathy and to provide timely support in the face of an offender's failure and relapse and allows them to be harbingers of hope to repeat offenders (Martin & Stermac, 2010).

The research on desistors' accounts of having a "prosocial narrative identity" has been taken up by the SPS and further explored for therapeutic use. This concept was not new to SPS psychologists in their work with violent offenders and helping these men to develop non-violent skills and self-constructs. Within the framework of using a cognitive behavioural approach to address antisocial personality patterns, cognitions, and negative peer associates, intervention staff engage offenders in exploring and developing for themselves a prosocial narrative identity that could potentially help them redefine themselves as they return to the community. It is hoped that having a positive self-identity construct will help them build a new life free from crime. The development of such narratives is facilitated within the group-based psychological intervention programmes conducted by CRS and psychologists.

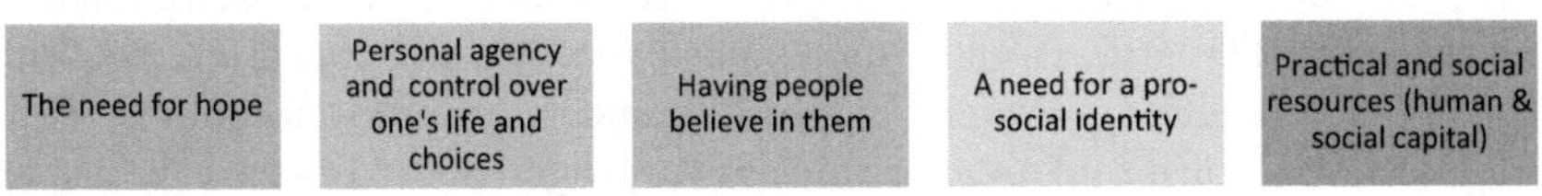

Figure 11.1 Essential elements of desistance in the offender population

Source: Adapted from McNeill and Weaver (2010)

The Good Lives Model posits that all human beings, including offenders, aspire to certain universal "goods" (Ward & Brown, 2004). Below is the list of the primary goods emphasised in the Good Lives Model:

- Life (including healthy living and functioning)
- Knowledge (how well informed an individual feels about things that are important to him or her)
- Excellence in play (hobbies and recreational pursuits)
- Excellence in work (including mastery experiences)
- Excellence in agency (autonomy, power, and self-directedness)
- Inner peace (freedom from emotional turmoil and stress)
- Relatedness (including intimate, romantic, and familial relationships)
- Community (connection to wider social groups)
- Spirituality (in the broad sense of finding meaning and purpose in life)
- Pleasure (feeling good in the here and now)
- Creativity (expressing oneself through alternative forms)

The relevance of considering these goods within a correctional population stems from the view that offenders pursue them using antisocial means. Hence rehabilitation efforts should go beyond the traditional framework of risk reduction to also include efforts to help offenders identify the goods that are most relevant to them and help them attain these goods in prosocial ways. Efforts in this regard can motivate offenders towards worthwhile pursuits, give them hope for the future, increase self-agency towards what is important for them, and equip them with the necessary skills to attain what they need for their future life.

The integrated criminogenic programme (ICP)

In 2010, work was under way to review existing criminogenic programmes, drawing from the latest research findings and incorporating desistance and Good Lives Model principles (Lipsey, Landenberger, & Wilson, 2007; McNeil & Weaver, 2010; Ward, 2010). The result was the development of a new innovative programme called the Integrated Criminogenic Programme (ICP), which would be offered to higher-risk offenders within a new through-care system.

Beyond improving programme design and delivery, effective psychology principles were also applied to develop an intervention milieu to house high-risk offenders undergoing rehabilitation. Such milieus within the SPS are called "transformational environments" to emphasise the aim of transforming the lives of prisoners. The first transformation milieu that was developed was the Pre-Release Centre (PRC), whereby high-risk offenders undergo 10 months of the ICP and vocational and other reintegrative programmes. Effective principles guided the operationalisation of the PRC, and prison staff selected to work in the PRC were trained to support prosocial change (Bourgon & Armstrong, 2005). SPS psychologists developed the MOST (Maximising Opportunities to Support Transformation) curriculum to equip prisoner officers working within the pre-release housing unit. The MOST curriculum drew from the evidence found in the core correctional practice literature (Dowden & Andrews, 2004). MOST training involves a series of classroom training and role plays, followed up by in vivo supervision and coaching within the PRC. Officers are taught how to support prisoners in their efforts to use problem-solving skills, role-model prosocial approaches to issues and relationships, and appropriately use their authority in managing offenders and challenging situations. This allows for better generalisation of prosocial skills practice by prisoners in their living environment.

To enable through care at the organisational level, the rehabilitation system was revamped to include a new Mandatory Aftercare Scheme (MAS) to enable the SPS to provide structured evidence-based rehabilitation services that straddle both prison and the community. The revamp was informed by the principles of effective rehabilitation covering the assessment of offenders, revised criminogenic programming, preparing prisoners for entry into the community through vocational skills and family programmes, developing milieus to support transformation, crafting community supervision, and casework aimed at increasing reintegration (Bogue et al., 2004; Bourgon & Armstrong, 2005). To implement the MAS, changes to legislation had to be made; this resulted in new legislation under the Conditional Remission System and changes to the *Prisons Act.* Legislative changes were also influenced by psychological principles that support rehabilitation and reintegration.

With these legislative changes, the SPS expanded its theatre of operations beyond the prison to the community. This resulted in the creation of the Community Corrections Command, which provides services to post-release offenders in the community and offenders in the form of different types of community-based programmes and sentences. The changes in the rehabilitation system and legislation enabled the SPS to change from a prison service to a correctional system.

The operational arm of the Community Corrections Command is supported by two sets of staff, one primarily supervising the offenders under "conditions" and the other providing case management services to offenders to support their reintegration. To achieve synergy between these two functions, with the aim of maximising community reintegration and ultimately to prevent offenders from reoffending, all staff are given training in evidence-based psychological skills. With the assistance of the University of Cincinnati, they receive specialised training in effective practices in community supervision (EPICS), an evidence-based set of skills that when used with offenders in the community contribute to a reduction in recidivism (Bonta et al., 2010; Bonta, Gutierrez, & Ashton, 2012).

Evaluation data for the prisoners that have undergone the ICP in the PRC and have received evidence-based casework during the period of conditional release and supervision in the community showed a significant decline in procriminal attitudes, better employment outcomes, and improved coping. The two-year recidivism rate of these offenders is lower than the rate for a comparison group of offenders who did not receive the ICP and casework, after matching for risk level and other relevant factors. These findings underscore the point that properly implemented evidence-based rehabilitation efforts can significantly reduce offenders' reoffending rates.

Psychological research in the SPS

Applied research and programme evaluation forms a critical part of psychological practice within the SPS. The development of this capability was gradual, commencing with the utilisation of overseas research evidence to guide local rehabilitation efforts. From this humble beginning, efforts were made to contextualise knowledge to the local offender population. Early research efforts from the year 2000 were focused on the psychometric validation of assessment tools and the development of local norms for assessment instruments such as the Level of Service Inventory-Revised (LSI-R) and the Self-Appraisal Questionnaire (SAQ) (Loza, Neo, Shahinfar, & Loza-Fanous, 2005; Neo, 2003). From these early studies, the first local actuarial risk screening instruments were developed. The Singapore Short Risk Scale (SPSRS), comprising nine items that can be quickly scored by prison officers, allowed the SPS to determine the risk levels of offenders in a much shorter time than that required to complete the longer and more comprehensive assessment using the LSI-R. The Institutional Violence Risk Scale (IVRS) provided prison officers with a relatively quick method of screening for the violence risk of prisoners, enabling better security screening to prevent violent incidents in prison. These scales have satisfactory predictive accuracy (Singapore Prison Service, 2006).

In 2006, the SPS produced a Correctional Research Compendium documenting 20 formal research projects commissioned by the service and a further 23 projects conducted by external parties and prison staff completing research projects as part of their tertiary academic requirements (Singapore Prison Service, 2006). The use of research knowledge and evidence to continually challenge and refine practice is one of the hallmarks of correctional practice in Singapore. Research is currently applied to three major areas within the SPS (see Table 11.1).

Table 11.1 Research areas within the SPS

Rehabilitation of Offenders	*Operational and Organisation Aspects of Running Prison*	*Ministry and National Level Projects*
Understanding the reintegration needs of offenders (2016) Understanding the offence pathways of female drug offenders (2015) Development of automated risk screening tool (i.e., STRAT) (2015)	Development of psychometric assessment tools for the selection of prison officers (2015)	Task force study on youth and drugs (2015)

Note: An overview on the different research topics categorised under three main areas in SPS

A recent development in the SPS involves the combination of using existing psychological knowledge of offender risk factors with data analytics to provide an actuarial risk score for all offenders entering the prison system. On the basis of a historical data set from 35,000 offenders, a risk probability is automatically computed for each offender entering the prison system. The development of this automated system, termed the Screening Tool: Risk Allocation Technique – General (STRAT-G), provides a highly efficient and accurate method that is useful for rehabilitation planning, prisoner management, and decision-making. While it does not replace the need for more individualised psychological assessments, it allows for a more efficient deployment of assessment and intervention resources. From the initial work with STRAT-G, the SPS has also been able to identify factors that predict violent offending within prison. This has led to the development of an automated screening system to identify prisoners with a higher probability of committing a violent act within the prison system. This spin-off from the development of STRAT-G has increased the SPS's capability in preventing and managing violent behaviour within the prison population. The use of psychological knowledge with data analytics has enabled the SPS to make better, more efficient, and effective organisational, operational, and rehabilitative decisions.

Prison research also extends to collaboration with other governmental agencies to address areas of national concern. Prison psychologists have been involved in two major inter-ministry research projects on drug offending. Such involvement enables psychology to make a valuable contribution to policies affecting the nation (Ministry of Home Affairs, June 2015a and 2015b).

Peering into the black box of rehabilitation: The use of programme evaluation

An effective correction rehabilitation system requires a robust system of programme evaluation. Evaluation can be used to guide the development, design, implementation, and refinement of rehabilitation practices to reach higher levels of effectiveness and efficiency. While effectiveness aims to reduce the recidivism rate, efficiency allows for the optimal use of resources and minimises wastage and duplication. A systematic and transparent system of evaluation allows all stakeholders to have a clear picture of the rehabilitation process and outcome. Towards this end, the SPS has a team of trained evaluators. Apart from collecting and analysing statistical information such as recidivism data, pre- and post-test psychometric results, and behavioural indicators, the SPS also incorporates the use of an evidence-based evaluation system called the Correctional Programme Checklist (Latessa & Holsinger, 1998; Lowenkamp, 2004). The Correctional Programme Checklist or CPC is a structured evaluation protocol that looks at an entire programme system and provides useful information on the different aspects of a rehabilitation system and whether these aspects meet the required standards necessary for reductions in recidivism. The use of the CPC can potentially optimise the various subcomponents (see Figure 11.2) to lead to greater reductions in offender recidivism.

Correctional Programme Checklist	Programme Leadership and Development
	Staff Characteristics
	Offender Assessment
	Treatment Characteristics
	Quality Assurance

Figure 11.2 Sub-components of the correctional programme checklist

Note and Source: An overview on the different aspects of a rehabilitation system evaluated by the Evidence-Based Correctional Programme Checklist. Adapted from O'Connor, Sawyer, and Duncan (2008).

To date, programme evaluation has served a number of purposes. Firstly, it has provided the assurance as to whether rehabilitation programmes have been effectively implemented. Secondly, it has given specific information as to which aspects need to be improved. Thirdly, it has provided valuable feedback to the different stakeholders, such as policymakers and funders of rehabilitation, programme designers, rehabilitation staff, and ground officers who run the programme. Fourthly, programme evaluation findings have been utilised for organisational learning.

Organisational learning is vital when organisations try to implement evidence-based principles in real-life systems. Such principles, often distilled from research, are usually presented as abstract concepts. Psychologists and CRS conversant with psychological theories and principles need to communicate them and work within the organisational dynamics and ground operational challenges. Correctional staff in management and operations are likely to find abstract psychological principles difficult to contextualise in the absence of local examples. The implementation of scientific evidence becomes a significant challenge with a diverse group of staff from different backgrounds. The use of the CPC provides a form, structure, and language to express these principles in organisational and operational terms, allowing for a diverse group of staff to arrive at a shared appreciation of the problems and challenges and to formulate solutions that take into consideration the complexities of a correctional system.

Increasing the force-multiplier effect of psychology

Psychologists and CRS make up about 7% of the staff of the SPS. Their smaller staff size compared to prison officers imposes physical limitations in terms of direct contact with and influence over offenders. Prison officers have greater and wider contact with prisoners. They are in a position to provide guidance and encouragement to the whole gamut of prisoners. Hence, equipping staff with the relevant psychological skills will enable them to play this role more effectively and extensively. Over the years, psychologists and CRS have been involved in training correctional staff in basic communication skills. A smaller subset of correctional staff has also been given specialised psychological training in critical incident stress management (CISM) and psychological peer support (Everly & Mitchell, 1999; Flannery, 2001). Psychological crisis management skills such as CISM training enable the SPS to professionally respond to and manage small- or large-scale crises.

While prison staff at the PRC receive a more advanced level of psychological skills, a more basic form is needed to enable more officers to use psychology-based skills in their work with offenders. From 2016, all prison officers will be provided with a basic set of skills derived from core correctional practice (CCP). With the use of CCP-informed skills, psychology becomes a potential force multiplier in enabling the staff to better influence change and increase the effectiveness of rehabilitation and operations in their daily interactions with prisoners.

To further extend the reach of effective practice principles, the SPS has also provided training to community volunteers working with offenders. A variety of training platforms and engagement sessions, including the co-hosting of the International Reintegration Puzzle Conference in 2014, have been used to share information on the RNR model of offender rehabilitation and encourage the use of evidence-based principles by the partners in rehabilitation work.

Conclusion

Psychology has played a significant and pivotal role in the development of the SPS. With the need to stem the high recidivism rate of prisoners, a rehabilitation pathway was undertaken by the service. Drawing from the PCC, the SPS adopted the RNR model of rehabilitation. Initial efforts in applying the model were aided by an enlightened leadership that brought about transformational change in the organisation. This change allowed psychology to take root in the SPS and enabled its application to the service's systems, structures, and processes. Psychology was applied to rehabilitation doctrine and practice, the management of prisoners, crisis management capabilities, organisational learning, staff and volunteer training, and policy development at the organisational and national levels. Since 1998, the overall recidivism rate has declined significantly. Current evaluation efforts have shown that evidence-based rehabilitation can lead to reductions in reoffending. Partnership with the community is an indispensable part of offender rehabilitation. Psychology has also been useful in enabling the community to use effective principles and practices in working towards the common goal of helping offenders reintegrate and remain in society as law-abiding and contributing citizens in Singapore.

Chapter summary points

- Psychology has been widely used in the practice and policy of risk assessment, rehabilitation and intervention, offender management, organisational and system change, and the community engagement work of the Singapore Police Service (SPS) since 2000.

- The application of psychology is made possible by the strong leadership and commitment towards transformational change in the SPS.
- In 2009, the Singapore Government formed an Inter-Ministry Committee on the Prevention of Reoffending (CPR), which recognised the need for rehabilitation to be expanded beyond the prison walls. This enabled psychology to take on an influential role in the development of new policies for effective rehabilitation.
- The Integrated Criminogenic Programme (ICP) was developed to offer higher-risk offenders within a new 'through-care' system in 2010. Effective psychology principles were also applied to develop an intervention milieu to house high-risk offenders undergoing rehabilitation. Such milieus are called "transformational environments". Officers were taught how to support prisoners in their efforts by equipping them with skills from the MOST (Maximising Opportunities to Support Transformation) curriculum.
- The combination of psychology and desistance research has enabled the SPS to break new grounds in offender rehabilitation.
- The SPS takes pride in the use of psychology in the areas of research, evaluation, offender risk assessment, and rehabilitation.
- Psychologists and correctional rehabilitation specialists (CRS) also create a multiplier effect in the application of psychology by sharing knowledge and working collaboratively with prison officers.

References

Andrews, D. A. (2001). Principles of effective correctional programs. In L. L. Motiuk & R. C. Serin (Eds.), *Compendium 2000 on effective correctional programming* (pp. 9–17). Ottawa, ON: Correctional Service Canada.

Andrews, D. A., & Bonta, J. (1995). *The level of service inventory: Revised.* Toronto, ON: Multi-Health Systems.

Andrews, D. A., & Bonta, J. (1998). *The psychology of criminal conduct* (2nd ed.). Cincinnati, OH: Anderson Publishing Co.

Andrews, D. A., & Bonta, J. (2010). *The psychology of criminal conduct* (5th ed.). Cincinnati, OH: Anderson Publishing Co.

Andrews, D. A., & Dowden, C. (2006). Risk principle of case classification in correctional treatment: A meta-analytic investigation. *International Journal of Offender Therapy and Comparative Criminology*, *50*(1), 88–100. doi: 10.1177/0306624X05282556

Andrews, D. A., Zinger, I., Hoge, R. D., Bonta, J., Gendreau, P., & Cullen, F. T. (1990). Does correctional treatment work? A psychologically informed meta-analysis. *Criminology*, *28*(3), 369–404. doi: 10.1111/j.1745-9125.1990.tb01330.x

Bogue, B., Campbell, N., Carey, M., Clawson, E., Faust, D., Florio, . . . Woodward, W. (2004). *Implementing evidence based practice in community corrections: The principles of effective intervention.* Washington, DC: U.S. Department of Justice, National Institute of Corrections.

Bonta, J., Bourgon, G., Rugge, T., Scott, T. L., Yessine, A. K., Gutierrez, L., & Li, J. (2010). *The strategic training initiative in community supervision: Risk-need-responsivity in the real world. User report 2010–01.* Ottawa, ON: Public Safety Canada.

Bonta, J., Gutierrez, L., & Ashton, J. (2012). *From case management to change agent: The evolution of "What Works" community supervision. User report 2012–01.* Ottawa, ON: Public Safety Canada.

Bourgon, G., & Armstrong, B. (2005). Transferring the principles of effective treatment into a "real world" prison setting. *Criminal Justice & Behavior, 32*(1), 3–25. doi: 10.1177/0093854804270618

Chua, C. K. (2012). *The making of captains of lives – Prison reform in Singapore 1999 to 2007.* Singapore: World Scientific.

Douglas, K., & Kropp, P. R. (2002). A prevention-based paradigm for violence risk assessment: Clinical and research applications. *Criminal Justice and Behavior, 29*(5), 617–658. doi: 10.1177/009385402236735

Dowden, C., & Andrews, D. A. (2004). The importance of staff practice in delivering effective correctional treatment: A meta-analytic review of core correctional practice. *International Journal of Offender Therapy and Comparative Criminology, 48*(2), 203–214. doi: 10.1177/0306624X03257765

Everly, G., & Mitchell, J. (1999). *Critical incident stress management (CISM): A new era and standard of care in crisis intervention.* Ellicott City, MD: Chevron Publishing.

Flannery, R. B. J. (2001). Assaulted Staff Action Program (ASAP): Ten years of empirical support for critical incident stress management (CISM). *International Journal of Emergency Mental Health, 24*, 104–118.

Gendreau, P., Little, T., & Goggin, C. (1996). A meta-analysis of adult offender recidivism: What works! *Criminology, 34*(4), 575–607. doi: 10.1111/j.1745-9125.1996.tb01220.x

Graham, H., & White, R. (2015). *Innovative justice.* London: Routledge.

Hart, S. D. (1998). The role of psychopathy in assessing risk for violence: Conceptual and methodological issues. *Legal and Criminological Psychology, 3*(1), 121–137. doi: 10.1111/j.2044-8333.1998.tb00354.x

Helliwell, J. F. (2011). Institutions as enablers of wellbeing: The Singapore Prison case study. *International Journal of Wellbeing, 1*(2), 255–265.

Kropp, P. R., & Hart, S. D. (2000). The Spousal Assault Risk Assessment (SARA) guide: Reliability and validity in adult male offenders. *Law and Human Behavior, 24*(1), 101–118. doi: 10.1023/A:1005430904495

Latessa, E. J., & Holsinger, A. (1998). The importance of evaluating correctional programs: Assessing outcome and quality. *Corrections Management Quarterly, 2*(4), 22–29.

Leo, T. (2012). *The introduction of evidence-based practice within an organization undergoing transformational change.* Tokyo: UNAFEI Resource Material Series No. 88.

Leong, L. (2010). *The story of the Singapore Prison Service: From custodians of prisoners to captains of lives.* Singapore: Civil Service College.

Leong, L. (2015). *Case study: Towards a society with offending.* Singapore: Civil Service College.

Lipsey, M. W., Landenberger, N. A., & Wilson, S. J. (2007). Effects of cognitive-behavioural programs for criminal offenders. *Campbell Systematic Reviews, 6*, 1–27.

Lowenkamp, C. J. (2004). *Correctional program integrity and treatment effectiveness: A multi-site, program-level analysis.* (Unpublished doctoral dissertation). University of Cincinnati, Cincinnati.

Loza, W., Neo, L. H., Shahinfar, A., & Loza-Fanous, A. (2005). Cross-validation of the Self- Appraisal Questionnaire: A tool for assessing violent and nonviolent recidivism with female offenders. *International Journal of Offender Therapy and Comparative Criminology*, *49*(5), 547–560. doi: 10.1177/0306624X04273433

Manfred, K. V., & Hellwig, T. (2011). *The captains of lives: Transformation journey of the Singapore Prison Service.* Singapore: INSEAD.

Martin, K., & Stermac, L. (2010). Measuring hope: Is hope related to criminal behavior in offenders? *Offender Therapy and Comparative Criminology*, *54*(5), 693–705. doi: 10.1177/0306624X09336131

Maruna, S. (2001). *Making good: How ex-convicts reform and rebuild their lives.* Washington, DC: American Psychological Association.

McMurran, M. (2009). Motivational interviewing with offenders: A systematic review. *Legal and Criminological Psychology*, *14*(1), 83–100. doi: 10.1348/135532508X278326

McNeill, F., & Weaver, B. (2010). *Changing lives.* Glasgow: Scottish Centre of Crime and Justice Research.

Ministry of Home Affairs. (2015a). *Behavioural analysis of young drug offenders* [Press Release]. Retrieved from https://www.mha.gov.sg/Newsroom/press-releases/PublishingImages/protecting-our-youths-from-drugs/Annex%20C%20Executive%20summary%20for%20TF%20Research%20Study.pdf

Ministry of Home Affairs. (2015b). *Protecting our youths from drugs* [Press Release]. Retrieved from https://www.mha.gov.sg/Newsroom/press-releases/Pages/Protecting-our-Youths-from-Drugs-.aspx

Neo, L. H. (2003). *The LSI-R: An appropriate risk/needs assessment tool for the Singapore correctional population? Internal research report.* Singapore: Singapore Prison Service.

O'Connor, T., Sawyer, B., & Duncan, J. (2008). A country-wide approach to increasing programme effectiveness is possible: Oregon's experience with the Correctional Program Checklist. *Irish Probation Journal*, *5*, 36–49.

Senge, P. M. (1990). *The fifth discipline – The art and practice of the learning organisation.* New York, NY: Doubleday.

Senge, P. M., Kleiner, A., Roberts, C., Roth, G., Ross, R., & Smith, B. (1999). *The dance of change: The challenges to sustaining momentum in learning organizations.* New York, NY: Doubleday.

Sim, S. (2015). Soh Wai Wah, Commissioner of Prisons, Singapore. In M. H. Durley & D. K. Das (Eds.), *Trends in corrections. Interviews with corrections leaders around the world, volume two* (pp. 199–214). Boca Raton, FL: CRC Press.

Singapore Prison Service. (2006). *Correctional research compendium.* Singapore: Singapore Prison Service.

Singapore Prison Service. (2013). *The courage to believe: Unlocking life's second chances.* Singapore: Singapore Prison Service.

Singapore Prison Service. (2015). *2015 Singapore Prison Service annual statistics release.* [News Release]. Retrieved from http://www.sps.gov.sg/sites/default/files/Press%20Release_PRIS%20Annual%20Statistics%20Release%202014_SG%20PRESS%20CENTRE_0.pdf

Tan, C. (2012, 19 April). *Extending aftercare for inmates by 2013* [Online News]. Retrieved from https://www.hometeam.sg/m/article.aspx?news_sid=20120419nIRDWB9zRgXf

Ward, T. (2010). The good lives model of offender rehabilitation: Basic assumptions, aetiological commitments, and practice implications. In F. McNeil, P. Raynor, & C. Trotter (Eds.), *Offender supervision: New directions in theory, research and practice* (pp. 41–64). New York, NY: Willan Publishing.

Ward, T., & Brown, M. (2004). The good lives model and conceptual issues in offender rehabilitation. *Psychology, Crime & Law*, *10*(3), 243–257. doi: 10.1080/10683160410001662744

12 The assessment and management of youth offenders in Singapore

Implementing the risk-need-responsivity framework

Chi Meng Chu and Gerald Zeng

Introduction

Assessments of the risk of recidivism are often used to inform judicial decisions in the criminal and juvenile justice systems (Olver, Stockdale, & Wormith, 2009). Decisions made by the criminal and juvenile justice systems reflect the basic values embraced by a society (Hoge, 2002) and indicate the types of behaviours that are tolerable within that society. Such decision-making processes typically take into consideration the personal and developmental needs of the young person when making sentencing decisions or pleading special conditions (Hoge, 1999, 2002; Young, Moline, Farrell, & Bierie, 2006). These factors then guide judicial decision-making processes to achieve appropriate and fair dispositions and to promote the effective management and rehabilitation of juvenile offenders (Hoge, 1999; Young et al., 2006).

Risk assessments are intended to predict future antisocial behaviours with the ultimate purpose of managing risk and preventing negative outcomes. Such assessments play an important role in the juvenile justice system (Bartol & Barol, 1998; Champion, 1998; Hoge, 2001; Krisberg & Howell, 1998; Melton, Petrila, Poythress, & Slobogin, 1997) and facilitate the formulation of decisions regarding adjudication and interventions efforts (Hoge, 2002). Young and colleagues (Young et al., 2006) observed that juvenile justice systems traditionally relied on unstructured clinical judgements and that this approach has been demonstrated to have poor reliability and validity; importantly, it also has a considerable detrimental impact on the youth offender and the community in that the former is not always dealt with consistently. In particular, the extant literature suggests that the indeterminacy of the decision criteria in juvenile justice systems allows for personal prejudices and biases to influence decision-making processes (Corrado & Turnbull, 1992; Grisso, Tomkins, & Casey, 1988; Hoge, 2002; Johnson & Secret, 1995; Mulvey & Saunders, 1982; Sanborn, 1996), thereby affecting dispositional outcomes.

Effective youth offender risk assessment seeks to inform decision-making processes and risk classification, especially in view of increasing demands for optimal resource allocation and the need to provide empirical evidence in judiciary processes. Moreover, it encourages professionals to be accountable for their assessment (and subsequent offender management) endeavours. This can only be made possible through the use of reliable and valid risk assessment measures that systemically assess the relevant risk and needs of offenders. It should be further noted that offender rehabilitation is most effective when interventions are matched to the risk level and needs of the offender and also take into consideration the individual's responsivity factors (Andrews & Bonta, 2010; Andrews, Bonta, & Wormith, 2011).

This chapter will describe the implementation journey of the risk-need-responsivity framework in Singapore as well as the relevant local research findings on the associated risk assessment measure that facilitates the systematic evaluation of youth offenders. The chapter concludes with a discussion on the future directions of implementing the risk-need-responsivity framework and the need to enforce adherence to the model throughout the sector.

Juvenile justice in Singapore

Singapore is an independent island-state in South East Asia with a land area of 718 square kilometres and a total population of 5.47 million[1] (Singapore Department of Statistics, 2015). Singapore is a busy international business hub and is heavily influenced by both Asian and Western cultures. With regard to crime statistics, youth[2] arrests account for approximately 10% of all arrests in Singapore (Singapore Police Force, 2015). Many statutes in Singapore are based on English common law (e.g., the *Criminal Procedure Code*, 2012); there are some statutes that are based on legislation from other jurisdictions (e.g., India), but these laws were actually formulated by the English in the 1800s. Therefore, similarities with other jurisdictions exist in the way that offences are defined in Singapore, but the exact language of the laws might differ.

Apropos the legislation and judiciary bodies, the Juvenile Court of Singapore was created with the passing of the *Children and Young Persons Ordinance* in 1949 (Subordinate Courts of Singapore, 2004, 2006). The Juvenile Court was subsequently renamed the Youth Court with the establishment of the Family Justice Courts, pursuant to the *Family Justice Act* (*Family Justice Act*, 2014). The *Children and Young Persons Act* (Chapter 38) (CYPA)[3] is the legislation that governs the proceedings in the Youth Court for youths aged 7 years to under 16 years (Kamal, 2002; Subordinate Courts of Singapore, 2004). The amended CYPA has been revised several times since 2001 to encompass more noncustodial options as well as to provide enhanced community orders to meet the various rehabilitation needs of juveniles (Kamal, 2002). The Magistrate of the Juvenile Court is assisted by a Panel of Advisers (which is comprised of court volunteers) and is supported by the Juvenile Probation Case Committee[4] to provide a more comprehensive analysis of the issues presented by each youth (Subordinate Courts of Singapore, 2001). In addition, the Magistrate considers the social investigation or pre-sentencing reports to provide a basis for dispositions.

In accordance with the principles of restorative justice, the Youth Court acknowledges the potential for positive change and seeks to reintegrate youth offenders into society (Subordinate Courts of Singapore, 2001, 2010). Youth offenders are held accountable for their offending behaviours and are asked to take responsibility for their actions and the consequences of these actions. Victims are also allowed to seek redress with the offender to increase the offender's awareness of the extent of harm caused by their misdeeds through victim-offender mediation.[5] This process is intended as a rehabilitation opportunity; specifically, it allows the offender to repair the harm and restore the relationship with the victim(s). Furthermore, the Youth Court seeks to empower parents to play a greater role in their child's rehabilitation, and they are given opportunities to take responsibility for their child's behaviours[6] (Subordinate Courts of Singapore, 2001, 2010). The Youth Court has the unique role of pursuing the fine balance between the youth's welfare and its state duty to uphold law and order (Kamal, 2002; Subordinate Courts of Singapore, 2001, 2004, 2010). Given the above-mentioned considerations, it appears that the risk-need-responsivity framework has an important role to play in the juvenile justice system in Singapore. In the next section, the main tenets of the risk-need-responsivity framework will be discussed.

Risk-need-responsivity framework

The risk-need-responsivity framework is underpinned by general personality and cognitive social learning (GPCSL) theoretical perspectives on criminal behaviour; in particular, the GPCSL approach posits that the criminal conduct of individuals is heavily influenced by the "Big Four" variables of antisocial cognition, past antisocial behaviour, antisocial personality patterns, and antisocial associates (see Andrews & Bonta, 2010 for a review). These four variables, together with difficulties pertaining to substance use, family and marital relationships, education and/or employment, and leisure activities, make up the "Central Eight" variables (see Figure 12.1) that are implicated in criminal offending behaviour (Andrews & Bonta, 2010). Meta-analyses of risk factors and criminogenic needs with various offender groups have enhanced our understanding of the risk factors that are associated with reoffending (e.g., Bonta, Law, & Hanson, 1998; Gendreau, Litte, & Goggin, 1996; Hanson & Morton-Bourgon, 2005; Lipsey & Derzon, 1998) and have provided empirical support for the "Big Four" as well as the "Central Eight" risk and need factors (see Andrews & Bonta, 2010; McGuire, 2004 for a review).

Figure 12.1 The "Central Eight" risk/need factors for criminal offending behaviour

The Central Eight	
The Big Four (Major Predictor Factors) • Antisocial cognition • Antisocial personality patterns • Antisocial associates • History of antisocial behaviour	The Moderate Four • Family and marital relationships • Education and/or employment • Substance use • Leisure activities

The risk-need-responsivity framework (Andrews & Bonta, 2010) posits that effective offender rehabilitation requires the accurate classification of the offender's level of risk and needs. Clinicians can make informed decisions about the levels of supervision as well as the type and intensity of the treatment interventions that are required when the risk level and needs of the offender are accurately identified and classified. The risk principle states that the levels of treatment and supervision should be matched with the risk level of the offender (Andrews, Bonta, & Hoge, 1990). Put differently, low-risk offenders should not be provided with intensive interventions so that interactions with higher-risk offenders are minimised (Andrews et al., 2011). This is because providing intensive rehabilitative programmes and supervision to low-risk offenders may actually increase their risk of recidivism through interaction with high-risk offenders within the programme (Andrews & Friesen, 1987; Andrews & Kiessling, 1980; Baird, Heinz, & Bemus, 1979; O'Donnell, Lydgate, & Fo, 1971). Overall, it is clear that the risk principle has implications for the level of service delivery as well as the usage and prioritisation of scarce resources.

The need principle states that interventions relating to offender rehabilitation should target dynamic criminogenic needs that are functionally related to criminal behaviour so as to reduce the risk of recidivism (Hoge, 2002). In addition, the responsivity principle articulates that the style and mode of intervention should match the offender's abilities and learning style. Regarding offender rehabilitation, interventions that adhere to all the risk-need-responsivity principles have been associated with significant reductions in recidivism rates, whereas those interventions that do not adhere to the risk-need-responsivity principles have poorer outcomes in terms of the reduction in recidivism rates (Andrews & Dowden, 2005).

As previously mentioned, the risk-need-responsivity principles have been shown to be hugely important for the assessment and rehabilitation aspects of offender management. The level of service risk assessment measures, which are associated with the risk-need-responsivity framework, are widely used assessment measures in many jurisdictions across the world (Andrews, Bonta, & Wormith, 2010). These measures include the Level of Service Inventory (LSI; Andrews, 1982), the Level of Service Inventory-Revised (LSI-R; Andrews & Bonta, 1995), the Level of Service/Case Management Inventory (LS/CMI; Andrews, Bonta, & Wormith, 2004), the Level of Service/Risk-Need-Responsivity (LS/RNR; Andrews, Bonta, & Wormith, 2008), the Youth Level of Service Inventory (YLSI; Andrews, Robinson, & Hoge, 1984), and the Youth Level of Service/Case Management Inventory (Hoge & Andrews, 2002, YLS/CMI; 2011).

Previously, assessments of risk and needs were often based on unstructured clinical judgements, and such a decision-making approach was criticised as being inaccurate and biased (Ægisdóttir et al., 2006; Grove, Zald, Lebow, Snitz, & Nelson, 2000; Monahan, 1981). Fortunately, with the advancement of risk assessment practices over the past three decades, there has been a consensus among professionals to adopt risk assessment measures that are structured and empirically based. These structured risk assessment measures provide a more valid and consistent assessment of risk of future offending behaviour and potential treatment needs (Hoge & Andrews, 2002) and reduce the potential for biases and unreliability. The suite of various YLS measures has been used in a variety of juvenile justice systems and correctional settings in different jurisdictions for assessing the risk of general recidivism and the criminogenic needs of youth offenders so as to guide judicial dispositions and make informed decisions regarding programme placements.

Youth level of service measures

Originally developed in Canada, the YLS measures have been successfully adapted for use in other international jurisdictions. Importantly, the YLS measures are objective and standardised actuarial measures that aim to meet the dual goals of assessing criminogenic risk and needs and guiding the formulation of appropriate case management plans (Hoge & Andrews, 2006). The current version (2.0) of the YLS/CMI contains six parts (see Table 12.1), with Parts I and II providing an assessment and summary of eight domains that correspond to the Central Eight risk and needs variables: prior or current offences/dispositions, family circumstances/parenting, education/employment, peer relations, substance abuse, leisure/recreation, personality/behaviour, and attitudes/orientation. Each of the 42 items among the eight domains are rated either "yes" or "no". The total number of endorsed items on each domain reflects the level of domain-specific criminogenic needs, and a total risk score can be computed by summing up the domain scores. Risk scores can then be classified into low, moderate, high and very high risk levels.

Part III: Assessment of Other Needs and Special Considerations constitutes a 51-item section that assesses the presence of non-criminogenic needs to improve the measure's responsivity and utility for assessing and providing individualised intervention and management of youth offenders. This part is divided into a Family/Parents sections and a Youth section, and items are rated either "yes" or "no". Part IV provides an overall summary of the risk level and needs of the client as well as a professional override, whereby the assessor may choose to lower or increase the assessed level of risk and need. Parts V and VI can then be used to detail programme/placement decisions and the case management plan for the youth, respectively.

Notably, there is a growing body of research on the predictive validity of the YLS measures among various youth offender populations. The YLS measures have been validated on male and female youths in both community and institutional settings as well as among various races, ethnicities, and indigenous populations (Andrews & Bonta, 2010; Brumbaugh, Hardison Walters, & Winterfield, 2009; Jung & Rawana, 1999; Matthews & Hubbard, 2008; Schwalbe, 2008). To date, most findings have consistently shown that the YLS measures are robust risk assessment instruments in predicting various outcomes, including rearrest, as well as general and violent recidivism (Catchpole & Gretton, 2003; Flores, Travis, & Latessa, 2004; Hoge & Andrews, 2006; Jung & Rawana, 1999; Upperton & Thompson, 2007; Welsh, Schmidt, McKinnon, Chattha, & Meyers, 2008).

Table 12.1 Components of the Youth Level of Service/Case Management Inventory 2.0

Part	*Description*
Part I – Assessment of Risks and Needs	• Provides the main assessment of eight domains that correspond to the Central Eight: o Prior or current offences/dispositions o Family circumstances/parenting o Education/employment o Peer relations o Substance abuse o Leisure/recreation o Personality/behaviour o Attitudes/orientation
Part II – Summary of Risks and Needs	• Provides a summary of the eight domains assessed in Part I. • Summaries of domain and total scores and their corresponding risk/need levels are provided (low, moderate, high, very high). • Normative scores and risk levels are also provided.
Part III – Assessment of Other Needs and Special Considerations	• 51-item section assessing the presence of non-criminogenic needs. • Divided into a section on family/parents (e.g., marital conflict, abusive father/mother) and a section on youth (e.g., history of bullying, low self-esteem).
Part IV – Final Risk/Need Level and Professional Override	• Provides an option to use a professional override for the assessor to raise or lower the assessed level of risk/need with justification. • Provides the final risk/need level.
Part V – Programme/ Placement Decision	• Provides a template for recommendation of placement and programmes for the assessed youth.
Part VI – Case Management Plan	• Provides a template for the recommended case management plan.

More recent meta-analytic studies on the YLS measures have indicated that the measures have modest to moderate predictive validity for general recidivism. In particular, Schwalbe (2007) found a mean weighted area under curve (AUC) of .64 on the basis of a review of 11 YLS studies. In an overlapping but larger sample of 19 studies, the mean-weighted correlation between YLS total scores and general recidivism was .32 (Olver et al., 2009). In their meta-analysis, Olver et al. (2009) reported that the YLS measures had lower predictive validity for general recidivism when they were used in other Western jurisdictions outside of Canada (mean-weighted correlation of .26 versus .35). They suggested that " 'international' differences contributed to the variability across studies" (p. 348).

In addition to the main 42-item scale, a screening version of the YLS/CMI has also been developed (YLS-SV, Hoge & Andrews, 2009). The YLS-SV is an eight-item measure that is designed to provide an initial screening of a set of risk factors and needs that correspond closely with domains of the YLS/CMI: history of conduct disorder, current school/employment problems, some criminal friends, alcohol/drug problems, leisure/recreation, personality/behaviour, family circumstances/parenting, and attitudes/orientation.

Implementation of the risk-need-responsivity framework in Singapore

To adopt an evidence-based framework and a structured risk assessment measure for assessing youth offenders in Singapore, an extensive review of existing offender rehabilitation frameworks and structured youth offender risk assessment measures was undertaken in 2001 by the Ministry of Social and Family Development (MSF; then the Ministry of Community Development and Sports). The risk-need-responsivity framework for offender rehabilitation was subsequently adopted at the Ministry of Social and Family Development (then the Ministry of Community Development and Sports) in 2003 (Chu, Ng, Fong, & Teoh, 2012). Concomitant with the implementation of the risk-need-responsivity framework, the Youth Level of Service/Case Management Inventory (YLS/CMI) was introduced as the principal youth offender risk assessment and case management measure. Following consultation with Professor Hoge (one of the authors of the YLS/CMI), the YLS/CMI scoring guidelines were initially localised so that the risk assessment measure would be culturally relevant to the Singapore youth offender population. For example, for the items in the prior or current offences/dispositions subscale, the term *convictions* was localised to follow legal terminology in Singapore. Similarly, for the items in the family circumstances/parenting and education/employment subscales, school and work contexts were localised to include the learning centres in youth correctional institutions and also compulsory military service for male youths. Localised examples were also included in the item descriptions for the various subscales to assist with the ratings (Chu et al., 2015). The YLS/CMI was then adopted by the Probation Service in 2003 for use in the assessment of youth offenders aged between 12 and 18 years. Its use has since grown, and it is currently being used by all agencies that come into contact with youth offenders; these agencies include the Singapore Police (screening version), the Central Narcotics Bureau, and the Singapore Prisons Service as well as non-governmental organisations that use the tool to assess antisocial youths. A brief summary of the use of the YLS/CMI in various agencies is presented in Table 12.2 below.

Importantly, the introduction of both the risk-need-responsivity framework and the YLS/CMI has helped to establish a systematic assessment of risk and needs for youth offenders and also to facilitate a common understanding of risk, need, and responsivity factors between professionals who are working with youth offenders and antisocial youths. Similarly, their implementation has also provided a structure by which youths' offending and antisocial behaviour may be investigated, leading to more focused and empirically based interventions for youth offenders (Chua, Chu, et al., 2014).

Table 12.2 Implementation of the risk-need-responsivity framework across agencies in Singapore

Agency	*Implementation and use*
Probation Service	In 2003, the Probation Service implemented the risk-need-responsivity framework in their assessments at the pre-sentencing phase of the juvenile justice system. Probation officers prepare pre-sentencing reports for the court using the YLS/CMI to assess the risk and needs of youth offenders. The measure assists probation officers to predict a youth offender's risk of recidivism and informs intervention planning and supervision intensity. As such, probation officers are better able to provide dispositional recommendations and directions on specific areas to focus on during intervention and case management. Youth offenders' risk and needs are assessed at the commencement and end of their court orders, and they are reassessed every six months or when summoned for court reviews. In addition, when they commit violations during their orders or when significant changes in their circumstances are observed, their risk and needs are assessed again using the YLS/CMI. This allows the practitioners to monitor youths' progress during their rehabilitation (Barnoski, 1998; Bonta, 2002) and to modify the case management plans and/or interventions to address their criminogenic needs whenever necessary.
Youth Residential Service	The risk-need-responsivity framework and the use of the YLS/CMI were successfully introduced to juvenile rehabilitation centres in 2011, which include youth residential correctional facilities such as the Singapore Boys' Home and the Singapore Girls' Home (Chu, Chu, et al., 2014). Similar to the Probation Service, youth offenders' risk and needs are assessed using the YLS/CMI at the commencement and end of their court orders, and they are reassessed every six months, when summoned for court reviews, or when they commit violations. This provides for systematic assessments of youth offenders with higher levels of risk and criminogenic needs. Similarly, it allows the caseworkers at the Juvenile Rehabilitation Centres to monitor progress and modify case management plans accordingly.
Central Narcotics Bureau	The Central Narcotics Bureau also adopted the risk-need-responsivity framework and the use of the YLS/CMI measure to assist their officers in classifying youths who have been arrested for drug-related offences (e.g., misuse of drugs) and thereafter to guide their decision as to whether to divert a juvenile from the courts. The Enhanced Supervision Scheme, which requires the evaluation of the risk levels of the youth drug offender and the appropriateness of intervention services, supports the use of the YLS/CMI in the management of these drug offenders. The implementation of the risk-need-responsivity framework and the adoption of the YLS/CMI allow the authorities to determine if a youth should receive low-intensity (e.g., community-based counselling and supervision) or high-intensity (e.g., institutionalisation in a drug rehabilitation centre) interventions.

(*Continued*)

Table 12.2 (Continued)

Agency	*Implementation and use*
Singapore Prison Service	Similarly, the Singapore Prison Service also adopted the risk-need-responsivity framework for the management and rehabilitation of youth offenders in their care in 2001; however, they did not fully implement the YLS/CMI as the primary risk assessment measure for youth offenders in the Reformative Training Centre until 2007. The YLS/CMI is conducted at the start and the end of the reformative training order. Assessment is also carried out to determine placement on community programmes that are designed to help youth offenders' transition and reintegration into the community.
Supervising Agencies for Beyond Parental Control Orders	The Beyond Parental Control (BPC) programme is a scheme through which caregivers may apply to the Juvenile Court to intervene with children and young persons deemed "beyond control" or "unmanageable". The court may issue an order for a child or young person to be placed under a court-appointed supervisor or to be sent to a place of safety, both for a period not exceeding three years. The BPC programme seeks to intervene with children and young persons who are believed to exhibit delinquent behaviour (e.g., running away, smoking, petty theft, etc.), and a key goal of the programme is to prevent them from escalating into offending. The risk-need-responsivity framework and the YLS/CMI have been used by the BPC programme since 2013 for the assessment of the risk of offending among its clients who display antisocial behaviour. Clients are first assessed prior to placement decisions in order to select appropriate interventions for the children in the programme. In particular, such assessment will mitigate the possibility of placing children who are lower risk in institutions with those who are higher risk. Clients are then assessed every six months until the end of the order as part of case management and the monitoring of intervention provided to clients. Additionally, the programme is currently considering the use of the screening version (YLS-SV) during the initial assessment phase when caregivers apply for BPC intervention.
Singapore Police Force	Although the Singapore Police Force has not as yet adopted the risk-need-responsivity framework, it worked with the Probation Service in 2012 to pilot a programme to assess youths at the point of arrest using the YLS-SV. The aim of the programme was to examine if the YLS-SV could assist with placement decisions, either placing youths in a pre-court diversionary programme or charging them on the basis of the severity of their offences and level of risk.

Research of the YLS measures in Singapore

Predictive validity and norms

Since 2009, several studies on the predictive validity of the YLS measures have been conducted in Singapore. Neo (2009) first developed norms for male youth offenders within the Singapore context (i.e., YLS/CMI total score: 0 to 10 = *low* risk, 11 to 19 = *moderate* risk, 20 to 26 = *high* risk, and 27 to 42 = *very high* risk). Subsequently, the predictive validity of the YLS/CMI and its screening version for assessing the risk of recidivism and identifying criminogenic needs in youth offenders were examined in several studies (e.g., Chu et al., 2012; Chu et al., 2015; Chu, Yu, Lee, & Zeng, 2014; Zeng, Chu, Koh, & Teoh, 2014), and the YLS measures were found to have adequate predictive validity for assessing the risk of violent ($AUC_{YLS/CMI\text{-}SV\_Male} = .62$), non-violent ($AUC_{YLS/CMI\text{-}SV\_Male} = .64$; $AUC_{YLS/CMI\text{-}SV\_Female} = .59$), and general recidivistic ($AUC_{YLS/CMI\_Male} = .65$; $AUC_{YLS/CMI\_Female} = .67$; $AUC_{YLS/CMI\text{-}SV\_Male} = .65$; $AUC_{YLS/CMI\text{-}SV\_Female} = .59$) outcomes but not sexual recidivism ($AUC_{YLS/CMI\_Male} = .29$). In addition, the risk cut-offs were useful in distinguishing the low-, moderate-, and high-risk community-based youth offenders in terms of time to recidivism. Chu et al. (2015) ascertained that the norms developed by Neo for community-based male offenders remained applicable, and they also derived the norms for community-based female offenders (i.e., YLS/CMI: 0 to 12 = *low* risk, 13 to 19 = *moderate* risk, and 20 to 42 = *high* risk). Their findings further suggested that strengths[7] and other special needs are also important in the assessment of youth offenders. In particular, incremental predictive validity was found for Part III: Assessment of Other Needs and Special Considerations, on top of the eight domains of the YLS/CMI ($\Delta R^2 = .062$), to predict general recidivism (AUC = .71).

The YLS/CMI and discrete groups

Even though the predictive validity of the YLS/CMI has been found to be generally adequate for youth offenders, different findings have been found for discrete groups, each with implications for the application and use of the YLS/CMI. A study by Lai, Zeng, and Chu (2015) demonstrated that the YLS/CMI was useful in differentiating the risk factors and criminogenic needs of violent and non-violent offenders. Furthermore, within the violent offender group, it was able to differentiate between offenders who committed only violent crimes (violent-only) and criminally diverse violent offenders (violent-plus). Violent-plus youths were found to have the highest levels of risk and criminogenic needs and the highest risk of violent and general reoffending; compared with non-violent youths, these youths had higher scores on all YLS/CMI domains and higher total risk scores.

In contrast, the violent-only youth offenders had similar total risk scores to non-violent youths, although the differences in risk for general and violent reoffending between both groups of youth offenders were nonsignificant. Violent-plus youth offenders were found to have a greater risk and need compared to violent-only youth offenders on five out of the eight domains of the YLS/CMI: prior and current offences/dispositions, family circumstances/parenting, education/employment, substance abuse, and attitudes/orientation.

In another study, Chng and colleagues (unpublished manuscript) showed the utility of other non-criminogenic needs as assessed in Part III of the YLS/CMI (in addition to the eight primary scales) when assessing youth offenders. Their study aimed to identify family subtypes of youth offenders and to explore the associations of these subtypes to offending outcomes. Eight family factors were used to examine family characteristics, including father's criminality, mother's criminality, sibling criminality, and non-intact family, that were coded through case reviews. The four other family factors were extracted from the YLS/CMI – marital conflict, psychiatric/emotional distress, and drug/alcohol abuse were extracted from the family/parents section of Part III of the YLS/CMI; the last factor was the family circumstance/parenting domain from Part I of the YLS/CMI.

Using latent class analysis, three classes of family were determined from the data: families with criminality (characterised by high levels of family criminality, non-intact family, and drug/alcohol abuse), poorly managed families (characterised by higher levels of poor parenting, non-intact family, and marital conflict), and intact functioning families (characterised by minimal family criminality, lower probability of being from a non-intact family, and lower levels of poor parenting). The intact functioning family class had a lower likelihood of recidivism compared to the other two family classes. However, there was no significant difference in the likelihood of reoffending among the families with criminality and poorly managed families classes. The findings point to the importance of family factors in reoffending and in assessing the various characteristics of families (as in the YLS/CMI) for case management and intervention.

The above-mentioned studies have demonstrated the utility of the risk-need-responsivity framework and the YLS/CMI in examining offender typology or risk factors and their associations with offending outcomes. However, other studies that have been conducted signal that caution should be exercised when using the YLS/CMI for certain groups and circumstances. As mentioned above, the YLS/CMI has been found inadequate for use in predicting sexual recidivism among youths who have offended both sexually and non-sexually (Chu et al., 2012; Lai et al., 2015). With regard to gender, only three out of the eight domains of the YLS/CMI have been found to predict general recidivism for females (prior and current offences/disposition, family circumstances/parenting, and attitudes/orientation), as compared to six domains for males (the exceptions being peer relations and personality/behaviour). Furthermore, only two of the other non-criminogenic needs as measured in Part III were associated with general recidivism (Chu et al., 2015). This may indicate that there may be some risk factors and needs relevant to female youth offenders that are not captured by the YLS/CMI (Chu et al., 2015).

Additionally, in a matched-control study conducted on youth offenders in Singapore, Li and colleagues (2015) found that care should be taken when using the YLS/CMI to assess maltreated youth offenders, despite its usefulness for predicting general recidivism in non-maltreated youth offenders. In particular, the unique contribution of childhood maltreatment on recidivism suggests that the YLS/CMI 2.0 overall risk ratings (derived from Singaporean norms) are not able to successfully differentiate maltreated offenders, especially those who are classified as low or moderate risk. In fact, the findings showed that the recidivism rates for maltreated offenders who were assessed as being low and moderate risk were not significantly different from those for non-maltreated offenders who were classified as being high risk. Given these findings, practitioners should be cautious when using the YLS/CMI 2.0 to assess maltreated youth offenders. These findings have important implications for risk classification and management. Notably, these findings could potentially affect the recommendations provided by probation officers to the courts for their pre-sentence assessments; they suggest that it may be useful to employ the professional override for the YLS/CMI overall risk rating when assessing maltreated youth offenders.

Taken together, it is apparent that the YLS measures are suitable for use within the juvenile justice system in Singapore. The aforementioned studies strengthen the implementation of the risk-need-responsivity framework for offender rehabilitation and promote evidence-based practice that is grounded in the nuances of the local setting. Such empirical endeavours present evidence to support the effectiveness of the YLS measures in systematically assessing risk as well as formulating case management plans. Hence, judicial decisions pertaining to youth offenders can be consistent and unbiased and youth offenders can receive appropriate interventions suited to their criminogenic needs.

Training

Professor Hoge was also instrumental in developing and conducting a series of workshops for professionals working in the youth justice system. Two types of training workshops have been conducted since 2011: one to train and certify users, the other to train the trainers. As part of the YLS/CMI certification programme, users were required to attend a two-and-a-half day training programme in which participants were equipped with (a) knowledge of the risk-need-responsivity framework and related research; (b) the principles of interviewing, scoring, and developing a case management plan using the YLS/CMI; and (c) hands-on scoring opportunities. Participants in the training programme had to complete an examination that measured their knowledge of the risk-need-responsivity framework and the YLS/CMI and had to pass with a score of 80% or higher. They were also required to rate the YLS/CMI using a test vignette with six or fewer scoring errors and then develop an appropriate case management plan linking the relevant risk and need factors. Regardless of the examination outcomes, participants received individualised feedback from the trainers. Additional support and coaching were provided to those who performed poorly before they were reassessed. Upon successful completion of the examination, participants were certified as YLS/CMI users and could conduct YLS/CMI assessments independently.

Nevertheless, they were encouraged to consult with more experienced YLS/CMI users should they encounter any difficulties.

Notably, some certified YLS/CMI users[8] were also selected for the train-the-trainer course that was conducted by Professor Hoge. This training provided an in-depth examination of the risk-need-responsivity framework and its research; hands-on scoring opportunities; and knowledge and practice of the delivery of the YLS/CMI training programme for users. Furthermore, participants had to submit two YLS/CMI assessments and corresponding case management plans to Professor Hoge for audit. Once qualified as trainers, these participants became responsible for conducting future YLS/CMI training for users within the Singapore juvenile justice system whenever necessary.

Centralising the practice of risk-need-responsivity and the use of the YLS: Multi-agency workgroup

To support the implementation of the risk-need-responsivity framework and the use of the YLS/CMI in the youth offender rehabilitation sector in Singapore, a multi-agency workgroup was established to be responsible for coordinating ongoing training and research efforts, applying local research data to the development of the YLS/CMI, disseminating local YLS/CMI research findings, looking into leveraging technology to develop a more sustainable model of training and data collection, and maintaining the quality of YLS/CMI risk assessments.

Since 2014, the training and certification of the YLS/CMI in Singapore has been centralised within the Social Service Institute of Singapore (SSI),[9] which provides the same two-and-a-half day programme and certification process. This has made the certification process more efficient by reducing the need for each agency to conduct their own in-house training. Importantly, the SSI also conducts annual recertification exercises, whereby existing users undergo a web-based course that refreshes and updates their current knowledge about using the YLS/CMI.

Overall, the risk-need-responsivity framework has enhanced the transparency and consistency of policy and decision-making processes that pertain to the assessment, adjudication, and management of youths who have committed offences. It also guides the development and improvement of various programmes to effectively target the specific criminogenic risk and needs of the youth population. Importantly, a common risk assessment and management framework allows the involved agencies to coordinate the interventions for the youth offender population better. In the next section, we examine some of the local research that has been conducted on the YLS measures.

Future directions

While the implementation of the risk-need-responsivity framework and the YLS/CMI has widened and become more coordinated since the early 2000s, much can be done to improve and extend the progress that has been made. It is important to continue to conduct checks and audits on the YLS/CMI training programmes and the recertification process. At the same time, it is crucial to engage new institutions that may be seeking to adopt the risk-need-responsivity framework into their practice. To this end, the SSI, the multi-agency workgroup, and current agencies are working to encourage agencies that work with youth offenders to adopt and implement the risk-need-responsivity framework and the YLS/CMI.

As they have been widely implemented in Singapore, the risk-need-responsivity framework and the YLS/CMI are featured in almost all current investigations on youth offenders in Singapore and will continue to be included in future studies. Together with continual checks and auditing of the use of YLS/CMI, the norms for various typologies of offenders and the predictive validity of the instrument for reoffending should be periodically reassessed. There are currently research programmes applying the risk-need-responsivity framework and the YLS/CMI to specific groups, such as investigating the risk and needs of female offenders and establishing norms for institutionalised youth offenders. Future studies could continue to test and identify groups for which the use of the YLS/CMI may be suitable and to examine how the instrument may be applied, in conjunction with other measures, for use in groups for whom it may not be as suitable (as mentioned above). As programmes of research continue to expand and data on Singaporean youth offenders are collected, it may also be of use to conduct cross-cultural comparisons with other jurisdictions in order to identify any similarities and differences in risk and need among youth offenders and how the YLS/CMI may be adapted to such differences. Finally, research is also required into issues regarding implementation such as the translation of assessment findings into effective case planning and management.

Conclusion

In summary, the adoption and implementation of the risk-need-responsivity framework and the YLS/CMI has expanded since their introduction into Singapore in the early 2000s. As more agencies have brought the framework and instrument into their practices, they have provided a centralised structure and common foundation from which the assessment and management of and research on youth offenders in Singapore can occur. As they become more established in the country, there is a need to ensure the continuation and expansion of coordination, education, and research among local and international institutions in order to further develop and inform responsive assessments and interventions for youth offenders.

Chapter summary points

- Multiple agencies in Singapore's youth justice system have adopted the risk-need-responsivity framework.
- Localised YLS/CMI scoring guidelines ensure cultural relevance.
- Research has shown that the YLS/CMI is suitable for use in Singapore.
- A standardised training and audit framework has improved the reliability of YLS ratings.

Notes

1 Total population of 5.47 million includes Singapore residents and non-residents. Singapore's resident population is about 3.87 million, of which 74.3% are Chinese, 13.3% are Malays, 9.1% are Indians, and 3.3% are of other races.
2 Youth arrests refer to children and young persons who are arrested for offences. Please see below for the definition of children and young persons under the *Children and Young Persons Act.*
3 In the *Children and Young Persons Act*, a "child" refers to a person who is below the age of 14 years and a "young person" refers to a person who is 14 years of age (or above) and under 16 years old.
4 The Juvenile Probation Case Committee's primary tasks are to review the progress of probationers and set procedural guidelines to ensure due process in the treatment of offenders on non-custodial sanctions. It also allows for the monitoring mechanisms at the Probation Service (e.g., case conferencing, the one-on-one supervision which every probation officer is entitled to, and a computerised case management system).
5 Mediation can be carried out through healing, enriching, and linking (HEAL) conferences, which provide victim-offender mediation. The conferences focus on the restoration of the victim through meeting the offender in circumstances that would be most comfortable to the victim. The victim and family can then be guided to further restoration programmes (Family Justice Courts of Singapore, 2015).
6 These are carried out through family conferences which provide a platform that brings together the youth, the youth's family, and professionals (e.g., psychologists, school, police, etc.) involved with the youth. The family conferences aim to involve the family in the youth's rehabilitation and reintegration into society by addressing issues such as reconciliation between the youth and the family, constructing social contracts to take steps to cultivate prosocial behaviour, and mandatory counselling for parents (Family Justice Courts of Singapore, 2015).
7 Strengths are purported protective factors that have utility in mitigating the level of risk that an individual poses and also possibly reducing the likelihood of recidivism. Strengths are assessed in the following domains of the YLS/CMI: *Family Circumstances/Parenting, Education/Employment, Peer Relations, Substance Abuse, Leisure/Recreation, Personality/Behaviour,* and *Attitudes/Orientation*). For example, for a youth who has very few risk factors in the family domain and whose parents are very supportive and exhibit good parenting practices, the assessor can indicate that the youth possesses a strength in this domain.
8 These users come from various institutions implementing and using the YLS/CMI in practice and research and include probation officers, corrections officers, social workers, and researchers.
9 More information on YLS/CMI training and about the instrument can be found at https://www.socialserviceinstitute.sg/Default.aspx.

References

Ægisdóttir, S., White, M. J., Spengler, P. M., Maugherman, A. S., Anderson, L. A., Cook, R. S., . . . Rush, J. D. (2006). The meta-analysis of clinical judgment project: Fifty-six years of accumulated research on clinical versus statistical prediction. *The Counseling Psychologist, 34*(3), 341–382. doi: 10.1177/0011000005285875

Andrews, D. A. (1982). *The Level of Supervision Inventory (LSI): The first follow-up.* Toronto, ON: Ontario Ministry of Correctional Services.

Andrews, D. A., & Bonta, J. (1995). *The Level of Service Inventory-Revised.* Toronto, ON: Multi-Health Systems.

Andrews, D. A., & Bonta, J. (2010). *The psychology of criminal conduct* (5th ed.). New Providence, NJ: Anderson.

Andrews, D. A., Bonta, J., & Hoge, R. D. (1990). Classification for effective rehabilitation: Rediscovering psychology. *Criminal Justice and Behavior, 17*(1), 19–52. doi: 10.1177/0093854890017001004

Andrews, D. A., Bonta, J., & Wormith, J. S. (2004). *The Level of Service/Case Management Inventory (LS/CMI).* Toronto, ON: Multi-Health Systems.

Andrews, D. A., Bonta, J., & Wormith, J. S. (2008). *The Level of Service/Risk-Need-Responsivity (LS/RNR).* Toronto, ON: Multi-Health Systems.

Andrews, D. A., Bonta, J., & Wormith, J. S. (2010). The level of service (LS) assessment of adults and older adolescents. In R. K. Otto & K. Douglas (Eds.), *Handbook of violence risk assessment* (pp. 199–225). New York, NY: Routledge.

Andrews, D. A., Bonta, J., & Wormith, J. S. (2011). The risk-need-responsivity (RNR) model: Does adding the Good Lives Model contribute to effective crime prevention? *Criminal Justice and Behavior, 38*(7), 735–755. doi: 10.1177/0093854811406356

Andrews, D. A., & Dowden, C. (2005). Managing correctional treatment for reduced recidivism: A meta-analytic review of programme integrity. *Legal and Criminological Psychology, 10*(2), 173–187. doi: 10.1348/135532505X36723

Andrews, D. A., & Friesen, W. (1987). Assessments of anticriminal plans and the prediction of criminal futures: A research note. *Criminal Justice and Behavior, 14*(1), 33–37. doi: 10.1177/0093854887014001004

Andrews, D. A., & Kiessling, J. J. (1980). Program structure and effective correctional practices: A summary of the CaVIC research. In R. R. Ross & P. Gendreau (Eds.), *Effective correctional treatment* (pp. 439–463). Toronto, ON: Butterworth.

Andrews, D. A., Robinson, D., & Hoge, R. D. (1984). *Manual for the Youth Level of Service Inventory.* Ottawa, ON: Carleton University, Department of Psychology.

Baird, S. C., Heinz, R. C., & Bemus, B. J. (1979). *Project report #14: A two-year follow-up.* Madison, WI: Department of Health and Social Services, Case Classification/Staff Deployment Project, Bureau of Community Corrections.

Barnoski, R. (1998). *Juvenile rehabilitation administration assessments: Validity, review and recommendations.* Olympia, WA: Washington State Institute for Public Policy.

Bartol, C. R., & Barol, A. M. (1998). *Delinquency and justice: A psychosocial approach* (2nd ed.). Upper Saddle River, NJ: Prentice Hall.

Bonta, J. (2002). Offender risk assessment guidelines for selection and use. *Criminal Justice and Behavior, 29*(4), 355–379. doi: 10.1177/0093854802029004002

Bonta, J., Law, M., & Hanson, K. (1998). The prediction of criminal and violent recidivism among mentally disordered offenders: A meta-analysis. *Psychological Bulletin, 123*(2), 123–142. doi: 10.1037/0033-2909.123.2.123

Brumbaugh, S., Hardison Walters, J. L., & Winterfield, L. A. (2009). *Suitability of assessment instruments for delinquent girls.* Washington, DC: U.S. Department of Justice, Office of Justice Programs, Office of Juvenile Justice and Delinquency Prevention.

Catchpole, R. E. H., & Gretton, H. M. (2003). The predictive validity of risk assessment with violent young offenders: A 1-year examination of criminal outcome. *Criminal Justice and Behavior, 30*(6), 688–708. doi: 10.1177/0093854803256455

Champion, D. J. (1998). *The juvenile justice system: Deliquency, processing, and the law.* Upper Saddle River, NJ: Prentice Hall.

Chng, G., Chu, C. M., Zeng, G., Li, D., & Ting, M. H. *Family characteristics linked to youth offending outcomes* (Unpublished manuscript).

Chu, C. M., Lee, Y., Zeng, G., Yim, G., Tan, C. Y., Ang, Y., . . . Ruby, K. (2015). Assessing youth offenders in a non-Western context: The predictive validity of the YLS/CMI ratings. *Psychological Assessment*, *27*(3), 1013–1021. doi: 10.1037/a0038670

Chu, C. M., Ng, K., Fong, J., & Teoh, J. (2012). Assessing youth who sexually offended: The predictive validity of the ERASOR, J-SOAP-II, and YLS/CMI in a non-Western context. *Sexual Abuse: A Journal of Research and Treatment*, *24*(2), 153–174. doi: 10.1177/1079063211404250

Chu, C. M., Yu, H., Lee, Y., & Zeng, G. (2014). The utility of the YLS/CMI-SV for assessing youth offenders in Singapore. *Criminal Justice and Behavior*, *41*(12), 1437–1457. doi: 10.1177/0093854814537626

Chua, J. R., Chu, C. M., Yim, G., Chong, D., & Teoh, J. (2014). The implementation of the risk-needs-responsivity framework across the youth justice services in Singapore. *Psychiatry, Psychology, and Law*, *21*(6), 877–889. doi: 10.1080/13218719.2014.918076

Corrado, R. R., & Turnbull, S. D. (1992). A comparative examination of the Modified Justice Model in the United Kingdom and the United States. In R. R. Corrado, N. Bala, R. Linden, & M. Le Blanc (Eds.), *Juvenile justice in Canada: A theoretical and analytical assessment* (pp. 75–136). Toronto, ON: Buttersworth.

Family Justice Act, Pub. L. No. 27 Singapore (2014).

Family Justice Courts of Singapore. (2015). *Youth court matters.* Retrieved from https://www.familyjusticecourts.gov.sg/Common/Pages/YouthMatters.aspx#programmes

Flores, A. W., Travis, L. F., & Latessa, E. J. (2004). *Case classification for juvenile corrections: An assessment of the Youth Level of Service/Case Management Inventory.* Cincinnati, OH: Division of Criminal Justice.

Gendreau, P., Litte, T., & Goggin, C. (1996). A meta-analysis of the predictors of adult offender recidivism: What works! *Criminology*, *34*(4), 575–608. doi: 10.1111/j.1745-9125.1996.tb01220.x

Grisso, T., Tomkins, A., & Casey, P. (1988). Psychosocial concepts in juvenile law. *Law and Human Behavior*, *12*(4), 403–437.

Grove, W. M., Zald, D. H., Lebow, B. S., Snitz, B. E., & Nelson, C. (2000). Clinical versus mechanical prediction: A meta-analysis. *Psychological Assessment*, *12*(1), 19–30. doi: 10.1037/1040–3590.12.1.19

Hanson, R. K., & Morton-Bourgon, K. E. (2005). The characteristics of persistent sexual offenders: A meta-analysis of recidivism studies. *Journal of Consulting and Clinical Psychology*, *73*(6), 1154–1163. doi: 10.1037/0022-006X.73.6.1154

Hoge, R. D. (1999). An expanded role for psychological assessments in juvenile justice systems. *Criminal Justice and Behavior*, *26*(2), 251–266. doi: 10.1177/0093854899026002006

Hoge, R. D. (2001). *The juvenile offender: Theory, research, and applications.* Boston, MA: Kluwer Academic.

Hoge, R. D. (2002). Standardized instruments for assessing risk and need in youthful offenders. *Criminal Justice and Behavior*, *29*(4), 380–396. doi: 10.1177/009385480202900403

Hoge, R. D., & Andrews, D. A. (2002). *Youth Level of Service/Case Management Inventory (YLS/CMI).* Toronto, ON: Multi-Health Systems.

Hoge, R. D., & Andrews, D. A. (2006). *Youth Level of Service/case Management Inventory (YLS/CMI): User's manual.* Toronto, ON: Multi-Health Systems.

Hoge, R. D., & Andrews, D. A. (2009). *Youth Level of Service/Case Management Inventory-Screening Version.* Toronto, ON: Multi-Health Systems.

Hoge, R. D., & Andrews, D. A. (2011). *Youth Level of Service/Case Mangement Inventory 2.0 (YLS/CMI 2.0): User's manual.* Toronto, ON: Multi-Health Systems.

Johnson, J. B., & Secret, P. E. (1995). The effects of court structure on juvenile court decision making. *Journal of Criminal Justice, 23*(1), 63–82. doi: 10.1016/0047-2352(94)00045-X

Jung, S., & Rawana, E. P. (1999). Risk and need assessment of juvenile offenders. *Criminal Justice and Behavior, 26*(1), 69–89. doi: 10.1177/0093854899026001004

Kamal, C. (2002). *Directions of juvenile justice reforms in Singapore.* Visiting Experts' Papers, 118th International Training Course, Resource Material Series No. 59 (pp 113–127). Tokyo: United Nations Asia and Far East Institute for the Prevention of Crime and Treatment of Offenders.

Krisberg, B., & Howell, J. C. (1998). The impact of the juvenile justice system and prospects for graduated sanctions in a comprehensive strategy. In R. Loeber & D. P. Farrington (Eds.), *Serious and violent juvenile offenders: Risk factors and successful interventions* (pp. 346–366). Thousand Oaks, CA: Sage.

Lai, V., Zeng, G., & Chu, C. M. (2015). Violent and nonviolent youth offenders: Preliminary evidence on group subtypes. *Youth Violence and Juvenile Justice, 14*(3), 313–329. doi: 10.1177/1541204015615193

Li, D., Chu, C. M., Goh, J. T. L., Ng, I. Y. H., & Zeng, G. (2015). Impact of childhood maltreatment on recidivism in youth offenders: A matched-control study. *Criminal Justice and Behavior, 42*, 990–1007. doi: 70.1177/0093854815598598.

Lipsey, M. W., & Derzon, J. H. (1998). Predictors of violent or serious delinquency in adolescence and early adulthood: A synthesis of longitudinal research. In R. Loeber & D. P. Farrington (Eds.), *Serious and violent juvenile offenders: Risk factors and successful interventions* (pp. 86–105). Thousand Oaks, CA: Sage.

Matthews, B., & Hubbard, D. J. (2008). Moving ahead: Five essential elements for working effectively with girls. *Journal of Criminal Justice, 36*(6), 494–502. doi: 10.1016/j.crimjus.2008.09.011

McGuire, J. (2004). *Understanding psychology and crime: Perspectives on theory and action.* Berkshire, UK: Open University Press.

Melton, G., Petrila, J., Poythress, N. G., & Slobogin, C. (1997). *Psychological evaluations for the courts: A handbook for mental health professionals and lawyers* (2nd ed.). New York, NY: Guilford.

Monahan, J. (1981). *Predicting violent behavior: An assessment of clinical techniques.* Beverly Hills, CA: Sage.

Mulvey, E. P., & Saunders, J. T. (1982). Juvenile detention criteria: State of art and guidelines for change. *Criminal Justice Abstracts, 14*, 261–289.

Neo, L. H. (2009). *A retrospective study of factors predicting breach and reoffending in local young offenders under the purview of RPRSD.* Rehabiliation, Protection and Residential Services Division (now Rehabilitation and Protection Group). Ministry of Social and Family Development, Singapore.

O'Donnell, C. R., Lydgate, T., & Fo, W. S. O. (1971). The buddy system: Review and follow-up. *Child Behavior Therapy, 1*(2), 161–169. doi: 10.1300/J473v01n02_03

Olver, M. E., Stockdale, K. C., & Wormith, J. S. (2009). Risk assessment with young offenders: A meta-analysis of three assessment measures. *Criminal Justice and Behavior, 36*(4), 329–353. doi: 10.1177/0093854809331457

Sanborn, J. B. (1996). Factors perceived to affect delinquent dispositions in juvenile court: Putting the sentencing decision into context. *Crime & Delinquency, 42*(1), 99–113. doi: 10.1177/0011128796042001006

Schwalbe, C. S. (2007). Risk assessment for juvenile justice: A meta-analysis. *Law and Human Behavior, 31*(5), 449–462. doi: 10.1007/s10979-006-9071-7

Schwalbe, C. S. (2008). A meta-analysis of juvenile justice risk assessment instruments: Predictive validity by gender. *Criminal Justice and Behavior*, *35*(11), 1367–1381. doi: 10.1177/0093854808324377

Singapore Department of Statistics. (2015). *Yearbook of statistics 2015*. Retrieved from http://www.singstat.gov.sg/docs/default-source/default-document-library/publications/publications_and_papers/reference/yearbook_2015/yos2015.pdf

Singapore Police Force. (2015). *Annual crime brief 2014*. Retrieved from http://www.spf.gov.sg/stats/crimebrief2014.html

Subordinate Courts of Singapore. (2001). *The Juvenile Justice Division*. Retrieved from http://app.subcourts.gov.sg/Data/Files/File/AR_2001/Juvenile.pdf

Subordinate Courts of Singapore. (2004). *Juveniles @ juvenile court*. Retrieved from http://app.subcourts.gov.sg/Data/Files/File/Research/RB34.pdf

Subordinate Courts of Singapore. (2006). *About juvenile justice – Role of juvenile court*. Retrieved from http://www.juvenilecourtofsingapore.gov.sg/abt_JJ_role_juvenilecourt.htm

Subordinate Courts of Singapore. (2010). *Philosophy – Restorative justice model*. Retrieved from http://app.subcourts.gov.sg/juvenile/page.aspx?pageid=3854

Upperton, R. A., & Thompson, A. P. (2007). Predicting juvenile offender recidivism: Risk-need assessment and juvenile justice officers. *Psychiatry, Psychology and Law*, *14*(1), 138–146. doi: 10.1375/pplt.14.1.138

Welsh, J. L., Schmidt, F., McKinnon, L., Chattha, H. K., & Meyers, J. R. (2008). A comparative study of adolescent risk assessment instruments: Predictive and incremental validity. *Assessment*, *15*(1), 104–115. doi: 10.1177/1073191107307966

Young, D., Moline, K., Farrell, J., & Bierie, D. (2006). Best implementation practices: Disseminating new assessment technologies in a juvenile justice agency. *Crime & Delinquency*, *52*(1), 135–158. doi: 10.1177/0011128705281752

Zeng, G., Chu, C. M., Koh, L. L., & Teoh, J. (2014). Risk and criminogenic needs of youth who sexually offended in Singapore: An examination of two typologies. *Sexual Abuse: A Journal of Research and Treatment*, *27*(5), 479–495. doi: 10.1177/1079063213520044

Part 3

Research and future directions

13 Singaporean police officers who responded to a major riot

A study of psychological reactions

Rong Cheng Lee, Majeed Khader, Ciping Goh, Hui Fen Ho, Yining Tham, Samantha Hui Fang Neo, and Jansen Ang

Introduction

While there is a growing body of evidence in North America and Europe examining the effects of policing on police officers' psychological well-being, little is known about developments in other parts of the world. Yet this knowledge would bolster the development of practices and programmes and the provision of support services in relation to the field of police psychology. In this chapter, the possible onset of traumatic stress symptomatology and psychiatric morbidity among police officers following a riot incident in Singapore is investigated. In addition, police officers' use of coping strategies is examined to better understand how they cope following such incidents.

The Singapore context

On the night of 8 December 2013, the Singapore Police Force (SPF) responded to a riot that lasted around two hours in the vicinity of Little India and involved about 400 Indian migrant workers. Little India is a neighbourhood that hosts traditional Indian businesses and shops, and it is also where many foreign workers congregate during the weekends. On the whole, locals and foreigners have coexisted peacefully in Singapore, even in crowded places like Little India during weekends when foreign workers typically spend their day off in their ethnic enclave. The riot was a unique and unexpected event for the nation and especially for the SPF given that it was the first riot in Singapore in 40 years. Although the SPF has performed public order duties and crowd management functions regularly in recent years (e.g., annual National Day celebrations; the provision of security for Singapore's hosting of international meetings such as the 2006 meeting of the International Monetary Fund), the Little India riot was arguably the first time in a long while that the SPF had to respond to a large-scale violent incident. About 300 officers were dispatched to the scene to manage the riot incident. During the incident, officers were faced with potential life-threatening situations (e.g., police officers were pelted with bricks and rocks, ambulances were set on fire, police cars were overturned) and violent perpetrators while trying to disperse the crowd and take control of the scene (Neo & Chia, 2013). The riot lasted for around two hours. The chaos resulted in 25 damaged emergency vehicles, in addition to five which were set on fire, and left 39 officers injured (Lim, 2014). While police officers undergo a rigorous regime of training before passing out of the police academy (e.g., taught crowd management skills, how to defuse violent situations, stress-coping skills for self-care), there are still concerns as to the level of impact their involvement in the Little India riot may have had on the police officers.

Riot policing and stress reactions

Policing as a vocation has been regarded as one of the most stressful occupations in the world due to the exposure to a wide range of critical incidents (Anshel, 2000; Rudofossi, 2007). Police critical incidents can be divided into two categories: very violent incidents, entailing active participation in events, and very depressing incidents, entailing confrontation with the repercussions of events (Carlier & Gersons, 1992; Larsson, Kempe, & Starrin, 1988). Examples of the former include shooting incidents, hostage takings, and riot situations; examples of the latter include dealing with seriously injured victims or corpses and disaster rescue work (Carlier, Lamberts, & Gersons, 1997).

One type of critical incident in the violent category is police management of riot situations, which involves interaction with violent individuals and managing aggressive crowds (Garbarino, Cuomo, Chiorri, Piattino, & Magnavita, 2012). This can be particularly stressful for police officers as they are required to make time-critical decisions and utilise appropriate strategies to protect the lives of others and property (Garbarino et al., 2012). Moreover, exposure to the death and suffering of human beings during these incidents can further exacerbate officers' stress levels (Robinson & Mitchell, 1993).

Involvement in critical incidents can subsequently result in acute stress reactions that are overwhelming for police officers, sometimes impeding their ability to cope and taking an emotional toll even on the most resilient officer (Kates, 1999; Mitchell & Bray, 1990; Pasciak & Kelley, 2013; Robinson & Mitchell, 1993). Stress symptoms can continue over a significant period of time (Robinson & Mitchell, 1993) and can possibly result in post-traumatic stress disorder (PTSD) (Carlier et al., 1997; Robinson & Mitchell, 1993; Stephens & Miller, 1998) and minor psychiatric morbidity (MPM) (Doctor, Curtis, & Isaacs, 1994; Ghosh, Chaudhury, & Zaman, 2011).

Post-traumatic stress disorder

PTSD has been found to be one of the possible outcomes resulting from involvement in critical incidents (Carlier et al., 1997; Robinson & Mitchell, 1993; Stephens & Miller, 1998). According to the Diagnostic and Statistical Manual of

Mental Disorder (5th ed.), an individual with PTSD may re-experience the traumatic event involuntarily (e.g., recurring nightmares), exhibit avoidance behaviour (e.g., consciously steering clear of external reminders related to the event), display symptoms of increased arousal (e.g., sleep disturbances or reckless behaviour), and present negative cognitions and mood (e.g., persistent and distorted sense of self-blame) (American Psychiatric Association, 2013). These symptoms may be present for at least a month and may cause significant impairment to the individual's daily functioning (e.g., affect their work performance).

Robinson and Mitchell (1993) examined the effects of critical incident stress on 100 American suburban police officers. Stressors included involvement in shooting incidents or attending to incidents involving the dead. The participants completed a questionnaire which included the Impact of Event Scale – Revised (Weiss & Marmar, 1997) to assess PTSD symptomatology according to the DSM-IV-TR (American Psychiatric Association, 2000) criteria. The results indicated that 13% of the sample met the diagnostic criteria for PTSD, which was high compared to the 7% figure for the US general population (National Institute of Mental Health, 2014). Similar results have been reported for police officers involved in critical incidents in the Netherlands and New Zealand (Carlier et al., 1997; Stephens & Miller, 1998).

However, it is less clear whether these effects are found across the world, especially in Asian contexts. Moreover, research examining post-traumatic stress symptomatology following specific types of critical incidents is limited. Therefore, the current research aimed to address these questions by determining the extent of trauma symptomology in police officers following a riot incident in Singapore.

Minor psychiatric morbidity

Psychological distress or disturbances to psychological well-being, otherwise referred to as minor psychiatric morbidity (MPM), have also been found to be an outcome of police work due to the stressful nature of the occupation (Doctor et al., 1994; Ghosh et al., 2011; Khader, 1995). Doctor et al. (1994) explored this relationship among a sample of 171 police officers in the United Kingdom. Through the administration of the General Health Questionnaire (GHQ), the results showed that 24% of the officers met the criteria for minor MPM. Khader's (1995) study also found similar results: Using the GHQ, more than 33% of 121 Singaporean police corporals were found to have MPM, which is higher than the national norm of 17% (Fones, Kua, Ng, & Ko, 1998). However, contrary to the aforementioned findings, Ghosh et al. (2011) found that in a sample of 116 police officers, none of the officers met the threshold for MPM in respect to policing work in India, although it is unclear if the GHQ was used in this study.

As the findings in the past literature are mixed, the results are too inconclusive to draw any firm implications. Moreover, studies have yet to examine the relationship between the experience of critical incidents and the subsequent onset of MPM. The studies discussed focused on the relationship between the police occupation as a whole and the development of possible MPM. Therefore, the current study aimed to address these issues by examining this relationship in the context of a riot incident in Singapore.

Coping strategies and stress

People try to cope with their stressors in various ways and have varying degrees of success. Efficient and adaptive coping skills can help individuals manage or even buffer against the effects of stress to maintain their psychological well-being (Foa, Davidson, & Frances, 1999). Coping responses may be broadly grouped into three categories: problem-focused coping, active emotional coping, and avoidant emotional coping (Carver & Scheier, 1994; Folkman & Lazarus, 1985; Holahan & Moos, 1987). Problem-focused coping involves proactive attempts to adjust the current situation so as to resolve the issue. Active emotional coping involves directly reducing stress levels through managing of one's emotions: for example, by the venting of emotions through exercise and talking to others about one's worries. Finally, avoidant emotional coping involves escaping from the current reality through non-engagement: some examples would include denying the existence of the stressor and doing nothing about it and also coping through the use of substances (e.g., smoking, alcohol).

Problem-focused coping and active emotional coping, rather than avoidant emotional coping, have been found to be useful for police officers to manage their operational stressors. Violanti (1992, 1993) found that compared with the use of avoidant emotional coping such as the avoidance or denial of the problem, the use of problem-focused coping such as devising plans to resolve a problem is more effective in decreasing officers' personal distress during simulated stressful police situations. Furthermore, the use of active emotional coping such as humour has been found to be useful in both training and actual policing situations (Papazoglou & Andersen, 2014). Avoidant emotional coping seems to be generally related to poorer psychological well-being in police officers after experiencing a traumatic event (Anshel, 2000), which is in line with the prevalent literature on trauma recovery. This suggests that avoidant emotional coping tends to be regarded as relatively maladaptive for police officers' well-being in the long run.

However, research suggests that police officers may sometimes turn to avoidant emotional coping/maladaptive coping strategies to deal with their stress. Cross and Ashley (2004) found that the use of maladaptive coping methods such as alcohol abuse, gambling, and unsafe sex were more common among police officers than the general population. Possible explanations for this include the pressures of police culture, such as loyalty and secrecy, that ultimately create barriers for officers in seeking help (Atkinson-Tovar, 2003; Follette, Polusny, & Milbeck, 1994; Plaxton-Hennings, 2004; Reiser & Geiger, 1984). The abuse of alcohol allows officers to maintain the tough guy image that is prevalent in police culture, which is incompatible with help-seeking behaviours (Cross & Ashley, 2004; Reiser & Geiger, 1984). Furthermore, the goodness-of-fit hypothesis of coping (Lazarus & Folkman, 1985) also posits that although it is generally more adaptive to employ problem-focused coping strategies, individuals do use emotion-focused (both active and avoidant) coping strategies to cope when they are unable to change the controllable stressor. Overall, these findings suggest that police officers may employ a range of both adaptive and maladaptive coping strategies to deal with occupational stress and traumatic incidents.

Culture plays a role in the use of coping strategies. For example, O'Connor and Shimizu (2002) studied the differences in coping styles among British and Japanese students and found that Japanese students, with a significantly lower sense of personal control, higher perceived stress, and negative mood compared to their British counterparts, employed more emotion-focused coping strategies when faced with stressful encounters. However, no differences between the two groups were found with regard to the use of problem-focused coping strategies. The authors explained that the differences found could be attributed to the difference in mindsets in the two cultures – an individualistic mindset in Western cultures and a collectivistic mindset in Eastern cultures, whereby individuals with a collectivistic mindset may find it more difficult to perceive stressors as being within their personal control (O'Connor & Shimizu, 2002). More research is thus required to understand if there are any differences in the coping strategies employed in the policing context in Eastern cultures compared to the Western context. Specifically, this study aimed to examine the coping strategies police officers employed following a riot incident in Singapore.

Objectives of study

As the Little India riot was a unique and unexpected event for the SPF, a study was conducted to examine the impact of this incident on the responding police officers. As the prevalent literature comes mostly from Western cultural sources, its application to the Asian, and more specifically the Singaporean, context arguably has limited ecological validity. In fact, there is little or no known research on the well-being of Singapore police officers after a critical incident such as managing a riot. The areas of interest include the possible onset of post-traumatic stress symptoms and MPM.

Method

Participants

The participants were Singaporean police officers who were physically present and directly engaged in policing duties during the riot incident. Eighty-four police officers (79 males and 5 females) participated in this study. The mean age of the participants was 27.07 years (standard deviation [*SD*] = 6.91; range 19–54). Participation was voluntary. Due to operational requirements and duties, some 36 of the officers involved in the incident were unable to participate in the current study.

Measures

The impact of event scale – revised (IES-R)

This scale consists of 22 items to assess current subjective distress for any specific life event (Weiss & Marmar, 1997). The scale includes a list of difficulties people sometimes experience after stressful events. The participants were required to indicate how distressing a particular difficulty had been during the previous 7 days with respect to the riot incident. Items were rated on a 5-point scale (0 = *Not at all*, 1 = *A little bit*, 2 = *Moderately*, 3 = *Quite a bit*, 4 = *Extremely*). Examples of the items include "Any reminder brought back feelings about it" and "I had trouble falling asleep". The scores of the participants were subsequently aggregated. The derived total score suggested the degree of distress the individual may be experiencing, with higher scores indicating a greater degree of traumatisation (Weiss & Marmar, 1997). As the IES-R is based on the PTSD diagnostic criteria presented in DSM-IV-TR rather than DSM-5, the PTSD diagnostic criteria of DSM-IV-TR, which include re-experiencing the traumatic event involuntarily (e.g., recurring nightmares), exhibiting avoidance behaviour (e.g., consciously steering clear of external reminders related to the event), and displaying symptoms of increased arousal (e.g., sleep disturbances or reckless behaviour) (American Psychiatric Association, 2000), were used in the study. A cut-off score of 34 was adopted as it provides good values on sensitivity and overall efficiency when benchmarked against the diagnosis of PTSD symptomatology using the MINI International Neuropsychiatric Interview (Morina, Ehring, & Priebe, 2013). The scale's Cronbach's alpha for the sample was .91.

The scores were further categorised into three subscales (intrusion, avoidance, hyperarousal) to get a more detailed understanding of an individual's stress response (Weiss & Marmar, 1997). Intrusion symptoms include nightmares and involuntary recurring thoughts, images, or feelings. Avoidance symptoms include attempts to dampen or avoid experiences associated with the traumatic event and the associated numbing of responsiveness. Hyperarousal symptoms include anger, irritability, exaggerated startle response, trouble concentrating, and hypervigilance. The computed Cronbach's alphas for the avoidance, intrusion, and hyperarousal subscales were .85, .86, and .66, respectively, for the present sample.

General health questionnaire (GHQ-12)

This 12-item scale was used to screen for the incidence of MPM (Goldberg & Williams, 1988). The GHQ-12 enquires about the respondents' current state and asked if it differs from their usual state using a four-point scale ("*Better than usual*", "*Same as usual*", "*Worse than usual*", and "*Much worse than usual*"; Goldberg & Williams, 1988). Likert scoring (0-1-2-3) was used over GHQ scoring (0-0-1-1) as the former is found to produce scores that are less skewed and have less kurtosis (French & Tait, 2004; Goldberg et al., 1997; Tait, Hulse, & Robertson, 2002). Examples of items include "Have you recently been able to concentrate on whatever you're doing?" and "Have you recently lost much sleep over worry?" (Goldberg & Williams, 1988). The total scores of the 12 items ranged from 0 to 36, where higher scores suggested the heightened possibility of the respondent having MPM. The default threshold of "more than 12" was used to flag participants who may possibly have post-incident mental well-being issues (Goldberg et al., 1997). The Cronbach's alpha for this sample was .73.

Brief COPE (BC)

This scale was used to discern the general coping responses adopted by the officers in relation to the Little India riot incident (Carver, 1997; Carver, Scheier, & Weintraub, 1989). The coping responses refer to the strategies or approaches an individual tends to adopt when reacting to stressors. The 28-item scale includes a list of statements which asked the participants to indicate what they had been doing and feeling since the riot incident. Items were rated on a four-point scale (1 = *I usually don't do this at all*, 2 = *I usually do this a little bit*, 3 = *I usually do this a medium amount*, 4 = *I usually do this a lot*). A total of 14 dimensions are covered by BC: self-distraction, active coping, denial, substance use, use of emotional support, use of instrumental support, behavioural disengagement, venting, positive reframing, planning, humour, acceptance, religion, and self-blame. Each coping dimension has two items, and the corresponding scores of the two items were averaged to derive the coping dimension score. Higher scores indicated a higher use of the corresponding coping responses by the participants. The mean scores for the 14 coping styles were ranked to ascertain the coping styles most and least commonly employed by the officers.

To better elucidate the adaptiveness of the coping strategies the officers employed as informed by relevant conceptual literature (Carver & Scheier, 1994; Folkman & Lazarus, 1985; Holahan & Moos, 1987), the 14 coping strategies were further grouped into three broad coping categories: problem-focused coping (i.e., active coping, planning, instrumental support, and religion), active emotional coping (i.e., venting, positive reframing, humour, acceptance, and emotional support), and avoidant emotional coping (i.e., self-distraction, denial, behavioural disengagement, self-blame, substance use). The Cronbach's alphas were .82 for problem-focused coping, .84 for active emotional coping, and .67 for avoidant emotional coping.

Procedure

A self-report questionnaire with the four scales was administered approximately a month after the incident to (a) delineate normal stress responses that people typically tend to exhibit immediately after experiencing a stressful event due to severe stress reactions of a morbid nature, and (b) lessen the interruption to police operations. The survey administration was conducted by the authors at various police premises over the course of one week to minimise the disruption to operational duties. Participants were informed about the aim of the research, and an emphasis was placed on data confidentiality and response anonymity to encourage frank and forthcoming responses. Questionnaire-specific instructions were given in the booklet, and participants were asked to read these instructions carefully. No time limit was imposed for the completion of the questionnaire, and participants were encouraged to provide their honest responses. All participants gave informed consent for this study.

Results

Post-incident traumatic responses

This current study examined the possibility of post-traumatic stress symptoms being exhibited by the police officers involved in the riot incident. The IES-R results showed that 75 (89%) officers involved in the riot incident did not report experiencing any significant distress due to the incident. However, nine officers (11%) reported experiencing a significant amount of post-traumatic stress symptomology. Of these nine officers, five (6%) scored in the range where post-traumatic stress symptomology was a clinical concern (Weiss & Marmar, 1997). The remaining four officers (5%) met the criteria for a probable diagnosis of PTSD, and the trauma experienced was seemingly enough to suppress their immune system's functioning (Weiss & Marmar, 1997). Table 13.1 presents the statistics for the sample of 84 officers and also indicates the associations of the various scores with post-traumatic stress symptoms.

The analyses showed that the five officers who displayed some post-traumatic stress symptoms indicated experiencing avoidance, intrusion, and hyperarousal symptoms occasionally. The other four officers that met the criteria for a probable

Table 13.1 Breakdown of the number of officers with possible post-traumatic stress symptomology ($N = 84$)

Score range	*Risk of developing PTSD (Weiss & Marmar, 1997)*	*Number of officers (%)*
Less than 24	No clinically significant post-incident distress.	75 (89)
24 or more	PTSD is a clinical concern. Those with scores this high who do not have full PTSD will have partial PTSD or at least some of the symptoms.	5 (6)
33 and more	Probable diagnosis of PTSD.	0 (0)
37 or more	Probable diagnosis of PTSD, and traumatic impact is high enough to suppress one's immune system's functioning (even 10 years after an impact event).	4 (5)

Note: $N = 84$

Table 13.2 Breakdown of the number of the officers who are likely to develop MPM ($N = 84$)

Score range	*Likelihood of having minor psychiatric morbidity (MPM)*	*Number of officers (%)*
Less or equal to 12	Not likely to develop MPM	82 (98)
More than 12	At risk of developing MPM	2 (2)

Note: $N = 84$

diagnosis of PTSD indicated experiencing symptoms of avoidance and intrusion on a moderate basis and hyperarousal symptoms occasionally.

General well-being and psychological distress

The present research also set out to discover if any incidence of MPM could be found in the police officers involved in the riot incident. With regard to the GHQ, two officers met the threshold criteria for MPM (2%). Table 13.2 shows the breakdown of the sample of 84 officers.

General coping strategies

The present study sought to find out the different coping strategies utilised by officers in relation to the riot incident. Table 13.3 presents the means of the 14 coping strategies for this sample using the BC scale, ranked from highest to lowest. The top four coping strategies used by the participants were acceptance ($M = 3.88$, $SD = 2.06$), humour ($M = 3.41$, $SD = 1.57$), positive reframing ($M = 3.36$, $SD = 1.92$), and active coping ($M = 3.32$, $SD = 1.64$), while the bottom four were substance use ($M = 2.06$, $SD = 0.28$), behavioural disengagement ($M = 2.15$, $SD = 0.52$), denial ($M = 2.22$, $SD = 0.68$), and self-blame ($M = 2.26$, $SD = 0.66$).

Table 13.4 shows the grouping of the 14 coping responses into the three broad categories of problem-focused coping, active emotional coping, and avoidant emotional coping. The highest mean score was for active emotional coping ($M = 16.08$, $SD = 6.21$), followed by problem-focused ($M = 12.79$, $SD = 5.28$) and lastly avoidant emotional ($M = 9.66$, $SD = 2.30$) coping. This suggests that the officers tended to use a range of active emotional coping responses more than problem-focused and avoidant emotional coping strategies in relation to the riot incident.

Discussion

The current study indicates that the majority of the officers handled the stress adequately during and after the riot incident. This is consistent with past literature that suggests that the majority of people are generally resilient and typically

Table 13.3 Brief COPE mean scores for officers (ranked from highest to lowest mean scores)

S/N	*Coping strategies*	*Definition*	*Mean score (SD)*
1	Acceptance	Acknowledge that the stressor is present and learn to live with it	3.88 (2.06)
2	Humour	Use of jokes to make light of the stressor	3.41 (1.57)
3	Positive reframing	Think about the stressful situation in a more positive way	3.36 (1.92)
4	Active coping	Work towards managing the stressor head-on	3.32 (1.64)
5	Religion	Increased praying or meditating	3.26 (1.80)
6	Self-distraction	Forget about stressor through partaking in other activities	3.18 (1.44)
7	Planning	Think about how to confront the stressor with a plan	3.18 (1.72)
8	Use of instrumental support	Ask others (e.g., family, friends) for advice when faced with stress	3.04 (1.40)
9	Use of emotional support	Confide in others (e.g., family, friends) for sympathy	2.94 (1.27)
10	Venting	Cathartic release of negative feelings	2.48 (0.88)
11	Self-blame	Criticise oneself	2.26 (0.66)
12	Denial	Reject the notion that the stressor is present	2.22 (0.68)
13	Behavioural disengagement	Give up trying to reach the goal in the face of the stressor	2.15 (0.52)
14	Substance use	Turn to drugs and/or alcohol for relief from stressors	2.06 (0.28)

only a small number of individuals are affected after experiencing a potentially stressful event (Devilly, Gist, & Cotton, 2006; Hodgkinson & Stewart, 1998; Kanel, 2011). Another perspective could be that the police riot management training currently in place (e.g., assessing the dynamicity of the situation; crowd management practices such as minimising instances of us versus them) may be deemed as effective in equipping police officers with the ability to cope competently with high-stress situations. However, as noted in this study, there was still a small group of officers affected by the riot incident. As such, there is a need for the SPF to be mindful and to extend the necessary care to the affected officers.

The results showed that approximately 11% of the officers experienced post-traumatic stress symptoms, which is roughly similar to the finding of 13% in Robinson and Mitchell's (1993) study on an American sample of police officers. The result was also higher than the life-time prevalence rate of PTSD for the

Table 13.4 Officers' endorsement of the different coping categories (ranked from highest to lowest mean scores)

S/N	*Coping categories*	*Definition*	*Total score (SD)*
1	Active emotional coping – Venting – Positive reframing – Humour – Acceptance – Emotional support	Managing one's emotions, such as venting one's emotional distress, or cognitively reframing a stressor's impact	16.08 (6.21)
2	Problem-focused coping – Active coping – Planning – Instrumental support – Religion	Taking an active stance towards overcoming the problem	12.79 (5.28)
3	Avoidant emotional coping – Self-distraction – Denial – Behavioural disengagement – Self-blame – Substance use	Regulating one's emotions, but involves more avoidance of the source of distress so as to minimise the stressor's impact on one's emotions	9.66 (2.30)

US general population, which is estimated to be about 7% (Kessler, Sonnega, Bromet, Hughes, & Nelson, 1995; National Institute of Mental Health, 2014). Unfortunately, direct comparison of this current study's results with previous studies (e.g., Carlier et al., 1997; Stephens & Miller, 1998) is challenging as different measurement tools have been used in studies.

The GHQ-12 results from the present study showed that about 2% of the sample officers had MPM after experiencing the incident, which is lower than the Singaporean national norm of 17% (Fones et al., 1998). This showed that the police officers in the current study seemed to be generally unaffected in terms of psychological well-being after their experience of a critical incident. While not a like-for-like comparison, it is interesting to note that the percentage of officers with MPM is much lower than the findings of previous studies done on police officers with respect to general policing duties (e.g., Doctor et al., 1994; Khader, 1995). There could be many possible reasons for the current study's findings. One reason is perhaps that the existing stress management measures and training courses have equipped the police officers adequately and buffered them against possible MPM. One of the aforementioned training courses is called SMART COP (an acronym for the scope of life skills and stress-busting areas that the course covers), and it serves to equip all police officers with easy-to-apply stress-relieving measures (e.g., deep-breathing exercises; think about what can be controlled versus what cannot; share concerns with loved ones). The incorporation of role-play and scenario-based learning arguably trained the police officers to better appreciate possible difficulties that could be faced on the ground and in turn helped them to cope with the stressors more competently (Diong et al., 2005; Moats, Chermack, & Dooley, 2008). The second reason is that perhaps the police officers were not affected much psychologically as there were no major casualties (i.e., no deaths) resulting from the incident. However, the present study was unable to conclusively provide a firm explanation for the phenomenon, and further investigation into the link between policing work and MPM needs to be undertaken.

The results showed that the top four most commonly adopted coping strategies were acceptance, humour, positive reframing, and active coping, and the four least commonly used methods were substance use, behavioural disengagement, denial, and self-blame. It seems that the police officers tended to accept and acknowledge that the riot/incident had happened and that they needed to do something to actively maintain law and order instead of getting mired in denial over the riot incident. Rather than engaging in maladaptive coping such as alcohol abuse for temporary relief or indulging in self-blame (Cross & Ashley, 2004; Reiser & Geiger, 1984), the officers for the most part attempted to look for silver linings amidst the dark clouds and to rethink the incident in a more positive manner. Making light of the situation, such as cracking jokes, also aided them in adopting different perspectives to resolve the issue at hand. Stoeber and Janssen (2011) postulated that positive reframing, acceptance, and humour are the most effective coping strategies when faced with setbacks as they help individuals to feel more satisfied at the end of the day, which is heartening to note as it means that the SPF officers are commonly using generally adaptive coping strategies. In addition, the participants tended to employ active emotion-focused coping strategies (acceptance, positive reframing, and humour) and problem-focused strategies (active coping) rather than avoidant emotional coping strategies (self-blame, substance use, denial, and behavioural disengagement), which have been found to correlate with a heightened risk of developing post-trauma stress issues (Schnider, Elhai, & Gray, 2007). Using solely emotional-focused coping strategies, and in particular avoidant emotional strategies, is apparently related to inferior overall psychological well-being in the long term, although avoidant emotional coping may be useful in helping individuals to cope in the short term (Coyne & Racioppo, 2000; Holahan & Moos, 1987). The use of active coping and cognitive reappraisal modes of coping and less use of avoidance coping strategies have also been found to be generally associated with better psychological and physical health in Singaporean police officers (Diong et al., 2005). As such, officers' inclinations to use more adaptive coping strategies (i.e., active emotional coping and problem-focused coping) may have buffered them from suffering severe post-trauma stress issues and helped them to maintain their mental well-being to some extent (Folkman & Lazarus, 1985; Holahan & Moos, 1987).

On the surface, this study's finding that active emotional coping strategies were used more frequently is consistent with O'Connor and Shimizu's (2002) research results to a certain extent. In accordance with their explanation, perhaps Singaporean police officers are similar to their counterparts in Japan, where a more collectivistic culture was found to result in an inclination towards using more emotional-focused coping responses compared to their British counterparts. However, O'Connor and Shimizu (2002) grouped both positive reframing and escape-avoidance coping strategies in the same category, which was not the case in the current study, where positive reframing was part of active emotional coping strategies and escape-avoidance coping was part of avoidant emotional coping strategies. There is thus a limitation in drawing similarity between this study's results and O'Connor and Shimizu's (2002) finding. A more targeted investigation is needed to ascertain the magnitude of the cultural effect on the coping responses used by police officers in different parts of the world and in relation to different contexts (e.g., operational and organisational).

Care and support for police officers

All in all, the findings seem to suggest that efforts to provide organisational support and care for police officers is important so as to not neglect the needs of affected officers, albeit the number of such officers is generally small. In the Singapore context, the Police Psychological Services Division (PPSD) of the SPF, as part of its organisational "duty of care", has in place various measures to help affected officers manage their stressors and return to normalcy (Khader et al., 2012). PPSD psychologists typically conduct group psychological debriefings (PD) for officers exposed to a potentially traumatic event using Everly and Mitchell's (2000) Crisis Intervention Stress Management (CISM) model. The CISM model is a multi-component crisis intervention programme designed to provide a structured supportive element to facilitate individuals' recovery from potentially traumatic experiences through the use of PD techniques such as "Demob, Defuse, and Debrief" (Everly & Mitchell, 2000). The PD provided by the PPSD serve to address the distress felt by officers and to attenuate the possibility of developing psychopathology. Also, one-to-one counselling sessions are conducted with officers who are more affected. Other than the aforementioned reactive and ad hoc measures, the PPSD also has proactive and preventive measures to help officers cope more effectively with stressors. Drawing from the findings of stress-related studies on police officers through collaborations with the National University of Singapore (e.g., Bishop et al., 2001; Diong et al., 2005), the PPSD has enhanced existing stress management programmes and workshops to better meet the needs of police officers and better prepare them to face future stressors (Khader et al., 2012).

Limitations

The current study has some limitations. First, as the study was conducted about a month after the riot incident, it is unclear whether the responses indicating the presence of certain post-traumatic stress symptoms on the IES-R were associated with acute stress disorder (ASD) or PTSD. Symptoms are more likely to be indicative of ASD if they were present for more than two days and less than four weeks; if the symptoms were to last longer than four weeks, it may be more suggestive of PTSD (American Psychiatric Association, 2013). As such, it could have been either ASD or PTSD at the point of the questionnaire's administration, and the current study was unable to differentiate between the two due to the timing of the survey administration.

Second, the present study may not have comprehensively captured all of the manifestations of post-trauma stress as there could be delayed expression in some of the research participants. Furthermore, as previously mentioned, the IES-R was used for this study; this measure is based on the now-obsolete DSM-IV-TR following the release of DSM-5. Although they may not exhibit signs and symptoms associated to post-traumatic stress initially, some officers may develop such symptoms after a period of time, typically about six months after the trauma incident (American Psychiatric Association, 2013). As such, future studies may consider incorporating assessment of disturbances to psychological well-being at different time points after the incident so as to ensure that officers who are affected are able to have the professional care they need.

Third, there was a lack of control groups. Due to the high operational demands of the SPF, it was particularly challenging to have a control group (i.e., a similarly sized group of police officers in the same unit). Although having a control group would have enabled us to reach a more informed conclusion (e.g., was the PTSD symptomatology reported an effect of being involved in the riot incident or was it more of a baseline level which the individuals tended to report?), the operational needs of the SPF were of higher priority to maintain law and order in Singapore. Even though one cannot confidently infer the exact effect that involvement in the Little India riot has had on the officers, the results, when compared to previous studies with a similar population, still offer some interesting insights as to the extent of the psychological reaction experienced by the police officers. Future studies should include a control group, where possible, to ascertain the true effects of involvement in a riot situation.

Though not investigated in the current study, it is interesting to note that the rates of PTSD incidence when exposed to potentially traumatic events was posited to be lower in police officers compared to other emergency services groups (e.g., medical technicians) due to two main reasons, namely the selection criteria of the organisation and self-selection (Marmar, Weiss, Metzler, & Delucchi, 1996). Pre-employment selection tests in the form of a psychometric assessment battery help organisations select individuals who have the tenacity to withstand repeated stressors. Moreover, individuals in the police force may have an inclination for the heightened risk involved with the job and be mentally prepared for the associated dangers of the job. Those who are unable to handle the challenges may also leave the job at an early stage. As such, future studies should focus on the possible difference in post-traumatic stress symptoms exhibited by police officers compared to the other emergency services groups.

Conclusion

The results of the present study showed that the majority of the officers involved in the Little India riot were not affected by this incident, despite the fact that such incidents occur in Singapore rarely. It is hypothesised that the regular training on dealing with such situations may have helped. Furthermore, measures to provide care and support for police officers who have responded to a critical incident are necessary. This study adds to the existing literature regarding the psychological effects of critical incident stress on police officers.

Chapter summary points

- On the night of 8 December 2013, officers of the Singapore Police Force (SPF) responded to a riot that lasted for around two hours in the vicinity of Little India which involved about 400 Indian migrant workers. This was the first riot in Singapore in 40 years.
- There were concerns that the SPF police officers might develop post-traumatic stress symptomatology and minor psychiatric morbidity (MPM) after being involved in a critical incident. However, most of the officers did not manifest signs of post-traumatic stress reactions.
- The Impact of Events Scale-Revised, General Health Questionnaire, and Brief COPE were used in the study.
- The results showed that the majority of the officers handled the stress adequately during and after the riot incident, which is consistent with past literature which suggests that the majority are generally resilient and that typically only a small number of individuals are affected after experiencing a potentially stressful event.
- The percentage of officers who experienced post-traumatic stress symptoms was small and is similar to the percentage found in a study done on American police officers.
- The percentage of officers who experienced MPM was much lower than the findings of previous studies done on police officers with respect to general policing duties, both in the Singapore and Western contexts.
- The top four most commonly adopted coping strategies were acceptance, humour, positive reframing, and active coping, which are generally adaptive coping strategies.
- The four least commonly used coping strategies were substance use, behavioural disengagement, denial, and self-blame, which are generally maladaptive coping strategies.
- Overall, the findings seem to suggest that the officers coped well after the riot incident. However, organisational support and care for police officers is still important so as to not neglect the needs of the small number of affected officers. Support and care are provided through proactive means (e.g., stress management programmes) and reactive measures (e.g., provision of psychological debriefing and counselling services).

References

American Psychiatric Association. (2000). *Diagnostic and statistical manual of mental disorders* (4th ed.). Washington, DC: Author.

American Psychiatric Association. (2013). *Diagnostic and statistical manual of mental disorders* (5th ed.). Washington, DC: Author. doi: 10.1176/appi.books.9780890425596

Anshel, M. H. (2000). A conceptual model and implications for coping with stressful events in police work. *Criminal Justice and Behaviour, 27*(3), 375–400. doi: 10.1177/0093854800027003006

Atkinson-Tovar, L. (2003). The impact of repeated exposure to trauma. *Law & Order, 51*(9), 118–123.

Bishop, G. D., Tong, E. M., Diong, S. M., Enklemann, H. C., Why, Y. P., Khader, M., & Ang, J. C. (2001). The relationship between coping and personality among police officers in Singapore. *Journal of Research in Personality, 35*(3), 353–374. doi: 10.1006/jrpe.2001.2319

Carlier, I. V. E., & Gersons, B. P. R. (1992). Development of a scale for traumatic incidents in police work. *Psychiatrica Fennica Supplementum, 23*, 59–70.

Carlier, I. V. E., Lamberts, R. D., & Gersons, B. P. (1997). Risk factors for posttraumatic stress symptomatology in police officers: A prospective analysis. *The Journal of Nervous & Mental Disease, 185*(8), 498–506. doi: 10.1097/00005053-199708000-00004

Carver, C. S. (1997). You want to measure coping but your protocol's too long: Consider the Brief COPE. *International Journal of Behavioral Medicine, 4*(1), 92–100. doi: 10.1207/s15327558ijbm0401_6

Carver, C. S., & Scheier, M. F. (1994). Situational coping and coping dispositions in a stressful transaction. *Journal of Personality and Social Psychology, 66*(1), 184–195. doi: 10.1037/0022–3514.66.1.184

Carver, C. S., Scheier, M. F., & Weintraub, J. (1989). Assessing coping strategies: A theoretically based approach. *Journal of Personality and Social Psychology, 56*(2), 267–283. doi: 10.1037/0022-3514.56.2.267

Coyne, J. C., & Racioppo, M. W. (2000). Never the twain shall meet? Closing the gap between coping research and clinical intervention research. *American Psychologist, 55*(6), 655–664. doi: 10.1037/0003-066X.55.6.655

Cross, L. C., & Ashley, L. (2004). Police trauma and addiction: Coping with the dangers of the job. *FBI Law Enforcement Bulletin, 73*(10), 24–32. doi: 10.1037/e311382005-006

Devilly, G. J., Gist, R., & Cotton, P. (2006). Ready! Fire! Aim! The status of psychological debriefing and therapeutic interventions: In the work place and after disasters. *Review of General Psychology, 10*(4), 318–345. doi: 10.1037/1089-2680.10.4.318

Diong, S., Bishop, G. D., Enklemann, H. C., Tong, E. M., Why, Y. P., Ang, J. C., & Khader, M. (2005). Anger, stress, coping, social support and health: Modelling the relationships. *Psychology & Health, 20*(4), 467–495. doi: 10.1080/0887044040512331333960

Doctor, R. S., Curtis, D., & Isaacs, G. (1994). Psychiatric morbidity in policemen and the effect of brief psychotherapeutic intervention – A pilot study. *Stress Medicine, 10*(3), 151–157. doi: 10.1002/smi.2460100304

Everly, G. S., & Mitchell, J. T. (2000). The debriefing "controversy" and crisis intervention: A review of lexical and substantive issues. *International Journal of Emergency Mental Health, 2*(4), 211–224.

Foa, E. B., Davidson, J. R. T., & Frances, A. (1999). The expert consensus guideline series: Treatment of posttraumatic stress disorder. *Journal of Clinical Psychiatry, 60* (Suppl. 16), 1–76.

Folkman, S., & Lazarus, R. (1985). If it changes it must be a process: Study of emotion and coping during three stages of a college examination. *Journal of Personality and Social Psychology, 48*(1), 150–170. doi: 10.1037/0022-3514.48.1.150

Follette, V. M., Polusny, M. M., & Milbeck, K. (1994). Mental health and law enforcement professionals: Trauma history, psychological symptoms, and impact of providing services to child sexual abuse survivors. *Professional Psychology: Research and Practice, 25*(3), 275–282. doi: 10.1037/0735-7028.25.3.275

Fones, C. S., Kua, E. H., Ng, T. P., & Ko, S. M. (1998). Studying the mental health of a nation: A preliminary report on a population survey in Singapore. *Singapore Medical Journal, 39*(6), 251–255.

French, D. J., & Tait, R. J. (2004). Measurement invariance in the General Health Questionnaire-12 in young Australian adolescents. *European Child & Adolescent Psychiatry, 13*(1), 1–7. doi: 10.1007/s00787-004-0345-7

Garbarino, S., Cuomo, G., Chiorri, C., Piattino, S., & Magnavita, N. (2012). Personality profiles of special force police officers. *Journal of Police and Criminal Psychology, 27*(2), 99–110. doi: 10.1007/s11896-011-9099-6

Ghosh, S., Chaudhury, P. K., & Zaman, R. U. (2011). Study of stress, quality of life & psychiatric morbidities in police personnel. *Asian Journal of Psychiatry, 4*(1), 79. doi: 10.1016/S1876-2018(11)60304-3

Goldberg, D., Gater, R., Sartorius, N., Ustun, T. B., Piccinelli, M., Gureje, O., & Rutter, C. (1997). The validity of two versions of the GHQ in the WHO study of mental illness in general health care. *Psychological Medicine, 27*(1), 191–197. doi: 10.1017/S0033291796004242

Goldberg, D., & Williams, P. (1988). *A user's guide to the General Health Questionnaire.* Windsor, UK: NFER-Nelson.

Hodgkinson, P. E., & Stewart, M. (1998). *Coping with catastrophe: A handbook of post-disaster psychological aftercare* (2nd ed.). London: Routledge. doi: 10.4324/9780203133422

Holahan, C. J., & Moos, R. H. (1987). Risk, resilience, and psychological distress: A longitudinal analysis with adults and children. *Journal of Abnormal Psychology, 96*(1), 3–13. doi: 10.1037/0021-843x.96.1.3

Kanel, K. (2011). *A guide to crisis intervention* (4th ed.). Belmont, CA: Thomson.

Kates, A. (1999). *CopShock: Surviving Post-traumatic Stress Disorder (PTSD).* Tucson, AZ: Holbrook Street Press.

Kessler, R. C., Sonnega, A., Bromet, E., Hughes, M., & Nelson, C. B. (1995). Posttraumatic stress disorder in the national comorbidity survey. *Archives of General Psychiatry, 52*(12), 1048–1060. doi: 10.1001/archpsyc.1995.03950240066012

Khader, M. (1995). *Stress and stress management programs in the Singapore Police Force.* (Unpublished Report). Singapore: Police Psychological Unit, Singapore Police Force.

Khader, M., Ang, J., Maan, D. S., Li, P. L., Min, T. S., Jayagowry, A., . . . Fen, H. H. (2012). Police psychology in Singapore: The red dot experience. *Journal of Police and Criminal Psychology, 27*(1), 24–32. doi: 10.1007/s11896-011-9094-y

Larsson, G., Kempe, C., & Starrin, B. (1988). Appraisal and coping processes in acute time-limited stressful situations: A study of police officers. *European Journal of Personality, 2*(4), 259–276. doi: 10.1002/per.2410020404

Lim, Y. L. (2014, 20 January). More police powers to secure order in Little India. *The Straits Times.* Retrieved from http://www.straitstimes.com/the-big-story/little-india-riot/story/new-bill-give-police-temporary-specific-powers-little-india-ar

Marmar, C. R., Weiss, D. S., Metzler, T. J., & Delucchi, K. (1996). Characteristics of emergency services personnel related to peritraumatic dissociation during critical incident exposure. *The American Journal of Psychiatry, 153*(7 Suppl.), 94–102. doi: 10.1176/ajp.153.7.94

Mitchell, J., & Bray, G. (1990). *Emergency services stress: Guidelines for preserving the health and careers of emergency services personnel.* Englewood Cliffs, NJ: Prentice Hall.

Moats, J. B., Chermack, T. J., & Dooley, L. M. (2008). Using scenarios to develop crisis managers: Applications of scenario planning and scenario-based training. *Advances in Developing Human Resources, 10*(3), 397–424. doi: 10.1177/1523422308316456

Morina, N., Ehring, T., & Priebe, S. (2013). Diagnostic utility of the Impact of Events Scale-Revised in two samples of survivors of war. *PLoS ONE, 8*(12): e83916. doi: 10.1371/journal/pone.0083916

National Institute of Mental Health. (2014). *Post-traumatic stress disorder among adults.* Retrieved from http://www.nimh.nih.gov/statistics/1ad_ptsd_adult.shtml

Neo, C. C., & Chia, A. (2013, 9 December). Little India riot: 19 injured, 27 arrested. *Today.* Retrieved from http://www.todayonline.com/singapore/riot-breaks-out-little-india

O'Connor, D. B., & Shimizu, M. (2002). Sense of personal control, stress and coping style: A cross-cultural study. *Stress and Health, 18*(4), 173–183. doi: 10.1002/smi.939

Papazoglou, K., & Andersen, J. P. (2014). A guide to utilizing police training as a tool to promote resilience and improve health outcomes among police officers. *Traumatology: An International Journal, 20*(2), 103–111. doi: 10.1037/h0099394

Pasciak, A. R., & Kelley, T. M. (2013). Conformity to traditional gender norms by male police officers exposed to trauma: Implications for critical incident stress debriefing. *Applied Psychology In Criminal Justice, 9*(2), 137–156.

Plaxton-Hennings, C. (2004). Law enforcement organizational behaviour and the occurrence of post-traumatic stress symptomatology in law enforcement personnel following a critical incident. *Journal of Police and Criminal Psychology, 19*(2), 53–63. doi: 10.1007/BF02813873

Reiser, M., & Geiger, S. P. (1984). Police officer as victim. *Professional Psychology: Research and Practice, 15*(3), 315. doi: 10.1037/0735-7028.15.3.315

Robinson, R. C., & Mitchell, J. T. (1993). Evaluation of psychological debriefings. *Journal of Traumatic Stress, 6*(3), 367–382. doi: 10.1007/BF00974135

Rudofossi, D. (2007). *Working with traumatized police officer-patients. A clinician's guide to complex PTSD syndromes in public safety professionals.* Amityville, NY: Baywood. doi: 10.2190/wwt

Schnider, K. R., Elhai, J. D., & Gray, M. J. (2007). Coping style use predicts post-traumatic stress and complicated grief symptom severity among college students reporting a traumatic loss. *Journal of Counselling Psychology, 54*(3), 344–350. doi: 10.1037/0022-0167.54.3.344

Stephens, C., & Miller, I. (1998). Traumatic experiences and post-traumatic stress disorder in the New Zealand Police. *Policing: An International Journal of Police Strategies & Management, 21*(1), 178–191. doi: 10.1108/13639519810206664

Stoeber, J., & Janssen, D. P. (2011). Perfectionism and coping with daily features: Positive reframing helps achieve satisfaction at the end of the day. *Anxiety, Stress & Coping, 24*(5), 477–497. doi: 10.1080/10615806.2011.562977

Tait, R. J., Hulse, G. K., & Robertson, S. I. (2002). A review of the validity of General Health Questionnaire in adolescent populations. *The Australian and New Zealand Journal of Psychiatry, 36*(4), 550–557. doi: 10.1046/j.1440-1614.2002.01028.x

Violanti, J. M. (1992). Coping strategies among police recruits in a high-stress training environment. *The Journal of Social Psychology, 132*(6), 717–729. doi: 10.1080/00224545.1992.9712102

Violanti, J. M. (1993). What does high stress police training teach recruits? An analysis of coping. *Journal of Criminal Justice, 21*(4), 411–417. doi: 10.1016/0047-2352(93)90022-F

Weiss, D., & Marmar, C. (1997). The Impact of Event Scale – Revised. In J. Wilson & T. Keane (Eds.), *Assessing psychological trauma and PTSD* 2 (pp. 168–189). New York, NY: Guildford.

14 The Little India riot in Singapore

A crowd psychology and behavioural analysis study

Vincent Yeh, Majeed Khader, Carolyn Misir, Jeffery Chin, Siew Maan Diong, Gabriel Ong, and Li Li Poh

Introduction

The Little India riot in 2013 was Singapore's worst major public order incident in more than four decades – the last riot seen in Singapore occurred in 1969. This inevitably came as a shock to many Singaporeans. Despite the violence and damage caused, the riot was considerably less severe than incidents that have occurred in other parts of the world. There was no loss of life; the riot remained contained in one small area, and it was dispersed peacefully by the police without the use of shots, tear gas, or water cannons on the rioters. This public order incident nevertheless sent a strong message to all that peace and stability cannot be taken for granted.

How the riot occurred

Little India is a historic cultural district in Singapore. It is a centre of commerce, dining, and recreation for the local ethnic-Indian population. As the Indian and Bangladeshi foreign worker populations in Singapore increased over the last decade, Little India naturally became a locus of activity among them. These workers typically head to Little India on Sundays (their most common day off) to meet friends and relatives, eat, drink, shop, and run errands such as remitting money to their families. It is also the only place from which there is private bus transport to bring these foreign workers back to their dormitories. They thus congregate at the boarding locations in Little India (i.e., Tekka Lane and Hampshire Road). This results in an intense concentration of human traffic in Little India, particularly on Sunday nights.

The riot of 2013 was sparked off by a fatal road traffic accident. The accident occurred near a bus boarding area where foreign workers were waiting to catch a ride back to their dormitories. The rioters were male foreign workers primarily from the construction industry. No Singaporeans were involved in this public order incident, which lasted approximately two hours.

The events unfolded as follows (Ministry of Home Affairs, 2014):

1 At about 9:20 pm on 8 December 2013 (Sunday), a bus carrying South Asian foreign workers was making a sharp left turn out of a small road. As the bus was completing its turn, a foreign worker who had been running alongside it fell into the path of the front left wheel of the bus. He died instantly. The bus stopped immediately. The worker's body was pinned under the left rear wheel.
2 A crowd of foreign workers formed around the bus and the mob turned against the bus driver and timekeeper. Both individuals eventually found shelter inside the bus with the help of a pro-social Indian worker who urged them to stay there. The mob continued to attack the vehicle.
3 Officers from the Singapore Police Force (SPF) and Singapore Civil Defence Force (SCDF) arrived shortly. They first removed the body from the scene. Then, the police and fire service/emergency officers escorted the passengers from the bus.
4 Subsequently, a concentrated group of rioters appeared. They became hostile and aggressive towards the SPF and SCDF officers. SPF and SCDF vehicles in particular became the target of their anger. Vehicles were attacked and overturned; some were burned. This continued until troops from the Special Operations Command (SOC), a specialist squad trained in riot control, arrived at the scene. Seeing the SOC officers, the rioters dispersed.
5 Thirty-seven police officers, twelve fire and emergency service officers, five auxiliary police officers, and eight members of the public were injured in the riot. Twenty-three emergency vehicles were damaged, six of which were overturned, and four set on fire by the rioters. A fifth vehicle also sustained fire damage from a burning vehicle next to it. The property damage caused was valued at over S$530,000.

This chapter discusses a psychological and behavioural analysis of the incident, discusses crowd psychology theories and their relevance to this incident, and indicates some lessons for crowd management.

Public order policing and theories of crowd psychology and behaviour

Public order policing is challenging. Its success during a crowd event is dependent on the public's acceptance of law enforcement officers' role in "public order maintenance" (Reiner, 1985, p. 123). Police actions during crowd events are constantly scrutinised and appraised by the public and the lack of sensitivity or excessive uses of force in managing a crowd bring the legitimacy of public order policing into question (Masterson, 1988; Scarman, 1981). Perceived illegitimacy of public order policing may embolden the crowd to react to police actions. Hence, constant communication of the intent and role of public order policing to the public during crowd events is imperative in building trust in the police's authority and its legitimacy.

Given the precarious nature of public order policing, it is important for law enforcement officers to be familiar with crowd behaviours, to understand their attitudes and behaviours so that they can appreciate the complexity and dynamic nature of crowd situations. This in turn allows law enforcement officers to better manage and respond to crowd behaviours during public order policing. In the last decade, researchers have emphasised the importance of crowd psychology theories in managing the crowds during public order policing (Hogget & Stott, 2010). They have highlighted that an understanding of crowd behaviour would have a direct impact on the type of tactics used during public order policing, which could in turn affect the outcome of crowd situations. Classical and contemporary theories on crowd psychology and behaviour, and their corresponding impact on public order policing, are often discussed in the field of social psychological research.

The classical theories of crowd psychology emerged in the European social sciences in the late nineteenth century and their most prominent theorists were the French scholars Gustave Le Bon and Gabriel Tarde. The central tenet underlying classical theories of crowd psychology is that when people are immersed in a crowd, they lose their ability to reason (i.e., become irrational) and behave in a destructive and uninhibited manner. Specifically, the processes of anonymity, suggestibility, and contagion negatively affect the prosocial standards of human behaviour in crowds. The idea of collective irrationality and its negative impact on social behaviour is captured in Gustav Le Bon's (2002) expression "Crowds are violent and destructive, they are characterised by an impulsive, barbarian nature and by the incapacity to reason". Gabriel Tarde, another key figure in crowd theory, identified largely with Le Bon's ideas, and stated that "The crowd is a wild beast which is in a state of delirium" (Tarde, 1968, p. 323).

In summary, the early theories of crowd psychology state that when in a crowd:

1 Individuals lose their sense of self;
2 Individuals unthinkingly follow the behaviour of the crowd;
3 Individuals feel a sense of power due to their numbers; and
4 There is a breakdown of social standards of behaviour.

Researchers began to contest classical theories of crowd psychology in the early 20th century (Zeitz, Tan, Grief, Couns, & Zeitz, 2009). Much of the criticism of Le Bon's and Tarde's theories revolved around the theme of irrational crowd thinking, which was deemed to be problematic (Borch, 2006). Contrary to earlier understanding of crowd psychology, McPhail's research on crowds and collective behaviour (2006) suggested that crowds appear rational in trying to achieve their specific goals. Specifically, there is "symbolic and rational" interaction between individuals in a crowd and individual actions are purposeful towards a particular goal. Hogget and Stott (2010) added to the criticism of classical theories by highlighting their problematic impact on public order policing tactics. They argued that the classical understanding of crowd behaviour could lead to a confrontational approach to managing public order policing through the utilisation of mass containment and dispersal tactics, which are likely to exacerbate the situation.

Contemporary theories of crowd psychology and behaviour

Currently, the elaborated social identity model (ESIM) is the most widely used theory to explain crowd behaviour as it accounts for ideological and structural settings (Reicher, 1996, 2001). The theory has since been further elaborated upon and applied to the policing context by other researchers (Drury & Reicher, 2000; Drury, Cocking, Beale, Hanson, & Rapley, 2005; Gorringe, Stott, & Rosie, 2012; Stott & Reicher, 1998; Stott, Adang, Livingstone, & Schreiber, 2007). ESIM posits that:

1. Individuals are able to act as one in a crowd because they share a common social identity. Specifically, individuals experience a shift in self-perception so that they identify themselves less in terms of their own characteristics and more in terms of those of the group.
2. The identity change of individuals in a crowd is related to context and environment. This means that group identities can change when there are interactions (depending on context and environment) between different groups. For example, the identities of crowd members can change during a protest when the riot police arrive.
3. Two characteristics are necessary for identity change to occur in an individual:
    - (a) Asymmetry in stereotypes held by the in-group (e.g., crowd) and out-group (e.g., police), and
    - (b) Asymmetry of power relations between groups.

Several studies have suggested that empowerment plays an important role in determining crowd mood and behaviour (Drury & Reicher, 2005; Drury et al., 2005). Based on their analyses, Drury and Reicher (2005) suggested that:

1. When crowd members perceive that they are being treated in what they view as an "illegitimate" manner, group boundaries extend to include those who may have been regarded formerly as outsiders by the in-group.
2. The extension of group boundaries leads to a sense of empowerment in the crowd.

Such phenomena are observed in various crowd situations (e.g., football hooliganism, public demonstrations). Stott, Hutchison, and Drury (2001) suggested that conflict and violent crowd behaviour between groups is likely to occur when one group perceives another in a stereotypical manner. For example, the police

Table 14.1 An overview of contemporary theories on crowd psychology and behaviour

In summary, contemporary theories on crowd psychology and behaviour suggest that: 1. Crowds are not irrational and unthinking entities. 2. Not all crowds are unruly or violent. 3. Identity change in members of a crowd is dependent on both the context and dynamic interactions between and within groups. 4. When group boundaries extend to include individuals formerly regarded as outsiders by the in-group, the crowd may experience a sense of empowerment.

may view all football supporters or protestors as troublemakers or a hostile group. Following which, football supporters and protestors are likely to unite (i.e., possess a shared identity) against what they perceive to be illegitimate police perceptions and bias against them. The social dynamics between the groups thus change due to a shift in identities: the police treat the whole crowd as disorderly while the crowd perceives the police to be against them. Subsequently, crowd members are likely to express hostility and antisocial behaviour towards the police. Table 14.1 presents an overview of contemporary theories on crowd psychology and behaviour.

Objectives of study

Given the limited amount of research on crowd psychology in the Asian context, the rare and unexpected occurrence of the Little India riot in Singapore provides an unprecedented opportunity for local researchers to contribute to the literature on crowd psychology. Specifically, this study seeks to:

1 Identify crowd behavioural characteristics by analysing the Little India riot, and
2 Highlight potential implications for law enforcement officers tasked with public order policing.

Method

Data for behavioural analysis

Due to the unexpected nature of such incidents, the researchers of this study were not present at the scene of the Little India riot to make behavioural observations of the rioters. Instead, the researchers were given a detailed briefing by the investigation team appointed by the Committee of Inquiry on the chronology of the incident in order to understand what happened. The researchers were also brought to the site of the incident by the investigation team in order to gain a better understanding of the environment in which the riot unfolded. Additionally, the researchers were given access to other resources that provided valuable insights into what may have occurred during the riot. These included:

1 Interview transcripts from personnel involved during the riot as well as eyewitnesses interviewed by the investigating officers,
2 Interview transcripts from deported foreign workers,
3 Video footage (without sound) recorded by closed-circuit television cameras in the vicinity,
4 Video footage recorded by members of the public who witnessed the riot, and
5 Photographs of the aftermath at the scene.

Following a detailed review of these resources, the researchers conducted follow-up interviews with key police and emergency services first responders from the SPF and the SCDF who had first-hand interactions with the crowd while on the scene. These interviews provided additional behavioural perspectives[1] that were not previously captured during interviews by the investigation team. While the researchers noted the importance of obtaining accounts of the foreign workers involved in the riot, it was not possible to conduct face-to-face interviews with them due to procedural constraints as they were on trial.

Analytical process

A comprehensive analysis of the incident was undertaken by a group of researchers which comprised psychologists from various Home Team departments.[2] The researchers first reviewed the scientific literature and research on crowd psychology theories prior to analysing the Little India riot data.

The video footage of the riotous scenes at various points during the incident were played, replayed, observed, and analysed by an assigned group of researchers. Their notes on rioters' behaviours were subsequently transcribed and served as the basis for analysis. These data were complemented by the interview transcripts that were made available to the researchers. The analytical approach adopted in this study was *thematic analysis*, a commonly used method for identifying, analysing, and reporting patterns (themes) within data.

Validity checks

Three procedures were employed to check the validity of these analytical conclusions. First, the researchers were divided into various groups, each tasked with the analysis of a specific data set. The assigned data set was analysed independently from each group, to be analysed separately by another for corroboration purposes to ensure the robustness of the analyses. The findings of similar data sets were checked to determine whether both groups had reached similar conclusions. In cases of differences, the groups met to discuss their interpretations and only findings on which they reached consensus were included.

Second, following the completion of the preliminary analysis, the findings were presented to a group of national-level professionals and experts from various multidisciplinary fields in an "expert critique session". This critique of the analysis and findings allowed the researchers to consider multiple and alternative perspectives on the issues examined, thus minimising the possibility of groupthink. Third, the final findings were compared to findings of other studies on public order incidents to examine whether they were coherent.

Findings

Following the comprehensive review of the available resources, thematic analysis revealed three key themes relating to the behavioural characteristics of the crowd during the Little India riot:

1 Rationality of the crowd.
2 Heterogeneity of the crowd.
3 Presence of identity within the crowd.

The findings suggest that the crowd was not irrational but rational. Several things suggest this. First, it was noted that the foreign workers were there not to riot per se but to fulfil their needs (e.g., waiting for a bus, catching up with compatriots, purchasing groceries). Second, it was also established that the angry rioters were targeting the bus driver and timekeeper, whom they apparently blamed for the death of their compatriot. The rioters eventually switched to targeting the first responders and their vehicles to vent their anger and frustrations, as they perceived them to be "siding" with the bus driver and timekeeper. These were not random attacks. Their choices to target (a) the bus driver and timekeeper, and subsequently (b) the first responders and their vehicles, were indicative of deliberation, suggesting rationality.

The findings also suggest heterogeneity of the crowd. It was observed that there were three distinct groups of foreign workers in the vicinity. The first group exhibited prosocial behaviours within the crowd (e.g., shielding the bus driver and timekeeper, attempting to persuade the rioters to stop their violence, warning the first responders to leave the ambulance as it was about to be set on fire by rioters). The second group comprised those involved in rioting and the destruction of property. The last group was the majority of the foreign workers present, bystanders who did not take part in the rioting.

Finally, the findings indicate a presence of group identity within crowd. Individuals do not lose their individual identity in crowds. Changes in the situation (i.e., the occurrence of the fatal traffic accident, the arrival of first responders) resulted in changes of identity within the crowd. The researchers are of the view that some members of the crowd had perceived the actions of the responding forces to be "illegitimate",[3] which may have created a sense of "us" versus "them" (i.e., formation of identity) – that the authorities were not responsive to their situation. When law enforcement officers arrived on the scene, they tried to prevent the rioters from damaging the bus, thus appearing to be protecting the bus driver and timekeeper.

Discussion

The findings of the behavioural analysis of the Little India riot appear to be congruent with the ideological and structural settings in crowd behaviour as postulated by the ESIM (Reicher, 1996, 2001). This reinforces the point that the conventional wisdom of treating crowds as "irrational" and "unthinking" is outdated. The findings of this study further highlight the importance of the dynamic interactions between groups (e.g., between the crowd and the first responders) and within groups, and their influence on crowd behaviours.

These findings have important implications for public order policing. Given that crowds are rational and their behaviours dependent on the dynamic interactions between and within groups, Hogget and Stott (2010) argued that by reducing the likelihood of an "us" versus "them" mentality developing (i.e., crowds accepting the role and actions of law enforcement officers in managing public order during crowd events), law enforcement officers are more able to adopt effective crowd management strategies. This involves the use of dialogue and communication to address potential misperceptions of law enforcement officers among crowds.

Four learning points on crowd management gleaned from this incident

Based on the key principles of contemporary theories on crowd psychology and behaviours, as well as international best practices for crowd behaviour management, this chapter suggests four guidelines which may be worthy of consideration for public order policing:

1. Obtain information about the crowd early and systematically

It is essential for law enforcement personnel to collect background intelligence about the members of a gathering crowd in order to understand their social identities, motives, and goals. Initial contact with groups at the commencement of law enforcement operations should be characterised by "low-impact visibility", with focus on information gathering and monitoring. Crowd members should be engaged via initial dialogue (e.g., polite interactions, non-aggressive postures) to gather information and intelligence about their intentions, demeanour, and concerns. This will provide more information which can then be used for violence de-escalation.

The United States Marine Corps report *Crowd behaviour, crowd control, and the use of non-lethal weapons* (Kenny et al., 2001) provides useful suggestions, such as appreciating the following:

1 Who are the members of the crowd and what is the overarching identity of the crowd? Understanding who they are would indicate what they might do.
2 What are the goals and purposes of the crowd being there? Understanding what the group wants to accomplish by assembling could determine the extent to which it can be accommodated/facilitated.
3 What is the composition of the crowd? Crowds are often heterogeneous, not homogeneous.
4 What are their traditional behaviours or social repertoires? Actions of crowd members are not universal and vary according to their culture and social practices.
5 What are the possible targets of violence? Riots in particular may focus on specific targets or facilities.
6 When and where will they disperse? Crowds have a life course. Knowing when and where crowds are likely to disperse affects planning and operations (e.g., dispersal avenues, traffic).
7 Explore their plans for subsequent gatherings. Plans for subsequent gatherings may be part of mobilisation instructions for crowd members.

2. Differentiate the crowd: Not all members of the crowd are the same

Collectively classifying rioters' actions as "mindless mayhem" or relying on discredited notions about crowds does not aid in the understanding of how to deal with them. The implication is that people in crowds act without thinking and that their acts thus lack sense or meaning. Similarly, the idea of "de-individuation", that people become anonymous and lose their sense of self in crowds, does not hold up. Recent research has shown that people are generally not anonymous to each other in groups and crowds; they do not lose their identity or control of their behaviour, instead they act in accordance with their group or social identity (Reicher et al., 2007).

Behaviour should not be generalised to all individuals in a crowd setting, as crowds are heterogeneous, containing people with different motivations, roles, and actions. By overgeneralising and responding collectively with force (i.e., an undifferentiated police response), law enforcement personnel risk provoking individuals who were not originally involved in violence, which could lead to an escalation in disorderly behaviour as it facilitates the "us versus them" mentality. It is thus useful to differentiate the members of the crowd and target the individuals engaged in violent behaviours rather than the crowd as a whole.

3. Facilitate the legitimate goals of the crowd

Crowds gather for various reasons: to watch a concert, to use public transport, and to protest. Law enforcement personnel should not assume that every crowd will necessarily become violent and volatile, though they have the potential to do so. Authorities may avoid violence and win cooperation by facilitating the majority of the crowd, who tend to have non-criminal intentions, to satisfy the purpose for which they are there. For example, in the Little India incident, most of those present were there to take the bus home and facilitating this (instead of stopping all traffic movement) would have reduced the size of the crowd and met the crowd's needs. This would similarly have reduced the likelihood of the "us" versus "them" mentality developing.

4. Communicate first and operate with a hierarchy of graduated tactics

It is important to plan communication with a crowd. During a crowd event, it is important to develop a means of addressing crowd members so that the authorities and the police can try to explain what they are doing and how it relates to the aims of the crowd, should unexpected events arise (i.e., facilitating legitimate goals). During crowd events, law enforcement officers must negotiate, educate, and maintain constant dialogue with organisers and crowd members. Law enforcement personnel must remain neutral regardless of the crowd's position and views.

However, in the event of crowd violence, law enforcement officers are advised to adopt a graduated escalation of their response to manage the crowd. This includes the use of more forceful measures to quell violence. When law enforcement officers respond with graduated escalation, police actions are more likely to be deemed justified, fair, and legitimate. Most members of the crowd are more likely to rationalise the actions of law enforcement personnel as "fair" since adequate verbal warnings were given. Members of the crowd are given ample opportunity to disengage from aggressive or violent acts. If arrests become necessary, law enforcement officers must convey to those who are arrested that they expect their cooperation. Such a graduated tactical approach is similar to the "dialogue policing" used by the Stockholm Police Department and the "communication police" of British law enforcement agencies, who engage and open a dialogue with members of the crowd initially with the option to use reasonable force should violence escalates. Table 14.2 presents a summary of four learning points on crowd management gleaned from the Little India riot.

Table 14.2 A summary of four learning points on crowd management gleaned from the Little India riot

In summary, four learning points on crowd management are gleaned from the Little India riot:
1 Obtain information about the crowd early and systematically.
2 Differentiate the crowd: not all members are the same.
3 Facilitate the legitimate goals of the crowd.
4 Communicate first and operate with a hierarchy of graduated tactics.

Chapter summary points

- Crowds are not irrational and unthinking entities.
- Crowds are heterogeneous in nature.
- Individuals do not lose their identity in crowds. Changes in the situation result in changes of identity within the crowd.
- It is important for law enforcement officers to be familiar with crowd behaviours, to understand their attitudes and behaviours so that they can appreciate the complexity and dynamics of crowd situations.
- Contemporary theories on crowd psychology and behaviours can offer useful advice for law enforcement officers in the area of public order policing.

Notes

1 These behavioural perspectives were not pertinent to the investigations and thus not pursued or captured by the investigation team during their interviews.
2 The Ministry of Home Affairs is also known as "the Home Team" in the Republic of Singapore. It is the ministry responsible for public safety, civil defence, and immigration. The psychologists (i.e., the researchers) involved in the behavioural analysis of the Little India riot are from the Home Team Academy, Singapore Police Force, Central Narcotics Bureau, Singapore Civil Defence Force, and the Singapore Prison Service.
3 This term is not used in the legalistic sense of whether an action is legal or illegal. Instead, it refers to whether an action is perceived to be fair or right in a particular context.

References

Borch, C. (2006). The exclusion of the crowd: The destiny of a sociological figure of the irrational. *European Journal of Social Theory*, *9*, 83–102. doi: 10.1177/1368431006060464

Drury, J., Cocking, C., Beale, J., Hanson, C., & Rapley, F. (2005). The phenomenology of empowerment in collective action. *British Journal of Social Psychology*, *44*, 309–328. doi: 10.1348/014466604X18523

Drury, J., & Reicher, S. D. (2000). Collective action and psychological change: The emergence of new social identities. *British Journal of Social Psychology*, *39*, 579–604. doi: 10.1348/014466600164642

Drury, J., & Reicher, S. D. (2005). Explaining enduring empowerment: A comparative study of collective action and psychological outcomes. *European Journal of Social Psychology*, *35*, 35–58. doi: 10.1002/ejsp.231

Gorringe, H., Stott, C., & Rosie, M. (2012). Dialogue police, decision-making, and the management of public order during protest crowd events. *Journal of Investigative Psychology*, *9*, 111–125. doi: 10.1002/jip.1359

Hoggett, J., & Stott, C. (2010). The role of crowd theory in determining the use of force in public order policing. *Policing and Society: An International Journal of Research and Policy*, *20*, 223–236. doi: 10.1080/10439461003668468

Kenny, J. M., McPhail, C., Waddington, P., Heal, S., Ijames, S., Farrer, D. N., . . . & Odenthal, D. (2001, 1 January). *Crowd behavior, crowd control, and the use of non-lethal weapons*. Retrieved from http://www.popcenter.org/problems/spectator_violence/PDFs/HEAP.pdf

Le Bon, G. (2002). *The crowd: A study of the popular mind.* Mineola, NY: Dover Publications.

Masterson, K. (1988). How can the police prevent minor incidents of public disorder from developing into major riots? *Police Journal*, *61*, 234–244. doi: 10.1177/0032258X8806100306

McPhail, C. (2006). The crowd and collective behaviour: Bringing symbolic interaction back in. *Symbolic Interaction*, *29*, 433–464. doi: 10.1525/si.2006.29.4.433

Ministry of Home Affairs. (2014). *Report of the Committee of Inquiry into the Little India riot on 8 December 2013.* Retrieved from http://www.mha.gov.sg/Newsroom/press-releases/PublishingImages/Pages/Report-of-the-Committee-of-Inquiry-into-the-Little-India-Riot-on-8-December-2013/Little%20India%20Riot%20COI%20report%20-%202014-06-27.pdf

Reicher, S. D. (1996). "The Battle of Westminster": Developing the social identity model of crowd behaviour in order to explain the initiation and development of collective conflict. *European Journal of Social Psychology*, *26*, 115–134. doi: 10.1002/(SICI)1099-0992(199601)

Reicher, S. D. (2001). The psychology of crowd dynamics. In M. Hogg & R. S. Tindale (Eds.), *Blackwell handbook of social psychology: Group processes* (pp. 182–208). Hoboken, NJ: Wiley-Blackwell.

Reicher, S. D., Stott, C., Drury, J., Adang, O., Cronin, P., & Livingstone, A. (2007). Knowledge-based public order policing: Principles and practice. *Policing*, *1*, 403–415. doi: 10.1093/police/pam067

Reiner, R. (1985). *The politics of the police.* London: Wheatsheaf.

Scarman, L. O. B. E. (1981). *The Brixton disorders, April 10–12 1981: Report of an inquiry by the Rt. Hon. the Lord Scarman, O.B.E. (Cmnd. 8427).* London: HMSO.

Stott, C., Adang, O., Livingstone, A., & Schreiber, M. (2007). Variability in the collective behaviour of England fans at Euro2004: "Hooliganism", public order policing and social change. *European Journal of Social Psychology*, *37*, 75–100. doi: 10.1002/ejsp.338

Stott, C., Hutchison, P., & Drury, J. (2001). "Hooligans" abroad? Intergroup dynamics, social identity and participation in collective "disorder" at the 1998 World Cup Finals. *British Journal of Social Psychology*, *40*, 359–384. doi: 10.1348/014466601164876

Stott, C., & Reicher, S. (1998). Crowd action as intergroup process: Introducing the police perspective. *European Journal of Social Psychology*, *28*, 509–529. doi: 10.1002/(SICI)1099-0992(199807/08)28:4<509::AID-EJSP877>3.0.CO;2-C

Tarde, G. (1968). *Penal philosophy.* Montclair, NJ. Patterson Smith.

Zeitz, K. M., Tan, H. M., Grief, M., Couns, P. C., & Zeitz, C. (2009). Crowd behavior at mass gatherings: A literature review. *Prehospital and Disaster Medicine*, *24*, 32–38. doi: 10.1017/S1049023X00006518

15 The psychology of violent extremism

What we know and what else we need to do

Leevia Dillon, Loo Seng Neo, and Majeed Khader

Introduction

Over the years, research examining the psychology of violent extremism has gathered momentum and grown substantially. Although early research on the psychology of violent extremism was centred mostly in psychoanalytic theory (see Borum, 2004), findings in recent years have proposed new explanations to better understand the psychological underpinnings of violent extremism at the individual level. For instance, studies have disputed the assumption that violent extremists are mentally unsound (Weatherston & Moran, 2003). This finding demonstrates how frighteningly normal and unremarkable, in psychological terms, those who engage in violent extremist activity are. In like manner, Cragin (2014) argues that most of the people who were exposed to the same enabling environments as those who became violent extremists were not radicalised. Even for those who have been influenced online by violent extremist ideology, only a small minority would eventually become radicalised. In fact, most of them would reject the use of violence (Rieger, Frischich, & Bente, 2013).

Thus, as a discipline, psychology has re-examined certain assumptions of violent extremism and offered new insights not only into the individual but also to the group dynamics and universal behavioural principles that expound on engagement in violent extremism (DeAngelis, 2009). Psychology has the potential to answer the questions of why an individual becomes a violent extremist, how violent extremist groups are formed, why the public react in a certain manner towards violent extremist acts, and how to create narratives to counter violent extremism. Such revelations have slowly gained the recognition and interest of law enforcement agencies, policymakers, and the academic community.

As a relatively new field of research within the context of violent extremism, the scientific discipline of psychology has introduced new insights and ways of analysing the phenomenon. This chapter therefore seeks to articulate the nature and direction of current psychological research on violent extremism from 2011 to 2015 and, in doing so, explore ways in which psychology might inform and improve our current understanding of violent extremism. The first section will explore the scientific and professional literature about the "psychology of violent extremism" by utilising a systematic review of four major academic databases.

The second section will analyse the literature review using thematic analysis to identify themes of interest from 2011 to 2015. The last section will delve into the future directions of research on the psychology of violent extremism.

Reviewing the literature on the psychology of violent extremism

To identify the relevant literature on the psychology of violent extremism, a review of major academic databases was conducted. Four databases (i.e., ScienceDirect, Psychology and Behavioural Sciences Collection [PBSC], JSTOR, and SAGE) were analysed using a systematic, iterative keyword strategy, mapping where possible onto existing subject headings. Of particular interest here is the acknowledgement that the literature review did not solely focus on literature relevant to violent extremism alone but also on both violent extremism and terrorism[1] since both terms have been used interchangeably, thus preventing any exclusion of relevant content. For the purposes of this chapter, a working definition of violent extremism would be "a willingness to use or support the use of

Table 15.1 Review of four academic databases on the psychology of violent extremism

Keywords	*Academic database*			
	ScienceDirect	*PBSC*	*JSTOR*	*SAGE*
Psychology AND Terroris*	3919	808	3877	7729
Psychology AND Terroris* AND Internet	870	17	2760	1794
Psychology AND Terroris* AND Radicali*	143	21	2347	655
Psychology AND Terroris* AND Internet AND Radicali*	45[a]	2[a]	359[a]	273[a]
Psychology AND Violent Extremis*	309	14	3795	1018
Psychology AND Violent Extremis* AND Internet	75	0	508	321
Psychology AND Violent Extremis* AND Radicali*	60	5	1028	290
Psychology AND Violent Extremis* AND Internet AND Radicali*	23[a]	0	188[a]	149[a]
Psychology AND Violent Extremis* AND Terroris* AND Internet AND Radicali*	38[a]	0	239[a]	225[a]

Note: The values represent the number of papers that were identified using the keywords.

a These values were consolidated to generate the total amount of potentially relevant papers (i.e., 1,541) across the four databases.

violence to further particular beliefs, including those of a political, social or ideological nature. This may include acts of terrorism" (Nasser-Eddine, Garnham, Agostino, & Caluya, 2011, p. 9).

Searches included terms such as psychology, violent extremis*, terroris*, Internet, and radicali*. Variations of the search terms were also used to ensure all available materials were included. This allowed the search strategy to be diverse enough to gather sufficient content that examines the psychology of violent extremism. An initial search conducted in December 2015 using the search terms generated a total of 1,541 potentially relevant papers across the four databases. The breakdown of these searches is summarised in Table 15.1. These papers were then appraised to determine if they warranted full review. As this chapter represents an exploratory attempt to document the nature and direction of current psychological research, the criteria for identifying relevant content adhered to the principles of purposive sampling (see Teddlie & Yu, 2007). In this context, this method involved selecting papers that were published from 2011 to 2015 for the purpose of currency. Furthermore, after the initial list was generated, papers that appeared repeatedly across all four databases were consolidated to reduce repetition. On the basis of the results of this appraisal, 534 papers were selected for full review.

Thematic analyses

To examine the current state of psychological research on violent extremism from 2011 to 2015, the 534 identified papers were analysed using thematic analysis to identify themes of interest. According to Braun and Clarke (2006), thematic analysis "is a method for identifying, analysing and reporting patterns [themes] within data – it organises and describes data set in rich details" (p. 79). Methodologically, this form of qualitative analysis is suited for highlighting key themes from a large body of qualitative data to understand how psychology has contributed to our understanding of violent extremism. For each paper, three independent raters were asked to identify themes that indicated the use of the psychological perspective in analysing violent extremism. Themes were rated as present when all three raters agreed on the presence of that theme for each paper. In cases of disagreements, the raters would discuss their decisions and address the differences until an agreement was reached.

In total, 10 general themes were identified (see Table 15.2): violent extremist tactics; gender; online discourse; public perception of violent extremism; counter violent extremism efforts; use of Internet by violent extremists for recruitment; group dynamics; violent extremist groups; risk assessment; and cyber threats.

Themes of the psychology of violent extremism

This section examines seven themes of the psychology of violent extremism. These were recurring themes in the scientific and professional literature that was published from 2011 to 2015, and they appeared in at least three years or more (see Table 2); for example, the theme *Online Discourse* was selected as it appeared in papers that were published in 2011, 2012, 2013, and 2015.

Table 15.2 Overview of themes where psychology is used to examine violent extremism

Themes	*Year*				
	2011	*2012*	*2013*	*2014*	*2015*
Violent extremist tactics[a] – Suicide bombing, stabbing, IEDs, exploitation of vulnerable population	√	√	√	√	
Gender – Female violence, women and violent extremism, gender differentiation	√			√	
Online discourse[a] – Propaganda, ideologies, narratives, violent extremist websites	√	√	√		√
Public perception of violent extremism[a] – Violent extremism reporting, ground-up online initiatives	√	√	√	√	√
Counter violent extremism efforts[a] – Counter narratives, deradicalisation, disengagement, resilience	√	√	√	√	√
Use of Internet by violent extremists for recruitment[a] – Communication, planning of attacks, radicalisation		√	√		√
Group dynamics[a] – In-group versus out-group, authority, group identity	√	√	√	√	√
Violent extremist groups – Islamic State in Iraq and Syria, Al-Qaeda, Liberation Tigers of Tamil Eelam, Animal Liberation Front, Earth Liberation Front		√			√
Risk assessment[a] – Motivation, behavioural indicators, propensity to violence and radicalisation process		√	√	√	√
Cyber threats – Cyberterrorism, hacking, cybercrimes	√				√

Note: The tick (√) indicates that there were papers being published in that particular year based on the theme.

a The themes selected were recurring themes in the scientific and professional literature that was published from 2011 to 2015, and they appeared in at least three years or more – they are elaborated in detail in the next section; for example, the theme *Online Discourse* was selected as it appeared in papers that were published in 2011, 2012, 2013, and 2015.

Violent extremist tactics: What modus operandi do violent extremists adopt and who are they targeting for recruitment?

In terms of violent extremist tactics, psychological research has provided insights into the symbolic meaning and intent behind the adoption of certain modus operandi and the vulnerable populations that perpetrate such attacks. There are many modus operandi that violent extremists use to conduct their attacks, ranging from knives to improvised explosive devices, suicide bombing, and weaponry. For example, in Europe and Australia, the most common method of attack is the use of an explosive device (Mullins, 2011). However, recent studies suggest an increase in the use of innocuous everyday objects such as knives (e.g., the murder of Lee Rigby in 2013). Though unsophisticated in nature, knives have also been utilised in acts of beheading by violent extremist groups (Radford, 2014). For example, James Foley was beheaded in August 2014 by the Islamic State in Iraq and Syria (ISIS), purportedly as a response to the United States airstrikes in Iraq. While the modus operandi may be brutal, the messages associated with the heinous act (e.g., to strike fear in enemies) are still able to attract and recruit new followers (Kruglanski, 2014). Furthermore, such acts do capture the attention of the world, as evidenced by the recirculation of these propaganda materials on various social media platforms, including mainstream news channels (Neo et al., 2016).

There are also studies that focus on the vulnerable groups which are prone to being recruited by violent extremist groups. For example, Mahan and Griset (2013) note that about 300,000 children have been recruited by violent extremist groups to conduct acts of violence. Many groups have used children to serve as lookouts, participate in suicide bombings, and carry supplies. Women are also playing an increasingly important role in conducting acts of violent extremism. While men continue to occupy the primary leadership roles, women have been recruited to perform various important roles such as carrying out logistics, recruiting new members, and, in some cases, more combatant roles, including suicide missions (Bloom, 2011). Furthermore, women have been documented serving as "enforcers of the law". An example is ISIS's Al-Khansaa Brigade, which is an all-women police enforcement unit whose members ensure that their female counterparts living in ISIS adhere to its rules and regulations (Eleftheriou-Smith, 2015).

Online discourse: How are violent extremists framing and disseminating their online propaganda material?

The role of psychology in the analysis of online discourse is to provide insights into the ways narratives are framed by violent extremists and the platforms on which such content is being disseminated. The advent of the Internet and the opportunity it offers have allowed violent extremists to expand the functionalities of their propaganda efforts beyond the boundaries of the traditional mainstream media (Conway, 2012; Edwards & Gribbon, 2013). In fact, violent extremist ideological narratives that are pervasive on the Internet have proven capable of gaining a foothold in the psyche of individuals who seek some form of justification for their frustration and anger over the plight of Muslims suffering in conflict zones (Hu, 2016). For instance, the romantic vision of a utopian caliphate has been exploited by the Islamic caliphate that ISIS has claimed to have established in Syria and Iraq to shape its audience's world views and attract new recruits.

Furthermore, it offers the opportunity for violent extremists such as Abu Bakr al-Baghdadi (leader of ISIS) to exploit the Internet to achieve greater impact and media publicity, albeit using fewer resources. It is essential to note that before the dawn of the Internet, he would have had to kill large numbers of people to grab the attention of supporters and media. In the same vein, Seib and Janbek (2011) observe that incidences of prisoner abuse in Abu Ghraib have been exploited in an attempt to galvanise recruits by citing retribution as their cause for violence. As Hussain and Saltman (2014) note, the exploitation of the Internet involves "rebranding many of their harsh ideas to make them sound benign and selecting emotive issues in order to elicit public sympathy" (p. 109). Thus, violent extremist groups will reframe their narrative and utilise it as an effective medium to communicate their beliefs, values, and reappraisals of events.

Research into hypermedia seduction for violent extremist recruitment (e.g., Bhui & Ibrahim, 2013; Dauber & Winkler, 2014) has hinted that features of these online platforms may influence how an individual reacts to violent extremists' online propaganda. Some have focused on the initial response of the user when he or she comes into contact with violent extremists' online platforms. After a brief initial confrontation with online radical content, it is envisaged that the individual would experience a range of emotions from apathy to repulsion to exhilaration that might influence his or her decision to either ignore the materials or to continue the search for more relevant materials (Neo, 2016). Others have examined users' initial impression of videos carrying the messages disseminated by violent extremists (Rieger et al., 2013). In fact, the sharp increase in online discourse and publications with violent extremist ownership indicates that it is an increasingly important means for violent extremists to achieve their cause (Lemieux, Brachman, Levitt, & Wood, 2014).

Public perception of violent extremism: How has the public reacted to violent extremism attacks?

In terms of the public perception of violent extremism, psychology can provide insights into the phenomenon of the bystander effect and the emergence of ground-up online initiatives in the aftermath of an attack. The bystander effect is a psychological phenomenon that occurs when individuals do not offer help to victims in the presence of others (see Darley & Latané, 1968). In the context of violent extremism, bystander effect studies have focused on identifying the reasons why individuals (i.e., those who have observed warning signs) are not reporting and proposing suggestions to overcome these barriers. From their empirical research, Williams, Horgan, and Evans (2016) found evidence that the relationship between the "associate gatekeepers" (i.e., individuals who witness warning signs) and potential violent extremists plays an important part in their willingness to intervene and their ability to recognise violent extremism in the making. In particular, there is the degree of fear in damaging that relationship. Williams et al. (2016) argue that the greatest barrier to vicarious help-seeking in CVE [counter violent extremism] contexts is not whether associate-gatekeepers can be trained to help their associates get the help they need. Instead, it suggests that among the next steps – the next challenges – are to develop the curricula and protocols for how associate-gatekeepers should respond (p. 63). Furthermore, Staub (2013) suggests that when bystanders do not react, the perpetrators may become emboldened in their actions. Therefore, it seems that the inaction of bystanders may result in an enduring violent extremism-related conflict (Schillinger, 2014).

Research has also examined the emergence of ground-up online initiatives in the aftermath of an attack (e.g., Giglietto & Lee, 2015; Lesaca, 2015). There have been many instances where social media has been utilised by members of the public to rally and unite the community to deal with the negativity following an attack. One example of such an initiative can be seen in the "#illridewithyou" social media campaign after the 2014 Sydney siege. This campaign has encouraged Australians to stand in solidarity with local Muslims by riding home with them and protecting them from possible anti-Muslim retaliation. The campaign emphasised the identity of "One Australia", recognising and regarding Muslim Australians as "fellow mates" who suffered the same national tragedy at the hands of Man Haron Monis. Examples of other popular online initiatives included "#IstandWithAhmed" and "#NotAllMuslims". These online developments provide valuable insights about the public's sentiments and perceptions with regard to violent extremism and, more importantly, the level of resilience within the community. Furthermore, given that such initiatives are community-led (i.e., free of the government's influence), they have an added sense of credibility and legitimacy as well as community solidarity (Spalek, 2014).

Efforts to counter violent extremism: How can we manage the threat of violent extremism?

Efforts to counter violent extremism efforts have focused on countering the pull of radical propaganda and inoculating individuals who are at risk (Liang, 2015). Psychological studies under this theme have centred on the development of counter narratives, deradicalisation, and disengagement. Effective counter narratives include well-defined objectives which seek to "create a competing narrative that strikes an emotional chord with potential militants weighing whether to join a violent extremist group" (Schmitt, 2013, para. 7). There are many types of narratives which include alternative (i.e., creation of proactive, positive content), strategic (i.e., condemnation of violent extremist-related attacks), ethical (i.e., highlighting violence as immoral way of achieving goals), ideological and religious (i.e., content is focused on theological debates by those with religious authority), tactical (i.e., content that emphasise on violence being less effective in the long run as compared to more peaceful methods) content and the use of humour and sarcasm (i.e., used to delegitimise violent extremists). However, new evidence suggests that the introduction of narratives that challenge an individual's extant belief system may be counterproductive and promote counterarguments and resistance. Researchers such as Garrett and Weeks (2013) note that individuals who adhere to beliefs consistent with their world views often experience resistance with maximum vehemence when they are exposed to messages that highlight inaccuracies that run counter to their beliefs. Garrett and Weeks further observed that extremists often find solidarity in sources that are ideologically similar. It seems reasonable to assume that in the marketplace of ideas, counter messages may inadvertently provoke extremists into defending their beliefs and viewing these messages from a biased perspective (Mielczarek & Perlmutter, 2014).

New developments (e.g., Dechesne, 2011; Reinares, 2012) in the area of deradicalisation and disengagement have revealed evidence of individuals disengaging from violent extremism due to a myriad of factors, such as fear, disillusionment with extremist group, unmet expectations, changes of one's lifestyle, and perceived ineffectiveness of the cause. It is essential to note that the terms *deradicalisation* and *disengagement* are two distinct concepts that have been used interchangeably (Horgan & Braddock, 2010). Deradicalisation is a process where an individual experiences a role change that is associated with a reduction of violent extremism-related behaviours. Psychological factors such as disillusionment, burnout, or the failure to reach expectations influence this process. In contrast, disengagement is the reduction of an individual's commitment and involvement in violent extremism. It also refers to initiatives that attempt to reduce the risk of recidivism with regard to violent extremism. Deradicalisation refers to changes in cognition (i.e., values and beliefs), while disengagement refers to behavioural changes but does not compel a cognitive change (Fink & Hearne, 2008).

Use of the Internet by violent extremists for recruitment: How are violent extremists using the Internet for recruitment?

An increasing amount of research has gone into the question of how the Internet has enhanced and contributed to the recruitment and radicalisation process. Serving as an effective conduit for communication, the Internet has allowed violent extremist groups to disseminate their propaganda messages more easily, and it has become the ideal platform for violent extremists to communicate with one another and with their followers (Aly, Weimann-Saks, & Weimann, 2014; Hussain & Saltman, 2014). Cohen, Johansson, Kaati, and Mork (2014) argue that the threshold for individuals to be influenced by radical ideology and engage in violent extremism-related behaviours is becoming lower due to the power of the Internet.

Weimann (2012) observes that almost all lone wolf attacks in recent years have involved the use of electronic social media. Violent extremists have utilised gradual inoculation to groom potential members and get them more involved in their activities via interaction on online media public platforms such as Ask.fm, Instagram, Facebook, and Twitter before encouraging them to move to private encrypted online platforms for further communication. Not only that, violent extremists have exploited the Internet to spread rumours and disinformation and deliver their threats, which are intended to instil fear and helplessness in their audience (Torok, 2013). Violent extremists have direct control over the messages pushed out into the Internet which enable them to paint a positive and powerful image about themselves while putting down their enemies. This, in turns, may create an illusion of power and demonstrate their strength, allowing them to push above their weight (Caiani & Kröll, 2015). Furthermore, the Internet has been transformed into a virtual training camp. For example, Barnes (2012) notes the ease with which one can use the Internet to access technical information, such as how to build an explosive device. Some of this technical information provides instruction not only on how to build the device but also on how to acquire the necessary parts.

Group dynamics: How do violent extremists behave within their group?

Social psychological research on violent extremist groups has highlighted the role of group dynamics. Some of this research includes concepts such as group polarisation, group identity, and the influence of authority. Brachman and Levine (2011) draw attention to the formation of online communities which enable like-minded individuals to find support and online materials. The General Intelligence and Security Service [AIVD] (2012) notes that even in cases of lone wolf attacks, the perpetrators have rarely been radicalised in complete isolation; there will be some form of interactions with like-minded individuals in these online communities. Acting as an "echo chamber", these online communities encourage group polarisation, which is a psychological phenomenon that occurs within a group where members engage in extreme decision-making. Group polarisation can abet individual radicalisation and lead to confirmation biases where they search for information that confirms their beliefs and reject opposing ones, thus leaving "a hard-core group that increasingly becomes radicalised" (Gupta, 2011, p. 39). The nature of group polarisation implies that individuals would regress from a myriad of mainstream influences to a narrow radical frame of reference.

Furthermore, studies have examined how the interactive element of these online communities facilitates the formation of new social norms and identity. These online platforms provide members with a sense of belonging while guaranteeing relative anonymity (Seib & Janbek, 2011). They create a sphere of influence where violent extremists can introduce new social conduct, routines, and behaviours expected of members. Such interactions may socialise the members to social circles with radical world views, thereby creating a ready-made antecedent for more radical ideology. In other words, as Caiani and Kröll (2015) suggest, "isolated individual 'consumers' can find a common identity through extreme right websites, convincing themselves that they are not alone, but instead part of a community, albeit a 'virtual' one" (p. 332).

Research has also examined the importance of authority figures within violent extremist groups. In particular, literature has focused on the charisma associated with radical preachers and violent extremist leaders. Charisma lies in violent extremist leaders' ability to recruit, radicalise, and lead their groups

(Nesser, 2011). Such authority figures play vital roles in the formation of the group ideology, strategic operations, and organisational success (Ligon, Harms, Crowe, Lundmark, & Simi, 2014). In the context of religion, these authority figures have issued fatwas and instructions for their followers to follow on the basis of their legitimacy and credibility. Of note, many violent extremists are not well versed in religion and have not had a religious upbringing (Bartlett & Miller, 2012). As a result, many of them will gravitate towards these authority figures without questioning the messages.

Risk assessment: How to assess the risk of violent extremists?

In endeavouring to assess the danger represented by the radicalisation of individuals, psychological research has looked into several areas of interest: motivations, behavioural indicators, and risk assessment tools. The motivations of violent extremists are extremely varied; each violent extremist is motivated to differing degrees in terms of their group and personal interests as well as ideology (Dean, 2014; Kruglanski et al., 2013). Common themes of motivation include perceived grievances, need for identity, need for affiliation, adventure, and fame (see Borum, 2014). For example, the quest for significance model developed by Kruglanski and Orehek (2011) is a framework delineating motivations that lead an individual to join a violent extremist group. The framework identifies three motivations of interest: (a) significance loss, (b) threat of significance loss, and (c) opportunity for significance gain. These factors may shape and restructure one's degree of susceptibility to being influenced and persuaded by radical rhetoric (Borum, 2011). Hence, there is the need to identify the causes and conditions which make people become attracted to violent extremist attitudes or behaviours.

There has been a great interest in developing behavioural indicators that can help to identify features synonymous with involvement in violent extremism and in turn identify individuals who may potentially become involved (Kebbell & Porter, 2011; Meloy, Hoffmann, Roshdi, & Guldimann, 2014). These warning behaviours can be viewed as indicators of an increasing or accelerating risk of committing a violent attack. In a similar fashion, Neo, Khader, Ang, Ong, and Tan (2014) have developed a three-domain (i.e., behaviour-ideology, group psychology, operational preparatory) framework to identify individuals who are at risk of getting involved in jihadi violent extremism. Eleven prevalent behavioural features (e.g., individuals pushing for terrorist ideals through violence; individuals showing a desire for revenge; the presence of a leader figure who espouses terrorist ideology) were derived from a list of 53 features after mapping them to 30 case studies. These features may be presented as reference points that law enforcement could utilise to prioritise their attention on areas that warrant further probing and to guide their preliminary investigations.

Another literature of interest is the risk assessment tools developed to measure the risk of an individual engaging in violent extremism. An example of a risk assessment instrument is the Violent Extremism Risk Assessment (VERA) developed by Pressman (2009). This tool is designed to assess incarcerated individuals in order to determine their potential for rehabilitation and propensity for violence (see Pressman & Flockton, 2012; Pressman, 2009). There are 31 items grouped correspondingly into five themes: (a) beliefs and attitudes (e.g., victims of perceived injustice), (b) context and intent (e.g., anger and expressed violent intent), (c) history and capability (e.g., criminal history), (d) commitment and motivation (e.g., moral superiority), and (e) protective factors (e.g., family support).

Psychology of violent extremism: The Singapore context

This section highlights some of the research conducted by the authors at the Home Team Behavioural Sciences Centre, Ministry of Home Affairs, Singapore. Three research areas were identified: (a) creating an early screening guide for jihadi violent extremism, (b) theorising a pathway for online radicalisation, and (c) developing a threat assessment screening tool for online violent extremism.

Creating an early screening guide for Jihadi violent extremism

The capability to detect and appreciate early warning signs would allow law enforcement and intelligence officers to better analyse behaviours which might indicate the likelihood of an attack. Hence, it is necessary to develop the knowledge and capability to identify possible violent extremism behavioural features for the purpose of intelligence gathering.

This research seeks to develop a screening guide for jihadi violent extremism with the intention of streamlining the huge amounts of raw intelligence into smaller amounts of data for further analysis. On the basis of the authors' collective experience in dealing with violent extremists and a review of the literature and pre-attack indicators developed by law enforcement agencies worldwide, 53 features of jihadi violent extremism belonging to three domains (behaviour ideology [BI], group psychology [G], and operational preparatory [O]) were identified. The first domain of behaviour ideology outlines the concept of ideology (e.g., "thought reformation" processes) and utilises psychological theories to examine its role in attitude and behaviour manifestations. The second domain of group psychology focuses on how the dynamics (e.g., leadership, membership, training and communication patterns) of violent extremist groups influence their members' attitudes and behaviours. The third domain of operations addresses the identification and assessment of activities that push violent extremist groups towards conducting their attacks.

To test the utility of the features, these domains were mapped against 30 jihadi violent extremist attacks from different parts of the world. The results suggest that there were 11 features that were evident in more than 50% of the 30 case studies (see Figure 15.1). The authors proposed that the identified 11 prevalent features may be presented as reference points of an early screening guide that practitioners could utilise to prioritise their attention on areas that warrant further probing and to guide their preliminary investigations. It is important to note that the features identified were not intended to constitute a risk assessment tool;

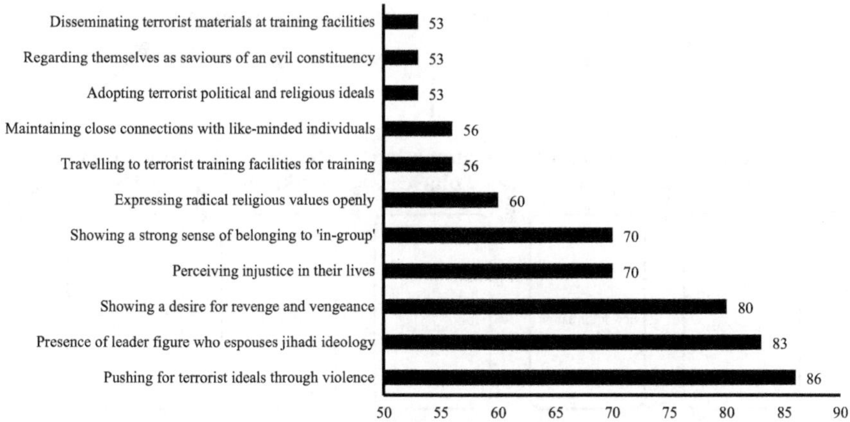

Figure 15.1 Eleven most prevalent features of Jihadi violent extremism across 30 terror attacks

they have to be used together with existing intelligence and operational markers of terrorist behaviours. The value of these features can be predicated on the behavioural and psychological perspective it offers to augment the operational knowledge of law enforcement agencies.

Theorising a pathway for online radicalisation, RECRO

This framework, which was adapted from Weimann and Von Knop's (2008) research on online violent extremism, was developed to enhance our understanding of the psychological processes of how an individual may engage with violent extremist-related narratives online and become radicalised. It was developed in response to the growing threat posed by Singaporeans who have been radicalised by online propaganda materials they have consumed over the Internet.

The framework consists of five phases: Reflection, Exploration, Connection, Operational, and Resolution [RECRO] (see Figure 15.2). The reflection phase details the triggers, needs, and vulnerabilities that an individual may have which increase his or her receptiveness to alternative belief systems. The exploration phase outlines the period where the individual begins making sense of the information put forth by violent extremists. The connection phase addresses the online interactions that the individual may proceed to establish with other like-minded people in a virtual community to reinforce his or her new world view. The resolution phase details the period where the individual encounters new circumstances that challenge the newly internalised world view and provide the momentum to translate his or her radical beliefs into action. Finally, the operational phase outlines the period where the individual is ready to commit acts of violence in furtherance of his or her radical objectives. By identifying the dyadic interaction between the Internet and the individual, this model offers a framework to

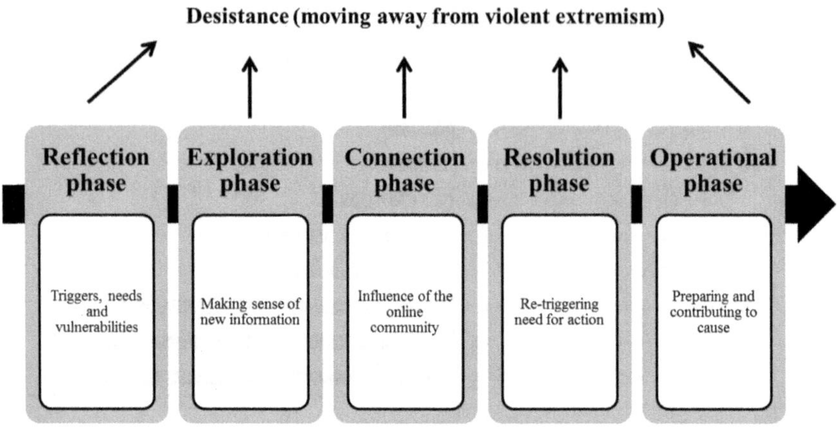

Figure 15.2 The RECRO framework of online radicalisation

organise the concepts, mechanisms, and processes that might be involved in the radicalisation process.

Developing an online violent extremism screening tool (OVEST)

The authors' research into the phenomenon of online violent extremism, as well as case studies on attacks (e.g., Boston Bombing, Sydney Siege, Charlie Hebdo shooting, Jakarta attacks) by radicalised individuals, suggests the need for measures to identify the early warning signs of individuals who may be engaging in online violent extremism (e.g., becoming ISIS supporters). This would, in turn, facilitate the assessment of an individual's potential risk for involvement in online violent extremism and prioritise intervention and threat management efforts.

However, the current state of international research on the identification of potential online violent extremists is in its infancy, and there are no established screening tools designed specifically to assess an individual's risk of becoming involved in online violent extremism. To address this gap, the authors developed an Online Violent Extremism Screening Tool (OVEST) to aid law enforcement and intelligence officers to identify these early warning signs of online violent extremism. OVEST is comprised of three general domains of interest: person-centric (risk) factors, system-centric (risk) factors, and protective factors. The first domain of person-centric factors addresses an individual's involvement in online violent extremism on the basis of their vulnerabilities, attitudes, emotions, and behaviours. The second domain of system-centric factors focuses on the cyber behaviours manifested by the individual on the basis of their consumption of violent extremist materials and their interactions with like-minded others in online communities. Finally, the third domain details the protective factors that reduce the individual's propensity to become radicalised.

It is essential to note that the research thus far undertaken by the authors has largely been conducted from a theoretical lens. In order to test and validate OVEST, they are currently in the process of validating the tool by mapping the associated factors with data collected via interviews with violent extremists in Indonesia.

Future research on the psychology of violent extremism

Analysing the themes of the psychology of violent extremism has identified several issues. The first is the need for a multidisciplinary approach to study the phenomenon of violent extremism. While the focus of this chapter is on psychology, this is not intended to suggest that the psychological approach provides the only, or even necessarily the best, analytic framework for understanding violent extremism. At the same time, it is clear that recent psychological research has gained ascendance as a reasonable and potentially human-centric line of inquiry that contributes to the overall understanding on violent extremism. While much progress has been made, much more is still needed. Thus, this chapter acts as an insight into an area that requires further attention, exploring the themes pertaining to violent extremism that have been raised by social science researchers.

The second issue revolves around the inability to predict future attacks well, despite many years of research and responding to the threat of violent extremism. Why is it that most researchers are not able to predict future attacks well? One reason could be that research has yet to provide a comprehension explanation for violent extremism and why it comes about in the first place (Khader, 2016). For example, the low base rate for violent extremism poses a major challenge to developing models for understanding what motivates violent extremists to do what they do before rather than after an attack. It is also confounded by the more general deficits in our understanding of the process through which individuals become involved in violent extremist activity. Another reason could be the diversity and variation of the phenomenon. Violent extremists are motivated by different causes, adopt different modus operandi, utilise different targeting strategies, and have different organisational structures. The vast differences make it difficult to generalise about psychological influences on violent extremism. Whatever the reasons, in order to be able to get better at predicting the threat of violent extremism, there is a need to appreciate the potential role played by psychological research paradigms (e.g., developing risk assessment for violent behaviours) in differentiating between and comparing high- and low-risk populations of violent extremist behaviour. This is critical because there is currently a lack of empirically based risk factors in this enterprise.

Finally, while research on the psychology of violent extremism has grown substantially in the last few years, there remain many unanswered challenges and unchartered territories of knowledge in the field. In particular, there is a need to design and conduct research within a framework of operationally relevant questions that may make violent extremism more understandable to practitioners who work to prevent and counter violent extremism. On the basis of the analysis of the above-mentioned themes, the authors identified several areas of research through which psychology can further our understanding of violent extremism.

Identify ways to reduce the bystander effect

The public plays an important role in countering violent extremism by reporting suspected violent extremism. However, as Williams and colleagues (2016) suggest, most individuals may express a reluctance to report due to the fear of the potential repercussions of such actions. There is therefore an urgent need to identify ways to overcome these barriers and reduce the bystander effect. While research on the bystander effect in the context of violent extremism is still in its infancy, there are valuable lessons to learn from research conducted in the domain of bullying and sexual assault (see Polanin, Espelage, & Pigott, 2012). Some of these bystander studies have also shown that training programmes on bystander intervention have led to real-world increases in bystander intervention behaviours. Some important questions that future psychological research needs to address are:

1 The need to design training programmes on bystander intervention for members of public to report suspected violent extremism.
2 The need to formulate a theory of bystander intervention for violent extremism and to suggest cultural-specific interventions for overcoming these barriers.

Develop risk assessment that is focused on cyber-related behaviour and content

Violent extremists have exploited the Internet to transform the way they operate on a historically unprecedented scale. This has several implications for practitioners. Firstly, online behaviours potentially provide an important source of open-source information from which law enforcement can glean intent. The observable remnants of online behaviours and chatter found in radical websites and social media accounts may provide valuable insights into the individual's world view and intentions. Secondly, such online observations can be used to triangulate offline intelligence gathered from other sources. This, in turn, allows the risk assessment to be carried out on multiple levels that involve data acquired from Internet content, other observed behaviours, reports, and background information. The addition of detailed cyber-behavioural indicators or evidence will make extant risk assessment approaches more robust and relevant.

However, while this might sound like a common sense solution, there are not many online risk assessment tools for violent extremism. There have been excellent early efforts with the development of the CYBERA (see Pressman & Ivan, 2016), but more research is needed to fully understand the early warning indicators of violent extremist action and determine the risk trajectories of individuals. It is clear, therefore, that the development of robust and cyber-focused risk assessment tools which allow one to analyse risk and determine the specific elements and indicators most pertinent to involvement in online violent extremism should continue to be an area for future psychological research. Some important questions are:

1 What are the risk and protective factors associated with online violent extremism?
2 How can we provide a more individualised and integrated picture of online violent extremism-related risk rather than just a tally or an accumulation of risk factors?
3 How may an individual's behaviour change over time and affect the risk he or she may pose?

Understand the transition from online to offline domain

From an operational perspective, it is clear that practitioners need to understand the interaction between individuals' online experiences and their offline experiences. However, research has yet to examine the dyadic interplay between individuals' engagement with violent extremist content online and their experiences offline; the transition from online to offline engagement as part of the larger psychological process of radicalisation remains poorly understood (Caiani & Kröll, 2015; von Behr, Reding, Edwards, & Gribbon, 2013). For example, while there are thousands of members of violent extremist online communities, very few become violent extremists in the real world. The "loudest" online members (i.e., those engaged in the most vigorous and aggressive forms of online interactions) may not, in fact, be the ones most likely to engage in violence. Likewise, the most passive ones are not automatically the most peaceful. Thus, understanding the transition between the online and offline worlds is essential if law enforcement practitioners are to understand how the next generation of potential violent extremists will be radicalised. Some important questions are:

1 Do some aspects of the online engagement reflect offline realities and impact real life?
2 Do online supporters and influencers manifest similar dynamics in the real world?

Conducting "cyber psychological autopsy" to understand how individuals become radicalised online

While the literature on radicalisation seems to abound with research on how people become radicalised, there are hardly any in-depth approaches that accurately assess the psychology and motivation of the individual (Khader, 2016; Klausen, Campion, Needle, Nguyen, & Libretti, 2015). Taking insights from the domains of criminal and health psychology, violent extremism researchers can consider extrapolating the principles behind the concept of "psychological autopsy" (see Isometsä, 2001; Lankford, 2012) to provide a much more complete explanation of behaviours associated with the radicalisation process. Such an approach may focus more on the individual's life experiences rather than just on the act of violence; amongst other things, it can potentially reveal deep insights into motivations, preferences for particular cyber platforms, the nature of interactions and the interconnectedness of these interactions, and the links between cyber-world and real-world interactions. Thus, it can provide a deep insight into the processes of radicalisation for the cyber age. Some important questions are:

1 How do we undertake a cyber autopsy of how an individual gets radicalised online?
2 How does an individual's narrative escalate or de-escalate, or do they become more or less active over time?

Chapter summary points

- The scientific discipline of psychology has introduced new insights and ways of analysing the phenomenon of violent extremism.
- Using a systematic review of four academic databases, themes on the psychology of violent extremism were identified (based on literature published from 2011 to 2015).
- The seven themes are: violent extremist tactics, online discourse, public perception of violent extremism, counter violent extremism efforts, use of Internet by violent extremists for recruitment, group dynamics, and risk assessment.
- Utilising a psychological perspective, the authors have embarked on three research projects in response to regional threats: creating an early screening guide for jihadi violent extremism; theorising a pathway for online radicalisation; and developing a threat assessment screening tool for online violent extremism.
- Future areas of research for the psychology of violent extremism have also been highlighted: the bystander effect in the context of violent extremism reporting; the development of risk assessments focusing on cyber-related behaviour; the transition of behaviours from the online domain to the offline domain; and performing a cyber psychological autopsy to enhance our understanding of radicalised individuals.

Note

1 There is no consensus in the literature regarding a universally accepted definition of violent extremism and terrorism in spite of decades of research (Schmid, 2013). According to Schmid (2011), the revised academic consensus definition of terrorism is as follows: "Terrorism refers on the one hand to a doctrine about the presumed effectiveness of a special form or tactic of fear-generating, coercive political violence and, on the other hand, to a conspiratorial practice of calculated, demonstrative, direct violent action without legal or moral restraints, targeting mainly civilians and non-combatants, performed for its propagandistic and psychological effects on various audiences and conflict parties" (p. 86).

References

Aly, A., Weimann-Saks, D., & Weimann, G. (2014). Making "noise" online: An analysis of the say no to terror online campaign. *Perspective on Terrorism*, *8*(5), 33–47. Retrieved from http://www.terrorismanalysts.com/pt/index.php/pot/article/view/376/html

Barnes, B. (2012). Confronting the one-man wolf pack: Adapting law enforcement and prosecution responses to the threat of lone wolf terrorism. *Boston University Law Review*, *92*, 1613–1662. Retrieved from http://papers.ssrn.com/sol3/papers.cfm?abstract_id=2177295

Bartlett, J., & Miller, C. (2012). The edge of violence: Towards telling the difference between violent and non-violent radicalisation. *Terrorism and Political Violence*, *24*, 1–21. doi: 10.1080/09546553.2011.594923

Bhui, K., & Ibrahim, Y. (2013). Marketing the "radical": Symbolic communication and persuasive technologies in jihadist websites. *Transcultural Psychiatry*, *50*(2), 216–234. doi: 10.1177/1363461513479329

Bloom, M. (2011). *Bombshell: The many faces of women terrorists.* Philadelphia, PA: University of Pennsylvania Press.

Borum, R. (2004). *Psychology of terrorism.* Tampa, FL: University of South Florida. Retrieved from https://www.ncjrs.gov/pdffiles1/nij/grants/208552.pdf

Borum, R. (2011). Radicalization into violent extremism I: A review of social science theories. *Journal of Strategic Security*, *4*(4), 7–36. doi: 10.5038/1944–0472.4.4.1

Borum, R. (2014). Psychological vulnerabilities and propensities for involvement in violent extremism. *Behavioral Sciences and the Law*, *32*, 286–305. doi: 10.1002/bsl.2110

Brachman, J. M., & Levine, A. N. (2011). You too can be awlaki! *The Fletcher Forum of World Affairs*, *35*(1), 25–46. Retrieved from http://www.fletcherforum.org/2011/01/20/brachmanlevine/

Braun, V., & Clarke, V. (2006). Using thematic analysis in psychology. *Qualitative Research in Psychology*, *3*(2), 77–101. doi: 10.1191/1478088706qp063oa

Caiani, M., & Kröll, P. (2015). The transnationalization of the extreme right and the use of the Internet. *International Journal of Comparative and Applied Criminal Justice*, *39*(4), 331–351. doi: 10.1080/01924036.2014.973050

Cohen, K., Johansson, F., Kaati, L., & Mork, J. C. (2014). Detecting linguistic markers for radical violence in social media. *Terrorism and Political Violence*, *26*(1), 246–256. doi: 10.1080/09546553.2014.849948

Conway, M. (2012). Introduction: Terrorism and contemporary mediascapes – reanimating research on media and terrorism. *Critical Studies on Terrorism*, *5*(3), 445–453. doi: 10.1080/17539153.2012.725979

Cragin, R. K. (2014). Resisting violent extremism: A conceptual model for non-radicalisation. *Terrorism and Political Violence*, *26*, 337–353. doi: 10.1080/09546553.2012.714820

Darley, J., & Latané, B. (1968). Bystander intervention in emergencies: Diffusion of responsibility. *Journal of Personality and Social Psychology*, *8*(4), 377–383. Retrieved from http://www3.nd.edu/~wcarbona/darley%20and%20latane%20-%20bystander%20intervention.pdf

Dauber, C. E., & Winkler, C. K. (2014). Radical visual propaganda in the online environment: An introduction. In C. K. Winkler & C. E. Dauber (Eds.), *Visual propaganda and extremism in the online environment* (pp. 1–30). Carlisle, PA: Strategic Studies Institute and U.S. Army War College Press. Retrieved from http://www.strategicstudiesinstitute.army.mil/pdffiles/PUB1213.pdf

Dean, G. (2014). *Neurocognitive risk assessment for the early detection of violent extremists.* New York, NY: Springer. doi: 10.1007/978-3-319-06719-3_3

DeAngelis, T. (2009). Understanding terrorism. *American Psychological Association.* Retrieved from http://www.apa.org/monitor/2009/11/terrorism.aspx

Dechesne, M. (2011). Deradicalization: Not soft, but strategic. *Crime, Law and Social Change, 5*(4), 287–292. doi: 10.1007/s10611-011-9283-8

Edwards, C., & Gribbon, L. (2013). Pathways to violent extremism in the digital era. *The RUSI Journal, 158*(5), 40–47. doi: 10.1080/03071847.2013.847714

Eleftheriou-Smith, L. M. (2015, 20 April). Escaped ISIS wives describe life in the all-female Al-Khansa Brigade who punish women with 40 lashes for wearing wrong clothes. *The Independent.* Retrieved from http://www.independent.co.uk/news/world/middle-east/escaped-isis-wives-describe-life-in-the-all-female-al-khansa-brigade-who-punish-women-with-40-lashes-10190317.html

Fink, N. C., & Hearne, E. B. (2008). Beyond terrorism: Deradicalisation and disengagement from violent extremism. *International Peace Institute.* Retrieved from http://www.ipinst.org/wp-content/uploads/publications/beter.pdf

Garrett, R. K., & Weeks, B. E. (2013). *The promise and peril of real-time corrections to political misperceptions.* Proceedings of the 2013 Conference on Computer Supported Cooperative Work, 1047–1058. doi: 10.1145/2441776.2441895

General Intelligence and Security Service [AIVD]. (2012). *Jihadism on the web: A breeding ground for jihad in the modern age.* Retrieved from https://www.aivd.nl/binaries/aivd_nl/documenten/publicaties/2012/02/14/het-jihadistisch-internet-kraamkamer-van-de-hedendaagse-jihad/summary-jihadism-on-the-web-en-20120214.pdf

Giglietto, F., & Lee, Y. (2015, 18 May). *To be or not to be Charlie: Twitter hashtags as a discourse and counter-discourse in the aftermath of 2015 Charlie Hebdo shooting in France.* Proceedings of the 5th Workshop on Making Sense of Microposts. Retrieved from http://ceur-ws.org/Vol-1395/paper_12.pdf

Gupta, D. K. (2011). Waves of international terrorism: An exploration of the process by which ideas flood the world. In J. E. Rosenfield (Ed.), *Terrorism, identity, legitimacy: The four waves theory and political violence* (pp. 30–43). New York, NY: Routledge.

Horgan, J., & Braddock, K. (2010). Rehabilitating the terrorists? Challenges in assessing the effectiveness of de-radicalization programs. *Terrorism & Political Violence, 22*, 267–291. doi: 10.1080/09546551003594748

Hu, W. (2016). Psychological effects of the threat of ISIS: A preliminary inquiry of Singapore case studies. In M. Khader, L. S. Neo, G. Ong, E. Tan, & J. Chin (Eds.), *Combating violent extremism and radicalisation in the digital era* (pp. 168–173). Hershey, PA: IGI Global. doi: 10.4018/978-1-5225-0156-5

Hussain, G., & Saltman, E. M. (2014). *Jihad trending: A comprehensive analysis of online extremism and how to counter it.* London: Quilliam Foundation. Retrieved from http://www.quilliamfoundation.org/wp/wp-content/uploads/publications/free/jihad-trending-quilliam-report.pdf

Isometsä, E. T. (2001). Psychological autopsy studies – A review. *European Psychiatry, 16*(7), 379–385. doi: 10.1016/S0924-9338(01)00594-6

Kebbell, M. R., & Porter, L. (2011). An intelligence assessment framework for identifying individuals at risk of committing acts of violent extremism against the West. *Security Journal, 25*(3), 212–228. doi: 10.1057/sj.2011.19

Khader, M. (2016). What we know and what else we need to do to address the problem of violent extremism online: Concluding chapter. In M. Khader, L. S. Neo, G. Ong, E. Tan, & J. Chin (Eds.), *Combating violent extremism and radicalisation in the digital era* (pp. 486–495). Hershey, PA: IGI Global. doi: 10.4018/978-1-5225-0156-5

Klausen, J., Campion, S., Needle, N., Nguyen, G., & Libretti, R. (2015). Toward a behavioral model of "homegrown" radicalization trajectories. *Studies in Conflict & Terrorism, 39*(1), 67–83. doi: 10.1080/1057610X.2015.1099995

Kruglanski, A. W. (2014, 28 October). Psychology not theology: Overcoming ISIS' secret appeal. *E-International Relations.* Retrieved from http://www.e-ir.info/2014/10/28/psychology-not-theology-overcoming-isis-secret-appeal/

Kruglanski, A. W., Bėlanger, J. J., Gelfand, M., Gunaratna, R., Hettiarachchi, M., Reinares, F., . . . Sharvit, K. (2013). Terrorism – A (self) love story: Redirecting the significance quest can end violence. *American Psychologist, 68*(7), 559–575. doi: 10.1037/a0032615

Kruglanski, A. W., & Orehek, E. (2011). The role of the quest for personal significance in motivating terrorism. In J. Forgas, A. W. Kruglanski, & K. Williams (Eds.), *The psychology of social conflict and aggression* (pp. 153–166). New York, NY: Psychology Press. Retrieved from http://public.psych.iastate.edu/caa/Classes/487Readings/KruglanskiOrehek2011.pdf

Lankford, A. (2012). A psychological autopsy of 9/11 ringleader Mohamed Atta. *Journal of Police and Criminal Psychology, 27*(2), 150–159. doi: 10.1007/s11896-011-9096-9

Lemieux, A. F., Brachman, J. M., Levitt, J., & Wood, J. (2014). Inspire magazine: A critical analysis of its significance and potential impact through the lens of the information, motivation, and behavioral skills model. *Terrorism and Political Violence, 26*(2), 354–371. doi: 10.1080/09546553.2013.828604

Lesaca, J. (2015, 19 November). Fight against ISIS reveals power of social media. *The Brookings Institution.* Retrieved from http://www.brookings.edu/blogs/techtank/posts/2015/11/19-isis-social-media-power-lesaca

Liang, C. S. (2015). Cyber jihad: Understanding and countering Islamic State propaganda (GCSP Policy Paper 2015/2). *Geneva Centre for Security Policy.* Retrieved from http://www.gcsp.ch/News-Knowledge/Publications/Cyber-Jihad-Understanding-and-Countering-Islamic-State-Propaganda

Ligon, G. S., Harms, M., Crowe, J., Lundmark, L., & Simi, P. (2014). The Islamic State of Iraq and the Levant: Branding, leadership culture and lethal attraction. *National Consortium for the Study of Terrorism and Responses to Terrorism (START).* Retrieved from https://www.start.umd.edu/pubs/START_ISIL%20Branding%20Leadership%20Culture%20and%20Lethal%20Attraction_Ligon_Nov2014.pdf

Mahan, S., & Griset, P. L. (2013). *Terrorism in perspective* (3rd ed.). Thousand Oaks, CA: Sage.

Meloy, J. R., Hoffmann, J., Roshdi, K., & Guldimann, A. (2014). Some warning behaviors discriminate between school shooters and other students of concern. *Journal of Threat Assessment and Management, 1*, 203–211. doi: 10.1037/tam0000020

Mielczarek, N., & Perlmutter, D. D. (2014). Big pictures and visual propaganda: The lessons of research on the "effects" of photojournalistic icons. In C. K. Winkler & C. E. Dauber (Eds.), *Visual propaganda and extremism in the online environment* (pp. 215–232). Carlisle, PA: Strategic Studies Institute and U.S. Army War College Press. Retrieved from http://www.strategicstudiesinstitute.army.mil/pdffiles/PUB1213.pdf

Mullins, S. (2011). Islamist terrorism in Australia: An empirical examination of the "home grown" threat. *Terrorism and Political Violence, 23*, 254–285. doi: 10.1080/09546553.2010.535717

Nasser-Eddine, M., Garnham, B., Agostino, K., & Caluya, G. (2011). *Countering Violent Extremism (CVE) literature review*. Edinburgh, Australia: Australian Government, Department of Defence, Command and Control Division, Defence Science and Technology Organisation (DSTO). Retrieved from http://dspace.dsto.defence.gov.au/dspace/bitstream/1947/10150/1/DSTO-TR-2522%20PR.pdf

Neo, L. S. (2016). An internet-mediated pathway for online radicalisation: RECRO. In M. Khader, L. S. Neo, G. Ong, E. Tan, & J. Chin (Eds.), *Combating violent extremism and radicalisation in the digital era* (pp. 197–224). Hershey, PA: IGI Global. doi: 10.4018/978-1-5225-0156-5

Neo, L. S., Khader, M., Ang, J., Ong, G., & Tan, E. (2014). Developing an early screening guide for jihadi terrorism: A behavioural analysis of 30 terror attacks. *Security Journal*. Advance online publication. doi: 10.1057/sj.2014.44

Neo, L. S., Shi, P., Dillon, L., Tan, J., Wang, Y., & Gomes, D. (2016). Why is ISIS so psychologically attractive? In M. Khader, L. S. Neo, G. Ong, E. Tan, & J. Chin (Eds.), *Combating violent extremism and radicalisation in the digital era* (pp. 149–167). Hershey, PA: IGI Global. doi: 10.4018/978-1-5225-0156-5

Nesser, P. (2011). Ideologies of jihad in Europe. *Terrorism and Political Violence, 23*(2), 173–200. doi: 10.1080/09546553.2010.53787

Polanin, J. R., Espelage, D. L., & Pigott, T. D. (2012). A meta-analysis of school-based bullying prevention programs' effects on bystander intervention behaviour. *School Psychology Review, 41*, 47–65. Retrieved from https://www.researchgate.net/publication/235220413_A_Meta-Analysis_of_School-Based_Bullying_Prevention_Programs%27_Effects_on_Bystander_Intervention_Behavior

Pressman, D. E. (2009). *Risk assessment decisions for violent political extremism*. Ontario: Carleton University. Retrieved from http://www.publicsafety.gc.ca/cnt/rsrcs/pblctns/2009-02-rdv/2009-02-rdv-eng.pdf

Pressman, D. E., & Flockton, J. S. (2012). Calibrating risk for violent political extremists: The VERA-2 structural assessment. *The British Journal of Forensic Practice, 14*(4), 237–251. doi: 10.1108/14636641211283057

Pressman, D. E., & Ivan, C. (2016). Internet use and violent extremism: A cyber-VERA risk assessment protocol. In M. Khader, L. S. Neo, G. Ong, E. Tan, & J. Chin (Eds.), *Combating violent extremism and radicalisation in the digital era* (pp. 391–409). Hershey, PA: IGI Global. doi: 10.4018/978-1-5225-0156-5

Radford, B. (2014). Why terrorists behead their victims. *Discovery News*. Retrieved from http://news.discovery.com/history/religion/why-terrorists-behead-their-victims-140822.htm

Reinares, F. (2012). Exit from terrorism: A qualitative empirical study on disengagement and deradicalisation among members of ETA. *Terrorism and Political Violence, 23*(5), 780–803. doi: 10.1080/09546553.2011.613307

Rieger, D., Frischich, L., & Bente, G. (2013). *Propaganda 2.0 psychological effects of right-wing and Islamic extremist internet videos*. Germany: German Federal Criminal Police Office. Retrieved from https://www.researchgate.net/publication/264829254_Propaganda_20_Psychological_effects_of_right-wing_and_Islamic_extremist_internet_videos

Schillinger, T. (2014). Bystander effect and religious group affiliation: Terrorism and the diffusion of responsibility. *International Journal of Peace and Conflict Studies*, *2*(3), 29–44. Retrieved from http://www.rcmss.com/2014/IJPCS-VOl2-No2/BYSTANDER%20EFFECT%20AND%20RELIGIOUS%20GROUP%20AFFILIATION_%20TERRORISM%20AND%20THE%20DIFFUSION%20OF%20RESPONSIBILITY.pdf

Schmid, A. P. (Ed.). (2011). *The Routledge handbook of terrorism research*. New York, NY/London: Routledge.

Schmid, A. P. (2013). *Radicalization, de-radicalization, counter-radicalization: A conceptual discussion and literature review* (ICCT Research Paper). The Hague: International Centre for Counter-Terrorism – The Hague. Retrieved from http://www.icct.nl/download/file/ICCT-Schmid-Radicalisation-De-Radicalisation-Counter-Radicalisation-March-2013.pdf

Schmitt, E. (2013, 4 December). A U.S. reply, in English, to terrorists' online lure. *The New York Times*. Retrieved from http://www.nytimes.com/2013/12/05/world/middleeast/us-aims-to-blunt-terrorist-recruiting-of-english-speakers.html

Seib, P., & Janbek, D. M. (2011). *Global terrorism and new media: The post Al-Qaeda generation*. New York, NY: Routledge.

Spalek, B. (2014). Community engagement for counter-terrorism in Britain: An exploration of the role of 'connectors' in countering takfiri jihadist terrorism. *Studies in Conflict & Terrorism*, *37*, 825–841. doi: 10.1080/1057610X.2014.941436

Staub, E. (2013). *Overcoming evil: Genocide, violent conflict and terrorism*. Oxford: Oxford University Press.

Teddlie, C., & Yu, F. (2007). Mixed methods sampling: A typology with examples. *Journal of Mixed Methods Research*, *1*(1), 77–100. doi: 10.1177/2345678906292430

Torok, R. (2013). Developing an explanatory model for the process of online radicalisation and terrorism. *Security Informatics*, *2*, 1–10. doi: 10.1186/2190-8532-2-6

von Behr, I., Reding, A., Edwards, C., & Gribbon, L. (2013). *Radicalisation in the digital age: The use of the internet in 15 cases of terrorism and extremism*. Santa Monica, CA: RAND Corporation. Retrieved from http://www.rand.org/content/dam/rand/pubs/research_reports/RR400/RR453/RAND_RR453.pdf

Weatherston, D., & Moran, J. (2003). Terrorism and mental illness: Is there a relationship? *International Journal of Offender Therapy and Comparative Criminology*, *47*(6), 698–719. doi: 10.1177/0306624X03257244

Weimann, G. (2012). Lone wolves in cyberspace. *Journal of Terrorism Research*, *3*(2), 75–90. doi: 10.15664/jtr.405

Weimann, G., & Von Knop, K. (2008) Applying the notion of noise to countering online terrorism. *Studies in Conflict & Terrorism*, *31*(10), 883–902. doi: 10.1080/10576100802342601

Williams, M. J., Horgan, J. G., & Evans, W. P. (2016). The critical role of friends in networks for countering violent extremism: Toward a theory of vicarious help-seeking. *Behavioural Sciences of Terrorism and Political Aggression*, *8*(1), 45–65. doi: 10.1080/19434472.2015.1101147

16 Expanding the study of procedural justice and legitimacy in Hong Kong

What has been done, and future directions

Kevin Kwok Yin Cheng

Introduction

Studies in the criminological and socio-legal literature exploring the relationships between procedural justice, legitimacy, and cooperation with legal authorities and compliance with the law have proliferated in the past two decades. Starting with Tom Tyler's influential work, *Why People Obey the Law* (1990), procedural justice studies have expanded in the United States (e.g., Sunshine & Tyler, 2003; Tyler & Fagan, 2008; Tyler & Huo, 2002) and other English-speaking countries such as the United Kingdom (e.g., Hough, Jackson, Bradford, Myhill, & Quinton, 2010; Jackson et al., 2012, 2013), Australia (e.g., Hinds & Murphy, 2007; Murphy & Cherney, 2012), and Canada (e.g., Sprott & Greene, 2010). In recent years, procedural justice and legitimacy has also attracted attention from other societies across the world, including Ghana (Tankebe, 2009a), Jamaica (Reisig & Lloyd, 2009), Israel (Hasisi & Weisburd, 2011), and Pakistan (Jackson, Asif, Bradford, & Zakar, 2014). This chapter focuses on the Hong Kong Chinese context, where the study of procedural justice and legitimacy is in its infancy.

The core argument of procedural justice theory, or the process-based model of regulation, is that the more people perceive that they have been treated in a procedurally just way by legal authorities such as the police and courts, the more they view the authority in question as legitimate and the more willing they are to cooperate with and defer to the authority. Tyler (2003, p. 285) notes that "[t]his model is explicitly psychological, viewing subjective judgments on the part of the public about the actions of the police and the courts as central to the effectiveness of legal authorities." This chapter is divided into three broad sections: the first section provides a general review of procedural justice and legitimacy; the second section discusses the current studies that have been done in Hong Kong, with a focus on young offenders and defence lawyers; and the third section offers some suggestions on future directions for studying procedural justice and legitimacy in Hong Kong and, by extension, other parts of the region as well.

Procedural justice and legitimacy: An overview

Drawing on social psychology, procedural justice theory argues that people's law-related conduct is associated with subjective assessments on how legal authorities treat them and other members of the public. Such appraisals of treatment consist of both the quality of decision-making by the authority and the quality of treatment by the authority (Tyler, 2003). Assessments of procedural justice can be further broken down into four factors: voice, neutrality, treatment with dignity and respect, and trustworthiness.

Voice, or level of participation, refers to the opportunity for people to express their views or their side of the story to the legal authority. People want to feel that the authority has sincerely considered their side of the story before making a decision such as an arrest or an adjudication of guilt. Neutrality refers to the notion that the decision-makers have based their decisions on facts and procedures and not on personal biases or opinions: for instance, police officers or judges can explain how they have applied certain rules to a particular situation. Treatment with dignity and respect refers to the subjective assessment regarding the manner in which people are treated by the legal authority. This includes treating people with politeness and courtesy and providing individuals with information such as when and where to appear in court. The important thing about treating people well is that legal authorities convey the message that the person is still a valuable member of society and that their rights and dignity will be upheld even if they are suspected of committing a crime. The final factor of trustworthiness involves the assessment of the character of the decision-maker and whether he/she is acting in the interests of, or doing right for, all the parties involved in a particular situation (Tyler, 2008).

Procedural justice ultimately enhances public cooperation and deference to legal authorities as it leads the public to view these authorities as legitimate. Legitimacy has been defined as a psychological property of authorities and "the belief that authorities, institutions, and social arrangements are appropriate, proper, and just" (Tyler, 2006, p. 376). Moreover, legitimacy is regarded as "a feeling of obligation to obey the law and to defer to the decisions made by legal authorities" (Tyler & Fagan, 2008, p. 235). Most procedural justice studies measure legitimacy through two main values: obligation to obey, and trust and confidence in legal authorities. Therefore, even if a person does not agree every time with the decisions of the legal authority in question, there is still an obligation and a trust to defer, cooperate, and comply because it is the appropriate, proper, and just response (Tyler, 2003).

All of this is important because legal authorities rely on public cooperation for the criminal justice system to operate successfully. The police rely on the public to follow directives, come forth as witnesses, and report crimes to them. Similarly, the courts need individuals to testify as witnesses and to serve as jury members. Conversely, when legal authorities have been found to treat people in procedurally unjust ways, this has led to people resorting to self-help and vigilantism (Tankebe, 2009b).

Numerous studies have demonstrated empirical support for the process-based model of regulation. For example, using a sample of over 1,400 Californian residents living in Oakland and Los Angeles, Tyler and Huo (2002) measured the residents' evaluations of the courts and their willingness to accept the courts' decisions and found that there was strong support for the salience of procedural justice. Using regression analyses and controlling for the demographic and other background characteristics of the respondents, they discovered that the perceived fairness of the court procedures was the primary factor influencing people's willingness to accept court decisions and their overall evaluations of the court system. The salience of procedural justice was evident irrespective of the respondents' gender, age, education level, city of residence, and race, where the sample was divided between Whites, Hispanics, and African-Americans.

The procedural justice literature has mainly been devoted to public perceptions of the police. A more recent study, for instance, focused on Muslim Americans' willingness to cooperate with and alert the police in respect to counterterrorism policing (Tyler, Schulhofer, & Huq, 2010). The study drew from a sample in New York City. Two prevailing models relating to the willingness to cooperate with the police were tested: the first is instrumental, contesting that individuals cooperate out of self-interest to do so; and the second is normative, arguing that procedural justice shapes legitimacy and in turn cooperation with the police. Legitimacy was found to directly influence respondents' willingness to assist and to alert the police with respect to counterterrorism policing. Two aspects of procedural justice, policy formation and policy implementation, positively influenced Muslim Americans' perception of the legitimacy of the police. Policy formation refers to the degree to which the authorities considered the views of the Muslim community in formulating anti-terrorism policing strategies. Policy implementation concerns the fairness of the decision-making process and the quality of treatment given by police officers.

Another study that should be mentioned for the purposes of this chapter is Jiang, Wu, and Wang's (2013) empirical study on citizens' perceived obligation to obey the law in Guangzhou, China. Following the same vein as previous procedural justice studies in the United States, citizens' obligation to obey the law was measured using both the instrumental and normative models. It was found that both the instrumental model, measured by perceived severity of punishment, and the normative model, measured by the legitimacy of legal authorities, played significant roles in shaping people's compliance with the law. The authors stressed that their study was exploratory in nature and that more research needs to be done to effectively compare findings between Western countries and China.

The Hong Kong context: Young people and lawyers

The study of procedural justice and legitimacy has only recently gained limited traction in Hong Kong, and the focus has been on young people and defence lawyers. Since its early colonial days, Britain imposed English law on all Chinese citizens in Hong Kong. Even now, after the handover of Hong Kong to the People's Republic of China in 1997, the previous common law system and institutions remain. Hong Kong courts can still look to English precedents and court cases from other common law jurisdictions such as Canada, Australia, and New Zealand to decide their cases. While these cases are not binding, they can be used to persuade the court. In Hong Kong's highest court, the Court of Final Appeal, one judge out of the five-member panel can be an acting or retired high court judge from another common law jurisdiction. The previous court system, legal profession, and laws remain largely intact (see Lo & Chui, 2012).

The study of juvenile delinquency and young offenders has always been a mainstay of criminological research in Hong Kong. Indeed, most criminological work in Hong Kong has been about juvenile and youth delinquency or crime (Xu, 2011). Moreover, like many other jurisdictions, young people in Hong Kong disproportionately come into contact with legal authorities. Scholars in Hong Kong have constantly pointed out that many young people get caught up in the criminal justice system for committing petty offences (Gray, 1994; Wong, 2000). According to Gray (1994), Hong Kong operates a *disciplinary welfare model* with respect to youth delinquency where the goal is to sentence young offenders in order to remove antisocial bonds and to strengthen positive bonds with family and school. This is primarily achieved through a sentencing tariff, where the court takes into account the welfare needs of the juvenile or young offender and matches it with the appropriate level of sentencing. Sentences focus on rehabilitation and discipline, such as probation, which involves supervision and adherence to conditions, and a detention centre, which involves physical toil that is meant to foster correction (Lo, 2008). The objective is to restore the offender back to a "normal" lifestyle (Gray, 1994, pp. 193–194).

Unlike the majority of procedural justice studies, the focus in Hong Kong has been on young people's perceptions of defence lawyers. The right to legal representation remains an integral part of Hong Kong's legal system. For instance, Article 35 of the *Basic Law*, Hong Kong's constitution, states: "Hong Kong residents shall have the right to confidential legal advice, access to the courts, choice of lawyers for timely protection of their lawful rights and interests or for representation in the courts, and to judicial remedies". This right extends to both adults and young people. Despite the handover of Hong Kong back to the People's Republic of China in 1997, the Hong Kong legal system continues in very much the same way as during its colonial era. A separate juvenile justice system has been in place in Hong Kong since 1932. Criminal proceedings in both adult and juvenile court are adversarial in nature, where lawyers are the main driving force of the proceedings.

The Hong Kong juvenile justice system stresses the importance of ensuring that youths understand the legal procedures and that their rights are protected (*Juvenile Offenders Ordinance* Cap. 226). Past studies in other jurisdictions have noted that young people are less likely to have an appropriate understanding of criminal justice proceedings and how to safeguard their own rights (e.g., Grisso, 1981). In this sense, lawyers play a vital role in ensuring that young defendants are legally represented and understand the procedure and that their rights are upheld.

A few studies in Canada have examined the relationship between procedural justice and legitimacy in lawyer-youth client interactions. Peterson-Badali, Care, and Broeking (2007) developed the Perception of Fairness in Lawyer-Client

Interactions Scale, which focuses on the four dimensions of procedural justice outlined above, and surveyed a sample of young offenders in a Canadian youth court. The young defendants were asked to rate their perceptions of how fairly their lawyers had treated them. A strong positive correlation was found between the young offenders' perception of how fairly their lawyers had treated them (measures of procedural justice) and their satisfaction with their lawyers. The youths were more satisfied when their lawyers were regarded as competent in terms of their legal skills and provided options for their young clients in terms of case directions. On the other hand, dissatisfaction was associated with a lack of responsiveness and respect from the lawyer.

In a similar study, Sprott and Greene (2010) also measured the views of a sample of young offenders in a Canadian youth court. They measured how the youths felt they had been treated by their lawyer, the prosecution, and the judge at their first appearance and after their sentencing. The surveys focused on perceptions of procedural justice on the four dimensions of respect, objectivity, participation, and trustworthiness. It was found that the young offenders' feelings on how procedurally just their lawyers and judges had been in their treatment of them affected their perceptions of the legitimacy of the juvenile justice system as a whole.

Study 1: Young offenders, youths-at-risk, and students

Drawing on the works of the Canadian studies outlined above, the first study in Hong Kong compared the perceptions of the procedural justice of defence lawyers between young offenders (N = 151), youths-at-risk (N = 262), and students (N = 744) (Chui & Cheng, 2015a). The age of the participants ranged from 14 to 22, with a mean age of 17. Just over half of the participants were male (N = 615; 53.2%), the rest being female (N = 539; 46.6%). The sample of young offenders that had direct experiences of having legal representation represents the group with the highest level of delinquency/criminality. Youths-at-risk are young people who are considered to be in negative conditions that create vulnerabilities which may lead them into criminality in the near future. They have also displayed some sort of deviant or antisocial behaviour such as dropping out of school, staying out late at night on the streets, or engaging in substance abuse, but they have never been formally charged and brought into the criminal justice system (see Lee, 2011). In this study, the youths-at-risk were referred by social outreach groups and had come to the attention of the police. Lastly, the student group, drawn from various secondary schools in Hong Kong, served as the reference group.

The main rationale for including three groups of youths as opposed to just young offenders is because perceptions of how fairly lawyers treat young clients extend to those without direct contact with lawyers. Such perceptions may come from vicarious experiences, such as from family members or friends who have been caught up in the criminal justice system. Overall, by comparing the three youth groups, the study of procedural justice and legitimacy with respect to young people would be expanded.

The participants (N = 1,157) were asked to fill out a questionnaire with assorted measures during the period from May 2012 to April 2013. Peterson-Badali et al.'s. (2007) Perception of Fairness in Lawyer-Client Interactions Scale was adopted for this study. This scale, which consists of 20 items, measures the four dimensions of procedural justice in lawyer-client interactions. Sample items include: "My lawyer gave me the chance to express my opinions and feelings" (participation); "My lawyer showed concern for my rights" (treatment with dignity and respect); "My lawyer had personal opinions and attitudes that affected the way he/she treated me" (objectivity; reverse-coded); and "My lawyer tried hard to do the right thing by me" (trustworthiness). For the two groups that had no prior experience of defence lawyers representing them, the wordings of the items were amended slightly: for instance, "My lawyer *would give* me the chance to express my opinions and feelings". Participants were asked to rate their agreement with each statement on a six-point Likert scale ranging from strongly disagree to strongly agree. A composite score was calculated on the basis of the mean scores of each item after taking into account reverse-coded items.

Like previous works, this study was interested in the relationship between procedural justice and legitimacy. More specifically, it tested whether perceptions of procedural justice in lawyer-youth client interactions would affect youths' views of the legitimacy of the criminal justice system. The measurements of the legitimacy of the criminal justice system drew on items from existing previous procedural justice studies, but slight wording changes were made to highlight the context of Hong Kong. These items focused on the dimensions of obligation and trust and confidence. Sample items included: "People should support the decisions made within the Hong Kong courts" and "Overall, I feel proud of our courts in Hong Kong". Participants were asked to rate their agreement with each statement on a five-point Likert scale ranging from strongly disagree to strongly agree. A composite legitimacy score was calculated on the basis of the mean scores of each item.

A number of other independent variables were measured as well. The youths' understanding about lawyers was measured using the Understanding about Lawyers Scale (Revised) (Peterson-Badali et al., 2007). This scale asks respondents a series of questions to test their knowledge about the role of defence lawyers. For instance, participants were asked whether their lawyers ought to follow their instructions, their parents' instructions, or the courts' instructions. Another question asks about participants' experience of the justice system aside from hiring lawyers, such as whether they had been a victim of crime, arrested by the police, or attended court before. Lastly, a number of demographic characteristics, including gender, age, and level of education, acted as control variables.

A series of ordinary least square regressions were conducted. The first set of regressions tested perceptions of fairness in lawyer-client interactions as the outcome variable. The results demonstrated that youths-at-risk were less likely than students to perceive lawyers as acting fairly in dealing with their clients and that older participants were less likely to regard lawyers as fair. However, the more understanding that youths showed towards lawyers, the more they perceived them as treating defendants in a procedurally fair way.

Another regression examined legitimacy of the criminal justice system as the outcome variable and inputted perception of fairness in lawyer-client interactions as an independent variable. Here it was found that females and those with a higher level of education held the criminal justice system to be more legitimate, but those who had previous experience of being arrested perceived the criminal justice system to be less legitimate. Most importantly, it was the perception of fairness in lawyer-client interactions that showed the strongest influence on perceptions of legitimacy. The more that youths thought that lawyers treated their young clients in procedurally just ways, the more they found the criminal justice system to be legitimate. There was no difference found between young offenders, youths-at-risk, and students.

Summary of findings:

- Students showed greater understanding about lawyers.
- Students also demonstrated more favourable perceptions of fairness in lawyer-client interactions compared with the other two groups.
- A better understanding about lawyers was positively associated with perceptions of fairness in lawyer-client interactions.
- A better perception of fairness in lawyer-client interactions was positively associated with legitimacy of the justice system.

Study 2: Young offenders and lawyers

The second study in Hong Kong, which was conducted between 2012 and 2013, focused exclusively on the experiences and perceptions of a sample of young offenders (*N* = 168) with respect to their lawyers (Chui & Cheng, 2015b). The majority of the sample was male (N = 137; 81.5%), with only 31 participants being female (18.5%). The age of the participants ranged from 14 to 21 years, with a mean age of 17.5 years. A slightly different approach was adopted for this study compared with Study 1. Participants were asked to respond to the Perception of Fairness in Lawyer-Client Interactions Scale, the Understanding about Lawyers Scale (Revised), and items relating to the legitimacy of the criminal justice system, other experiences with the criminal justice system, and demographic characteristics. In addition, they were asked to indicate their satisfaction with their lawyers using the Satisfaction with Lawyers scale (Peterson-Badali et al., 2007). They were also asked about the type of legal representation that they had – either private or public. The purpose was to determine whether young offenders' satisfaction with lawyers would influence their views on the legitimacy of the criminal justice system.

Sample items for the Satisfaction with Lawyers scale include: "I was satisfied with the advice that my lawyer gave me"; "I was satisfied with the way my lawyer handled my case"; and "I would use my lawyer again". Participants were asked to rate their agreement with each statement on a six-point Likert scale ranging from strongly disagree to strongly agree. A composite satisfaction score was calculated on the basis of the mean scores of each item.

Besides a purely quantitative methodological approach, additional interviews were conducted with 30 participants in order to add meaning and supplement the statistical results. This mixed methods approach made for a more comprehensive study and combined the strengths of both quantitative and qualitative methods (Creswell & Plano Clark, 2011).

Similar to the first study, regression analyses were first conducted for perception of fairness in lawyer-client interaction. The only variable that demonstrated any significance was type of legal representation; namely, young defendants who had a private lawyer were more inclined to perceive that their lawyer had treated them in a procedurally fair manner. The Perception of Fairness in Lawyer-Client Interactions Scale was also divided separately into its four subscales of participation, treatment with dignity and respect, objectivity, and trustworthiness (which corresponded to the four dimensions of procedural justice). Regressions were run for each dimension as the outcome variable, and once again, young defendants with private lawyers were more likely to rate their lawyers more highly in each of the four dimensions.

Next, regression analyses were conducted for satisfaction with lawyers as the outcome variable, with participation of fairness in lawyer-client interaction included as an independent variable. Two variables stood out. First, once more, those who had hired a private lawyer were more satisfied with their lawyers than those who had a public lawyer. Second, perception of fairness in lawyer-client interaction positively correlated with participants' satisfaction with their legal representatives. Another analysis measured the four dimensions of procedural justice as separate independent variables. Only the dimensions of participation and trustworthiness demonstrated statistical significance on satisfaction with lawyers. The final set of analyses used legitimacy as the outcome variable. It was found that perception of fairness in lawyer-client interaction and satisfaction with lawyers had a positive influence on young offenders' perception of the legitimacy of the criminal justice system.

In the qualitative phase of the study, young offenders were asked why there was such a difference between private and public lawyers, especially with respect to the dimensions of participation and trustworthiness. The lack of participation that young offenders felt with respect to their interactions with their lawyers was likely caused by the structural limitations of the Duty Lawyer Scheme in Hong Kong. The Duty Lawyer Scheme provides free public lawyers to defendants for their first appearance in the lower courts (called the Magistrates' Courts, in which the Juvenile Courts are also housed). There are no full-time public lawyers in Hong Kong; rather, private practising lawyers appear on behalf of the Duty Lawyer Scheme on given dates and adopt the role of duty lawyers. Each morning in court, defendants meet their duty lawyer right before their court appearance. Each duty lawyer is likely to be assigned 10 to 12 cases at a time. Given the number of cases and the time restrictions, the young offenders revealed that they may only get to meet with their legal representative for approximately 10 minutes. Because of the short time frame, duty lawyers go through the case with the defendant quickly, often not giving ample opportunity for defendants to voice their concerns or express their views in any in-depth manner.

This is contrasted with the experiences of young offenders who were able to afford private lawyers. Among the sample, 50 young offenders (29.8%) had a private lawyer and 118 young offenders (70.2%) used the services of duty lawyers. Private lawyers meet with their clients in a more private setting on multiple occasions over the course of a longer period of time. Young offenders expressed that they were given opportunities to discuss with their lawyers for much longer and could go home and think about matters that they wanted to raise and then raise them in subsequent meetings with their lawyers.

In terms of trustworthiness, young offenders were less trusting of duty lawyers because they viewed them as employees of the government. The Duty Liaison Office, where defendants meet their duty lawyer, is housed within the Magistrates' Courts. Moreover, young offenders know that duty lawyers are subsidised by the government. Indeed, duty lawyers hold the same disciplinary welfare goals as other criminal justice actors (see Cheng, Chui, & Ong, 2015). Thus, compared with duty lawyers, private lawyers are seen to act independently, and their loyalty is primarily to their clients' interests.

Summary of findings:

- Young defendants who had a private lawyer were more inclined to perceive that their lawyers had treated them in a procedurally fair manner.
- Perception of fairness in lawyer-client interaction positively correlated with participants' satisfaction with their legal representatives.
- Participation and trustworthiness demonstrated statistical significance on satisfaction with lawyers.
- Young defendants felt that there was a lack of participation in interactions with publicly funded lawyers.
- Young defendants were less trusting of duty lawyers because they viewed them as employees of the government.

Future directions

This section focuses on future directions for procedural justice studies in Hong Kong and Asia. The above studies illustrate the salience of procedural justice in positively influencing the public's perception of the legitimacy of legal authorities. As noted, legitimacy has traditionally been operationalised by the two factors of obligation to obey and trust and confidence in procedural justice. However, in recent years, this conceptualisation of legitimacy has been challenged for being too narrow. There have been calls to examine other possible dimensions of legitimacy (Bottoms & Tankebe, 2012). In particular, the traditional conceptualisation of legitimacy has been challenged empirically when procedural justice was measured outside the Anglo-American context.

Tankebe (2009a), for example, used household surveys to collect citizens' perceptions of the police in Ghana and discovered that obligation to obey the police had no effect on peoples' willingness to cooperate with the police. He posited that in Western societies such as the United States, obligation to obey legal authorities is based on some shared moral values between the power holder and the governed. In a place like Ghana, where citizens have little alternative but to obey the police, obedience is based on fear. Therefore, the element of obligation is put in question, and it begs the question of whether legitimacy ought to be comprised of other dimensions.

In a widely cited piece, Bottoms and Tankebe (2012) contended that legitimacy should include other normative expectations, or what is referred to as shared values. These expectations are effectiveness, distributive fairness, and procedural fairness. Authorities need to justify to individuals that they are effective in wielding the power that has been granted to them; for instance, the police must show that they are effective in combatting crime and the judiciary must demonstrate effectiveness in convicting the guilty and acquitting the innocent. Authorities must also show that decisions are distributed fairly between people of different classes and demographic characteristics. Finally, individuals must perceive that they are treated impartially, honestly, and with respect. These utilitarian dimensions appear to be more profound in societies where there is a deficiency of shared moral values between the authorities and the governed.

All this suggests that there may be a gap between the values and norms of the general populace, who in the context of Hong Kong are mainly Chinese, and the legal institutions, which in large part were modelled after the English legal system. It is important to test which dimensions – effectiveness, distributive fairness, procedural fairness, or even moral alignment –best contribute to legitimacy in this context. Or are there other dimensions that have not been considered yet?

Moreover, there is an increasing use of Chinese in legal proceedings, principally in the lower courts known as the Magistrates' Courts in Hong Kong. Here, the procedures and trials are often conducted in Cantonese, the primary dialect of the local population. It would be useful to measure the public's and the defendants' perceptions of Chinese court proceedings. It has been noticed that the use of Chinese in court proceedings offers a greater opportunity for judges to directly engage with defendants and for parties, such as defendants and witness, to express their own views more naturally and colloquially (Ng, 2009). By conducting trials in Chinese, would defendants and witnesses be regarded as being given greater voice and participation? Would this enhance the trustworthiness of judges? Would parties feel that they are better treated when they are communicated with in their own language? Would these factors heighten moral alignment between defendants, witnesses, and the public and the courts and by extension improve the legitimacy of the courts?

Police legitimacy, which dominates the procedural justice literature, is conspicuously absent in Hong Kong studies and is scarce in other Asian societies as well. In particular, greater attention should be paid to young people's perceptions of police legitimacy. As discussed, young people are the most frequent group to come into contact with legal authorities, and police officers are often the first point of contact. Do the police treat young persons in a procedurally just way?

Does procedural justice influence police legitimacy and in turn lead to greater willingness to cooperate with the police? Does this apply only to youths who have been charged or brought into the police station suspected of a crime, or also to people who encounter police on the streets, for example in random ID checks? Strategies to enhance relations between the police and young people are especially important given the recent tensions between them during protests. Given that many of the demonstrators were students, there should be a focus on how to defuse hostilities and improve their cooperation with the police in the future.

What have also been missing are measurements with respect to compliance with the law. Since young people disproportionately come into contact with law enforcement and are thought of as the most deviant age group, it is imperative that there be more inquiries into what enhances young people's compliance with the law. In other words, the link between procedural justice, legitimacy, and compliance should be ascertained in the Hong Kong Chinese context and in different societies in Asia as well.

Chapter summary points

- Procedural justice theory argues that the more people perceive that they have been treated in a procedurally just way by legal authorities, the more they view the authority in question as legitimate and the more willing they are to cooperate with and defer to the authority.
- There is a paucity of research on procedural justice in Asia.
- In Hong Kong to date, studies have focused on lawyer-youth client interactions.
- Overall, there is support for procedural justice theory as the more that young people perceive that lawyers treat their clients in procedurally just ways, the more they will consider the justice system to be legitimate.
- Future studies in Asia should examine other proposed dimensions of legitimacy, such as effectiveness and moral alignment, as well as perceptions of other legal authorities such as the police.

References

Bottoms, A., & Tankebe, J. (2012). Beyond procedural justice: A dialogic approach to legitimacy in criminal justice. *Journal of Criminal Law & Criminology*, *102*, 119–170. doi: 0091-4169/12/10201-0119

Cheng, K. K., Chui, W. H., & Ong, R. (2015). Providing justice for low-income youths: Publicly funded lawyers and youth clients in Hong Kong. *Social & Legal Studies*, *24*(4), 577–593. doi: 10.1177/0964663914559867

Chui, W. H., & Cheng, K. K. (2015a). Young people's perception of lawyers in Hong Kong: A comparison between offenders, youth-at-risk and students. *International Journal of Law, Crime and Justice*, *43*(4), 481–495. doi: 10.1016/j.ijlcj.2014.12.001

Chui, W. H., & Cheng, K. K. (2015b). Perceptions of fairness and satisfaction in lawyer-client interactions among young offenders in Hong Kong. *Journal of Mixed Methods Research*. Advanced online publication. doi: 1558689815593834

Creswell, J. W., & Plano Clark, V. L. (2011). *Designing and conducting mixed methods research* (2nd ed.). Thousand Oaks, CA: Sage.

Gray, P. (1994). *Inside the Hong Kong Juvenile Court: The decision-making process in action* (Research paper series no. 23). Hong Kong: Department of Social Work and Social Administration, University of Hong Kong.

Grisso, T. (1981). *Juveniles' waiver of rights: Legal and psychological competence.* New York, NY: Plenum.

Hasisi, B., & Weisburd, D. (2011). Going beyond ascribed identities: The importance of procedural justice in airport security screening in Israel. *Law & Society Review*, *45*(4), 867–892. doi: 10.1111/j.1540-5893.2011.00459.x

Hinds, L., & Murphy, K. (2007). Public satisfaction with police: Using procedural justice to improve police legitimacy. *Australian & New Zealand Journal of Criminology*, *40*(1), 27–42. doi: 10.1375/acri.40.1.27

Hough, M., Jackson, J., Bradford, B., Myhill, A., & Quinton, P. (2010). Procedural justice, trust, and institutional legitimacy. *Policing*, *4*(3), 203–210. doi: 10.1093/police/paq027

Jackson, J., Asif, M., Bradford, B., & Zakar, M. Z. (2014). Corruption and police legitimacy in Lahore, Pakistan. *British Journal of Criminology*, *54*(6), 1067–1088. doi: 10.1093/bjc/azu069

Jackson, J., Bradford, B., Hough, M., Myhill, A., Quinton, P., & Tyler, T. (2012). Why do people comply with the law? Legitimacy and the influence of legal institutions. *British Journal of Criminology*, *52*(6), 1051–1071. doi: 10.1093/bjc/azs032

Jackson, J., Bradford, B., Stanko, B., & Hohl, K. (2013). *Just authority? Trust in the police in England and Wales.* Abington, UK: Routledge.

Jiang, S., Wu, Y., & Wang, J. (2013). Citizens' obligation to obey the law: An empirical study of Guangzhou, China. *International Journal of Offender Therapy and Comparative Criminology*, *57*(4), 495–518. doi: 10.1177/0306624X11434005

Lee, F. W. (2011). *Nurturing the pillars of society: Understanding and working with the young generation in Hong Kong.* Hong Kong: Hong Kong University Press.

Lo, S. H. C., & Chui, W. H. (2012). *The Hong Kong legal system.* Singapore: McGraw-Hill Education (Asia).

Lo, T. W. (2008). Custodial sentences and correctional services. In W. H. Chui & T. W. Lo (Eds.), *Understanding criminal justice in Hong Kong* (pp. 224–247). Cullompton, Devon: Willan Publishing.

Murphy, K., & Cherney, A. (2012). Understanding cooperation with police in a diverse society. *British Journal of Criminology*, *52*(1), 181–201. doi: 10.1093/bjc/azr065

Ng, K. H. (2009). *The common law in two voices: Language, law, and the postcolonial dilemma in Hong Kong* (2nd ed.). Stanford, CA: Stanford University Press.

Peterson-Badali, M., Care, S., & Broeking, J. (2007). Young people's perceptions and experiences of the lawyer-client relationship. *Canadian Journal of Criminology and Criminal Justice*, *49*(3), 375–402. doi: 10.3138/cjccj.49.3.375

Reisig, M. D., & Lloyd, C. (2009). Procedural justice, police legitimacy, and helping the police fight crime: Results from a survey of Jamaican adolescents. *Policing & Society*, *12*(1), 42–62. doi: 10.1177/1098611108327311

Sprott, J. B., & Greene, C. (2010). Trust and confidence in the courts: Does the quality of treatment young offenders receive affect their views of the courts? *Crime & Delinquency*, *56*(2), 269–289. doi: 10.1177/0011128707308176

Sunshine, J., & Tyler, T. (2003). The role of procedural justice and legitimacy in shaping public support for policing. *Law & Society Review*, *37*(3), 513–548. doi: 10.1111/1540-5893.3703002

Tankebe, J. (2009a). Public cooperation with the police in Ghana: Does procedural fairness matter? *Criminology*, *47*(4), 1265–1293. doi: 10.1111/j.1745-9125.2009.00175.x

Tankebe, J. (2009b). Self-help, policing, and procedural justice: Ghanaian vigilantism and the rule of law. *Law & Society Review*, *43*(2), 245–269. doi: 10.1111/j.1540-5893.2009.00372.x

Tyler, T. (1990). *Why people obey the law*. New Haven, CT: Yale University Press.

Tyler, T. (2003). Procedural justice, legitimacy, and the effective rule of law. *Crime and Justice*, *30*, 283–357.

Tyler, T. (2006). Psychological perspectives on legitimacy and legitimation. *Annual Review of Psychology*, *57*, 375–400. doi: 10.1146/annuarev.psych.57.102904.190038

Tyler, T. (2008). Procedural justice and the courts. *Court Review*, *44*(1–2), 26–31.

Tyler, T., & Fagan, J. (2008). Legitimacy and cooperation: Why do people help the police fight crime in their communities? *Ohio State Journal of Criminal Law*, *6*, 231–275.

Tyler, T., & Huo, Y. J. (2002). *Trust in the law: Encouraging public cooperation with the police and courts*. New York, NY: Russell Sage Foundation.

Tyler, T., Schulhofer, S., & Huq, A. Z. (2010). Legitimacy and deterrence effects in counterterrorism policing: A study of Muslim Americans. *Law & Society Review*, *44*(2), 365–401. doi: 10.1111/j.1540-5893.2010.00405.x

Wong, D. S. W. (2000). Juvenile crime and responses to delinquency in Hong Kong. *International Journal of Offender Therapy and Comparative Criminology*, *44*(3), 279–292. doi: 10.1177/0306624X00443003

Xu, J. (2011). Hong Kong, the state of criminology. In S. X. Zhang, R. Barberet, & C. J. Smith (Eds.), *Routledge handbook of international criminology: An international perspective* (pp. 411–418). London/New York, NY: Routledge.

Epilogue

A combined etic-emic approach to psycho-criminology

Samuel M. Y. Ho and Heng Choon (Oliver) Chan

Introduction

The 16 chapters in this book provide an overview of topics related to psycho-criminology in Singapore and Hong Kong. The two selected territories are largely ethnic Chinese and both were under British rule for more than 100 years (Singapore from 1819 to 1959; Hong Kong from 1841 to 1997) (Abshire, 2011; Carroll, 2007). The legal and rehabilitation practices of both locations were largely inherited from the British system, but each has modified the Western approach to cater to its own unique situation and developed new approaches during this process. We first highlight practices common to the two locations. We argue towards the end of this chapter that the combined etic-emic approach of (Ho & Cheung, 2007) can be used to inform future research and the practice of psycho-criminology, not only in the Asian context but also around the world.

A great leap forward

It is undeniable that the legal systems and rehabilitation services for offenders in both Singapore and Hong Kong have significantly developed in recent decades. A notable change is the move from a punishment-oriented approach to a rehabilitation-oriented approach (see Chapters 6, 7 and 11). The formation of the inter-ministry Committee on the Prevention of Reoffending (CPR) in Singapore in 2009 (Chapter 11) and the enactment of the Rehabilitation Centres Bill in Hong Kong in 2001 (Chapter 6) both played important roles in promoting progress. This top-down approach appears to be very effective in generating sustainable change in both territories, and should be considered by practitioners in other countries.

The rehabilitation approach

Singapore and Hong Kong share some common elements in their rehabilitation approaches to offending behaviour. As mentioned earlier, both have adapted rehabilitation programmes from Western countries, the common elements of which represent universally accepted principles of rehabilitating offending behaviour. Two of these common elements are outlined below.

Empirically supported approach to assessment and treatment

The empirically supported approach proposes that the practice and dissemination of intervention should be demonstrably efficacious in producing its desired effect (Chamless & Hollen, 1998). Consistent with current international practices, both Singapore and Hong Kong have a strong preference for empirically supported approaches to offender rehabilitation (Chapters 7 and 11). A notable example mentioned by authors from both locations is the development of empirically validated risk assessment tools to inform treatment. Such tools are used in the treatment of youth offenders in Singapore (Chapter 12) and serious violent offenders in Hong Kong (Chapter 9). Systematic studies have been conducted to validate the assessment instruments. In Hong Kong, the assessment package led to the establishment of the Violence Prevention Programme (VPP) and in Singapore, systematic training in use of the assessment tools was developed to ensure their accurate administration. Although the empirically supported approach is not without controversies (Chamless & Ollendick, 2001), it is widely accepted as the gold standard for the development and selection of intervention programmes in psychotherapy, and thus should continue to be a focus in the years to come.

Population-sensitive approach

A punishment-oriented approach assumes that harsh penalties can reduce recidivism and that the strategy applies to all offenders, regardless of gender, age and type of offence. This one-size-fits-all philosophy is not applicable to the rehabilitation approach to criminal justice (Miller, Gregory, & Iovanni, 2005) currently adopted by both cities. There are many examples of population-sensitive practices in this book, not only in rehabilitation services but also in the legal system. These include special measures to facilitate child testimony in court (Chapter 2), legitimacy of the insanity defence and adjudicative competence in court (Chapters 3 and 4), a new gender-specific facility for female offenders (Chapter 8), and treatment protocols tailored to sex offenders (Chapter 10), serious violent offenders (Chapter 9), and youth offenders (Chapter 11). Population-sensitive approaches lead to better outcomes and should be further developed in the future.

A combined etic-emic approach to psycho-criminology

A casual reader will notice that almost all of the practices mentioned in this book are adopted from the West, probably due to the strong history both cities have with Great Britain. Elsewhere, we have argued that there are generally three approaches to adopting assessment and treatments from other cultures: the etic approach, the emic approach, and the combined etic-emic approach (Ho & Cheung, 2007; Ho et al., 2014). The etic approach assumes that theories and practices are universal and can be transferred to other cultures with little modification. This approach is widely adopted by psychologists and criminologists, especially in the development of assessment tools. The two chapters on assessments (Chapters 9 and 12) provide examples of this approach in both cities. The emic approach, in contrast, proposes that behaviour is culture-specific. Practitioners should develop empirically supported assessment and treatments sensitive to the local context. To our knowledge, the emic approach is not common in Singapore or Hong Kong, and there are no examples of it in this book. Ho and Cheung (2007) argued that the etic and emic approaches represent two extremes and have their own limitations. They proposed that a combined etic-emic approach could be more viable when developing culturally sensitive assessments and interventions. Elements that appear to be universal can be identified first and other emic elements can be added based on specific cultural and population characteristics. The Sex Offenders' Evaluation and Treatment Unit (ETU) described in Chapter 10 is a good example of the etic-emic approach. Cognitive behavioural strategies that have strong empirical support across cultures were incorporated into the programme (the etic component). Other approaches (a strength-based approach and positive psychotherapy) were added based on the unique characteristics of the clientele. Another noteworthy example is the Psychological Gymnasium (PSY GYM) of the Correctional Services Department in Hong Kong (Chapter 8), which uses the cognitive behavioural paradigm (the etic component) in conjunction with other approaches (expressive art and positive psychotherapy) to cater for local needs. The etic-emic approach is not only relevant to offender rehabilitation but also to the legal system. Chapter 5 compares the judicial systems of Hong Kong, Mainland China, South Korea, and Japan. Each country represents a different degree of etic-emic combination. We recommend that the combined etic-emic approach should be considered in the development of legal systems and rehabilitation services in Asia.

The challenge ahead

Three of the final four chapters (Chapters 13, 14, and 15) point to riot, terrorism, and violent extremism as major challenges to be faced by law enforcers and legal experts. Rioting and terrorism are more than pure criminal behaviour. Theoretical frameworks should be used to analyse these phenomena. The Elaborated Social Identity Model (ESIM) (Drury & Reicher, 2000) (Chapter 14) is one such framework. We recommend that appropriate training be implemented to inform law enforcers of this model. Consistent with the etic-emic approach mentioned above, we hope more research will be conducted in future to examine whether emic components can be added to enhance the validity of this model in the Asian context.

References

Abshire, J. E. (2011). *The history of singapore*. Santa Barbara, CA: Greenwood Publishing Group.

Carroll, J. M. (2007). *A concise history of Hong Kong*. Hong Kong: Hong Kong University Press.

Chamless, D. L., & Hollen, S. D. (1998). Defining empirically supported therapies. *Journal of Consulting and Clinical Psychology*, *66*(1), 7–18. doi: 10.1037/0022-006X.66.1.7

Chamless, D. L., & Ollendick, T. H. (2001). Empirically supported psychological interventions: Controversies and evidence. *Annual Review of Psychology*, *52*, 685–716. doi: 10.1146/annurev.psych.52.1.685

Drury, J., & Reicher, S. D. (2000). Collective action and psychological change: The emergence of new social identities. *British Journal of Social Psychology*, *39*, 579–604. doi: 10.1348/014466600164642

Ho, S. M. Y., & Cheung, M. W. L. (2007). Using the combined etic-emic approach to develop a measurement of interpersonal subjective well-being in Chinese populations. In A. D. Ong & M. van Dulmen (Eds.), *Oxford handbook of methods in positive psychology* (pp. 139–152). New York, NY: Oxford University Press.

Ho, S. M. Y., Rochelle, T. L. R., Law, L. S. C., Duan, W., Bai, Y., Shih, S.-M., & Wang, G.-L. (2014). Methodological issues in positive psychology research with diverse populations: Exploring strengths among Chinese adults. In J. T. Pedrotti & L. M. Edwards (Eds.), *Perspectives on the intersection of multiculturalism & positive psychology* (pp. 45–57). New York, NY: Springer Science + Business Media B.V.

Miller, S. L. M., Gregory, C., & Iovanni, L. (2005). One size fits all? A gender-neutral approach to a gender-specific problem: Contrasting batterer treatment programs for male and female offenders. *Criminal Justice Policy Review*, *16*, 336–359. doi: 10.1177/0887403404273944

Index

For Product Safety Concerns and Information please contact our EU representative GPSR@taylorandfrancis.com Taylor & Francis Verlag GmbH, Kaufingerstraße 24, 80331 München, Germany

Batch number: 10725973

Printed by Printforce, the Netherlands